Guide to the
Mammals of Pennsylvania

GUIDE TO THE

Mammals

OF PENNSYLVANIA

JOSEPH F. MERRITT

RUTH ANNE MATINKO, *Editor*

HAL S. KORBER, *Photographer*

DAVID M. ARMSTRONG, *Scientific Consultant*

For Ron — with my best wishes, Joe

University of Pittsburgh Press for

The Carnegie Museum of Natural History

Published by the University of Pittsburgh Press, Pittsburgh, Pa. 15261
Copyright © 1987, University of Pittsburgh Press
Manufactured in the United States of America
10   9   8   7   6   5   4   3

Illustrations of skulls (except of Norway rat) by K. Simpson, taken from
T. Lawlor, *Handbook to the Orders and Families of Living Mammals* (Eureka,
Calif.: Mad River Press, 1979). Illustration of Norway rat skull by H. Douglas
Pratt, reprinted by permission of Louisiana State University Press, from George H.
Lowery, Jr., *The Mammals of Louisiana and Its Adjacent Waters*. Copyright ©
1974 by George H. Lowery, Jr.

Range maps researched and compiled by Arlynn Adamerovich;
all distribution maps drawn by William Nelson.

All other illustrations drawn by Linda A. Witt.

Drawings on pages 36, 37, 67 (bottom), and 146 are adapted from *The Wild
Mammals of Missouri* by Charles W. and Elizabeth R. Schwartz by permission
of the University of Missouri Press. Copyright 1981 by the Curators of the
University of Missouri.

The drawing on page 169 is adapted from *The Encyclopedia of Mammals*, edited
by Dr. David Macdonald. © 1984 by Equinox (Oxford) Ltd. Reprinted by permission of Facts On File, Inc., New York.

Library of Congress Cataloging-in-Publication Data

Merritt, Joseph F.
   Guide to mammals of Pennsylvania.

   Bibliography: p. 387.
   Includes index.
   1. Mammals—Pennsylvania—Identification.
I. Matinko, Ruth Anne. II. Title.
QL719.P4M47   1987   599.09748   87-40157
ISBN 0-8229-3563-5
ISBN 0-8229-5393-5 (pbk.)

To my children

Jeff and Kellie

and

In memory of my parents

Robert E. Merritt and

June A. Merritt

Contents

Preface

Pennsylvania is endowed with a fascinating and varied assemblage of mammals. I believe that an understanding of their natural history is a key to ensuring that these animals will be preserved for future generations to cherish and enjoy. To enhance that understanding, I have written this guide. I hope it finds its place not only on the bookshelves of those persons studying the lives of our Pennsylvania mammals but also in the hands of those individuals who traipse through the woods to learn more about the habits and habitats of our rich mammalian fauna.

Organization, Rationale, and Resources

To set the stage for the discussion of Pennsylvania's mammalian inhabitants, I begin this guide by describing the characteristics of mammals and by introducing the reader to the environment of Pennsylvania. The first chapter traces mammals from their rather obscure beginnings as "mammal-like reptiles" to their present-day role as the most sophisticated and diverse group of animals inhabiting Earth.

The rather extensive discussion of the environment in the following chapter details those features that molded the Pennsylvania landscape, namely its geologic history, physiography, drainage, vegetation, and climate. This chapter will be of particular interest to scholars and students.

The bulk of this guide consists of accounts of the 63 wild mammals known to occur within Pennsylvania today. Although three species of marine mammals (the harbor seal, hooded seal, and harbor porpoise) have occasionally been sighted in the lower Delaware River, they are considered to be wandering individuals and are not included. The species accounts are organized by order, family, genus, and species and arranged in conventional phylogenetic sequence. The classification of mammals in this guide and the vernacular and scientific names of each species are based on the *Revised Checklist of North American Mammals North of Mexico* (Jones et al., 1982), with minor exceptions.

Throughout the series of species accounts, each new order and family of mammals is introduced with a brief description of its salient characteristics. To help the reader to identify families and orders more easily, I have provided a line drawing of a representative skull for each family and illustrations of diagnostic external features when applicable.

For each species account, I have used the mammal's common name as the title. Each account begins with a telegraphic list of information that first gives the scientific name and its derivation from Latin or Greek. If a given species is represented by one or more subspecies within the Commonwealth, their names are listed alphabetically. Because many Pennsylvania mammals have several common names, I next list the most familiar alternatives under the heading "Also Called."

For ready reference and as a means of quickly distinguishing between mammals, ranges in body measurements and weights for adult animals are given. These maximum and minimum values are presented in metric units followed parenthetically by the less accurate U.S. units. Wherever possible, measurements were derived from *Mammals of Pennsylvania* (Doutt et al., 1977). Occasionally, I consulted references such as Hall (1981) and Chapman and Feldhamer (1982) for measurements and weights of uncommon or extirpated species. For detailed instructions on taking external measurements of mammals, I refer the reader to Hall (1981) and DeBlase and Martin (1981).

When available, life history attributes such as population density, home range, and longevity are included in the introductory list. These are representative of a given species throughout its geographic range in North America. Depending upon available data, longevity is given either as the maximum life span of individuals of a species or as the average range of the life span.

The geographic ranges of each species in the Commonwealth and throughout North America are depicted on distribution maps at the beginning of each account. These geographic ranges are based on currently known distribution patterns. It is important to note, especially for distribution within the Commonwealth, that these maps are deliberately conservative; additional field-work will surely extend the known limits of many Pennsylvania mammals. Further, be aware that the distribution of a given species is a product of its ecological tolerances. For example, although the Pennsylvania range map indicates that the muskrat occurs throughout the entire state, these amphibious mammals are restricted to aquatic habitats, namely marshes, ponds, lakes, and slow-moving creeks. The distribution maps are derived from the thorough state-wide research effort of the Pennsylvania Mammal Survey (1946–1951) and augmented by recent work of the Mammal Committee of the Pennsylvania Biological Survey (see Genoways and Brenner, 1985).

To enhance identification, a photograph of each of the species in its natural environment is provided. Of the 63 species the only mammals not depicted are the Maryland shrew (*Sorex fontinalis*) and the pygmy shrew (*Sorex hoyi*); they look so much like the masked shrew (*Sorex cinereus*) that usually only through careful examination by an expert can the three species be distinguished. Color photographs are supplied when coloring is an important distinguishing feature.

The narrative part of each account begins with a section called "Description," which presents the general characteristics of each species with emphasis on features distinguishing similar species. The "Ecology" section includes the mammal's preferred habitat, its food habits, major predators, and a summary of its external and internal parasites. The next section, entitled "Behavior," covers activity periods, temperament, nests, locomotion, vocalizations, and social behavior. Behavioral and physiological attributes such as communal nesting, torpidity, and hibernation are also discussed under "Behavior." The section "Reproduction and Development" is reserved for information pertaining to gestation periods of each species, litter sizes, and numbers of litters produced per year. When available, a description of the growth and development of young is undertaken. Wherever possible, information in each of the above sections is derived from studies conducted in Pennsylvania or adjacent states. Throughout the accounts, illustrations are used to supplement textual references to characteristic "signs" indicative of activities of mammals, such as nests and homes, tree scratches, and even partially eaten nuts.

Within certain accounts, I have included an additional section called "Status in Pennsylvania." This heading is reserved for those species in the Commonwealth designated as endangered, threatened, or vulnerable, or as having an undetermined status as defined by the Pennsylvania Biological Survey in its report *Species of Special Concern in Pennsylvania* (Genoways and Brenner, 1985). Within this section, the basis of this status classification and various recommendations of the Survey are summarized. The reader is alerted to a species of special concern by a "Status in Pennsylvania" entry in the list that begins the account.

In addition to the 63 species known to occur in Pennsylvania today, 10 other mammals suspected to occur in Pennsylvania or having occurred here within historic times are dealt with briefly in the chapters entitled "Species of Uncertain Occurrence" and "Extirpated Species." Each species falling within these categories is briefly discussed with respect to general characteristics such as size and color, natural history, and past and present status within the Commonwealth. These sections are based on the Pennsylvania Biological Survey's report *Species of Special Concern in Pennsylvania* (Genoways and Brenner, 1985) and the recent work of Williams et al. (1985).

The appendix to this guide, "Observing Mammals in the Wild," is designed to aid the reader in identifying mammals when their presence is evidenced only by tracks in snow or mud or by a skull found in the forest. The first section, "Selected Tracks," includes prints and typical gait patterns of representative species of Pennsylvania mammals arranged in conventional phylogenetic sequence. By combining evidence from these close-up prints with an interpretation of gait patterns, you may be able to identify the mammal that left a "sign" behind. Murie (1954), Halfpenny (1986), and my own examination of tracks in nature served as the bases for the illustrations.

The second section of this appendix presents the dental formulae for all genera of wild mammals and many domesticated mammals in Pennsylvania. Also included are formulae for humans, species of uncertain occurrence, and extirpated species. The text explains how to use these dental formulae as a tool in mammal identification.

Glossary, References, and Index and Checklist

Where necessary throughout the text, I employed scientific vocabulary. My intention was not to impress or confuse the reader. Rather, the use of a technical vocabulary permitted precise statements where everyday language would be misleading or would compromise the book's scientific accuracy. Technical terms repeated throughout the guide are defined in the "Glossary."

Although I wrote this guide with a general audience in mind, I took steps to meet the needs of students and scientists. Derived from an extensive literature review, this guide is an up-to-date compendium of information on Pennsylvania mammals. To enhance the flow and readability, I omitted all literature citations from the text except those that document direct quotations or exceptional data. Readers interested in detailed reviews or papers, reference texts, or even popular field guides for further reading should refer to "Selected References," which is organized by subject and arranged by mammalian taxa.

Throughout the guide, I have relied heavily on the series *Mammalian Species* published by the American Society of Mammalogists. These complete, yet succinct accounts are available for many of the mammals of Pennsylvania. Persons interested in subscribing to the *Mammalian Species* series should write to Dr. H. Duane Smith, Secretary-Treasurer, American Society of Mammalogists, c/o Dept. of Zoology, Brigham Young University, Provo, Utah 84601.

The book's index has been adapted to serve also as a checklist of animals observed. When you have spotted and identified a mammal in your wanderings through Pennsylvania, put a check in the circle next to its common name. As you begin to fill up these circles, you will be driven to look even harder for these often elusive creatures.

Acknowledgments

Since joining the staff of The Carnegie Museum of Natural History in 1979, I have seen the need for an up-to-date text that the general public, as well as researchers, students, and naturalists, could use to gain a fuller appreciation for and understanding of the fascinating mammals in Pennsylvania. Numerous individuals deserve great thanks for making this much-overdue guide possible.

The book's editor, Ruth Anne Matinko, began working on the project while Program Specialist for Publications at The Carnegie Museum of Natural History. In addition to editing, proofreading, and wordprocessing the manuscript, Ruthie served as project administrator and coordinated the efforts of the many individuals involved in making the book a reality. It was through her persistence and encouragement that the project stayed alive.

Special congratulations and thanks must go to our photographer, Hal S. Korber. Through fine-tuned skills, ingenious techniques, and many months of painstaking work, Hal produced an extraordinary documentation of the mammals of Pennsylvania. His work evidences his sensitivity to and knowledge of our state's wildlife resources.

The production of the guide also drew upon the talents of Linda A. Witt, who superbly executed the tracks and spot illustrations throughout the text. She is also to be commended for tolerating my eccentric nature.

My research assistant Arlynn Adamerovich was an indispensable member of the team. Lynn thoroughly researched recent literature on Pennsylvania mammals and reviewed each account. She also researched and compiled the distribution maps, worked with Hal in acquiring animals to photograph and setting up props, and occasionally covered for me in the office so that I could have some quiet time to write. During the early stages of the book's development, Cassandra Barton, Martin Friday, Katherine Hook, and Diane Schnupp served as my research assistants and aided in the literature search.

Dozens of others generously contributed their time, energy, and expertise to make this publication scientifically accurate. I extend very special thanks to Dr. David Armstrong of the University of Colorado for taking on the monumental task of being our scientific consultant. Having published a variety of similar guides, Dr. Armstrong ably reviewed and critiqued the manuscript. Dr. James Halfpenny, also of the University of Colorado and author of *A Field Guide to Mammal Tracking in Western America*, reviewed the track illustrations, and Paul G. Wiegman of the Western Pennsylvania Conservancy helped by reviewing the chapter on the environment of Pennsylvania.

I would also like to thank the staff of the Pennsylvania Game Commission for their assistance, in particular, Donald C. Madl, Dennis Jones, and Gary L. Alt. Further, Dr. Charles E. Rupprecht of the Rabies Unit of the Wistar Institute and Dr. John W. Cable of the Pennsylvania Department of Agriculture provided current information on the incidence of rabies in Pennsylvania mammals. Dr. Gordon L. Kirkland, Jr., kept us abreast of his current research on *Sorex hoyi* and *Sorex fontinalis*, and we consulted with Dr. Henry Croft, Jr., regarding animal diseases.

The list of individuals involved in the development of *Guide to the Mammals of Pennsylvania* does not stop here. Dr. Elizabeth Mertz, Program Assistant for Publications at The Carnegie Museum of Natural History, was responsible for securing photographs not available through Hal Korber and contributed to the environment chapter. She also proofread sections of the manuscript, as did my good friend Mary Jo Kelly. Thanks must also go to Louise Craft, Program Specialist—Publications at CMNH, who gave the manuscript its final copy-editing.

Dr. Timothy E. Lawlor granted us permission to reproduce illustrations of skulls from his *Handbook to the Orders and Families of Living Mammals*. A variety of photographers, credited in the photograph captions, also generously gave us permission to publish their work.

In acquiring the animals for live photography and in assisting photographer Hal Korber, the following individuals are acknowledged: Michael Adamerovich, Charles Bier, J. Michelle Cawthorn, C. Ray Chandler, William Gompers, Dr. John Hall, Sam Houston, Dan Jenkins, Paulette Johnson, Ross Korber, Ralph Kozlowski, David Krapp, Gilbert O. Lenhart, Janet Marvin, Al Pedder, Carol Porton, Meg Scanlon, Tom Serfus, and Gordon Whitcomb. Special thanks to Fred Rimmel, Bob Ealy, and Karen Ealy.

Finally, I acknowledge The Claude Worthington Benedum Foundation which, through the Benedum Endowment for Public Programs at The Carnegie Museum of Natural History, provided the financial support to get this project off the ground.

INTRODUCTION

Defining a Mammal

The class Mammalia is composed of about 4,060 living species arranged in 138 families which in turn are grouped into 20 orders. Mammals range in size from the tiny Kitti's hog-nosed bat, weighing about 1.5 grams (0.05 oz.), to the massive blue whale, weighing up to 160,000 kilograms (180 tons).

Compared with the five million or more kinds of animals living on Earth today, the variety of mammals is rather small. They make up less than 0.5 percent of all the animal species now known, whereas insects account for about 80 percent of the total. Although mammal species are greatly outnumbered by all other animal groups, their essence derives from their sophistication in form, function, and, especially, behavior. Further, the class Mammalia contains the largest animals, some of the most abundant animals, many domesticated animals, pets, and game species. Probably most noteworthy is the fact that humans are mammals, too.

Evolutionary History

Mammals are newcomers in the evolutionary picture. They evolved from a primitive group of reptiles (the therapsids) in the Triassic Period of the Mesozoic Era only some 230 million years ago during the "Age of Reptiles." This was a time when reptiles, including the popular dinosaurs, dominated a landscape marked by shallow inland seas and a hot, humid climate. The dog-sized early mammals were probably quite obscure.

At the end of the Cretaceous Period, some 65 million years ago, ruling reptiles nearly became extinct. Following their demise, mammals underwent a remarkable adaptive radiation. This led to the dominant position of mammals in the Cenozoic Era. During the past 65 million years, a time aptly called the "Age of Mammals," these animals have diversified into a great variety of ecological niches. They occur in marine and fresh water, underground, and in the air, as well as in trees and on the ground. They range from polar regions to the tropics on all continents and in all seas of the world.

Living members of the class Mammalia are divided into three major groups, differentiated on the basis of their reproductive anatomy. First, the monotremes are the only living mammals that lay eggs. They consist of only one species of platypuses in the family Ornithorhynchidae and two species of echidnas in the family Tachyglossidae. They are found only in Australia, Tasmania, and New Guinea. Second are the marsupials. Most of these mammals have pouches in which to carry the young; their young are born in an undeveloped "embryonic" stage and attach to the mother's nipples, commonly located within the pouch. There are some 258 species of marsupials residing principally in South America and the Australian region. Third, and by far the largest group of mammals, are the placentals, mammals whose females have a true placenta. This group consists of some 3,700 species residing throughout the world and includes humankind. The placenta is a complex of embryonic and maternal membranes that permits a two-way exchange of nutrients and oxygen between the blood of the mother and that of the developing embryo. In many mammals, the placenta is passed with the newborn at birth and commonly called the "afterbirth."

Characteristics of Mammals

Probably the most well-known characteristic of a mammal is its mammae or breasts. (The word *mammal* is derived from the Latin word *mammalis,* meaning "breasts.") In females, these specialized skin glands produce milk to nourish the young; in males, they are rudimentary and nonfunctional. All mammals, except the monotremes (platypuses and echidnas), have teats or nipples to facilitate the transfer of milk to the young. In monotremes, the milk flows from pores in the skin rather than from nipples.

Having hair during some stage of development also defines a mammal. In some mammals, such as whales and dolphins, hair is limited to a few bristles on the nose or is entirely lacking except during embryonic development. A multicellular derivative from reptilian scales, hair was an important evolutionary advance for mammals. As a body covering, hair provides insulation and thus permits maintenance of a high and relatively constant body temperature, despite fluctuating air temperature. Reptiles lack this "endothermy" or warm-bloodedness and must maintain body temperature by finding shelter from excessive heat or by absorbing heat from the environment.

The lower jaw of mammals is unique among vertebrates since it is composed of only a single pair of bones, the dentaries, which articulate directly with the skull. Evolutionary changes in the jaw bones of amphibians and reptiles resulted in yet another unique mammalian structure, the presence of three tiny, sound-conducting bones in each middle ear: the incus, malleus, and stapes. Further, a bony shelf or secondary hard palate separating the nasal passage from the mouth typifies mammals. Crocodiles and alligators are the only other animals that have a hard palate resembling that found in mammals.

With the exception of the monotremes, anteaters, pangolins, and baleen whales, all adult mammals have teeth. Mammalian teeth are set in sockets, occur in two developmental sets—namely deciduous and permanent teeth—and are differentiated into four different types adapted for assorted functions. The four types of teeth are incisors, canines, premolars, and molars. Teeth of mammals are often described numerically in a "dental formula." This formula describes the upper and lower dentition of the jaw and is useful in identifying mammals when only the skull is available for study.

A combination of other anatomical characteristics helps to distinguish mammals from other vertebrates. Mammals have:

- A muscular diaphragm separating the lungs from the abdominal cavity.

- A four-chambered heart in which the aorta, the large vessel that carries blood away from the heart, turns to the left. (In birds, the aorta turns right; reptiles have two aortas, a left and a right.)

- Nonnucleated mature red blood cells. Because they are generally bioconcave discs, the red blood cells have a greater surface area available to transport oxygen to the tissues. As a result, these cells greatly aid in permitting the high levels of activity necessary for the survival of mammals.

- Seven cervical vertebrae. Exceptions are the manatee (*Trichechus*) and the two-toed sloth (*Choloepus*), which have six; the anteater (*Tamandua*), which has eight; and the three-toed sloth (*Bradypus*), which has nine.

- A double occipital condyle forming the articulation for the skull upon the first vertebra of the neck.

- A phalangeal formula (the number of bones in the fingers and toes) of 2-3-3-3-3 (two bones in the thumb, or the big toe, and three bones in each of the other digits).

- Limbs positioned directly below the body instead of sprawling to the side as in reptiles.

Finally, the brain of mammals is greatly enlarged, and its complex anatomy permits efficient processing and integration of information. Because of the well-developed learning centers in the brain, mammals show the greatest degree of individual variability of behavior and the most sophisticated learning ability of any animal.

Environment of Pennsylvania

Encompassing an area of 117,412 square kilometers (45,333 sq. mi.), the Commonwealth of Pennsylvania extends from coastal plains bordered by the Delaware River on the southeast, across ridges and valleys of the Appalachian Mountains, and on to the Appalachian Plateaus in the west and north. The different areas of the state exhibit distinct patterns of geology, physiography, drainage, soils, climate, and, ultimately, vegetation. Such diversity in the environment creates the complex patchwork of different habitats which are home for the state's varied mammalian fauna. To fully understand the lives of these animals, one must know about the environments where they reside.

Most of Pennsylvania's 63 species of mammals occupy a broad array of ecological settings distributed throughout our state. Several species, however, exhibit more restricted distributional patterns, some isolated to a specific plant community or physiographic zone. This chapter is designed to set the stage for understanding the distribution of our mammals by presenting a picture of Pennsylvania's complex environmental mosaic. As you read about a specific species, you may find it helpful to refer back to this chapter in order to visualize its environment more accurately.

The Land

Having a picture of the physiography of a region is vital to understanding the distribution of its flora and fauna. The form of the land influences the distribution of soils and surface water, which are intimately linked with climate. Hence, these factors act in concert to determine the vegetation on which mammals either directly or indirectly depend for their sustenance and, ultimately, survival.

Pennsylvania's mountain ridges, valleys, and plateaus were formed over long periods of time. During much of the Paleozoic Era (600 to 225 million years ago), shallow inland seas, with drainage patterns from east to west, covered what is now the midwestern United States. The relationship of land and sea was then nearly opposite to that of today. The ancient inland seas spread and receded, and the land underwent several episodes of uplift. Sediments from the sea and river bottoms accumulated and consolidated over time into the rock beds of limestones, sandstones, and shales that today underlie Pennsylvania. During part of the time, vast swamps spread over the region and later became coal beds.

Toward the end of the Paleozoic Era, rock layers folded to form great mountains. After that, the land mass was subjected to a gradual wearing down by erosion, chiefly by water, and to sinking and subsidence, until only a flat plain remained. Rivers then flowed northward or toward the coastal plain in the east. During the last 10 million years, uplift again raised the land somewhat, causing rivers to flow faster and to deepen their channels. Softer rocks eroded away, while more resistant ones remained.

In relatively recent geologic time, continental glacial sheets extended into the northeastern and northwestern parts of the state, rearranging the landscape by carving out shallow lakes, altering drainage patterns, scouring the surface of the land, leaving a mantle of till, and depositing piles of rocky debris.

In the current instant of geologic time, Pennsylvania is a tectonically quiet area with little seismic activity. Only a few earthquakes have been reported, and these have been of low intensity. Today, most of Pennsylvania lies within a physiographic division called the Appalachian Highlands, an area dominated by the Appalachian Mountains, which run southwest to northeast from Alabama to Maine. Flanking the mountains on either side are plateaus which give way to plains. The Pennsylvania Topographic and Geologic Survey divides Pennsylvania into seven major land divisions, called physiographic provinces (see figure 1).

COASTAL PLAIN PROVINCE

The southeastern edge of the Commonwealth, near Philadelphia, incorporates a narrow strip of the Atlantic Coastal Plain. This region, not a part of the Appalachian Highlands, is an elevated sea bottom typified by gently rolling hills, fresh and brackish marshes, and fresh intertidal mud flats. The last are unique communities to the Potomac, Delaware, and Hudson rivers.

The abundance of wetlands in this province provides optimal habitat for mesic-adapted mammals such as the fascinating marsh rice rat. Although best represented in southern states, *Oryzomys palustris* reaches the northern limit of its geographic range within the tidal flats of the Delaware River. There, it shares its habitat with the more common meadow vole and muskrat.

PIEDMONT PROVINCE

West of the Coastal Plain lies the Piedmont Province, a region about 90 kilometers (60 mi.) wide, with rolling hills dissected by many small streams. Bisecting this province is the Susquehanna River.

The Piedmont Province is divided into three distinct sections. The Piedmont Uplands and the Conestoga Valley sections are marked by low, rounded hills, rocky gorges, and fertile plains. Farther west at a slightly higher elevation is the Triassic Lowland Section, an uplifted, hilly plain dotted by outcrops of rocky woodlands. This section is unique in having two famous volcanic structures of the Triassic Period (246–208 million years ago): the Cemetery Ridge in Adams County (see figure 2) and the Palisades of the Hudson, located in nearby New Jersey. Today, much of the Piedmont Province is cleared for farmlands.

NEW ENGLAND AND BLUE RIDGE PROVINCES

The New England and Blue Ridge provinces extend into Pennsylvania as narrow prongs, the New England from the northeast, the Blue Ridge from the south. Both are typified by closely spaced ridges of igneous and metamorphic rock and form deep eroded valleys. The rugged, well-forested South Mountain in the Blue Ridge Province and, to a lesser degree, the Reading Hills in the New England Province provide suitable habitat for many mammals in the midst of a highly populated agricultural region.

VALLEY AND RIDGE PROVINCE

The Valley and Ridge Province, which contains most of the state's mountains, is divided into two sections—the Great Valley Section and the Appalachian Mountain Section. The Great Valley Section, in the eastern portion of the province, is marked by a broad plain about 30 kilometers (20 mi.) wide, regionally known as Lehigh, Lebanon, or Cumberland Valley. It is characterized by low, undulating hills incised by slow-moving watercourses.

Four major rivers traverse the Great Valley Section—the Susquehanna, Schuylkill, Lehigh, and Delaware. These meandering rivers serve as the principal north-south avenues of drainage for much of eastern Pennsylvania. Most of the southern Valley and Ridge Province drains to the north and east to the Juniata River and, ultimately, to the Susquehanna River, which drains

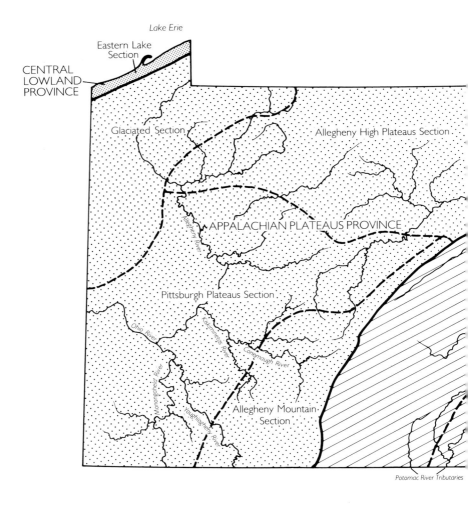

Source: Adapted from map by Bureau of Topographic and Geologic Survey of Pennsylvania Department of Environmental Resources.

Figure 1. Physiographic Provinces of Pennsylvania

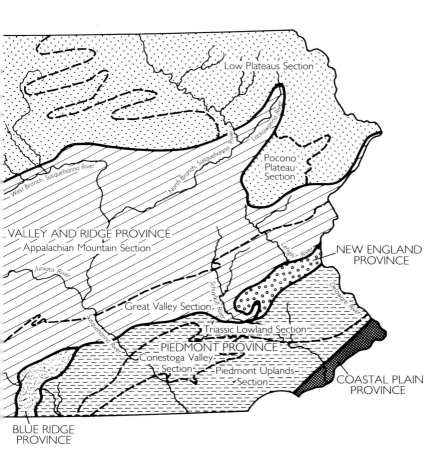

Low Plateaus Section

North Branch, Susquehanna River

Lackawanna River

West Branch, Susquehanna River

Pocono
Plateau
Section

VALLEY AND RIDGE PROVINCE
Appalachian Mountain Section

Juniata River

Lehigh River

NEW ENGLAND
PROVINCE

Schuylkill River

Great Valley Section

Delaware River

Susquehanna River

Triassic Lowland Section

PIEDMONT PROVINCE
Conestoga Valley
Section
Piedmont Uplands
Section

COASTAL PLAIN
PROVINCE

BLUE RIDGE
PROVINCE

Figure 2. Counties of Pennsylvania

much of eastern Pennsylvania. The Potomac River system drains most of Franklin County along the southern tier of the province.

Bordering the Great Valley Section on the west is a forest-covered mountain ridge known at various points along its length as Blue, Kittatiny, or First Mountain. This parallel ridge, a remnant of the great mountain-building period at the end of the Paleozoic Era, rises some 300 meters (990 ft.) above sea level. It forms the eastern boundary of the Appalachian Mountain Section of the Valley and Ridge Province.

Within the Appalachian Mountain Section, the Appalachian Mountains proper, a belt some 80 to 110 kilometers (50–70 mi.) wide, traverse the Commonwealth in a northeast-southwest direction. There, interspersed with farmed lowlands, lie long, narrow, parallel, forest-covered mountain ridges created by past upbending of sedimentary rock chiefly of Paleozoic age. These ridges are capped with a hard coating of resistant sandstones, as shown by the abundance of rocky talus slopes.

Here, residing in habitats typified by the oak and pine forests of southern Bedford, Fulton, and Franklin counties, may be found an intriguing mammal—the eastern spotted skunk. This petite skunk, noted for its acrobatic performances, reaches the northeastern-most limit of its geographic range in the southern regions of this province.

APPALACHIAN PLATEAUS PROVINCE

Most of western and northern Pennsylvania lies within the Appalachian Plateaus Province, an elevated plateau with river valleys cutting through flat-topped ridges to form an eroded, uneven landscape. Six physiographic sections constitute this province: Allegheny Mountain Section, Pocono Plateau Section, Pittsburgh Plateaus Section, Allegheny High Plateaus Section, Glaciated Section, and Low Plateau Section.

The Allegheny Mountain Section lies along the eastern margin of the Appalachian Plateaus Province. Its topography varies from rolling hills to deeply cut mountain canyons. The eastern border of this section is formed by the Allegheny Front—a long, sharp escarpment rising some 300 meters (990 ft.) above the valley floor and progressing some 480 kilometers (300 mi.) in an arching, northeastern path. In the northeast, this long front rises in the form of the Moosic Mountains, which rim the Pocono Plateau Section. This section has a thin mantle of glacial till and is marked by cool, moist forests with numerous lakes and wetlands which preclude agricultural development but invite recreational activities.

Also in the Allegheny Mountain Section lie ridges of dense, resistant sandstones, namely Chestnut Ridge, Laurel Mountain, and Negro Mountain. Here, located in southern Somerset County in the Negro Mountains, is Mt. Davis, the highest peak in the Commonwealth (980 m or 3,210 ft.).

The Allegheny Mountain Section is marked by many limestone caves, well-concealed by deep forests. These caves provide optimal habitat for many mammals, especially bats like the little brown myotis, big brown bat, and eastern pipistrelle. Another denizen of caves is the elusive eastern woodrat. This mild-mannered "pack rat" is noted for its tendency to raid campsites and cabins for "treasures," which it subsequently deposits in its own home.

The major rivers draining the Allegheny Mountain Section include the Youghiogheny River and its tributaries the Casselman River and Laurel Hill Creek, which flow west to meet the Monongahela River near Pittsburgh. To the north, much of the Laurel Highlands is drained by the Conemaugh River with its major tributary, Loyalhanna Creek. The Conemaugh flows westward, forming the Kiskiminetas River and ultimately reaching the Allegheny River north of Pittsburgh.

The rugged Allegheny Mountain Section yields on the west to the broad valleys and uplands of the Pittsburgh Plateaus Section. Here lie three major rivers—the Ohio, formed in Pittsburgh by the Monongahela, flowing northward from the West Virginia highlands, and the Allegheny, flowing southward from the Allegheny High Plateaus Section. The immediate tributaries of these spectacular rivers have incised the plateau surface, rendering deep V- and U-shaped valleys lined with extensive sandstone outcrops.

To the north of the Pittsburgh Plateaus Section, the Allegheny High Plateaus Section spans the northcentral part of the state. Here, the topography is mesa-like in appearance because of resistant horizontal beds of Mississippian and Devonian sandstone. The highest elevations in this section are in northcentral Potter County, where ridges reach an elevation of about 790 meters (2,590 ft.) above sea level. Except for the narrow lake plain of the Central Lowland Province (see below), all of northwest Pennsylvania is drained by tributaries of the Allegheny River and, to a lesser degree, by those watercourses leading to the Ohio River.

Eastward, the Allegheny High Plateaus Section declines in elevation to some 121 meters (400 ft.) in the valley of the North Branch of the Susquehanna River. The eastern half of the Allegheny High Plateaus Section is characterized by many deep, precipitous V-shaped canyons reaching 300 meters (990 ft.) in depth, molded by the West Branch of the Susquehanna River and its tributaries.

Framing the Allegheny High Plateaus Section on the west and east are the only areas of the Commonwealth ever subjected to glacial activity. The Glaciated Section on the west and the Low Plateaus Section on the east are characterized by features such as drumlins, eskers, and kettle-hole bogs and are dotted with small lakes and swamps. In the Glaciated Section, an 8- to 16-kilometer-wide (5 – 10 mi.) band of terminal moraine deposits marks the southern limit of the last glaciation in Pennsylvania. This moraine—consisting of scattered clays, sands, pebbles, and boulders—extends over 160 kilometers (100 mi.) through parts of Beaver, Lawrence, Butler, Venango, Mercer, Crawford, Warren, and Erie counties. Although lakes are typically small in the glaciated sections of the Commonwealth, the Glaciated Section contains the largest natural lake in the state. Conneaut Lake in Crawford County measures about 4 kilometers (2.5 mi.) long and 1 kilometer (0.6 mi.) wide.

CENTRAL LOWLAND PROVINCE

The Eastern Lake Section of the Central Lowland Province comprises an 80-kilometer (50 mi.) strip of land ranging from 3 to 8 kilometers (2 – 5 mi.) wide and bordering the southeastern portion of Lake Erie. This area of former lake deposits is now dry land characterized by gently rising terraces, except where streams have dissected underlying Devonian shales and sandstones to produce gorges up to 30 meters (100 ft.) deep. A prominent physiographic feature of this region is Presque Isle, a 10-kilometer (6.2-mi.) semicircular peninsula composed of sand deposits extending into Lake Erie and enclosing a shallow bay.

Climate

Like topography, climate plays an important role in the animal life of a region. It has an immediate effect on mammals, which must live within its extremes of heat and cold and adapt to its dry or wet conditions. Climate also affects the vegetation on which mammals depend for food and shelter.

Pennsylvania has a humid, continental climate marked by hot summers and cold winters. Prevailing winds are from the west. Because of the topographic diversity and the geographic position of the state between polar and tropical air masses, local weather patterns exhibit great variations. Areas south and east of the mountain systems have a more moderate climate and a longer growing season than other areas. To the west and north of the mountains, arctic fronts commonly produce harsh weather.

The annual temperature in Pennsylvania averages 10° C (50° F), ranging from extremes in some areas of −40° C (−40° F) to 43° C (109.4° F). The growing season extends from 100 days in the Allegheny High Plateaus Section in Potter County of northcentral Pennsylvania to as long as 205 days in the Piedmont and Coastal Plain provinces in the southeast. Both temperature and length of growing season are influenced by elevation.

Topography and altitude also influence the rainfall of a region. In Pennsylvania, annual precipitation averages 105 centimeters (40 in.). The maximum precipitation for the state occurs in the highlands of Somerset County between Laurel Ridge and the Allegheny Front, ranging from 125 to 140 centimeters (50−55 in.) per year. Because of the rainshadow effect of the Allegheny Front, precipitation lessens appreciably within the intermontane valleys of the Valley and Ridge Province. The lowest annual precipitation, averaging less than 100 centimeters (40 in.) per year, occurs at lower elevations of the North Branch of the Susquehanna and Lackawanna River valleys of northeastern Pennsylvania and in the Eastern Lake Section and Ohio Valley.

During winter months, all of Pennsylvania receives snow. The lightest snowfall takes place in the southeast corner of the Commonwealth; maximum snowfall occurs on the Pocono Plateau and in the Allegheny Mountain Section, with annual averages of 125 to 220 centimeters (50 and 85 in.) respectively. In the northern sections of the state, snowcover may persist from mid-November to mid-March.

Vegetation

Pennsylvania is endowed with a diverse array of plant communities. These range from the mature northern hardwood forests of the Pocono Plateau Section and the Valley and Ridge Province to the fresh intertidal marshes of the lower Delaware River. During the past 300 years of settlement, the original environment of the state has changed greatly. This change is apparent from reading the species accounts of those mammals no longer residing in Pennsylvania (see "Species of Uncertain Occurrence" and "Extirpated Species"). Today, less than 1 percent of the virgin forests remain—as a result of clearing, repeated logging, burning, and reforestation. Although virgin forests and grasslands have virtually disappeared, many wild and unspoiled habitats still remain to support the interesting mammalian fauna of Pennsylvania.

FORESTS

Pennsylvania may be divided into six major natural forest zones, each of which is named according to its dominant tree species (see figure 3). The following accounts of forest communities within the Commonwealth follow Kuchler (1964) and Erdman and Wiegman (1974). It is important to note that many of these forest types overlap, especially in western Pennsylvania where four exist.

Appalachian Oak Forest
The most widespread forest community in Pennsylvania is the Appalachian Oak Forest. It is composed of many different species of oaks such as red, white, black, scarlet, and chestnut mixed with hemlock and pines. Other hardwoods contributing to this forest type include maples, hickories, yellow poplar, and beech. This forest is well represented on well-drained loamy soils of hilltops, lower mountain slopes, and valleys usually at elevations below 600 meters (2,000 ft.). In the eastern United States, the Appalachian Oak Forest follows the Appalachian Mountain chain from New York, through Pennsylvania, to northern Georgia.

Northern Hardwoods Forest
Northern Hardwoods Forests are composed principally of sugar maples, yellow birch, beech, and hemlock, interspersed with white pine, oaks, and maples. Prior to extensive logging and forest fires during the late 19th century, this forest type was common throughout Pennsylvania. Today, stands of Northern Hardwoods Forests are found in northern sections of the state and extend south along the plateau summits and steep slopes of the western part of the Valley and Ridge Province, where this forest type is best represented in cool, moist ravines and on slopes that face north. In many other areas of the state, original forests of this type probably have been replaced by communities of mixed oak.

Mixed coniferous and deciduous forest habitat, typical of northcentral Pennsylvania.

Hemlock forest habitat.

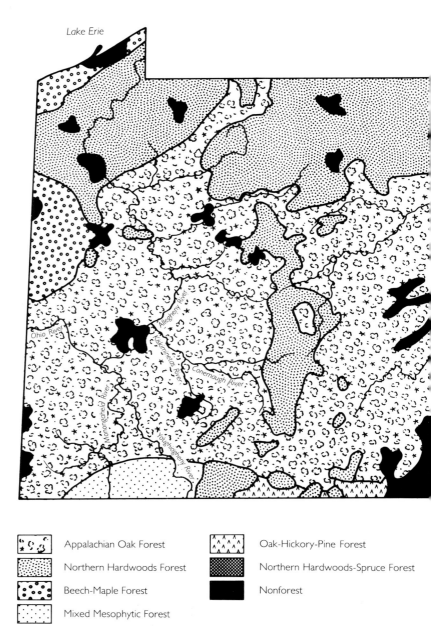

Appalachian Oak Forest

Northern Hardwoods Forest

Beech-Maple Forest

Mixed Mesophytic Forest

Oak-Hickory-Pine Forest

Northern Hardwoods-Spruce Forest

Nonforest

Source: Adapted from Kuchler (1964) and Ferguson (1968).

Figure 3. Forest Communities of Pennsylvania

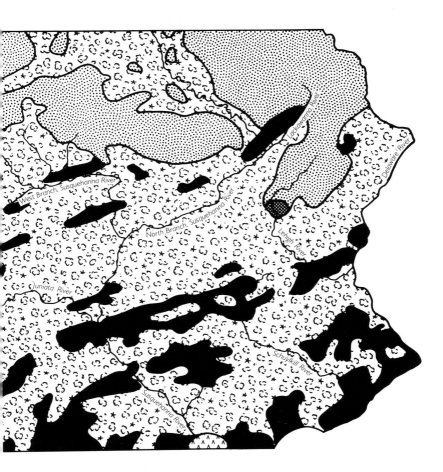

Note: This map indicates potential natural vegetation, that is, not only plants that exist in Pennsylvania today but also those that would occur today if humans were not present and if plant succession were condensed into a single moment. It is as precise as possible in depicting the plant communities in Pennsylvania; unfortunately it is not possible to illustrate the great local variations caused by differences in topography and climate and by human activities.

Deciduous forest habitat of northcentral Pennsylvania.

Beech-Maple Forest
The Beech-Maple Forest community formerly occupied the
boundaries of the Glaciated Section of northwestern Pennsylvania and was dominated principally by beech and sugar maples
interspersed with hickory, ash, and other hardwoods. Today, because of lumbering and farming, the composition of this forest
type has changed, replaced by hemlock and northern hardwood
communities in ravines and beech and sugar maple communities
in plateau areas. One of the last virgin Beech-Maple Forests is
located in Tryon-Weber Woods, near Conneaut Lake, Crawford
County (Erdman and Wiegman, 1974). In the United States, this
forest type occurs from Indiana and Michigan eastward through
Ohio and into New York.

Mixed Mesophytic Forest
The Mixed Mesophytic Forest is the most diverse of all forests in
eastern United States. It ranges from northern Alabama through
six states to its northernmost point in southwestern Pennsylvania. This predominantly southern forest consists mainly of
sugar maple, buckeye, beech, yellow poplar, white oak, red oak,
and basswood. Like the Beech-Maple Forest, the Mixed Mesophytic Forest is found primarily in river valleys or on moist
slopes.

Oak-Hickory-Pine Forest
The Oak-Hickory-Pine Forest is also best represented in southerly latitudes. In Pennsylvania, it reaches its northern limit within the Valley and Ridge and Piedmont provinces of the extreme south-central and southeastern part of the state. This forest type ranges throughout the southeastern United States and consists of a mixture of oaks, white pine, pitch pine, and Virginia pine. In the Commonwealth, it occurs mainly on serpentine barrens along dry, rocky ridges characterized by shallow, acid soils. An under-story of greenbriers and dwarf blueberries is common.

Northern Hardwoods-Spruce Forest
This forest type formerly occurred on the plateaus of Pennsylvania but—because of extensive lumbering, agricultural activities, and fires—is now rare throughout the Commonwealth. The best example of this northern forest is in Hickory Run State Park in the Pocono Plateau Section (Erdman and Wiegman, 1974). Common throughout New England, the Northern Hardwoods-Spruce Forest is characterized by red spruce, sugar maple, yellow birch, beech, and hemlock. It occupies cool, moist, well-drained soils that commonly support a lush carpet of *Sphagnum* moss and herbaceous plants such as Labrador tea, bog rosemary, and cranberries.

FARMLANDS, GRASSLANDS, OLD FIELDS, AND WETLANDS

Although forests cover much of Pennsylvania and provide food and shelter for many of the state's mammals, farmlands, grass-lands, old fields, and wetlands also supply suitable habitats. These plant communities are scattered throughout the state and are often ephemeral in existence. For example, farmland that no longer is cultivated may soon revert to a grassland community.

Grasslands, a common feature of the Pennsylvania landscape, are distributed between mountain ridges in the Appalachian Mountain Section or as broad lowland plains in the Great Valley Section. In addition, throughout much of Pennsylvania, communities composed of exotic species of grasses are being created as a by-product of surface mine reclamation. Many grasslands are, in fact, old field communities undergoing various stages of succession, reverting back to a forest community. As grasslands are established, one of the first mammals to colonize them is the woodchuck. The meadow vole also finds grassland communities to be an optimal habitat.

Farmland habitat.

Grassland habitat.

Old field habitat.

Wetlands habitat, typical of northwestern Pennsylvania.

Wetland communities such as swamps, marshes, bogs, and tidal flats are best represented in the two glaciated sections of the state and along the lower Delaware River in southeastern Pennsylvania. In the northwest, large lakes such as Pymatuning and Conneaut in Crawford County provide abundant swamps and wet meadows that support populations of aquatic mammals such as muskrats and minks. To the east, within the Pocono Plateau Section, are cool, moist, northern forests dotted with a plentiful supply of lakes, swamps, bogs, and ravines dissected by fast-moving mountain streams. This habitat is inviting to aquatic mammals such as the river otter. Within this region, forested valleys marked with abundant northern hardwoods also serve as home for another major semiaquatic mammal, the beaver.

Wetlands in the form of fresh intertidal mud flats are rare in the Commonwealth. A few can be found in the lower reaches of the Delaware River, and some of the finest marshes occur on Presque Isle on Lake Erie. Wetlands along the Delaware River grade from freshwater marshes of cattail, bullrushes, and sedges to brackish marshes supporting cordgrass, saltgrass, and other estuarine vegetation. These tidal marshes support an abundance of muskrats and also mark the northern limit of the geographic range of the marsh rice rat in North America.

MAMMALS OF PENNSYLVANIA

POUCHED MAMMALS

Order Marsupialia

The order Marsupialia is one of the most primitive orders of living mammals. It is first known from the Cretaceous Period in North America, some 130 million years ago. Because members of the order have remained structurally unchanged for the past 50 million years, they are commonly called "living fossils" of the class Mammalia.

Marsupials range in size from the tiny, 5-gram (0.2-oz.), insectivorous marsupial "mouse" of Australia to the huge, grass-eating, great gray kangaroo, which reaches 2 meters (6.6 ft.) in height and weighs approximately 90 kilograms (198 lbs.). There are marsupial "moles," "mice," "flying squirrels," "cats," and rabbit-like marsupials, as well as "woodchucks" and dog-like marsupials. In total, living representatives of Marsupialia consist of 16 or so families, broken down into some 80 genera and more than 200 species. Today, marsupials are restricted to only two geographic strongholds: the Australian region and the New World tropics.

Marsupial mammals differ from placental mammals in many ways. The most conspicuous difference is the presence of a fur-lined pouch (marsupium) on the abdomen of most female marsupials. This pouch serves as home for "embryonic" young that attach to nipples and are carried until they are capable of caring for themselves. Although the pouch is well developed in the Virginia opossum of the New World and other marsupials such as phalangers, kangaroos, wombats, bandicoots, and koalas, some marsupials have no pouch.

Marsupials can also be distinguished from placentals by the nature of the placenta. All marsupials except bandicoots have a "choriovitelline" or yolk sac placenta. Here, the fetal-maternal connection is weak and of short duration—about 12 days in the opossum. In contrast, placental mammals have a "chorioallantoic" placenta which permits a more effective exchange of materials between fetal and maternal circulations for a longer period. Lastly, female marsupials are distinguished by having a vagina and uterus that are divided by a septum, and in males the scrotum is located in front of a forked penis.

Only one family of marsupial mammals resides in North America, the Didelphidae (New World Opossums). It is represented by the Virginia opossum, which is established as far north as southeastern Canada (Ontario) and has been introduced into sections of western United States.

New World Opossums

Family Didelphidae

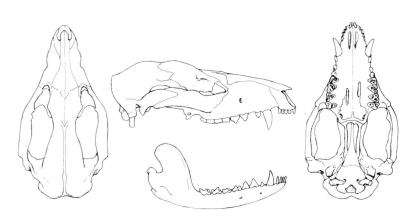

Skull of a didelphid (*Didelphis*, × ⅜).

The didelphids are the oldest-known family of marsupials. Although they presently reside primarily in tropical and subtropical areas, they originated in North America. Perhaps because of competition with evolving placental mammals, the didelphids were extirpated from the continent until the immigration from the tropics of the Virginia opossum within relatively recent geologic time. Today, the family comprises 12 genera with 66 species ranging from southeastern Canada to southern Argentina.

This age-old family of marsupials is quite diverse. Members range in size from the tiny mouse opossum of tropical rain forests, measuring only 12.3 centimeters (5 in.) in length, to the large Virginia opossum, which reaches some 90 centimeters (35 in.) and weighs up to 4.5 kilograms (10 lbs.). Many didelphids are arboreal and notably omnivorous (Virginia opossum), some are highly aquatic and carnivorous (water opossum), and still others are largely insectivorous (mouse opossum).

Didelphids are characterized by long noses and long, naked, prehensile tails. Their feet have five distinct digits, and the "great" toe (hallux) of their hindfoot is opposable and clawless. A marsupium or pouch is present in some genera but reduced or absent in others.

In Pennsylvania, the family Didelphidae is represented by only one species, *Didelphis virginiana.*

Virginia Opossum

SCIENTIFIC NAME
Didelphis virginiana (From the
Greek words *didelphis*, meaning
"double womb," and *virginiana*,
meaning "of Virginia." *Opossum*
derived from the Algonquin
Indian name *apasum*.)

SUBSPECIES IN PENNSYLVANIA
Didelphis virginiana virginiana

ALSO CALLED
Opossum, 'possum, brer 'possum,
white face

TOTAL LENGTH
650–900 mm (25.4–35.1 in.)

LENGTH OF TAIL
217–375 mm (8.5–14.6 in.)

WEIGHT
1.8–4.5 kg (4–10 lbs.)

MAMMAE
Six pairs arranged in horseshoe
configuration with one mamma in
the middle

POPULATION DENSITY
0.1–1/ha (Less than 1/acre)

HOME RANGE
4.0–24.3 ha (10–60 acres)

LONGEVITY
Up to 3 yrs. in the wild

Description

With its cone-shaped head,
pointed snout, small beady eyes,
and naked scaly tail, the Virginia
opossum does not look like any
other mammal of Pennsylvania
and is easily identified. Its long,
coarse, shaggy fur appears grayish
white, because of white underfur
and black-tipped overfur. The
adult opossum measures about the
size of a large house cat but with
shorter legs and a heavier body.
Males are larger than females. The
rat-like tail of the opossum is prehensile, that is, adapted for grasping or wrapping around objects
such as tree limbs. Its ears are thin
and leaf-like. In older opossums,
both the edges of the ears and tip
of the tail may be missing because
of frostbite sustained during periods of cold weather.

Opossum tracks can be easily

Virginia opossum (*Didelphis virginiana*).

identified. Both the forefeet and hindfeet of *D. virginiana* have five toes. All have claws except the hindfoot big toe, which has no claw and resembles a thumb in its grasping capability.

Ecology

Although the opossum has many primitive features, including a low level of intelligence, it has a wide distribution throughout Pennsylvania and northward as far as southern Canada. Some attribute the opossum's success to its generalized habitat requirements, omnivorous and opportunistic food habits, and high reproductive rate.

The opossum can live in a wide variety of habitats, ranging from dense, wooded areas to farmlands. It prefers the forest edge, close to streams or ponds, but also frequents towns and cities where household compost bins and garbage dumps tempt it with abundant food. A poor digger, *D. virginiana* commonly nests in abandoned dens and burrows of other animals such as the woodchuck, fox, and raccoon or in cavities of trees, logs, rock piles, or brush and wood piles. It also hides under buildings and even in drainpipes.

Just as the opossum lives almost anywhere, it also eats just about anything. Although the bulk of its diet consists of animal foods, chiefly insects and carrion, the opossum also eats plant material such as grapes, blackberries, pokeberries, and acorns. As a scavenger, it spends much time feeding on road-kills. This habit, coupled with nearsightedness,

poor hearing, and a slow, ambling gait, accounts for its frequent demise on highways.

In addition to killing opossums accidentally with their automobiles, some people, especially south of the Mason-Dixon line, harvest the opossum to make 'possum stew, which they feast upon with yellow corn bread and browned yams. Foxes, bobcats, dogs, hawks, and great horned owls also prey upon the opossum, and starvation and adverse winter weather kill many, especially young of the second litter. External parasites of *D. virginiana* include fleas and ticks, and it is parasitized internally by flukes, tapeworms, and roundworms. Further, the opossum is known to harbor the rabies virus and to contract the diseases tularemia and leptospirosis.

Behavior

In late autumn and during winter, the opossum is relatively inactive, especially on extremely cold days, but it does not hibernate. It usually stays in its nest made of grass and leaves. Primarily nocturnal, the opossum usually becomes active soon after dark. In the beam of automobile headlights, *D. virginiana* can be seen waddling slowly along roadsides. It might also be running, but the top speed for the opossum is only about 7.4 kilometers per hour (5 mi./hr.). When running, the opossum puts its entire foot on the ground and swings its tail awkwardly from side to side.

Just as it runs slowly, the opossum climbs and swims slowly but adeptly. It climbs hand over hand while using its prehensile tail as a "fifth leg." It swims about 1.1 kilometers per hour (0.7 mi./hr.) and, with little difficulty, covers distances up to 100 meters (330 ft.).

Its running and swimming ability offers little advantage when the opossum is faced with predators. If threatened, it may growl or hiss, crouch and defend itself, or run. The most common defense for *D. virginiana*, however, is to "play 'possum." This unique behavior of pretending to be dead is common and may result from merely seeing an enemy.

When playing 'possum, the opossum rolls over, becomes limp, closes its eyes, drools with its lips parted and tongue hanging out, and exposes its front cheekteeth in a sinister grin. This catatonic state can last from several minutes to six hours, during which time the heart beat slows considerably. The reasons for this behavior are not known. It may be caused by a type of nervous paralysis or may function as a passive defense. As an additional defense tactic, the opossum may defecate or exude a foul-smelling, greenish secretion from paired anal glands.

Reproduction and Development

Perhaps because it is a one-of-a-kind mammal in the United States, many myths have clouded the true picture of the life processes of *D. virginiana*. One particularly outrageous falsehood is that the male opossum copulates through the nose of the female, with the female "blowing" the embryos through her nostrils into the pouch! This imaginative, but mistaken notion is probably based on two observations: First, the male opossum has a forked penis, and, second, the female nuzzles her pouch shortly before her young appear there.

Females become sexually mature at one year of age. In Pennsylvania, opossums usually mate two times annually, in late February or March and in June or July. During copulation, the forked penis of the male delivers spermatozoa to the paired uteri of the female. Only 13 days later, 4 to 25 embryo-like young, the size of honeybees, emerge. These young are pink-skinned, hairless, and blind, each weighing about 0.13 grams (0.005 oz.) and measuring about 13 millimeters (0.5 in.). It is reported that an entire litter of newborn opossums can fit into a teaspoon!

When the young are being born, the mother sits up with her neck arched and her head down as the

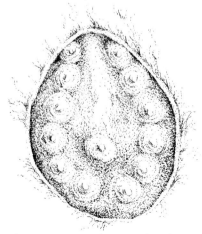

An opossum pouch, opened to show arrangement of mammae.

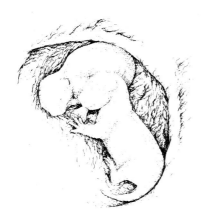

Two-week-old opossums attached to nipples within the pouch.

(2 in.) in only about 16.5 seconds, with no aid from their mother. Once inside the pouch, each individual lucky enough to find one of the mother's 13 nipples takes hold immediately. The nipples enlarge, forming a bulb within the mouth of the suckling young that remain attached until the time of weaning, some two months later.

Although as many as 25 young may be born, the entire litter cannot survive. Some young do not reach the pouch; others do not find a nipple or attach to a nonfunctional nipple. Pouched young average about eight in number and remain attached to the nipples for 50 to 65 days after birth. When they finally leave the pouch, they climb over the mother and ride on her back for another month. By the age of three to four months, the young are learning to care for themselves.

youngsters—with their well-developed, muscular forelegs and sharp claws—start to move, hand over hand, up the hair of her belly into her pouch. They traverse this distance of about 50 millimeters

SHREWS AND MOLES

Order Insectivora

The order Insectivora consists of a diverse group of mammals including shrews, hedgehogs, moles, and the tenrecs of Madagascar. Representatives of the order inhabit most of the land masses of the world except polar regions, Australia, and much of South America. Dating back to the Cretaceous Period, about 130 million years ago, this ancient order includes the earliest placental mammals.

No single characteristic defines Insectivora. Instead, the uniqueness of the order is derived from a combination of many characteristics. Almost all insectivores have five clawed toes on each foot, a long snout, and tiny beady eyes. The fur of these small mammals is often lax and dense, and the brain is comparatively simple. Their teeth are marked by small, sharp cusps adapted for eating invertebrates and insects, which form a major part of their diet. Living representatives of Insectivora include seven families, of which two are represented in Pennsylvania: the Soricidae (shrews) and the Talpidae (moles).

Shrews
Family Soricidae

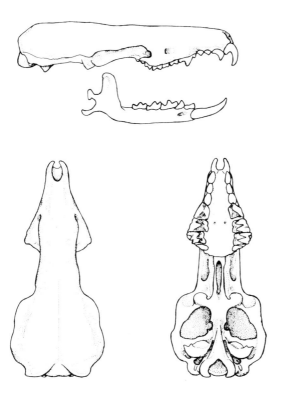

Skull of a soricid (*Crocidura*, × 1 ½).

Shrews are mouse-like in appearance, but, in contrast to mice, they have a long, pointed nose; a short, dense coat of fur; and a continuous row of needle-sharp teeth. Whereas mice have four toes on their forefeet, shrews have five clawed toes on each foot. The eyes are small and vision is poorly developed, but their hearing and smelling abilities are acute. Because male shrews do not have a scrotum and the testes are contained within the body cavity, determining the sex of shrews is difficult. Male shrews of the genus *Sorex* possess side glands which produce a substance that attracts the female, and ovulation is induced by the act of copulation.

The family Soricidae is the largest family of insectivores and includes the world's smallest land mammal, the pygmy white-toothed shrew (*Suncus etruscus*) of the Old World. This tiny animal weighs less than 2 grams (0.07 oz.), slightly less than the weight of one copper penny. The family is represented by eight species in Pennsylvania.

Masked Shrew

SCIENTIFIC NAME
Sorex cinereus (*Sorex* is Latin for
"shrew"; *cinereus* is Latin for
"ash-colored.")

SUBSPECIES IN PENNSYLVANIA
Sorex cinereus cinereus

ALSO CALLED
Cinereus shrew, common shrew,
long-tailed shrew, copper shrew,
shrew-mouse

TOTAL LENGTH
75–110 mm (3–4.3 in.)

LENGTH OF TAIL
28–48 mm (1.1–1.9 in.)

WEIGHT
3.4–5.5 g (0.1–0.2 oz.)

MAMMAE
Three pairs

POPULATION DENSITY
3–25/ha (1–10/acre)

HOME RANGE
0.2–0.6 ha (0.5–1.5 acres)

LONGEVITY
Up to 18 mos. in the wild; up to 2
yrs. in captivity

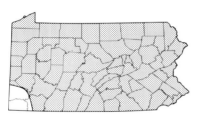

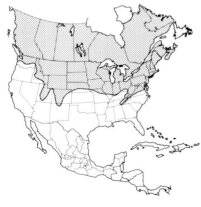

Description

The masked shrew is one of the
smallest of the eight shrews inhabiting Pennsylvania. Its eyes
are minute, its "mask" is barely
visible, and inconspicuous ears are
hidden under the thick, soft fur of
this mouse-like animal. *Sorex
cinereus* is brownish on the back
with a silvery or grayish tint on
the underside. A seasonal molt
occurs in spring and again in
autumn.

The masked shrew closely resembles the pygmy shrew and the
Maryland shrew. The latter actually was once thought to be
a subspecies of *S. cinereus*. To
distinguish these species, one
must examine specimens very
carefully. Often, only a review of
their cranial morphology verifies
identification. When *S. cinereus* is
viewed from the side, five unicuspid teeth are visible, whereas
the pygmy shrew has only three.
In general appearance, the rare
pygmy shrew and the Maryland

Masked shrew (*Sorex cinereus*).

shrew are smaller than the masked shrew. The darker brown dorsal color and the shorter, more constricted snout of the Maryland shrew also help to separate it from the masked shrew.

Other species of shrews are easier to distinguish from *S. cinereus*. The smoky shrew is larger than the masked shrew and has a darker underside. Compared with the masked shrew, the long-tailed shrew is also larger and has a longer, thicker tail. The tail of the least shrew is much shorter than that of the masked shrew.

Ecology

The masked shrew resides in a wide variety of habitats but seems to prefer moist woodlands. In Pennsylvania, it lives in moist, cool forests with abundant rocks, stumps, and ferns. Here, it forages and builds its nests under logs, in old stumps, and under clumps of vegetation. Its small, globular nests, constructed of grasses and dried leaves, measure about 7.5

centimeters (3 in.) in diameter. The masked shrew can also be found in old fields with a well-developed ground cover.

Like most shrews, the masked shrew is a voracious eater, feeding primarily on invertebrates. It is reported to eat more than three times its own body weight each day! It usually locates its food by touch and smell; its sense of sight is poorly developed. Unlike other small mammals such as mice, voles, and squirrels, the masked shrew does not cache food.

During summer, the masked shrew feeds on insects—including larvae of moths and beetles—centipedes, millipedes, spiders, slugs, snails, earthworms, and plant material. It also consumes mice and salamanders. In winter, the masked shrew's menu is mostly insect eggs and pupae. Because it eats larvae, *S. cinereus* acts as a natural control on larch sawflies in Canada. This small shrew may also prove to be important in controlling the gypsy moth in Pennsylvania.

Predators of the masked shrew

include snakes, hawks, owls, weasels, foxes, and house cats. Many mammals will kill this tiny animal, but most will not eat it because it has an offensive odor.

Behavior

Active throughout the year, the masked shrew does not hibernate and may leave tracks on top of the snow even during subzero weather. Although active both day and night, it usually forages just after dusk. When foraging, the masked shrew tends to follow runways made by itself or by other small mammals. This fact, coupled with its general nocturnal activity and small size, explains why the masked shrew is seldom observed in the wild. Actually, *S. cinereus* is one of the most widely distributed mammals in North America and is often abundant.

The masked shrew is an extremely nervous, high-strung animal. Every movement it makes is rapid. When it becomes frightened, its heart may beat 200 times per minute. In fact, *S. cinereus* could die of fright from loud noises or handling.

Reproduction and Development

The breeding season of the masked shrew begins in early spring and lasts until autumn. Because shrews can breed at the age of two months, young born in spring bear a litter by late summer. As many as three litters may be produced each year.

Litters of 2 to 10 tiny young are born after a gestation period of approximately 18 days. At birth, the young weigh about 0.1 gram (0.0035 oz.) and are blind, naked, and helpless. When they reach about nine days old, hair appears on the pups; a few days later, their eyes open. When disturbed in the nest, young masked shrews may exhibit an interesting behavior known as "caravaning": Weanlings follow behind the mother in a straight-line procession, each maintaining contact with the rump of the one in front by burying its nose in the fur near the tail. At about three weeks old, the young are weaned and must begin to care for themselves. Throughout the pregnancy and during this developmental stage, the male remains with the family.

Maryland Shrew

SCIENTIFIC NAME
Sorex fontinalis (*Sorex* is Latin for "shrew"; *fontinalis* is Latin meaning "of or from a spring or fountain.")

TOTAL LENGTH
An average of 85.6 mm (3.3 in.)

LENGTH OF TAIL
An average of 33.3 mm (1.3 in.)

WEIGHT
2.3–4.5 g (0.08–0.16 oz.)

MAMMAE
Three pairs

POPULATION DENSITY
3–25/ha (1–10/acre)

HOME RANGE
0.2–0.6 ha (0.5–1.5 acres)

LONGEVITY
Up to 18 mos. in the wild

STATUS IN PENNSYLVANIA
Undetermined

Description

The Maryland shrew is extremely difficult to distinguish from the masked shrew. (See page 43 for a photograph of the masked shrew.) Although historically it has been viewed as a subspecies of *S. cinereus*, recent reports based on statistical analyses of external and skull morphology indicate that the Maryland shrew is a distinct species.

The Maryland shrew is slightly smaller than the masked shrew, and its back is darker brown, especially on the rump. Further, unlike the silvery or grayish underside of the masked shrew, the belly of the Maryland shrew is a brownish gray. *S. fontinalis* also has a distinctly bicolored tail—dark above and light below. These color variations show greatest contrast in animals inhabiting eastern Pennsylvania. However, the two species can best be distinguished by cranial morphology. Like the masked shrew, *S. fontinalis* possesses five unicuspid teeth, rather than three as in the pygmy shrew. It also has a shorter, more constricted snout.

Ecology

The Maryland shrew resides in the south-central and southeastern counties of Pennsylvania east of the Allegheny Mountains, where it shows habitat overlap with the masked shrew. Here, habitats tend to be moist and include sedge-grass meadows, woodlands, and hedgerows in early successional areas.

The menu of the Maryland shrew consists of small insects and their larvae, annelids, and other invertebrates. Nests are commonly located below stumps or logs or within an underground tangle of roots. These tiny nests are very similar to those of the masked shrew and are composed of grass and leaves. The Maryland shrew is also reported to use abandoned ground nests of the white-footed mouse.

Behavior and Reproduction

Because *S. fontinalis* was regarded for years as the same species as the masked shrew, differences in natural history and behavior of

the two species are unknown at present. It is reported that the breeding season for the Maryland shrew begins in late February and lasts until late September. This shrew probably produces between two to three litters of four to six young each year. The gestation period is approximately 18 days. The development of young has not been studied for the Maryland shrew but is probably very similar to that of the young of the masked shrew.

Status in Pennsylvania

Very little is known about the life history and ecology of the Maryland shrew in Pennsylvania, largely because of taxonomic questions and the inability of researchers to distinguish between this shrew and the more common masked shrew. As a result, the status "undetermined" was assigned to *S. fontinalis* by the Pennsylvania Biological Survey in its report *Species of Special Concern in Pennsylvania* (Genoways and Brenner, 1985). The report recommends the establishment of a research effort to gain more knowledge of the present ecological status of this shrew in Pennsylvania with emphasis on defining its habitat requirements.

Water Shrew

SCIENTIFIC NAME
Sorex palustris (*Sorex* is Latin for "shrew"; *palustris* is Latin for "swamp" or "marsh.")

SUBSPECIES IN PENNSYLVANIA
Sorex palustris albibarbis; *Sorex palustris punctulatus* (West Virginia water shrew)

ALSO CALLED
Northern water shrew, white-lipped water shrew, big water shrew, Cope's water shrew, eastern marsh shrew, black and white shrew

TOTAL LENGTH
144–158 mm (5.6–6.2 in.)

LENGTH OF TAIL
65–72 mm (2.5–2.8 in.)

WEIGHT
10–15 g (0.4–0.5 oz.)

MAMMAE
Three pairs

POPULATION DENSITY
Unknown

HOME RANGE
Unknown

LONGEVITY
Up to 18 mos. in the wild

STATUS IN PENNSYLVANIA
Undetermined

S. p. albibarbis
S. p. punctulatus

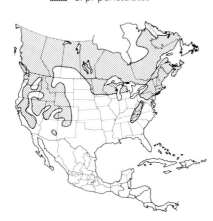

Description

The water shrew can easily be distinguished by the combination of its large size and long, bicolored tail. The only shrew in Pennsylvania weighing more than the water shrew is the northern short-tailed shrew.

Unlike the other shrews of Pennsylvania, the water shrew is semiaquatic and lives along mountain streams and in bogs. It is physically adapted to life in water, and these adaptations offer other distinctive characteristics by which to identify *S. palustris*. One unique feature of the water shrew is its large, broad hindfeet. (See the illustration for a comparison of the hindfeet of the water shrew and the smoky shrew.) The third and fourth toes of the water shrew's hindfeet are slightly webbed, and all toes have con-

Water shrew (*Sorex palustris*).
Photo by Roger W. Barbour.

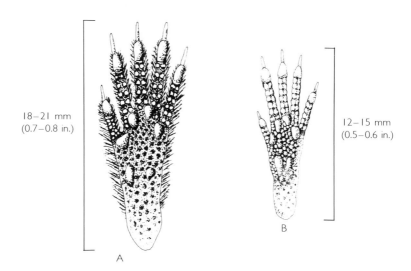

18–21 mm
(0.7–0.8 in.)

12–15 mm
(0.5–0.6 in.)

A

B

A. Hindfoot of a water shrew showing fringe of hairs.
B. Hindfoot of a smoky shrew.

spicuous stiff hairs along the sides. Both the webbing and the fringe of hairs increase the water shrew's swimming efficiency.

The fur of the water shrew is also adapted to its aquatic lifestyle. Quite dense, the fur does not allow water to penetrate it but traps air bubbles that retard wetting and enhance buoyancy. When swimming underwater or crawling on the stream bottom, the water shrew looks like a small silver submarine or a self-propelled bubble!

As with most shrews, the eyes of the water shrew are minute, and its ears are small and hidden under its bicolored coat that is black above and silver below. The spring molt occurs during late May and early June; the autumn molt takes place in September.

Ecology

Like the long-tailed shrew, the water shrew is restricted to a very specific habitat in Pennsylvania. As a result, its population is distributed in small pockets of optimal habitat, and the numbers of individuals found in these areas are generally low. This pattern contrasts with the more generalized distribution of the northern short-tailed and masked shrews.

Optimal habitat for this semi-aquatic insectivore is near mountain streams with rocky bottoms. Surrounding forests commonly are characterized by hemlock, spruce, and rhododendron—plants typical of high elevations in Pennsylvania. The water shrew's nests of dried moss can be found within bank-side burrows, under boulders, or in streamside tangles of roots.

The diet of the water shrew consists principally of small aquatic animals such as snails, worms, small fish and their eggs, and insects including nymphs of caddis flies, stone flies, and mayflies. Terrestrial invertebrates are also consumed. The water shrew is commonly preyed upon by fish such as trout and bass, by minks, otters, weasels, snakes, and, occasionally, hawks and owls. Parasites of *S. palustris* include fleas, tapeworms, and roundworms.

Behavior and Reproduction

The water shrew is active year-round, at any time of the day or night, with peaks of activity at sunrise and sunset. On a given day, this insectivore forages excitedly for short periods and then suddenly drops off to sleep. Because the eyes of the water shrew are poorly developed, it uses its keen senses of touch, hearing, and smell when foraging. Its ability to remain underwater for 15 seconds also increases the hunting success of *S. palustris*.

In addition to being an adept underwater swimmer, the water shrew is known to walk or glide on water. One report documented a water shrew running more than 1.5 meters (5 ft.) across the smooth surface of a pond (Jackson, 1961)! This impressive achievement is allowed by feet fringed with stiff hairs which can hold small globules of air and, thus, act as a sort of hydrofoil.

The breeding season of the water shrew extends from late March to August or September. Following a gestation period of about 21 days, *S. palustris* annually produces two or three litters of four to eight young. Females born in early spring may be capable of breeding in the same year.

Status in Pennsylvania

Two subspecies of the water shrew reside in Pennsylvania. The West Virginia water shrew (*S. p. punctulatus*) is reported to occur near Tumbling Cove Run in the Negro Mountains, Somerset County. The presence of this subspecies is known from only one capture of one specimen. The second Pennsylvania subspecies of water shrew (*S. p. albibarbis*) inhabits counties of central and northeastern Pennsylvania.

Populations of both subspecies occur in generally remote montane habitats characterized by plant communities of hemlock, spruce, and rhododendron in close proximity to creeks with a rocky bottom; and they exhibit narrow habitat requirements. As a result of this restricted distribution, knowledge of this shrew is scarce. The status of "undetermined," thus, was assigned to both subspecies of water shrew by the Pennsylvania Biological Survey in its report *Species of Special Concern in Pennsylvania* (Genoways and Brenner, 1985). The recommendation of the Survey includes establishing a research program aimed at delimiting populations in the Commonwealth and intensively studying the local distribution and ecology of *S. palustris*.

Smoky Shrew

SCIENTIFIC NAME
Sorex fumeus (*Sorex* is Latin for "shrew"; *fumeus* is Latin for "smoky.")

SUBSPECIES IN PENNSYLVANIA
Sorex fumeus fumeus

ALSO CALLED
Smoky Mountain shrew, northern smoky shrew, gray shrew

TOTAL LENGTH
110–126 mm (4.3–5 in.)

LENGTH OF TAIL
45–50 mm (1.8–2 in.)

WEIGHT
5–11 g (0.2–0.4 oz.)

MAMMAE
Three pairs

POPULATION DENSITY
2–15/ha (1–6/acre)

HOME RANGE
Unknown, probably slightly larger than the masked shrew

LONGEVITY
14–17 mos. in the wild

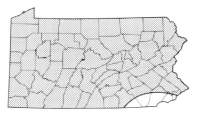

Description

The smoky shrew—close to the same size as the long-tailed shrew—is one of the largest shrews of the genus *Sorex*. It changes color with the seasons, but, because it loses hair from the entire body at once, it does not show the molt line common in deer mice and many other rodents. The May or June molt yields a summer coat of dull brown with a yellowish belly. Another molt in late September or early October results in the winter pelage of dark gray fur with slightly paler underparts. The feet of the smoky shrew are pale yellow, and the tail is bicolored, brown above and yellowish below.

Like all shrews, the smoky shrew is rarely seen alive. This small mammal may be found dead on a doorstep as the product of house cat foraging. Its long snout would verify the find as a shrew. Differentiating it from other

Smoky shrew (*Sorex fumeus*).

shrews of the genus *Sorex* is difficult but possible.

There are four species of shrews that might be confused with the smoky shrew, but can be distinguished as follows. The long-tailed shrew has a longer, thicker tail, and its belly fur is the same color as the back. The masked and Maryland shrews are smaller and browner with paler underparts. The water shrew is larger and blacker with stiff hairs along the sides of its hindfeet, and it lives near mountain streams.

Ecology

The smoky shrew prefers moist, cool forests. It lives under rotting logs and stumps and in rocky outcrops with lush vegetation and good accumulations of humus and leaf mold. In southern counties of Pennsylvania, *S. fumeus* is commonly associated with hemlock ravines and rocky habitats in maple-beech-birch forests. In northern counties, it can be found in spruce zones and *Sphagnum* bogs. Because there appears to be a strong similarity and overlap of habitats occupied by the smoky shrew and long-tailed shrew, the two species may be competitive.

Sorex fumeus eats food similar to that of most other shrews. This diet includes centipedes, millipedes, earthworms, sowbugs, small salamanders, and plant matter. The smoky shrew also feeds upon carrion, when available.

The smoky shrew, like other small forest mammals, is preyed upon by snakes, owls, hawks, foxes, weasels, and house cats. It harbors a variety of external parasites including mites, chiggers, and ticks. Internal parasites such as roundworms also infest *S. fumeus*.

Behavior and Reproduction

The smoky shrew is active year-round, throughout the day and night. Its nests of chewed-up leaves are spherical, approximately the size of a baseball, and located about 10 to 48 centimeters (5–20 in.) below the ground or in hollow logs or stumps. Burrow systems below ground or under leaf litter commonly radiate from the nest. Because the smoky shrew is not well adapted for digging, it often uses tunnels made by other small animals such as the red-backed vole, southern bog lemming, northern short-tailed shrew, or star-nosed mole.

The smoky shrew breeds from late March through September. Its young are born following a gestation period of approximately three weeks. As many as three litters of two to eight young are produced each year. Because a postpartum heat exists, another litter is on its way soon after the birth of the first litter. At birth, smoky shrews are altricial—blind, toothless, hairless, and pink throughout. In one month, they are weaned and on their own.

Long-tailed Shrew

SCIENTIFIC NAME
Sorex dispar (*Sorex* is Latin for
"shrew"; *dispar* is Latin for
"unlike" or "dissimilar.")

SUBSPECIES IN PENNSYLVANIA
Sorex dispar dispar

ALSO CALLED
Rock shrew, gray long-tailed shrew,
big-tailed shrew, longtail shrew

TOTAL LENGTH
110–135 mm (4.3–5.3 in.)

LENGTH OF TAIL
50–64 mm (2–2.5 in.)

WEIGHT
4–6 g (0.14–0.2 oz.)

MAMMAE
Three pairs

POPULATION DENSITY
Unknown, probably less than 5/ha
(2/acre)

HOME RANGE
Unknown, probably similar to the
masked shrew

LONGEVITY
Up to 18 mos. in the wild

Description

The nose of *S. dispar* is the longest, in proportion to the rest of the
body, of any Pennsylvania mammal. Nonetheless, the long-tailed
shrew is often confused with the
smoky shrew, especially during
winter when both of these small
insectivores are slate colored. At
that time of the year, one way to
tell the two species apart is by
looking at the belly hair. The
belly hair of the smoky shrew is
lighter in color than the rest of the
body hair; the hair all over the
long-tailed shrew is uniform. During summer, the long-tailed shrew
turns brownish with slightly paler
underparts. The tails of these two
shrews are also quite different.
The long-tailed shrew's tail is
thicker, rope-like, and indistinctly
bicolored.

Ecology

Sorex dispar has distinctive habitat requirements. This rare shrew

Long-tailed shrew (*Sorex dispar*).
Photo by Roger W. Barbour.

is restricted to cool, moist, very rocky areas in both deciduous and mixed forests. It is commonly found near mountain streams and eats small invertebrates such as centipedes and spiders. Its other common name, rock shrew, is derived from the fact that it forages in deep, subterranean tunnel systems among rocky outcrops where there is little or no soil but rather a loose accumulation of boulders.

The long-tailed shrew is well adapted for its life in boulder piles. Its long, slender body permits fine-tuned navigation of its labyrinth-like home, and its long tail facilitates balancing while climbing.

External parasites of the long-tailed shrew include fleas, ticks, mites, and chiggers. No information is available on the internal parasites or predators of *S. dispar*.

Behavior and Reproduction

Because it is difficult to capture the long-tailed shrew within its home of boulders, very little is known about its behavior. The breeding season probably extends from early spring to late summer, with one to two litters produced annually, with two to five young per litter.

Pygmy Shrew

SCIENTIFIC NAME
Sorex hoyi (*Sorex* is Latin for "shrew"; *hoyi* is a patronym in honor of Dr. Phila Romayne Hoy, American physician and naturalist. Although many authors assign the pygmy shrew to the genus *Microsorex*, a recent systematic study concluded that *Microsorex* is a subgenus of *Sorex*; this arrangement is followed here.)

SUBSPECIES IN PENNSYLVANIA
Sorex hoyi thompsoni

TOTAL LENGTH
84–91 mm (3.3–3.5 in.)

LENGTH OF TAIL
32–33 mm (1.2–1.3 in.)

WEIGHT
2.3–4.1 g (0.08–0.14 oz.)

MAMMAE
Four pairs

POPULATION DENSITY
0.5/ha (Less than 1/acre)

HOME RANGE
0.2 ha (0.5 acre)

LONGEVITY
Unknown

STATUS IN PENNSYLVANIA
Undetermined

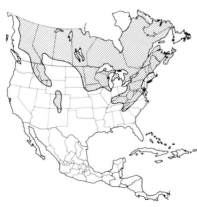

Description

The pygmy shrew, approximately the same weight as a dime, is the smallest mammal in North America and probably the smallest land mammal in the world. Its small size is rivaled only by the Old World pygmy shrews, *Sorex minutus* and *Suncus etruscus.*

Like other shrews, *S. hoyi* has small, black, beady eyes; a pointed nose; and tiny ears hidden beneath its fur. But, its small size and short tail easily distinguish the pygmy shrew from other shrews in Pennsylvania except the masked and Maryland shrews. (See page 43 for a photograph of the masked shrew.) From these, the pygmy shrew can be separated with certainty only by an examination of the unicuspid teeth at the front of the toothrow. When viewed from the side, only three unicuspid teeth are visible in *S. hoyi*, whereas five unicuspids are visible in the masked and Maryland shrews.

The short, velvety fur of the pygmy shrew varies in color from reddish brown to grayish brown on its back with paler sides and a whitish or grayish belly. During winter, the pelage changes to olive brown with smoky gray underparts. Indistinctly bicolored, the tail is brown above and paler below. The sexes are colored alike, and juveniles resemble adults in color. Typically, a spring molt occurs in late April or early May; the autumn molt takes place from late October to early November.

Ecology

In North America, the pygmy shrew inhabits a variety of ecological settings. It ranges from boreal spruce forests and *Sphagnum* bogs to dry cutover woodlands, cultivated land, and even rural gardens. Although this shrew shows great flexibility in its habitat requirements, it is most abundant in mesic montane habitats.

Until 1984, the pygmy shrew had never been captured in Pennsylvania; today, it is known to reside in three counties of the Plateau and Mountain sections of the Commonwealth (Franklin, Centre, and Clearfield counties). In Franklin County, the pygmy shrew is reported from a riparian hemlock ravine interspersed with scattered hardwoods. Here, the forest floor supports a lush layer of litter, also suitable habitat for the Maryland, smoky, and northern short-tailed shrews and the meadow vole. Farther north, in Centre County, *S. hoyi* resides in open montane bogs characterized by sedges and shrubs such as blueberry and leatherleaf encircled by forests of black spruce, balsam fir, white pine, and hemlock. Co-inhabitants of this community include the masked, smoky, long-tailed, and northern short-tailed shrews in addition to the meadow vole and meadow jumping mouse. No published information is available at this time to document the specific habitats of the pygmy shrew in Clearfield County.

The pygmy shrew is probably widespread throughout much of western Pennsylvania. Historically, its poor representation perhaps reflects inappropriate trapping methods. This tiny shrew is captured better by pitfall traps than traditional live traps or breakback traps.

The diet of the pygmy shrew closely resembles that of the more common masked shrew. Larvae of butterflies, moths, flies, and beetles are its major food. *Sorex hoyi* also consumes invertebrates such as slugs and earthworms and carcasses of dead animals. The high metabolic rate of this tiny mammal necessitates almost incessant feeding; this voracious shrew eats over twice its weight in food per day! When food is available in abundance, *S. hoyi* may cache it.

Predators of the pygmy shrew include most carnivorous mammals and probably other shrews. Its life below leaf litter probably affords some immunity from avian predators, but garter snakes and black rat snakes probably take their toll on this small animal. In addition, the pygmy shrew residing in rural areas is no doubt subject to predation by house cats. The parasites of *S. hoyi* include fleas, mites, ticks, and intestinal tapeworms.

Behavior and Reproduction

The pygmy shrew is active year-round. During winter, it has been observed traveling on the surface of the snow and is surely active in the subnivean environment, as are other shrews. Its small size permits *S. hoyi* to forage in tunnels of large beetles, earthworms, and other fossorial invertebrates.

The pygmy shrew is active both day and night, employing many short foraging bouts interrupted by brief periods of deep sleep. Its movements are rapid and erratic. It runs with its tail held straight out from its body. It is a capable climber and can jump as high as 11 centimeters (4.3 in.). Although its vision is poor, the pygmy shrew has keen senses of smell, touch, and hearing.

Sorex hoyi held in captivity is known to emit short, high-pitched squeaks. One biologist reported observing an agitated shrew sit up on its hindlegs, kangaroo-style, produce several whispering and whistling musical sounds, and then abruptly discharge a strong, musky odor.

The reproductive biology of the pygmy shrew is poorly understood. Available evidence indicates that, in Pennsylvania, this shrew produces one or two litters per year, during late spring and summer. The gestation period is unknown. Litter size probably ranges from five to eight young born in an altricial state.

Status in Pennsylvania

Until very recently, the pygmy shrew was reported from adjacent New York, Ohio, Maryland, and West Virginia but only from fossils recovered from Pleistocene cave deposits in Pennsylvania. New capture records show that *S. hoyi* is probably more widespread in the Commonwealth than previously known.

The Pennsylvania Biological Survey assigned the pygmy shrew the status of "undetermined" in its report *Species of Special Concern in Pennsylvania* (Genoways and Brenner, 1985). The Survey recommends that an intensive program of pitfall trapping be initiated in montane habitats of the Allegheny Mountains to search for the presence of *S. hoyi*. Data from the research would provide information on the distributional patterns, life history, and ecological requirements of this fascinating and little-known small mammal.

Northern Short-tailed Shrew

SCIENTIFIC NAME
Blarina brevicauda (*Blarina* is a coined name given by J. E. Gray in 1838; *brevicauda* is from the Latin words *brevis,* meaning "short," and *cauda,* meaning "tail.")

SUBSPECIES IN PENNSYLVANIA
Blarina brevicauda kirtlandi;
Blarina brevicauda talpoides

ALSO CALLED
Blarina, short-tailed shrew, mole shrew, bob-tailed shrew, shrew mouse

TOTAL LENGTH
100–132 mm (3.9–5.1 in.)

LENGTH OF TAIL
18–32 mm (0.7–1.2 in.)

WEIGHT
12.0–23.5 g (0.4–0.8 oz.)

MAMMAE
Three pairs

POPULATION DENSITY
2–25/ha (1–10/acre)

HOME RANGE
0.2–0.4 ha (0.5–1 acre)

LONGEVITY
Up to 2 yrs. in the wild; up to 33 mos. in captivity

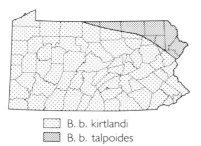

::::: B. b. kirtlandi
▓▓▓ B. b. talpoides

Description

The northern short-tailed shrew can be distinguished from other shrews in Pennsylvania by the combination of its large size, short tail, and dark slate color. The only other shrew with a short tail, the least shrew, is smaller, has a dark brownish-colored back with ashy gray underparts, and has 30 teeth instead of 32.

Ecology

The northern short-tailed shrew, the most abundant and wide-spread shrew in Pennsylvania, frequents a variety of moist habitats including deciduous, coniferous, and mixed forests, old fields, meadows, brushy thickets, and grasslands. Habitats lacking a well-developed layer of leaf litter and humus, such as dry ridges and

Northern short-tailed shrew (*Blarina brevicauda*).

shale banks, usually do not support a population of this semi-fossorial insectivore.

The diet of *B. brevicauda* is diverse. It feasts on invertebrates such as spiders, centipedes, slugs, snails, and earthworms. Being fairly large, *B. brevicauda* also preys upon salamanders, mice, voles, and, occasionally, birds. Although it prefers animal food, the northern short-tailed shrew also eats various fungi and plant material such as roots, nuts, fruits, and berries. During winter, it feeds mostly on insect larvae and pupae and, thus, serves as an important check on larch sawflies and may help to control the gypsy moth in Pennsylvania.

The northern short-tailed shrew is known to practice food hoarding or caching, a behavior well known for rodents such as squirrels. Food items cached include beechnuts, earthworms, insects, snails, plant material, and even small mice and voles.

Blarina brevicauda is one of the rare venomous mammals. Its submaxillary glands produce a venom similar to that of reptiles such as the cobra. The venom is released through a pair of ducts opening near the base of the lower incisors. Here, teeth project forward, forming a groove which facilitates the flow of venom into a wound as the shrew bites its prey. The poison quickly immobilizes small prey. If it is not consumed immediately, the prey is cached in a comatose state and, thus, is available as a fresh source of food for a period of time after capture. When humans are bitten, they may experience considerable irritation and localized swelling that could last up to three days.

Predators of *B. brevicauda* include hawks, owls, snakes, opossums, raccoons, foxes, weasels, and house cats. Many mammals kill this shrew, but most do not eat it because of its offensive smell. Its characteristic musky odor, produced by three large scent glands, is important to the shrew in establishing territories and in recognition of individuals.

Behavior

The northern short-tailed shrew is extremely active, nervous, and rather pugnacious. In confinement, it is intolerant of other small mammals, even individuals of its own species; it commonly fights and often kills other northern short-tailed shrews. Its well-developed repertoire of vocalizations extends from low and high ranges audible by humans to inaudible ultrasonic ranges. Ultrasonic vocalizations are used to detect objects in dark burrow systems by means of echolocation.

The northern short-tailed shrew is well adapted for winter survival. The density of its fur increases in winter, and it caches food. In addition, although active day or night even during frigid weather, it restricts its activity to the subnivean environment, only briefly venturing to the surface. Compared with temperatures above, the environment below the snowcover is quite warm and stable. By remaining in this zone, the shrew conserves energy for temperature

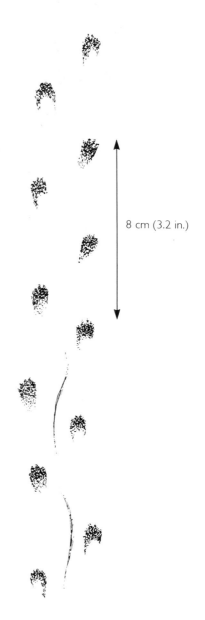

8 cm (3.2 in.)

Tracks of a short-tailed shrew in snow.

regulation and, therefore, requires less food during winter when prey is scarce. *Blarina brevicauda* also saves energy by remaining active only about 7 to 16 percent of the day, with long sleeping periods and brief, intermittent high levels of activity.

Only recently, *B. brevicauda* has been found to cope with harsh Pennsylvania winters in another way. This fascinating shrew is well endowed with a high-energy, heat-producing tissue called brown adipose tissue (brown fat), located between its shoulder blades. Brown fat allows for rapid heat production because of its abundant mitochondria which generate heat by means of oxidation of fatty acids. In response to cold temperatures, the brown fat acts like a heating blanket for vital organs such as the heart, lungs, and central nervous system. This rapid heat source permits the shrew to forage in cold zones and still mantain a normal body temperature and metabolic rate essential for proper body functions.

Two distinct types of nests are constructed by the northern short-tailed shrew: a breeding nest and a smaller resting nest. Both types of nests are generally located from 15 to 40 centimeters (6–16 in.) below ground or under logs, stumps, or old boards. They are made of grasses, sedges, and leaves arranged in the form of a hollow ball. Resting nests are about the size of a large apple, whereas breeding nests are considerably larger, ranging in diameter from 15 to 20 centimeters (6–8 in.). Both nests have from one to three openings radiating to elaborate underground burrow systems. Specific sites within the burrow systems are used as caching locations and also as "latrine" sites. Like most mammals, *B. brevicauda* does not defecate in the nest.

Reproduction and Development

The breeding season for the northern short-tailed shrew extends from mid-March to September. Females produce two to three litters per year of four to eight young, following a gestation period of 21 days.

Like other shrews, the northern short-tailed shrew is altricial at birth—naked, blind, wrinkled, dark pink, and about the size of a honeybee. By one week after birth, the young have hair and weigh about 6 grams (0.2 oz.) but still lack teeth. By the third week of life, the upper incisors show through the gums and the eyes open. Shortly thereafter, the young begin leaving the nest. They are capable of breeding when nearly three months old.

Least Shrew

SCIENTIFIC NAME
Cryptotis parva (*Cryptotis* is from
the Greek words *kryptos*, meaning
"hidden," and *otos*, meaning
"ear"; *parva* is Latin for "small"
or "petty.")

SUBSPECIES IN PENNSYLVANIA
Cryptotis parva parva

ALSO CALLED
Bee shrew, little short-tailed
shrew, small short-tailed shrew,
field shrew, small *Blarina*

TOTAL LENGTH
75–89 mm (2.9–3.5 in.)

LENGTH OF TAIL
13–20 mm (0.5–0.8 in.)

WEIGHT
4–6 g (0.1–0.2 oz.)

MAMMAE
Three pairs

POPULATION DENSITY
2–5/ha (1–2/acre)

HOME RANGE
0.17–0.23 ha (0.42–0.57 acre)

LONGEVITY
Up to 2 yrs. in the wild

STATUS IN PENNSYLVANIA
Undetermined

Description

Like other shrews, the least shrew
has small, black, beady eyes; a
long nose; five toes on each foot;
and ears hidden beneath its fine,
velvety fur. It can be distinguished
from other shrews of Pennsylvania
by its small size, short tail, and
dark brown back and ashy gray
belly. The least shrew most closely
resembles the northern short-
tailed shrew, which is larger, more
slate colored, and has 32 teeth instead of 30. The seasonal molt in
the adult least shrew takes place
in spring and early autumn.

Ecology

In contrast to most of Pennsylvania's shrews, *C. parva* is not an
inhabitant of moist, mature forests. Rather, it lives in early suc-

Least shrew (*Cryptotis parva*).
Photo by John R. MacGregor.

cessional communities such as old fields, abandoned pasturelands, and meadows of bluegrass, orchard grass, and weedy herbs.

Because of its high metabolic rate, the least shrew eats large quantities of food—as much as 60 to 100 percent of its body weight every 24 hours. Its diet, like that of other shrews, consists largely of invertebrates such as spiders, centipedes, millipedes, earthworms, and sowbugs. Unlike most shrews, the least shrew caches dead insects in its burrows for future consumption. *Cryptotis parva* also eats small salamanders and frogs. In addition, it is known for feeding on larvae and pupae and for entering beehives, a unique habit

from which the common name *bee shrew* is derived.

Owls are probably the major predator of the least shrew. House cats are also a threat to this diminutive shrew, as are many snakes and other predatory mammals. Ectoparasites include fleas, mites, and chiggers, and internal parasites consist of tapeworms, roundworms, and flukes.

Behavior

The least shrew is active year-round, at all hours of the day and night, but its activity is greatest during evening hours. It commonly forages in runways of meadow voles and, although not a noisy animal, is known to utter high-pitched chirpings and clicking sounds.

Under rocks, logs, stumps, or old boards, *C. parva* builds globular nests of dried grass and leaves. These nests, which measure 75 to 125 millimeters (3–5 in.) in diameter, are usually not far below ground. They have two entrances which give way to tunnels to the surface.

The least shrew is gregarious and colonial—a habit uncommon to most other North America shrews, which are belligerent and intolerant of one another when in close range. One scientist discovered 31 adult least shrews sharing a single nest in the wild (McCarley, 1959). Other reports indicate that this communal nesting tendency is common during winter months. For a small mammal with a high metabolic rate and a breathing rate of 70 breaths per minute, communal nesting aids in conserving heat during frigid winter weather.

Reproduction and Development

The breeding season for *C. parva* in Pennsylvania is not well known; it probably extends from March to late November. During this relatively long period, females probably produce three litters with an average litter size of five young, following a gestation period of 21 to 23 days. Females born in spring are capable of breeding during the same year.

When born, least shrews are naked, blind, translucent pink, and weigh about 0.3 gram (0.01 oz.). When they reach two weeks of age, they are fully haired and their eyes are open. At three weeks, they are weaned. Presumably, both parents care for the offspring; pairs of adults have been found in the nests with the young.

Status in Pennsylvania

Populations of the least shrew in Pennsylvania are widely scattered, and their densities are not great. This species characteristic, coupled with the failure of conventional small mammal trapping techniques, in part accounts for the poor knowledge of the biology of *C. parva* in the Commonwealth.

The paucity of information about the least shrew prompted the Pennsylvania Biological Survey to classify the least shrew as "status undetermined" in its report *Species of Special Concern in Pennsylvania* (Genoways and Brenner, 1985). The Survey recommended that pitfall traps be used in an extensive least shrew trapping effort. The data derived from the research would add to the understanding of the local distribution and population dynamics of *C. parva* in Pennsylvania.

Moles

Family Talpidae

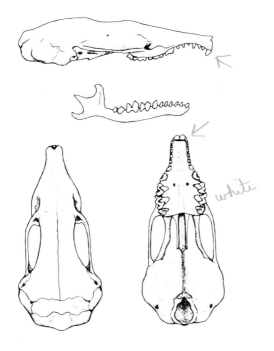

Skull of a talpid (*Scapanus*, × 1½).

The moles are a family of mammals especially adapted to fossorial (burrowing) life. They have a cylindrical, stout body with greatly enlarged and modified forefeet, arms, and shoulders. Their spade-like forefeet, with broad palms turned permanently outward, provide effective digging tools. Their shortened, flattened humeri (upper arm bones) increase leverage and provide ample surface area for attachment of their powerful digging muscles. Also, the pelvic girdle and hindlimbs of moles are greatly reduced, enabling them to turn easily in a narrow tunnel.

The head is conical, and the neck, short and muscular. There are no external ear pinnae (flaps); the openings are hidden beneath soft, velvety fur, which lies in any direction. The eyes, the size of pinheads, are hidden in the fur and serve little use. In

Underside of an eastern mole showing spade-like foot.

50 cm (20 in.)

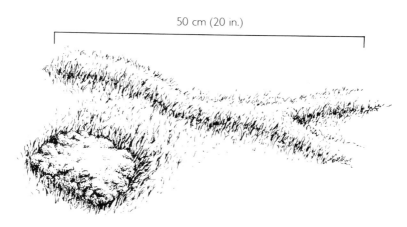

Molehill and surface tunnel of a mole.

some moles, the eyes lie beneath the skin. Like shrews, moles have teeth with needle-sharp cusps, which are adapted to their diet of insects and other invertebrates.

Living moles are currently classified into about 15 genera and 30 species residing in North America, Europe, and Asia. The three species found in Pennsylvania are regarded as pests by farmers, gardeners, and golf-course groundkeepers. Since their role as tillers of soil and consumers of soil insects is unsurpassed in the animal world, they are highly beneficial to humans. Widespread extermination of moles may cause a resurgence of harmful insect pests that reside in soil.

Hairy-tailed Mole

SCIENTIFIC NAME
Parascalops breweri (*Parascalops* is Latin for "large, rounded forefeet that act as a shield"; *breweri* is for Brewer, a zoologist.)

ALSO CALLED
Brewer's mole, Brewer's hairy-tailed mole

TOTAL LENGTH
145–168 mm (5.7–6.5 in.)

LENGTH OF TAIL
23–35 mm (0.9–1.4 in.)

WEIGHT
40–64 g (1.4–2.2 oz.)

MAMMAE
Four pairs

POPULATION DENSITY
3–27/ha (1–11/acre)

HOME RANGE
0.1 ha (0.2 acre)

LONGEVITY
3–4 yrs. in the wild

Description

The hairy-tailed mole is distinguished from other eastern United States moles by its small size and the presence of a short, hairy tail. It wears a velvety coat ranging from dark slate to black with slightly paler underparts. Its head is triangular, with minute ears covered by fur and ears that lack pinnae (flaps). As in other moles, the palms of its forefeet are enlarged and nearly circular in outline.

Females are generally smaller than males. The spring molt for *P. breweri* begins as early as late March and is complete by mid- or late May. The autumn molt begins in mid-September and is completed by mid-October.

Ecology

The hairy-tailed mole is common in Pennsylvania, where it prefers sandy loam soils with a good vege-

Hairy-tailed mole (*Parascalops breweri*).

tative cover. It seldom occupies extremely wet or dry areas or zones where soils have a high clay content. The plant community type is unimportant, and acceptable habitats range from grassy and brushy areas to mature forests.

Like many shrews, the hairy-tailed mole is a voracious eater and may consume up to three times its weight in food per day. Its main food consists of the larvae of beetles. It also eats other insects (both adults and larvae), snails, spiders, millipedes and centipedes, earthworms, sowbugs, and roots. *Parascalops breweri* consumes very little plant material.

Dogs, cats, foxes, and snakes pose the greatest threat to the hairy-tailed mole. Because *P. breweri* visits the surface of the ground at night, owls also prey on this species. In addition, the northern short-tailed shrew may kill unprotected nestling moles. Fleas, mites, and lice are common external parasites of the mole, and internal parasites include roundworms and spiny-headed worms.

Behavior and Reproduction

Active both day and night year-round, the hairy-tailed mole does not hibernate or undergo torpidity. Like all moles, it spends most of its life below ground in a complex system of tunnels which may remain in use for up to eight years. During its foraging, the hairy-tailed mole employs surface tunnels and deep tunnels, both measuring about 3.7 centimeters by 2.5 centimeters (1.5 in. × 1 in.). Surface tunnels are easily recognized in loose soils by the presence of ridges which may follow surface features such as boulders or logs. Deep tunnels, in contrast, are usually located between 25 to 45 centimeters (10–18 in.) below ground and serve as nest locations and wintering sites.

Molehills, produced by soil that has been pushed up during the construction of deep tunnels, also act as a clue to the presence of this mole. The hills of *P. breweri*, having a diameter of approximately 15 centimeters (6 in.) and a height of 7.5 centimeters (3 in.), are smaller then those of its relative the star-nosed mole. In autumn, molehills tend to be more common, because moles are actively digging deep tunnels in preparation for winter.

The hairy-tailed mole builds nests for resting, breeding, and wintering. Resting nests are about 8 centimeters (3 in.) in diameter and are merely enlargements of a tunnel. Breeding nests, on the other hand, are placed in larger spherical cavities about 30 centimeters (12 in.) below ground, measure about 15 centimeters (6 in.) in diameter, and are composed of dry leaves. The most elaborate nest is the winter nest, sometimes found at depths of 41 centimeters (16 in.) below ground. This nest measures about 20 centimeters by 15 centimeters (8 in. × 6 in.) and is composed of a bulky mass of well-packed leaves and grass.

The eyesight of *P. breweri* is poorly developed; it can only discriminate between light and dark. Its sense of smell, on the other hand, is well developed, and it can detect food as far away as 6 centimeters (2 in.). Both its sense of smell and touch are concentrated in its moist, pink nose, which is in constant motion when the mole is searching for food. Hearing undoubtedly plays a role in food acquisition and in social behavior, but little direct evidence of this is available.

The hairy-tailed mole is solitary for most of the year except during the mating period. Breeding occurs in early March, and four to five young are born following a gestation period of about four to six weeks. Only one litter is produced each year. The young are born hairless and toothless, and their eyes are covered by skin. They remain in the nest for approximately one month after birth, when they begin eating solid food. Females are able to reproduce at 10 months of age.

Eastern Mole

SCIENTIFIC NAME
Scalopus aquaticus (*Scalopus*
combines the Greek words
skalops, meaning "to dig," and
pous, meaning "foot"; *aquaticus*,
from a Latin word meaning "water
dwelling," is a misnomer applied
to the species by Linnaeus in 1758
probably because of the mole's
webbed feet.)

SUBSPECIES IN PENNSYLVANIA
Scalopus aquaticus aquaticus

ALSO CALLED
Common mole, ground mole,
common shrew-mole, garden
mole, naked-tailed mole

TOTAL LENGTH
143–205 mm (5.6–8 in.)

LENGTH OF TAIL
19–38 mm (0.7–1.5 in.)

WEIGHT
65–140 g (2.3–4.9 oz.)

MAMMAE
Three pairs

POPULATION DENSITY
Unknown

HOME RANGE
0.3–1.0 ha (0.7–2.5 acres)

LONGEVITY
3–4 yrs. in the wild

Description

The eastern mole is easily identified by the combination of its
short, naked tail and its greatly
enlarged, spade-like forefeet.
These forefeet are usually held
with the palms facing outward
and are broader than long with
heavy claws adapted for digging.
The long, pointed nose, naked
at the tip, further distinguishes
S. aquaticus from the star-
nosed mole.

The eastern mole wears a coat
of short, dense, velvety fur that
ranges in color from black with a
silver sheen to gray and brown. Its
small ears are concealed in the fur,
and its minute eyes are covered by
thin membranes (fused eyelids).
The winter pelage of the eastern
mole is slightly darker than that
of summer, and males may have
an orange stripe on the underside

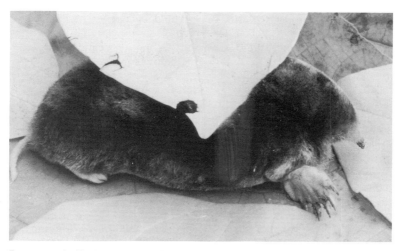

Eastern mole (*Scalopus aquaticus*).
Photo by John R. MacGregor.

because of a secretion of their abdominal skin glands. The eastern mole undergoes seasonal molts in spring and autumn.

Ecology

Unlike the star-nosed mole, the eastern mole tends to avoid wet, loose soils and swamps. Preferring well-drained, sandy soils, *S. aquaticus* makes its home in southeastern Pennsylvania. Its tunnels can be found in forests, fields, lawns, golf courses, cemeteries, and meadows.

Although *S. aquaticus* allegedly feeds on grasses and tubers, it, in fact, eats soil invertebrates—mainly earthworms and insects, both larvae and adults—and, to a lesser degree, vegetable matter. In captivity, this mole is quite omnivorous; it devours corn, wheat, tomatoes, apples, potatoes, seeds, and even mice. One captive eastern mole was reported to consume about 32 percent of its body weight per day.

Because of its subterranean habits and musky odor, the eastern mole has few natural predators. If the opportunity arises, foxes, skunks, owls, hawks, and snakes may consume moles. Domestic dogs and cats occasionally dig up a mole but rarely eat it because of its offensive odor. Flooding of subterranean burrows probably causes the highest mortality to the eastern mole. If this mole makes its tunnel system in a golf course, lawn, or garden, it may be killed by humans.

A number of external parasites have been reported for *S. aquaticus:* fleas, biting and sucking lice, mites, chiggers, and even parasitic beetles. Internal parasites include tapeworms, roundworms, and spiny-headed worms.

Behavior

Scalopus aquaticus does not hibernate and is active both day and night year-round. Its tunnel systems are generally of two types: those just beneath the surface and those more permanent tunnels deeper underground. The surface tunnels, more conspicuous than those of the hairy-tailed mole, form the characteristic ridges well known to gardeners. They are used mainly for foraging and are normally dug at a rate of about 3 to 6 meters (10–20 ft.) per hour.

The mole builds its tunnels by moving its broad forefeet sideways, using alternating sidestrokes. The dirt is then passed under the body to the hindfeet and kicked to the rear. Once a pile of dirt accumulates behind the mole, it makes a U-turn in its burrow and pushes the dirt, with one of its forefeet, into an unused section of the tunnel or to the surface of the ground by way of a vertical tunnel. As a result of these excavations, molehills are created. The eastern mole is reported to construct up to 31 meters (102 ft.) of tunnel per day. To repair damaged tunnels, the mole burrows beneath the damaged area and pushes up the floor of the old burrow.

The deeper, more permanent tunnels used by *S. aquaticus* are located about 25 centimeters (10 in.) below ground. These deeper burrows are commonly dug in spring and are marked only by a circular mound of dirt on the ground surface. Within these deep burrows, the eastern mole builds its nest lined with roots, grass, and leaves. The nest chamber measures about 10 to 20 centimeters (4–8 in.) in diameter and is used as a maternity site as well as a haven from heat and cold. A special location in the complex of tunnels is established for a "latrine."

Reproduction and Development

The eastern mole commences breeding in early spring. Following a gestation period of about four weeks, a litter of two to five young is born. They are pink, blind, and hairless. By 10 days old, the young have a coat of fine, velvety fur. When about four weeks of age, they leave the nest and fend for themselves. The eastern mole is usually capable of breeding at about one year of age.

Star-nosed Mole

SCIENTIFIC NAME
Condylura cristata (*Condylura*
means "three processes of the
tail"; *cristata* means "crested,"
referring to the fleshy tentacles of
the nose.)

SUBSPECIES IN PENNSYLVANIA
Condylura cristata cristata

ALSO CALLED
Long-tailed mole, black mole,
swamp mole

TOTAL LENGTH
175–204 mm (6.8–7.9 in.)

LENGTH OF TAIL
65–84 mm (2.5–3.3 in.)

WEIGHT
37–76 g (1.3–2.7 oz.)

MAMMAE
Four pairs

POPULATION DENSITY
2–41/ha (1–16/acre)

HOME RANGE
Unknown

LONGEVITY
3–4 yrs. in the wild

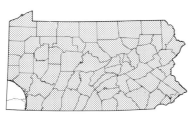

Description

The star-nosed mole is unique
among mammals in having 22
fleshy tentacle-like appendages
around the tip of its nose. These
nose tentacles are highly sensitive
tactile organs, called Eimer organs,
that work as a unit. With poorly
developed eyesight and only a
moderately developed sense of
smell, the star-nosed mole uses
this impressive snout and long
whiskers to probe and search out
prey. Its whiskers are located on
the sides of the snout, on the sides
of the eyes and ears, and even on
the forefeet. With so many touch
receptors, the star-nosed mole has
a better-developed sense of touch
than any other mole.

Except for its prominent pink
snout, the star-nosed mole is covered with a dense, coarse coat of
black or dark brown fur. This
waterproof coat is only one of the
star-nosed mole's adaptations for

Star-nosed mole (*Condylura cristata*).
Photo by Dwight R. Kuhn.

Head of a star-nosed mole.

aquatic life. Its dark, scaly, rat-like tail—almost one-third of its total length—acts as a rudder when the mole is swimming. Also, its long, spade-like forefeet provide "paddling power." The forefeet seem to extend from the sides of the head, because of the foreshortening of the neck and the entire shoulder region. Each of the five stubby toes of the forefeet is equipped with a heavy claw longer than the toe itself.

Condylura cristata is further distinguished by having 44 teeth characterized by low, sharp cusps; the number is exceeded in North America only by the 50 teeth of the opossum.

Ecology

The star-nosed mole, the only semiaquatic mole, spends time both underground and in water. Preferring water-saturated soils, it can be found in deep, mucky soils of wet bottom lands as well as on steep slopes and in wet areas of high ridges. It often builds tunnels near marshy areas or streams; these tunnels commonly open directly into water. In southwestern Pennsylvania, the star-nosed mole may be found in wet bottom lands of alder, silky dogwood, and arrowwood with an understory of skunk cabbage, green hellebore, marsh marigold, cattails, and rushes. In contrast, the star-nosed mole of northwestern Pennsylvania is known to occur in hay meadows of timothy, red clover, and orchard grass, where it has been found beneath stacks of spoiled hay.

Adept at swimming and diving, the star-nosed mole hunts mostly along stream bottoms where it finds aquatic invertebrates such as worms and insects, namely larvae of caddisflies, midges, and stoneflies. *Condylura cristata* also eats crustaceans, molluscs, and small fish. During winter, it forages below the ice in frozen ponds and streams and is highly dependent on bottom-dwelling prey. When foraging in its tunnel system, the star-nosed mole searches for earthworms, grubs, and other invertebrates. It is a voracious eater and consumes 50 percent or more of its body weight each day.

The star-nosed mole falls prey to a legion of predators including great horned owls, barn owls, screech owls, red-tailed hawks, skunks, foxes, weasels, and snakes. It is also frequently caught by house cats and is not immune to predation by large fish. *Condylura cristata* is infected by a number of external parasites including mites and fleas and internal parasites such as roundworms and tapeworms.

Behavior

Condylura cristata is active year-round both day and night. Like other moles, it spends a little less than half the day sleeping. In contrast to most insectivorous mammals, it is rather social and gregarious, sharing tunnels and runways with other moles of the same species. Star-nosed moles live in small colonies; some biologists believe that they reside in pairs during winter and that males disperse in the spring when the young are born.

Unlike other burrowing mammals, such as pocket gophers, which dig by holding their forefeet beneath their bodies, the star-nosed mole digs with its forelimbs held to the side. Like the hairy-tailed and eastern moles, *C. cristata* constructs two types of tunnels, one shallow and one deep. The shallow tunnels, a product of the mole's constant foraging activity, are not as pronounced and regular as those of other species of moles. Located near the ground surface, the tunnels form a visible ridge of soil well known to golf-course groundkeepers.

The deeper tunnel system, sometimes located several meters

below the ground surface, is more permanent and used for resting, rearing young, and foraging during winter when the ground surface is frozen. As with the hairy-tailed and eastern moles, excavation of deep tunnels produces the well-known molehills which may measure up to 25 centimeters (10 in.) in diameter. When forming molehills, the mole does not carry dirt onto the surface but forces it up from deep in the tunnel. Hence, their molehills never have the central hole found in crayfish mounds.

Nests of *C. cristata* are always located above the high-water level and close to food resources. An enlarged section of the tunnel is chosen for the spherical nest made of dead leaves, straw, and grasses. These nests measure approximately 15 centimeters (6 in.) in diameter.

Reproduction and Development

The star-nosed mole does not show the prolific reproductive potential of rodents such as mice and voles. Each year, females bear only one litter of three to seven young, following a comparatively long gestation period of about 45 days. Breeding commences in early spring, and the young are born in May and June.

Newborn moles are naked, blind, pinkish, and about 50 millimeters (2 in.) long; they weigh 1.5 grams (0.05 oz.). When they are about 10 days old, hair appears. Young develop rapidly and leave the nest when they are four weeks old, at which time they weigh about 33 grams (1.5 oz.). Both females and males can breed at about 10 months of age.

BATS

Order Chiroptera

Bats are the only true flying mammals and date back to the
Eocene Epoch about 50 million years ago. With 17 families,
about 170 genera, and some 850 species, bats make up the second largest mammalian order in terms of numbers of species,
second only to the rodents. Bats are divided into two distinct
suborders: the Megachiroptera (flying foxes) and Microchiroptera
(all other bats). The Megachiroptera inhabit the tropics and sub-
tropics of the Old World, whereas the Microchiroptera are distributed throughout the world.

The name *Chiroptera*, "hand-winged," refers to the characteristic that makes bats unique: Since bats have wings, they exhibit
true flight. The wing of the bat is composed of a very thin, double-
layered skin membrane (patagium) stretched over greatly elongated finger bones (phalanges). This membrane runs along the side
of the body, over and between the forearm, hand, and finger bones,
and connects to the hindleg. The short, clawed thumb (pollex) is
free of the wing membrane and is used for grasping.

Most bats also have an interfemoral or tail membrane (uropatagium) which unites the legs, body, and tail. Another cartilaginous structure, the calcar, extends back from the foot along
the free edge of the tail membrane and helps to support this membrane. The calcar varies with different species of bats and may be
used in their identification. (See the illustration in "Plain-nosed
Bats: Family Vespertilionidae.")

Other adaptations enhancing flight include a keeled sternum,
which anchors the pectoral muscles that support the wings, and
a knee, which is directed backward and upward, permitting bats
to hang upside down by their toes. This posture facilitates "take
off"; a bat can spread its wings, release its toe hold, and quickly
become airborne.

Bats are nocturnal and habitually fly in darkness, when their
small eyes are clearly of little use. As a consequence, they use
their extremely acute auditory and tactile receptors and navigate
by echolocation or sonar. They emit ultrasonic sounds through
the nose or mouth. As these sound waves strike objects such as
insects, the echo is reflected to the bat, which then pursues and

entraps the prey in its interfemoral membrane or its wing and commonly consumes the insect in flight.

The ears of bats are relatively large and well developed with a prominent leaf-like flap inside the pinna called a tragus, which also aids in echolocation. This structure varies greatly within the Microchiroptera and is useful in species identification.

Bats show great diversity in food habits. The diets of some bats include plant items such as fruit, nectar, and pollen. Carnivorous bats include fish-eating bats and those that prey on birds, rodents, and even other bats. Most bizarre are the true vampire bats, which feed exclusively on the blood of large mammals and birds in the New World tropics. Contrary to popular belief, these bats do not suck blood from their victims; rather, they make a small incision in their prey, inject an anticoagulant into the incision to prevent clotting, and lap free-flowing blood. Although diets vary greatly within the Microchiroptera, many bats, including all bats of Pennsylvania, feed on insects.

Plain-nosed Bats

Family Vespertilionidae

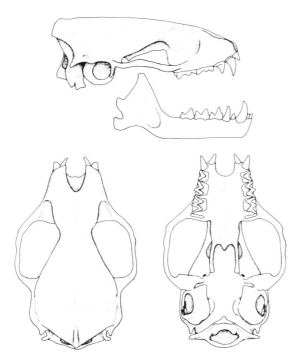

Skull of a vespertilionid (*Eptesicus*, × 2½).

In Pennsylvania, all bats belong to the family Vespertilionidae, the most common North American family of bats. Morphological characteristics defining the family include a complete interfemoral membrane, a tail which reaches to the back edge of the interfemoral membrane but not beyond it, and a muzzle which lacks leaf-like flaps. The incisors of vespertilionids are small, and the molars are characterized by well-developed, W-shaped cusps adapted for an insect diet.

Vespertilionids are mainly nocturnal and feed upon flying insects captured in the air. Because their food supply is not avail-

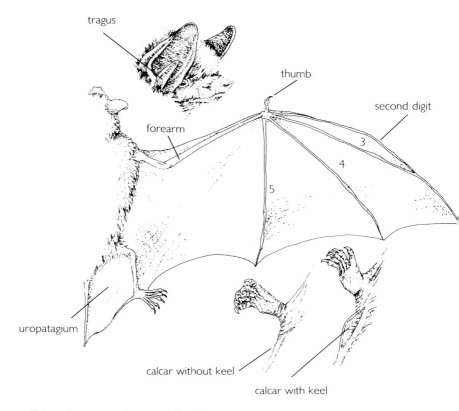

External anatomy of a vespertilionid bat.

able year-round, bats of Pennsylvania either hibernate during winter or migrate to warmer climates.

Vespertilionidae is the largest family in the order Chiroptera and consists of approximately 300 species and 35 genera with a worldwide distribution. Eleven species representing six genera occur in Pennsylvania.

Little Brown Myotis

SCIENTIFIC NAME
Myotis lucifugus (*Myotis* is
from the Greek words *mys*, for
"mouse," and *otis*, meaning "ear";
lucifugus is derived from two
Latin words meaning "light
fleeing.")

SUBSPECIES IN PENNSYLVANIA
Myotis lucifugus lucifugus

ALSO CALLED
Little brown bat, common bat,
blunt-nosed bat, LeConte's bat,
cave bat

TOTAL LENGTH
79–94 mm (3.1–3.7 in.)

LENGTH OF TAIL
32–44 mm (1.2–1.7 in.)

LENGTH OF EAR
12–16 mm (0.5–0.6 in.)

LENGTH OF FOREARM
33–41 mm (1.3–1.6 in.)

WEIGHT
6–9 g (0.2–0.4 oz.)

MAMMAE
One pair

LONGEVITY
Up to 25 yrs. in the wild

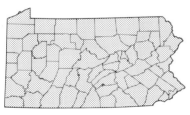

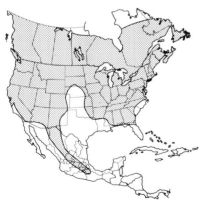

Description

The little brown myotis has a
well-furred face; small, beady
eyes; and a broad, blunt muzzle.
The hair on its back is dark to
buffy brown with long, metallic
tips that give *M. lucifugus* its
characteristic glossy sheen. The
underside of this bat is rather pale,
usually with a grayish tinge. Its
annual molt occurs in July, with
new pelage simultaneously growing in under the old fur. As a result, distinct molt lines are not
discernible.

The ears of the little brown
myotis are dark brown and relatively short and rounded, with a
rather short, blunt tragus that is
less than half the length of the
pinna. When laid forward, the ears
reach to the nostrils but not beyond. The calcar generally lacks a
keel or may be weakly keeled.

Myotis lucifugus differs from
similar species as follows: Keen's

Little brown myotis (*Myotis lucifugus*).

myotis has a longer tragus, paler and less glossy pelage, and longer ears than the little brown myotis. When laid forward, the ears of Keen's myotis reach well beyond the nose. Indiana myotis has a definite keel on the calcar, smaller feet with shorter hairs on the toes, and a duller pelage. Actually, no single characteristic separates the little brown myotis from other bats in Pennsylvania. It is rather nondescript, and identification is facilitated by employing a process of eliminating the other more distinctive species.

Ecology

The little brown myotis is the most common bat in Pennsylvania. Single males and barren females may be found roosting in a wide variety of places: barns, attics, caves, mine tunnels, hollow trees, in the loose bark of trees, under house shutters and eaves, and even in picnic pavilions. During summer, nursery colonies normally roost in attics of buildings warm enough to foster rapid growth of the young. Both nursery colonies and roosts are usually close to water.

Like other bats of the genus *Myotis*, little brown myotis feeds mainly on flying insects such as beetles, mosquitoes, moths, bugs, and flies. Its nightly foraging begins shortly after sunset and is concentrated near ponds and streams where it can be seen drinking water on the wing. It forages again prior to dawn. Most foraging occurs about 3 to 6 meters (10–20 ft.) above water or land. Prey is located by echolocation, captured while flying, quickly transferred to a sort of "basket" formed by the curling forward of the uropatagium, and then quickly transferred to the bat's mouth.

The little brown myotis has a voracious appetite, consuming large numbers of insects each night. It may fill its stomach in an hour or two, consuming half its body weight per night. A colony of 100 *M. lucifugus* reportedly consumed 19.2 kilograms (42 lbs.) of insects during a four-month summer period. These large quantities of food are necessary to support the high metabolic rate necessary for a bat's flight.

Following foraging, the little brown myotis will return to its roost and alight with its head in an upright position while hooking its thumbs and hindfeet to an object. It then quickly turns its head down and hangs by its hindfeet.

For the most part, the little brown myotis is free from natural predators, although minks, raccoons, hawks, owls, snakes, bass, and house cats occasionally prey on it. The worst enemy of the little brown myotis and bats in general is mankind. Because *M. lucifugus* forms large congregations during hibernation and while in maternity colonies, it is extremely vulnerable to human activity. Many bats hibernating in caves are killed or their hibernation process is disturbed—which indirectly may kill them. When disturbed and forced to fly, bats use up their stored fat reserves. If disturbances continue, fat may be depleted and, thus, the bats will not survive the winter.

Maternity colonies, frequently found in attics of houses, are commonly eliminated by various techniques ranging from shooting with BB guns to eradication by automobile exhaust fumes. The best way to deal with the problem of having bats in the attic is to prevent their entry by sealing all outside entrance holes.

A high mortality in *M. lucifugus* can also be attributed to natural causes. Many bats are killed by cave floods, and large numbers perish in storms during migration. Further, they are occasionally found impaled on barbed-wire fences or entangled in burrs on burdock plants.

The little brown myotis harbors external parasites such as chiggers, fleas, ticks, wing mites, and bat bugs. Internal parasites include tapeworms and roundworms. *Myotis lucifugus* also is known to carry and transmit rabies.

Behavior

Little brown myotis flies at an average speed of 20.3 kilometers per hour (13 mi./hr.) but can reach speeds of up to 35 kilometers per hour (22 mi./hr.). When moved experimentally as far as 432 kilometers (270 mi.) from its home site, *M. lucifugus* returned to its original location, thus demonstrating a strong homing tendency.

By early autumn, the little brown myotis has put on fat amounting to about one-third of its body weight in preparation for hibernation. At this time, a phenomenon called "swarming" may occur, when large numbers of *M. lucifugus* congregate around cave entrances. The purpose of this behavior is not fully known, but it may serve a prenuptial function and familiarize the young with locations for possible places to hibernate (hibernacula).

By late autumn in Pennsylvania, many bats will gather in caves and abandoned mine shafts to hibernate. Sites characterized by high humidity and above-freezing temperatures are preferred as hibernacula. During hibernation, metabolism and body temperature drop greatly, resulting in lowered respiration and heartbeat. This deep sleep may be interrupted periodically, at which time the bat may drink water but will not feed.

Reproduction and Development

Little brown myotis mates in early autumn, prior to hibernation, and sperm is stored in the female's uterus during winter. Actual fertilization occurs in spring when the bat emerges from hibernation. At this time, females disperse to warmer quarters and establish maternity colonies, with as many as 1,000 or more females sharing one site. Following the period of hibernation, males venture out and lead bachelor lives throughout summer. After a gestation period of 50 to 60 days, a single, black, naked, blind offspring is born, usually in late May or early June. During parturition, the female hangs by her thumbs (which is upside down for a bat). She forms a "basket" with her upturned uropatagium. This "basket" is used to catch the offspring following the half-hour labor.

At birth, a young bat weighs about 1.5 grams (0.05 oz.)—about one-quarter of the weight of the mother. Normally, the offspring is left to cling to the roost when the mother forages. If surprised in the roost, however, the mother takes the young bat into flight. She does this by carrying it in crosswise fashion with the infant attached to one nipple with its hindlegs tucked under the mother's opposite armpit.

The newborn grows rapidly and begins to fly in the roost at about three weeks of age. It begins foraging for insects at about four weeks of age, when the colony is disbanded. At about eight months of age, *M. lucifugus* reaches sexual maturity.

Keen's Myotis

SCIENTIFIC NAME
Myotis keenii (*Myotis* is from the Greek words *mys,* meaning "mouse," and *otis,* meaning "ear"; *keenii* is a patronym recognizing the Reverend John Henry Keen, who collected the type specimen in 1894.)

SUBSPECIES IN PENNSYLVANIA
Myotis keenii septentrionalis

ALSO CALLED
Keen's bat, eastern long-eared bat, acadian bat

TOTAL LENGTH
79–91 mm (3.1–3.5 in.)

LENGTH OF TAIL
36–40 mm (1.4–1.6 in.)

LENGTH OF EAR
14–18 mm (0.5–0.7 in.)

LENGTH OF FOREARM
34.6–38.8 mm (1.3–1.5 in.)

WEIGHT
6–9 g (0.2–0.4 oz.)

MAMMAE
One pair

LONGEVITY
Up to 18½ yrs. in the wild

STATUS IN PENNSYLVANIA
Vulnerable

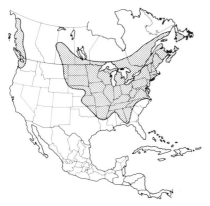

Description

Keen's myotis closely resembles the little brown myotis in both color and size. The two bats are also commonly found in the same hibernaculum. To distinguish between these two species, one must look at a combination of characteristics.

The most obvious external feature separating Keen's myotis from the little brown myotis is the size of the ear. In *M. keenii,* the ear, when laid forward, extends well beyond the tip of the nose instead of just reaching the tip as in the little brown myotis. Further, in *M. keenii,* the tragus is long (more than one-half the length of the ear), narrow, and pointed.

Another distinguishing feature is the dorsal hair. Although the pelage of *M. keenii* is similar in color to that of the little brown

Keen's myotis (*Myotis keenii*).
Photo by Richard K. LaVal.

myotis, the dorsal hair of Keen's myotis is more silky than glossy and has a brassy rather than coppery hue. Also, the wing membrane of *M. keenii* extends to the base of the toes, and the calcar is slightly keeled. Another similar species, the Indiana myotis, has a definite keel on the calcar, smaller feet and ears, and a duller pelage.

Ecology

Little is known about the ecology of *M. keenii*. It is found throughout Pennsylvania but is less common than the little brown myotis. Keen's myotis roosts behind shutters, in attics, hollow trees, or natural crevices. In summer, it prefers forested habitats and, thus, can be found hanging in picnic pavilions. It is here, in its summer retreats, that Keen's myotis is usually observed (unlike the little brown myotis, which is more commonly observed in its winter quarters).

During winter, *M. keenii* can be found hibernating in caves or mines with the little brown myotis, the big brown bat, and the eastern pipistrelle. Although hibernating colonies may include as many as 100 to 350 individuals, Keen's myotis is less gregarious than the little brown myotis. Maternity colonies—located in attics, roofs or barns, and cavities of trees—range in size from 3 to 30 individuals.

Little is known about the feeding activity of Keen's myotis. Mammalogists suspect, however, that it is similar to that of the little brown myotis. Both species seem to exhibit two major foraging periods. One begins shortly after dusk with a return to the night roosting site. A second foraging period occurs prior to dawn with a return to a different roosting site for daytime use. During their foraging, the bats fly over trees and ponds—mainly upland rather than in lowland forests—in search of small insect prey.

External parasites of *M. keenii* include bat bugs, mites, and chiggers. Tapeworms and roundworms are common internal parasites, and Keen's myotis is known to harbor the rabies virus.

Behavior and Reproduction

As with other bats in Pennsylvania, mating of Keen's myotis occurs in autumn prior to hiber-nation. Copulation has been observed under natural conditions. Males mount females from the rear and hold on by grasping the females by the back of the neck with their teeth. Because no detailed studies on the life history of this bat have been written, little is known about its reproductive biology. Young are born in late June and early July, and one offspring is born per year.

Status in Pennsylvania

Keen's myotis may be widespread in Pennsylvania, but densities are low and its distribution is localized and irregular. It seems to be most common during summer in the Commonwealth, whereas hibernating colonies are rare and consist of very few individuals. Because of its poor winter representation, *M. keenii* was assigned the status of "vulnerable" by the Pennsylvania Biological Survey in the report *Species of Special Concern in Pennsylvania* (Genoways and Brenner, 1985). The Survey recommends further study by qualified mammalogists to map the distribution and abundance of Keen's myotis in the Commonwealth.

Indiana Myotis

SCIENTIFIC NAME
Myotis sodalis (*Myotis* is from the
Greek words *mys*, meaning
"mouse," and *otis*, meaning "ear";
sodalis means "companion or
comrade," referring to the
tendency of this bat to hibernate
in large groups.)

ALSO CALLED
Pink bat, social bat, Indiana bat,
companion bat, Wyandotte cave
bat, cluster bat

TOTAL LENGTH
71–90 mm (2.8–3.5 in.)

LENGTH OF TAIL
28–42 mm (1.1–1.6 in.)

LENGTH OF EAR
10–14 mm (0.4–0.5 in.)

LENGTH OF FOREARM
36–40.6 mm (1.4–1.6 in.)

WEIGHT
6–9 g (0.2–0.4 oz.)

MAMMAE
One pair

LONGEVITY
Up to 20 yrs. in the wild

STATUS IN PENNSYLVANIA
Endangered

STATUS IN UNITED STATES
Endangered

Description

The Indiana myotis is a small,
brownish bat similar in size and
general appearance to the little
brown myotis. In fact, until its
description in 1929, the Indiana
myotis was confused in collections
with the little brown myotis.
A combination of many characteristics should be used to differentiate these two species.

Compared with the little brown
myotis, the Indiana myotis has a
definite keel on the calcar and
smaller feet with shorter hairs on
the toes. The color of the Indiana
myotis is dull, grayish chestnut
rather than the distinctive bronze
of the little brown myotis. An additional distinctive feature is the
tricolored fur of *M. sodalis:* Three
color bands run from the tip to
the base of each hair. Color variations of blotched or white-spotted

Indiana myotis (*Myotis sodalis*).
Photo by John R. MacGregor.

individuals also occur, although rarely, in some populations. Adults molt once each year during mid-June, and sexes are generally the same size.

Ecology

At one time, a total of about 5,000 *M. sodalis* individuals were estimated to live in Pennsylvania. One

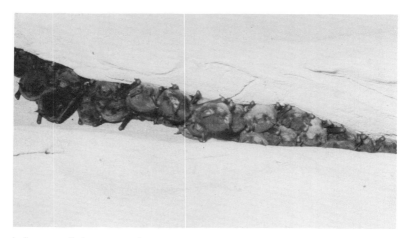

Indiana myotis in cave crevice.
Photo by John R. MacGregor.

cave in Centre County was recorded in 1932 as housing a group
of 2,000 individuals, and a 1965
count estimated 1,000 Indiana
myotis in a mine in Blair County.
A recent population survey of all
known cave sites for *M. sodalis* in
Pennsylvania revealed, however,
that only 150 individuals can still
be found in the Commonwealth.
All records of *M. sodalis* in Pennsylvania are from caves or abandoned tunnels.

Because the majority of the
total estimated population of the
Indiana myotis hibernates in certain large caves in Kentucky, Missouri, Indiana, and Illinois, much
of the information about this bat
is derived from studies of those
populations. The summer diet of
M. sodalis from Indiana includes
flies, moths, wasps, beetles, members of the order Homoptera
(cicadas, leafhoppers, aphids, and
scale insects), and caddisflies.

Predators of the Indiana myotis
are minks, black snakes, and
screech owls. External parasites
include mites and bat bugs, and
internal parasites such as roundworms and tapeworms are reported to occur.

Behavior and Reproduction

In late summer, *M. sodalis* begins
to accumulate fat for hibernation.
As with the little brown myotis,
swarming behavior occurs near hibernation sites during autumn.
Most mating occurs at this time,
and fertilization is delayed until
spring.

The Indiana myotis selects
medium- to large-sized caves. Optimal wintering sites are located
close to the cave entrance. Here,
temperatures are cool during midwinter, hovering between 4° to 6°C
(39°–43° F). During the hibernation period, individuals occasionally awaken every 8 to 10 days for
about an hour, at which time they
may seek warmer temperatures
deeper within the interior of the

cave. These periodic bursts of activity caused early biologists to believe erroneously that the Indiana myotis was not a true hibernator.

Within a cave, *M. sodalis* forms dense, radiating clusters of about 2,700 bats per square meter (250/ sq. ft.) on rough ceilings or side-walls. This behavior, which is distinctive for the species and ac-counts for the vernacular name *cluster bat*, helps biologists to dif-ferentiate *M. sodalis* from the little brown myotis, which forms semidense clusters along surfaces that have definite projections for hooking claws. While closely hud-dled in a cluster, the Indiana myotis folds its wings tightly against its body. It begins to leave the hibernaculum in mid-March, with females departing before males.

Data on the summer activity of *M. sodalis* are meager. It probably does not use buildings as summer roosts and appears to be less toler-ant of high temperatures than other bats such as the little brown myotis. Some groups of males probably remain near the hiber-nacula during summer, but it is not known where the majority of males go. Adult females do not form large maternity colonies as

the little brown myotis does. Rather, they bear their young in hollow trees or beneath tree bark. The Indiana myotis appears to produce a single offspring an-nually, in late June or early July.

Status in Pennsylvania

The U.S. Fish and Wildlife Service has placed the Indiana myotis on its list of endangered species. The entire species population is be-lieved to have decreased signifi-cantly throughout its range in the United States and is now threat-ened with extinction. The "en-dangered" status has also been assigned to all populations of *M. sodalis* in Pennsylvania by the Pennsylvania Biological Survey in the report *Species of Special Con-cern in Pennsylvania* (Genoways and Brenner, 1985). The Survey recommends that the distribution of colonies of the Indiana myotis be mapped by qualified mam-malogists and that new caves sup-porting colonies of the species immediately be placed off limits to all human activity to eliminate disturbance, especially during the crucial period of hibernation.

Small-footed Myotis

SCIENTIFIC NAME
Myotis leibii (*Myotis* is from
the Greek words *mys,* meaning
"mouse," and *otis,* meaning "ear";
leibii is a patronym recognizing
Dr. George C. Leib, collector of
the type specimen. This species
was once known as *M. subulatus.*)

SUBSPECIES IN PENNSYLVANIA
Myotis leibii leibii

ALSO CALLED
Least myotis, least brown myotis,
Leib's myotis, least brown bat

TOTAL LENGTH
74–80 mm (2.9–3.1 in.)

LENGTH OF TAIL
31–34 mm (1.2–1.3 in.)

LENGTH OF EAR
12–15 mm (0.5–0.6 in.)

LENGTH OF FOREARM
30–36 mm (1.2–1.4 in.)

WEIGHT
3–8 g (0.1–0.3 oz.)

MAMMAE
One pair

LONGEVITY
Up to 12 yrs. in the wild

STATUS IN PENNSYLVANIA
Threatened

Description

The small-footed myotis is the
smallest bat in Pennsylvania and
eastern North America. An adult
may weigh as little as 3 grams
(0.1 oz.), about the weight of a
ruby-throated hummingbird. Its
vernacular name is derived from
its tiny feet, which measure only
8 millimeters (0.3 in.) long.

The dorsal pelage of *M. leibii*
is pale yellowish brown to golden
brown. Black ears and membrane
and a black mask provide a distinctive contrast, as does the belly
hair, which varies from pale buff
to whitish in color. The calcar of
M. leibii has a definite keel. The
small-footed myotis is distinguished from the other three species of *Myotis* in Pennsylvania by
the combination of its small size,
black face, small feet, and short
forearms.

Small-footed myotis (*Myotis leibii*).
Photo by John R. MacGregor.

Ecology, Behavior, and Reproduction

Very little is known about the ecology of the small-footed myotis. During summer, buildings probably serve as roosting sites; maternity colonies of 12 to 20 individuals have been found in such localities. During winter, *M. leibii* favors caves and mine tunnels as its hibernation site. It is commonly found near the cave entrance, where temperatures are just slightly above freezing.

The small-footed myotis is reported to enter hibernation later than most other bats in Pennsylvania and may even show periodic short movements during winter. Although cave colonies of 100 to 120 individuals have been reported from Pennsylvania, *M. leibii* seems to be rather solitary and does not commonly form clusters within caves. It tends to hibernate in a horizontal position, unlike many bats, and it nestles between cracks and crevices, unlike most *Myotis* species, which hang in the open. *Myotis leibii* has even been found hibernating under rocks on the cave floor. In Pennsylvania, most sightings have been in caves within hemlock forests at elevations of approximately 600 meters (2,000 ft.) in Centre, Mifflin, Franklin, and Fayette counties.

The summer food habits of *M. leibii* in Pennsylvania are unknown but are presumed to be similar to those of the little brown myotis. Unique is the movement of *M. leibii* during foraging. In a slow, fluttering movement, the small-footed myotis forages over or near ponds and streams. This slow flight is rather atypical for a bat of such small size.

Little is known about the reproductive biology of the small-footed myotis. Following a two-month gestation period, a single offspring is born annually, probably in early July.

Status in Pennsylvania

Because of its rarity in Pennsylvania and because recent research has indicated a severe reduction in numbers, *M. leibii* has been assigned the status of "threatened" by the Pennsylvania Biological Survey in the report *Species of Special Concern in Pennsylvania* (Genoways and Brenner, 1985). To understand the distribution and biology of *M. leibii* in the Commonwealth and prevent the species from becoming endangered, the Survey recommends that qualified mammalogists conduct additional mapping and further study. Because the species is known to occur in sites with the endangered Indiana myotis, caves and mines occupied by the species should immediately be closed to human traffic to eliminate disturbance.

Silver-haired Bat

SCIENTIFIC NAME
Lasionycteris noctivagans
(*Lasionycteris* is from the Greek
words *lasio*, meaning "hairy," and
nycteris, meaning "bat";
noctivagans combines the Latin
words *noctis*, meaning "night,"
and *vagans*, meaning
"wandering.")

ALSO CALLED
Silver-black bat, silver bat, silvery
bat, silvery-haired bat, black bat

TOTAL LENGTH
95–112 mm (3.7–4.4 in.)

LENGTH OF TAIL
36–48 mm (1.4–1.9 in.)

LENGTH OF EAR
14–17 mm (0.5–0.7 in.)

LENGTH OF FOREARM
37–44 mm (1.4–1.7 in.)

WEIGHT
6–10 g (0.2–0.4 oz.)

MAMMAE
One pair

LONGEVITY
Up to 12 yrs. in the wild

STATUS IN PENNSYLVANIA
Undetermined

Description

The silver-haired bat can easily be
distinguished from all other bats
in Pennsylvania by its distinctive
color, the same for both sexes.
The dorsal pelage of *L. noctivagans* is long and blackish
brown with a silvery white, frosted
appearance. The underparts are
slightly duller than the back. The
only similar species is the hoary
bat with its white dorsal hair, but
the hoary bat is much larger than
the silver-haired bat and has a
distinctive, heavily furred
uropatagium.

   Lasionycteris noctivagans has
naked ears with rounded tips. As
broad as they are long, the ears,
when laid forward, barely reach
the nostrils. The tragus of the
silver-haired bat is broad and
blunt. The wings are black and
naked, but the uropatagium is
furred on the back. The calcar is
not keeled. This medium-sized bat

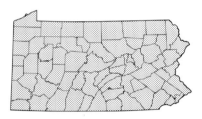

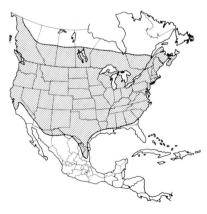

Silver-haired bat
(*Lasionycteris noctivagans*).
See plate 1, following page 172. Photo
by Robert Wayne Van Devender.

is slightly smaller than the big
brown bat but larger than any
of the *Myotis* species found in
Pennsylvania.

Ecology

Not fond of open country, the
silver-haired bat resides mainly in
coniferous and mixed forests
throughout Pennsylvania. Although groups of three and four
individuals are occasionally seen,
this bat is usually solitary and can
be found roosting singly in dense
foliage of trees, under loose bark,
in hollow trees, in woodpecker
holes, and even in birds' nests. Although most *L. noctivagans* in
Pennsylvania probably migrate
south for winter, some may hibernate in hollow trees, rock crevices, and other sheltered sites in
forest communities. During migration, this bat occupies buildings, rock crevices, woodpiles,
and, occasionally, caves and mine
tunnels.

The silver-haired bat emerges at
dusk and forages near ponds and
streams. Here, it feeds on many
different insects such as moths,
beetles, house flies, caddisflies,
true bugs, and flying ants. It forages close to the ground. Its slow,
erratic flight, characterized by
twists and glides, may be observed
as it forages on insects attracted
by the light of a campfire. Because
the silver-haired bat does not form
large maternity colonies or large
aggregations in caves, it has been
spared direct harassment by humans. Extensive deforestation and
forest management over the last
two centuries in Pennsylvania,
however, may have reduced available roosting sites for this bat.

Natural predators of *L. noctivagans* include owls, hawks, and
striped skunks. Mites, bat flies,
fleas, and bat bugs infest the silver-
haired bat externally, and its internal parasites include roundworms
and tapeworms. *Lasionycteris
noctivagans* is also known to be
susceptible to the rabies virus.

Behavior and Reproduction

A migratory species in Pennsylvania, the silver-haired bat flies south, probably between September and October. The return migration in spring probably occurs between late April and June. Migratory routes are unknown.

Little is known about the reproduction of *L. noctivagans.* Breeding probably takes place during the autumn migration, and, as with other bats, delayed fertilization occurs. The silver-haired bat usually produces twins, born in late June and early July, following a 50- to 60-day gestation period. Born pink with black wings, the young are naked and wrinkled, and their eyes are closed. They grow rapidly and fly by the age of three to four weeks of age. Most females with young roost alone, but there is evidence that small maternity colonies occasionally are formed. Most young males and females mature sexually during their first summer.

Status in Pennsylvania

There are no reliable reports of large winter or summer colonies of this bat from Pennsylvania. In addition, because very little is known about the biology of *L. noctivagans* in the Commonwealth, the status of "undetermined" has been assigned by the Pennsylvania Biological Survey in the report *Species of Special Concern in Pennsylvania* (Genoways and Brenner, 1985). The Survey recommends that research be undertaken, specifically during summer, to assess the distribution and abundance of the silver-haired bat in Pennsylvania. An effort should be made to determine if silver-haired bats captured in the state are breeding summer residents or merely migrants passing through Pennsylvania on their way to northern localities.

Eastern Pipistrelle

SCIENTIFIC NAME
Pipistrellus subflavus (*Pipistrellus* is from the Italian word for "bat"; *subflavus* combines the Latin words *sub*, meaning "almost," and *flavus*, meaning "yellow.")

SUBSPECIES IN PENNSYLVANIA
Pipistrellus subflavus subflavus

ALSO CALLED
Georgian bat, pygmy bat, southern pipistrelle, pipistrel, butterfly bat

TOTAL LENGTH
80–89 mm (3.1–3.5 in.)

LENGTH OF TAIL
36–49 mm (1.4–2 in.)

LENGTH OF EAR
12.4–14.1 mm (0.5–0.6 in.)

LENGTH OF FOREARM
31.4–34.1 mm (1.2–1.3 in.)

WEIGHT
6–11 g (0.2–0.4 oz.)

MAMMAE
One pair

LONGEVITY
Up to 15 yrs. in the wild

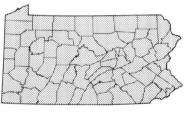

Description

The eastern pipistrelle is one of the smallest bats in Pennsylvania, second only to the small-footed myotis. It can be distinguished from other bats in the state by its yellowish brown, fluffy, tricolored fur. Its hairs are dark at the base, yellowish brown in the middle, and dark at the tip; the pelage is somewhat paler on the belly than on the back. The sexes are colored alike, but females are heavier than males.

The ears of *P. subflavus* are tan, naked, and thin, slightly longer than broad, with rounded tips. When laid forward, they reach just beyond the tip of the nose. Another distinguishing feature of *P. subflavus* is the short, blunt tragus, unlike the pointed tragus of all *Myotis* species.

The wing membrane of the eastern pipistrelle is naked except for the anterior third of the uro-

Eastern pipistrelle (*Pipistrellus subflavus*).

patagium. The calcar is not keeled, and the thumb is very large, about one-fifth the length of the reddish-colored forearm. The delicate skull may be distinguished from that of all other bats in Pennsylvania by a count of 34 teeth.

Ecology

During summer, the eastern pipistrelle roosts in the foliage of trees, crevices of cliffs, caves, mines, and, occasionally, in buildings. Common in Pennsylvania, this delicate, unobtrusive bat forages in forests and along the edges of woodlands with streams and ponds. It begins foraging earlier in the evening than most other bats. Its flight is comparatively weak, characterized by slow, erratic, fluttery movements. Because of its small size and flight pattern, *P. subflavus* may be mistaken for a large moth. Its prey tends to be quite small and includes mainly leafhoppers, planthoppers, small flies, moths, true bugs, beetles, and wasps.

Little is known about the predators of the eastern pipistrelle, but the hoary bat and the leopard frog are reported to kill it. Natural catastrophes, such as cave flooding and severe snowstorms, and the failure of young bats to store sufficient fat for hibernation are known to result in high mortality for the eastern pipistrelle. External parasites include chiggers, mites, and fleas, whereas endoparasites are flukes and roundworms. *Pipistrellus subflavus* is also known to harbor the rabies virus.

Behavior and Reproduction

The eastern pipistrelle is one of the first bats in Pennsylvania to enter hibernation and one of the last to depart in spring. It commonly hibernates in mine tunnels and caves and shares these sites with *Myotis* species and the big brown bat. Rather unsocial, *P. subflavus* does not hibernate in clusters. It hangs by its feet, usu-ally alone, in deep parts of caves where temperatures remain fairly constant, around 11° to 13° C (52°–55° F). Reports indicate that during hibernation droplets of moisture may condense on the fur of *P. subflavus,* and the bat may appear to be pure white when seen in the beam of a flashlight. The eastern pipistrelle is said to inhabit more caves in the eastern United States than any other bat.

Copulation and insemination of females take place in autumn, occasionally during hibernation, or in spring at the time of ovulation. In Pennsylvania, parturition occurs between mid-June and mid-July. Following this, *P. subflavus* leaves its hibernaculum and establishes maternity roosts in barns, buildings, trees, rock crevices, or caves. During this time, sexes are segregated, with males usually roosting singly in trees.

Two young, each weighing approximately 2 grams (0.07 oz.), are usually born to each female following a 44-day gestation period. As with other bats, the offspring are naked and pink, with their eyes closed. When the young reach three weeks of age, they begin to fly. They probably do not mate in their first year.

Big Brown Bat

SCIENTIFIC NAME
Eptesicus fuscus (*Eptesicus* is
from the Latin words for "house
flier"; *fuscus* is Latin for "brown,"
referring to this bat's color.)

SUBSPECIES IN PENNSYLVANIA
Eptesicus fuscus fuscus

ALSO CALLED
House bat, barn bat, serotine bat,
Carolina bat

TOTAL LENGTH
97–115 mm (3.8–4.5 in.)

LENGTH OF TAIL
35–48 mm (1.4–1.9 in.)

LENGTH OF EAR
16–19 mm (0.6–0.7 in.)

LENGTH OF FOREARM
39–53.6 mm (1.5–2.1 in.)

WEIGHT
11–16 g (0.4–0.6 oz.)

MAMMAE
One pair

LONGEVITY
Up to 19 yrs. in the wild

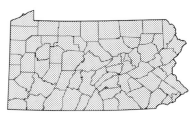

Description

The big brown bat is easily distinguished from all other bats in
Pennsylvania by its large size, long
fur, and two-toned color, which is
easily revealed when the fur is
separated by blowing on it. The
base of each hair is blackish,
whereas the outer half is brown,
and the hair of the underside is
paler than that on the back.

The black wings and interfemoral membrane lack hair,
whereas the short black ears are
furred at their base. The tragus of
E. fuscus is broad and rounded,
and the calcar is keeled, extending
slightly less than halfway down
the edge of the uropatagium. Male
and female big brown bats are
similar in color, with females
being slightly larger than males.

Big brown bat (*Eptesicus fuscus*).
Photo by Robert Wayne Van Devender.

Ecology

The big brown bat is common and resides in many different ecologic communities in Pennsylvania. Maternity communities are frequently situated in attics, barns, and even chimneys. Favored hibernation sites include caves and abandoned mine tunnels, although

E. fuscus also is reported to hibernate in buildings. Summer roosts include natural sites such as hollow trees and rock crevices. During daytime, *E. fuscus* may roost under windowsills or eaves, in cracks or crevices, or behind shutters of city or country homes. Because it readily roosts in occupied buildings, the big brown bat is the most likely bat for Pennsylvanians to see flying into their homes at night.

Foraging for the big brown bat begins shortly before dusk. The bat remains active until approximately five hours after sunset, at which time it returns to its roost. In captivity, *E. fuscus* has been shown to consume one-third of its weight in food each day and in nature is known to fill its entire stomach within a half-hour of foraging.

Eptesicus fuscus is a comparatively slow, leisurely flier and remains between 5 to 10 meters (16.5 – 33 ft.) off the ground or water when foraging. Like other bats of Pennsylvania, the big brown bat captures and consumes its food on the wing. Occasionally, however, it brings large prey to the roost to devour it.

Because of its large size, the big brown bat is able to eat large beetles, specifically ground and scarab beetles, which contribute almost half of the total volume of its food. Wasps, flying ants, house flies, caddisflies, stoneflies, and leafhoppers are also eaten. Surprisingly, moths are not one of the more common foods of the big brown bat.

Eptesicus fuscus has few natural enemies, although weasels, barn owls, screech owls, and snakes occasionally prey on it. Because of their close proximity to humans, maternity colonies in buildings are subject to frequent harassment and extermination. External parasites include fleas, mites, chiggers, ticks, and bat bugs. Tapeworms and flukes infest *E. fuscus* internally, and the rabies virus has been found to occur in this bat.

Behavior

For the most part, the big brown bat is fairly sedentary and demonstrates comparatively short seasonal movements and impressive homing instincts. Banding studies indicate that most remain within a 50-kilometer (30-mi.) radius of their summer and winter roosts. In addition, individuals transported and released as far as 720 kilometers (450 mi.) from their roosting sites are able to return to this home site within only four or five days. Biologists believe, based on this information, that most big brown bats hibernate in the vicinity of their summer roosts.

The big brown bat holds off hibernation until very late in autumn; it seems to be more tolerant of cold than most Pennsylvania bats. When going into hibernation, *E. fuscus* does not congregate in large groups as do many other bats. Instead, each individual finds its separate spot in the cave or tunnel, preferring cool, dry sites near the entrance.

During winter hibernation, the big brown bat employs energy from fat reserves that may constitute almost 30 percent of its body weight before hibernation. It reduces its metabolism which, in turn, is accompanied by a lowered rate of breathing and a lowered body temperature, approximating that of the hibernaculum with a range between $-1°$ to $18°$ C ($30°–64°$ F). When the bat is aroused, its normal body temperature reaches about $37°$ C ($98.6°$ F), the same as for humans.

Reproduction and Development

Most mating of *E. fuscus* takes place in autumn prior to hibernation, although periodic matings occur during winter. As with other bats, the sperm remains dormant in the female during the hibernation period. Fertilization occurs in early spring, and maternity dens are established shortly thereafter. These colonies may consist of as many as 200 individuals, although usually there are fewer than 100 bats per colony.

Young are born in June, following a gestation period of about two months. Normally two young are born to each female, and, in a given maternity colony, nearly all the young are born within approximately 48 hours of one another. This fact indicates that ovulation followed by delayed fertilization occurs nearly simultaneously in females and may be the result of some external cue such as an increase in temperature.

Young are born in an altricial state: naked, with closed eyes, and weighing about 3 grams (0.1 oz.). The mother nurses her own young and returns to her own after foraging. Growth is rapid. The young are weaned and able to fly alone by three to four weeks of age. When two months old, they are as large as their parents, and by autumn most males and about 50 to 75 percent of the females are sexually mature.

Red Bat

SCIENTIFIC NAME
Lasiurus borealis (*Lasiurus* is
from the Greek words *lasi,*
meaning "shaggy," and *urus,*
meaning "tail"; *borealis* is from
the Latin word for "northern.")

SUBSPECIES IN PENNSYLVANIA
Lasiurus borealis borealis

ALSO CALLED
Tree bat, northern bat, leaf bat,
New York bat

TOTAL LENGTH
94–112 mm (3.7–4.4 in.)

LENGTH OF TAIL
42–54 mm (1.6–2.1 in.)

LENGTH OF EAR
9–13 mm (0.4–0.5 in.)

LENGTH OF FOREARM
37–43 mm (1.4–1.7 in.)

WEIGHT
7–14 g (0.2–0.5 oz.)

MAMMAE
Two pairs

LONGEVITY
Up to 12 yrs. in the wild

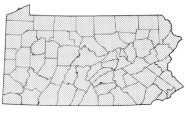

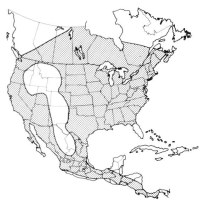

Description

The red bat is easily distinguished
from all other bats in Pennsylvania by a combination of its
brick red color, buffy white patch
on the front of each shoulder, and
its heavily furred uropatagium.
The tips of the hair on the back
and breast are "frosted" with
white. This is one of the few bats
in which the sexes are different
colors; males are redder and less
frosted than females. Females are
slightly larger than males.

The short ears of *L. borealis* are
rounded and pale colored. Its
short, broad tragus has a slight forward curve at the top and is less
than half the length of the ear.
The hindfeet are covered with
hair, and the calcar is keeled. In
flight, a characteristic V-shaped
silhouette can be seen, resulting
from the joining of the long, extended tail and the interfemoral
membrane.

Red bat (*Lasiurus borealis*).
See plate 2, following page 172. Photo
by Robert Wayne Van Devender.

Ecology

Optimal habitats of *L. borealis* include forest-edge communities, orchards, overgrown fields, and city parks. It seldom is found in caves and mines but occasionally enters buildings. A solitary species, the red bat spends the summer daytime hours hanging amidst the foliage of a deciduous tree, well concealed in the leaves. It shows a strong tenacity for specific roosting sites and returns to the same twig or branch for several days at a time.

The red bat is one of the first bats to become active after sundown, when it may be seen foraging above the treetops in a slow, fluttering, erratic flight pattern. Later in the evening, it tends to forage closer to the ground, maneuvering in straight flight patterns or in very wide circles. When foraging in a straight path, *L. borealis* has been reported to fly at speeds of up to 64 kilometers per hour (40 mi./hr.), averaging approximately 13 kilometers per hour (8 mi./hr.). It has also been observed flying near city street lights, preying on insects at-

tracted by the lights. Occasionally, it may alight on the poles to pick up moths.

The red bat consumes a variety of insects but seems to prefer moths. Other prey include planthoppers, leafhoppers, flies, beetles, and flying ants as well as crickets, cicadas, and true bugs, captured from the ground and on the foliage of trees and shrubs.

In eastern North America, one of the most important predators of the red bat is the blue jay, which attacks primarily the young. Other predators include opossums, domestic cats, skunks, sharp-shinned hawks, kestrels, merlins, great horned owls, and various snakes. Fleas, bat bugs, mites, and ticks are reported to be external parasites of the red bat, whereas flukes and tapeworms infest it internally. Rabies reportedly occurs in this bat.

Behavior

As with the hoary bat and the silver-haired bat, the red bat is a migratory species in Pennsylvania and flies as far south as Bermuda during September and October. Unlike migrating songbirds, it does not gather in premigratory flocks but advances southward singly. Males and females migrate at different times and also have different summer ranges.

Unlike most bats, *L. borealis* seems to be unusually well adapted to cold weather. It responds to subfreezing temperatures by lowering its body temperature and metabolism and, thus, becoming torpid. In this lethargic state, body functions occur at rates much slower than normal. To survive low temperatures, it also has special physical features such as short, rounded ears which minimize heat loss; thick, insulating fur; and a heavily furred uropatagium.

Reproduction and Development

The red bat breeds from August to October, a little earlier than most other bats in Pennsylvania. Copulation actually commences during flight but ends on the ground. Fertilization is delayed until spring, and, following a gestation period of 80 to 90 days, one to four young are born to each female in early summer. This litter size is high for bats, and the female *L. borealis* has four mammae with which to nurse her large brood.

Young red bats are born hairless, with their eyes closed, and weigh about 0.5 gram (0.02 oz.) each. Females with their young usually roost singly in trees rather than establishing large maternity colonies. Young bats cling to their mothers' fur with their teeth, hindfeet, and thumb claws. When the mothers change their roosting sites, they fly with the young. During daily foraging, however, young are left at the roost clinging to a leafy nest.

By three to five weeks of age, when young red bats open their eyes, they have a short, dense pelage and weigh about 4 to 5 grams (0.14–0.18 oz.) each. At about six weeks of age, they have mastered flying and are weaned, at which time they begin a solitary life.

Seminole Bat

SCIENTIFIC NAME
Lasiurus seminolus (*Lasiurus* is from the Greek words *lasi*, meaning "shaggy," and *urus*, meaning "tail"; *seminolus* refers to the Seminole Indian region where the bat was first known.)

ALSO CALLED
Mahogany bat

TOTAL LENGTH
108–114 mm (4.2–4.4 in.)

LENGTH OF TAIL
44–52 mm (1.7–2 in.)

LENGTH OF EAR
7–13 mm (0.3–0.5 in.)

LENGTH OF FOREARM
35–45 mm (1.4–1.8 in.)

WEIGHT
7–14 g (0.2–0.5 oz.)

MAMMAE
Two pairs

LONGEVITY
Unknown

STATUS IN PENNSYLVANIA
Undetermined

Description

Like the red bat, the Seminole bat has small, rounded ears; a furred uropatagium; and a white patch of fur on each shoulder. So similar are the two species that, for many years, biologists thought *L. seminolus* represented a color phase of the red bat. Nonetheless, despite their similar size and appearance, the Seminole bat can be distinguished from the red bat by its dark mahogany brown fur "frosted" with white. Also, in contrast with the red bat, the sexes of *L. seminolus* are similar in appearance.

Ecology, Behavior, and Reproduction

As the name implies, the Seminole bat is native to southeastern United States, specifically to the homeland of the Seminole Indians. In late summer, the bat wan-

Seminole bat (*Lasiurus seminolus*).
Photo by Roger W. Barbour.

ders northward; Pennsylvania and southern New York represent its northernmost reach. In Pennsylvania, it is documented from specimens found in autumn in Hopewell, Berks County, and from the shore of the Susquehanna River near the mouth of Fishing Creek, Lancaster County.

Lasiurus seminolus is abundant in southeastern United States from eastern North Carolina to eastern Texas. There, it is mainly a tree-roosting bat, associated with clumps of Spanish moss in oak forests. A solitary species like the red bat, the Seminole bat hangs during the day at 1 to 4.5 meters (3.5 – 15 ft.) above ground. The well-camouflaged roosting site has clear areas below that permit a downward fall into flight.

In its homeland, *L. seminolus* is active year-round, becoming torpid during periods of cold weather. Because only a few specimens have been found in northern areas such as Pennsylvania and New York, biologists believe that the Seminole bat is only a migrant to the Commonwealth.

The foraging zone of the Seminole bat is concentrated over watercourses, pine barrens, oak woodlands, and cleared land. It feeds on scale insects, aphids, leafhoppers, flies, and small beetles. It is reported to consume about 1.5 grams (0.05 oz.) of insects per hour and descends periodically to the ground to feed on insects such as crickets. *Lasiurus seminolus* tends to limit activity to evening hours when temperatures hover above 21° C (70° F). Because the behavior and roosting habits of the Seminole bat are similar to those of the red bat, the Seminole bat is probably subjected to similar predation pressure.

In the south, young Seminole bats are born in late May and early June. As with the red bat, the Seminole bat may give birth to as many as four young. Offspring are capable of flight at about three weeks of age.

Status in Pennsylvania

Because it is not known whether *L. seminolus* breeds in Pennsylvania, individuals recorded from southeastern counties are interpreted as "wandering vagrants" from the south. The Pennsylvania Biological Survey, hence, assigned the status of "undetermined" to the Seminole bat in its report *Species of Special Concern in Pennsylvania* (Genoways and Brenner, 1985). Before its status can be clarified, more data are needed on the biology of this species in the state. The Survey recommends that a study involving sky-netting be implemented in suitable forested areas to determine whether the species is a summer resident.

Hoary Bat

SCIENTIFIC NAME
Lasiurus cinereus (Lasiurus is from the Greek words *lasi,* meaning "shaggy," and *urus,* meaning "tail"; *cinereus* comes from the Latin word for "ashen" or "gray.")

SUBSPECIES IN PENNSYLVANIA
Lasiurus cinereus cinereus

ALSO CALLED
Great northern bat, gray bat, frosted bat

TOTAL LENGTH
133–145 mm (5.2–5.7 in.)

LENGTH OF TAIL
52–61 mm (2–2.4 in.)

LENGTH OF EAR
18 mm (0.7 in.)

LENGTH OF FOREARM
46–55 mm (1.8–2.1 in.)

WEIGHT
25–30 g (0.9–1.1 oz.)

MAMMAE
Two pairs

LONGEVITY
Unknown

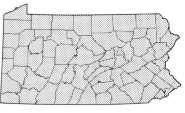

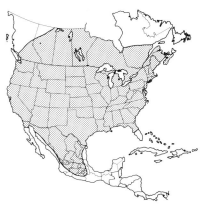

Description

The best single characteristic distinguishing the hoary bat from all other bats in Pennsylvania is its very large size; it is the largest bat in eastern North America. Its "hoary" color—chocolate brown, frosted with white—is also quite distinctive. In addition, the hoary bat has distinctive markings: On each shoulder is a yellowish white patch which may span the chest, and near each wrist is a cream-colored spot. Its throat is yellow or buff colored, and the fur of the underparts is paler than that on the back. Males and females are similar in color, although females are slightly larger.

The interfemoral membrane of *L. cinereus* is heavily furred. Its ears are short, broad, rounded, lightly furred, and rimmed with black. The tragus resembles that of the red bat. The calcar is twice as long as the foot and has a nar-

Hoary bat (*Lasiurus cinereus*).
See plate 3, following page 172. Photo
by Robert Wayne Van Devender.

row keel. The wings are long and narrow. The annual molt of the hoary bat takes place in July.

Ecology

The hoary bat is very similar to the red bat in its ecological requirements. A solitary bat, it roosts primarily among foliage of both coniferous and deciduous trees near the forest's edge. Its roost of leaves, located about 3 to 5 meters (10–17 ft.) above ground, is covered from above but is open below.

Lasiurus cinereus emerges late in the evening to forage. A strong flier, it can be recognized by its swift, direct flight and may reach speeds of up to 96 kilometers per hour (60 mi./hr.). Very little is known about the food habits of the hoary bat, but biologists suspect that, like its close relative the red bat, *L. cinereus* prefers to eat moths. Other insects in its diet include flies, grasshoppers, beetles, dragonflies, wasps, and termites.

The principal predators of the hoary bat are humans, hawks, owls, and snakes. Death also occurs when females with young are dislodged from trees and, thus, subjected to predation from many sources. Although the information about the parasites of *L. cinereus* is limited, mites and tapeworms are known to infest it, and the incidence of rabies is reported to be high.

Behavior

Lasiurus cinereus is a migratory species. Pennsylvania probably represents the southern edge of its summer range and the northern limit of its winter range. The wintering sites of the hoary bat are not well documented, and no specific migratory routes have been described. Circumstantial evidence indicates that this bat may winter in the southern states, in the mountains of Mexico, and even in northern Central America. Quite tolerant of cold, the hoary bat may possibly remain in Pennsylvania to hibernate. Its pelage has even more insulation than that of the hardy red bat.

The hoary bat is quite aggressive. When handled, it employs a threatening posture by widely opening its mouth, rigidly spreading its wings, and emitting a hissing/clicking call.

Reproduction and Development

Breeding occurs in early spring. During late May to early June, twins are born, following a gestation period of about 90 days. As with the red bat, this species does not form maternity colonies. Rather, young are born as the mother hangs in her leafy roost. The sexes are segregated during parturition and for most of the summer. They come together for breeding and then during migration in late summer and early autumn.

Newborn hoary bats are blind, are covered lightly with silvery gray hair, and weigh about 5 grams (0.18 oz.). Their eyes open at about 10 to 12 days after birth, and they grow rapidly. By three weeks old, they weigh between 9 and 10 grams (0.32–0.35 oz.). During their developmental stage, the young cling to their mother during the day but shift to a leaf or twig when she forages at night. By the age of 33 days, the young begin to fly and are soon weaned.

Evening Bat

SCIENTIFIC NAME
Nycticeius humeralis (*Nycticeius* combines the Greek word *nyktos,* meaning "night," and the Latin word *eius,* meaning "belonging to"; *humeralis* is from the Latin words *humerus,* meaning "upper arm," and *alis,* meaning "pertaining to.")

SUBSPECIES IN PENNSYLVANIA
Nycticeius humeralis humeralis

ALSO CALLED
Twilight bat, black-shouldered bat

TOTAL LENGTH
92−95 mm (3.6−3.7 in.)

LENGTH OF TAIL
35−42 mm (1.4−1.6 in.)

LENGTH OF EAR
11 mm (0.4 in.)

LENGTH OF FOREARM
33−39 mm (1.3−1.5 in.)

WEIGHT
10 g (0.4 oz.)

MAMMAE
One pair

LONGEVITY
Up to 5 yrs. in the wild

STATUS IN PENNSYLVANIA
Undetermined

Description

With its dark brown color and black ears and membranes, the evening bat looks like a miniature version of the big brown bat. *Nycticeius humeralis* is distinguished, however, by its notably smaller size and by the fact that its skull has only one pair of upper incisors instead of two. The evening bat also resembles the little brown myotis in size and color but can be distinguished from all *Myotis* species by its shorter tragus, which is blunt rather than slender and pointed. Further, the evening bat has a unique dental formula with a total of 30 teeth—the fewest of any bat in Pennsylvania.

The wings and uropatagium of the evening bat lack fur, and the calcar is usually not keeled. The belly of *N. humeralis* is slightly paler in color than the back, and young are considerably darker

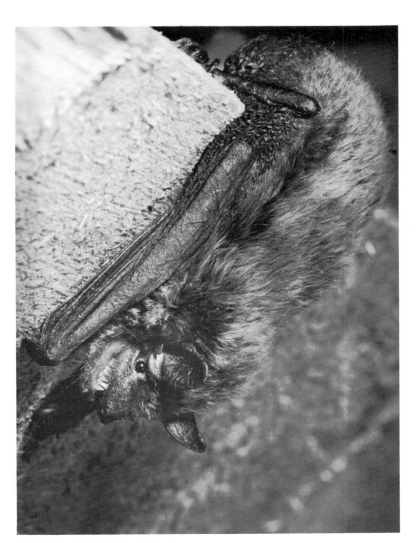

Evening bat (*Nycticeius humeralis*).
Photo by Roger W. Barbour.

than adults. Its small ears are thick and leathery.

Ecology

Pennsylvania represents the northern limit of the geographic range of the evening bat, although a westward range extension reaches the southern Great Lakes region. Rare in Pennsylvania, *N. humeralis* is reported only from Bucks, Cumberland, and Greene counties.

The evening bat roosts primarily in attics and other man-made structures. It also takes refuge in hollow trees and sometimes under loose bark. It is one of the few bats that does not commonly roost in caves.

Around twilight, the evening bat begins foraging in a slow, deliberate flight pattern. It initially flies above the treetops but, as darkness approaches, will forage closer to the ground. The diet of *N. humeralis* is generalized, and prey includes insects such as beetles, moths, leafhoppers, scale insects, true bugs, and flies.

Although skunks, raccoons, and snakes capture and consume the evening bat, its main enemies are humans, who eradicate maternity colonies from buildings. External parasites of the evening bat include mites and bat bugs, whereas internal parasites are tapeworms and roundworms.

Behavior, Reproduction, and Development

Little is known about the activities of *N. humeralis* in Pennsylvania. A maternity colony found on the campus of Waynesburg College confirms that the evening bat breeds in Pennsylvania, but the knowledge of its reproductive biology is derived from populations living in more southern states.

As with most other bats, mating of the evening bat occurs in autumn and winter, with the implantation of embryos delayed until spring. Maternity colonies may house hundreds of individuals and are commonly established in old buildings. Natural sites such as hollow trees support smaller colonies.

Females in the northern part of their range usually bear two young during mid-June. At birth, newborns weigh about 2 grams (0.07 oz.) and are naked and pink except for their dark feet, wings, ears, and lips. For the first two weeks following birth, mothers nurse only their own young. After that, they nurse any young indiscriminately. Young evening bats are able to fly at three weeks of age, and weaning begins about one week later.

Status in Pennsylvania

Because little is known about its distribution and biology, the status of "undetermined" has been assigned to the evening bat by the Pennsylvania Biological Survey in its report *Species of Special Concern in Pennsylvania* (Genoways and Brenner, 1985). Further research and protection of maternity colonies and summer mist-netting of this bat are necessary to evaluate properly the status of *N. humeralis* in the state.

RABBITS AND HARES

Order Lagomorpha

Lagomorpha is a very old order, derived from primitive placental mammals during Paleocene times, about 62 million years ago. The order comprises two living families, the Leporidae (rabbits and hares) and the Ochotonidae (pikas), and is represented today by approximately 12 genera and 62 species. Leporidae occur naturally on all continents except Australia and Antarctica. In Australia, the European rabbit, *Oryctolagus*, was introduced by humans, resulting in dire ecological consequences to the native fauna. Ochotonidae reside only in Asia and the mountains of western North America.

The word *lagomorpha* is derived from two Greek words meaning "hare shaped," which aptly describes the physical appearance of most members of this order except for the pikas. Members of the pika family are chunky little mammals resembling guinea pigs.

Lagomorphs have been a rather confusing group from a taxonomic standpoint. Although once thought to be closely related to rodents, lagomorphs are now thought to resemble artiodactyls (even-toed hoofed mammals) in many fundamental characteristics. Nonetheless, they are unique in having two pairs of ever-growing upper incisors. The front pair is rodent-like with a broad groove on the front surface. The second pair is peg-like and situated directly behind the first. These teeth are small and lack a cutting edge.

Other characteristics of Lagomorpha include the presence of a highly perforated upper jaw bone, testes anterior to the penis, an indistinct or small tail, and fur covering the soles of the feet. Also, lagomorphs are vegetarians and known to practice coprophagy (the reingestion of fecal material), which permits them to obtain essential nutrients from material as it passes through their alimentary canal a second time.

Rabbits and Hares

Family Leporidae

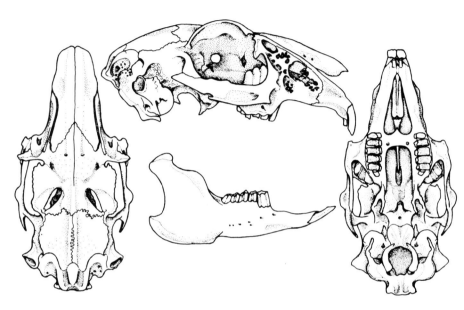

Skull of a leporid (*Lepus,* × ⅔).

Rabbits and hares are well known to almost everyone, because of their tiny cottony tufted tail, long ears, large hindfeet adapted for hopping, and their visibility during twilight hours. In addition, they are popular because they are edible.

The fossil record for the leporids dates back to the Eocene Epoch of North America, about 45 million years ago. Today, 10 genera and approximately 43 species occur naturally on all continents except Australia and Antarctica. They occupy diverse habitats ranging from tropical forests to deserts to alpine tundra; in northern latitudes their populations are reported to undergo cyclic fluctuations.

Leporids are commonly divided into two groups, rabbits and hares. Rabbits give birth to blind, naked young in a well-defined nest. Hares bear young that have hair and open eyes in a sheltered spot in the open. Two species of rabbits (*Sylvilagus*) and one species of hare (*Lepus*) occur in Pennsylvania.

Eastern Cottontail

SCIENTIFIC NAME
Sylvilagus floridanus (*Sylvilagus* combines the Latin word *silva,* meaning "forest," and the Greek word *lagos,* meaning "hare"; *floridanus* is the Latinized name for the state of Florida, where the type specimen was first described.)

SUBSPECIES IN PENNSYLVANIA
Sylvilagus floridanus mallurus;
Sylvilagus floridanus mearnsii

ALSO CALLED
Rabbit, cottontail, bunny, cotton hare, gray rabbit, brush rabbit, powderpuff

TOTAL LENGTH
382–488 mm (14.9–19 in.)

LENGTH OF TAIL
32–72 mm (1.2–2.8 in.)

WEIGHT
1–1.5 kg (2.2–3.3 lbs.)

MAMMAE
Four pairs

POPULATION DENSITY
8–11/ha (3–5/acre)

HOME RANGE
1–2.8 ha (2.5–6.9 acres)

LONGEVITY
Less than 2 yrs. in the wild; up to 10 yrs. in captivity

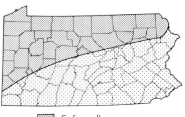

S. f. mallurus
S. f. mearnsii

Description

The eastern cottontail, the most common leporid in Pennsylvania, has long, coarse fur that is brownish or grayish, sprinkled with black on the back. The underparts are white except for a buffy throat, and the short tail is dark above and white beneath. A distinctive rusty patch marks the nape of the neck, and a white ring encircles the eyes. As with all leporids, the soles of the feet of *S. floridanus* are densely furred, with five toes on the forefeet and four toes on the hindfeet. Females are slightly larger than males.

The adult eastern cottontail undergoes two molts each year. The spring molt occurs from March to August; the autumn molt begins in late September and yields the winter pelage by early November.

Eastern cottontail (*Sylvilagus floridanus*).

The eastern cottontail does not turn white in winter as does the larger snowshoe hare.

Sylvilagus floridanus closely resembles the slightly smaller, rare New England cottontail. Although each has a few unique characteristics, it is difficult to distinguish between them in the field. The ears of the eastern cottontail are long, pointed, and sparsely furred on the inside. The New England cottontail, on the other hand, has comparatively short, rounded ears that are heavily furred on the inside. Also, a white blaze is usually present on the forehead of *S. floridanus* but not on that of the New England cottontail. In contrast to the difficulty experienced in distinguishing these rabbits in the field, they are easily differentiated on the basis of cranial characters.

Ecology

The eastern cottontail resides in various habitats throughout Pennsylvania. Although no single plant community is preferred, optimal habitats include brushy areas with profuse herbaceous vegetation such as cutover forests, thickets, and agricultural areas. *Sylvilagus floridanus* is less numerous in dense forests with poorly developed groundcovers of herbaceous plants and in very open grasslands.

The food habits of *S. floridanus* are as varied as the plant communities in which this rabbit resides. It does exhibit, however, some distinct food preferences. As gardeners will attest, staples in the diet of this rabbit include green beans, peas, lettuce, cabbage, and other treasured garden produce. Besides exhibiting this opportunistic feeding tactic, the eastern cottontail during spring, summer, and autumn also eats herbaceous plants such as clovers and various grasses including orchard grass, timothy, redtop, blue grass, and poverty grass. At twilight, rabbits can be seen on lawns foraging on the leaves of dandelions and plantain. During winter, when snow covers the ground and herbaceous plants are sparse, the bark of woody plants such as blackberry, raspberry, sumac, witch-hazel, apple, and wild black cherry is a staple.

Many factors keep eastern cottontail population densities in check. Domestic dogs and cats, skunks, raccoons, foxes, owls, hawks, and snakes are efficient predators. Mowing and plowing operations as well as adverse weather kill many nestling young each season. Because rabbits commonly forage in brushy areas along roadsides, highway mortality is also high. Lastly, *S. floridanus* is an important game animal in Pennsylvania and other states, and millions are harvested each year.

External parasites of the eastern cottontail include fleas, mites, chiggers, and ticks, whereas tapeworms and roundworms infect the rabbit internally. *Sylvilagus floridanus* also harbors botflies, and the bacterial disease tularemia or "rabbit fever" affects it. Although tularemia is transmitted primarily by tick bites, humans can become infected by contact with diseased rabbits.

Behavior

The eastern cottontail is a solitary animal, active day and night year-round. It is most active around twilight and spends its days resting in a "form"—a small, scratched-out depression in a clump of grass or under a brush pile. On warm summer days, a cottontail can be observed "sunbathing." Upon detecting an intruder with its acute vision or keen sense of hearing, the cottontail may initially freeze; it maintains a motionless, squatting position to escape notice. If this tactic fails, it flees by taking long leaps interrupted by a series of evasive, zigzag hops. Often, it doubles back to its point of origin by a circuitous route. When escaping a predator, *S. floridanus* may attain a speed of up to 29 kilometers per hour (18 mi./hr.). Although usually silent, the eastern cottontail may emit a piercing, high-pitched cry and scratch with its hindfeet if molested.

In addition to using its "form" as a resting site during the day, *S. floridanus* uses underground dens of woodchucks as a temporary home and/or during periods of heavy snow. As the time of parturition approaches, the female, or doe, excavates a small depression reaching about 13 centimeters (5 in.) below ground and measuring about 10 to 13 centimeters (4–5 in.) in diameter. She lines the nest first with dry grass and then with a layer of fur which she plucks from her shoulders, flanks, and legs.

Reproduction and Development

The first litter arrives in March or April, following a gestation period of about 30 days. Litter size ranges from three to eight, averaging five. Newborn cottontails are altricial—blind, naked, and helpless—and are placed in the shallow nest. At birth, they are about 10 centimeters (4 in.) long and weigh about 25 grams (1 oz.). As the young develop, the mother nurses them at dawn and dusk only and keeps them covered within the confines of the nest. She usually rests nearby at the "form" and will defend her young from intruders. Within one week of birth, the eyes open. As the young reach two weeks of age, they are the size of a chipmunk, are fully furred, and begin to emerge from the crowded nest. Weaning occurs at about five weeks of age, at which time the young are independent and begin foraging alone.

Females may breed in their first season, but males generally do not. Females may raise from five to seven litters each year, resulting in production of up to 35 young annually. This high biotic potential is offset by severe juvenile mortality and the many other population checks mentioned earlier.

New England Cottontail

SCIENTIFIC NAME
Sylvilagus transitionalis
(*Sylvilagus* combines the Latin
word *silva*, meaning "forest," and
the Greek word *lagos*, meaning
"hare"; *transitionalis* refers to the
habitat transition between grass
and forest.)

ALSO CALLED
Wood rabbit, mountain rabbit,
mountain cottontail

TOTAL LENGTH
382–425 mm (14.9–16.6 in.)

LENGTH OF TAIL
43–52 mm (1.7–2 in.)

WEIGHT
0.7–1.2 kg (1.5–2.6 lbs.)

MAMMAE
Four pairs

POPULATION DENSITY
Unknown

HOME RANGE
0.2–0.7 ha (0.5–1.7 acres)

LONGEVITY
4–5 yrs. in the wild

STATUS IN PENNSYLVANIA
Undetermined

Description

The New England cottontail
closely resembles the eastern
cottontail in external appearance
but is slightly smaller, has shorter
and more rounded ears, and, most
importantly, usually has a distinct
black spot between the ears. As
the vernacular name *wood rabbit*
suggests, *S. transitionalis* prefers
heavy forests. This ecological factor also is useful in distinguishing
the New England cottontail and
the eastern cottontail.

These two rabbits differ only
slightly in color, and neither turns
white in winter. Both are buffy
brown washed with gray and
sprinkled with black. The underparts vary from white to pale buff.
The anterior outer edge of the ear
of *S. transitionalis* is lined with
a black border, and the inside of
its ear is more heavily furred than
that of the eastern cottontail.

Female New England cottontails

New England cottontail (*Sylvilagus transitionalis*).
Photo by James F. Parnell.

are slightly larger than males. Unlike the eastern cottontail, *S. transitionalis* undergoes only one molt each year, in late summer. Although difficult to distinguish in the field, these rabbits can be easily differentiated by cranial morphology.

Ecology

The New England cottontail prefers dense forests, as compared with the eastern cottontail, which shows a more generalized habitat preference, focusing on successional areas peripheral to forests. In Pennsylvania, *S. transitionalis* inhabits forests at high elevations throughout the mountains of the northeastern, central, and southwestern parts of the state. The plant communities in which it resides vary from coniferous to deciduous forests with a lush herbaceous groundcover.

The summer diet of the New England cottontail includes mainly grasses and legumes and lesser amounts of seeds and fruits of herbs and shrubs. During winter, *S. transitionalis* consumes bark, twigs, and buds of maple and oak in addition to parts of many herbs and shrubs. The food habits of this rabbit seem to be more restricted than those of the eastern cottontail. Like other lagomorphs, *S. transitionalis* reingests fecal material.

The overall number of *S. transitionalis* in Pennsylvania has slowly declined during the past half century, in part because of the elimination of forests for agricultural lands and roadways. External parasites of the New England cottontail include ticks and fleas, and this rabbit is infected with the botfly. Internal parasites are tapeworms, roundworms, and various protozoans.

Behavior and Reproduction

The New England cottontail is rather secretive and, as a result, very little is known about its activities. In general, it seems to behave like the eastern cottontail. When handled, however, the New England cottontail is reported to struggle vigorously and squeal loudly, whereas the eastern cottontail is more docile and has a tendency to freeze. Both rabbits of Pennsylvania use their hindfeet as an effective defense.

Little is known about the reproduction of the New England cottontail, but courtship behavior is probably similar to that of the

eastern cottontail. Reproductive activity begins in late December or January. In late March and April, following a gestation period of 28 days, three to eight young, averaging five, are born. The young are placed in a nest measuring about 10 centimeters (4 in.) deep and 13 centimeters (5 in.) wide. The nest is located slightly below ground, lined with the mother's fur, and covered with twigs and leaves. Unlike the eastern cottontail, which places its nest in a relatively open habitat, the New England cottontail locates its nest in heavily wooded areas.

In Pennsylvania, usually three litters are produced each year. The period of lactation is reported as 16 days. As with the eastern cottontail, juvenile mortality of *S. transitionalis* is high, and the rabbit faces much predation pressure.

Crossbreeding of *S. transitionalis* and the eastern cottontail has been reported to occur in the wild. Research is under way to determine the frequency of mating between these two distinct species and the nature of the hybrids of such matings.

Status in Pennsylvania

Because of inadequate information on its abundance and distribution in Pennsylvania, the New England cottontail has been classified as "status undetermined" by the Pennsylvania Biological Survey in its report *Species of Special Concern in Pennsylvania* (Genoways and Brenner, 1985). The Survey recommends that suitable habitats within the range of *S. transitionalis* be maintained and that guidelines be established to regulate importation, release, or transportation of all members of the genus *Sylvilagus* in the Commonwealth to maintain the biological integrity of populations of the resident New England cottontail.

Snowshoe Hare

SCIENTIFIC NAME
Lepus americanus (*Lepus* is Latin
for "hare"; *americanus* is Latin
for America.)

SUBSPECIES IN PENNSYLVANIA
Lepus americanus virginianus

ALSO CALLED
Varying hare, snowshoe rabbit,
white rabbit, gray rabbit, big
brown rabbit, brown jackrabbit,
swamp jackrabbit

TOTAL LENGTH
473–520 mm (18.4–20.3 in.)

LENGTH OF TAIL
40–61 mm (1.6–2.4 in.)

WEIGHT
1.5–1.6 kg (3.3–3.5 lbs.)

MAMMAE
Three pairs

POPULATION DENSITY
2–12/ha (1–5/acre)

HOME RANGE
4–10 ha (10–25 acres)

LONGEVITY
4–5 yrs. in the wild

STATUS IN PENNSYLVANIA
Vulnerable

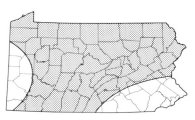

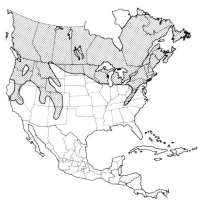

Description

The snowshoe hare is one of the
four Pennsylvania mammals that
turn white in winter. This fact,
coupled with the large size of the
snowshoe hare, helps to distinguish
it from the other two leporids found
in the Commonwealth.

The pelage of *L. americanus*
is thick and soft. In summer,
the hare is colored rusty brown
sprinkled with black. It has an indistinct line of darker brown hairs
along the midline, grading to an
olive-brown color on the flanks.
The top of the tail is black, and
the throat and belly are white.
During autumn, the guard hairs
are replaced by new white hairs,
casting a snow-white appearance
(although the underfur remains
brown). During winter in Pennsylvania, the snowshoe hare is white
except for the black tops of its
ears and a slight brown tint on the
head and legs. It remains white

Snowshoe hare (*Lepus americanus*) in winter.

until March, at which time a second molt occurs, giving way to the brown summer pelage. Timing of the autumn and spring molts is controlled principally by day length.

Lepus americanus has unusually large hindfeet with four long toes. These toes are heavily furred, an adaptation that aids in insulation. Also, the toes can be widely separated. Because of the increased surface area provided by these "snowshoes," the hare can travel on top of deep snow.

Ecology

Prior to logging activities, the snowshoe hare exhibited a wide distribution throughout Pennsylvania. Although the Pennsylvania Game Commission has restocked hares in regions with suitable habitats, this native of the Commonwealth presently has a very limited range.

The snowshoe hare is most common in mountainous sections of the northern half of Pennsylvania. In the northwest, it inhabits high ridges marked by mountain laurel and rhododendron. Farther

Snowshoe hare (*Lepus americanus*) in summer.
Photo by Jack Kirkley, Western Montana College.

east in the Pocono region, *L. americanus* favors mature forests with swamps and bogs at high elevations. In the Allegheny Mountains of northcentral Pennsylvania, it resides on steep, heavily forested slopes typified by hemlock, rhododendron, and mountain laurel with a lush, brushy understory. Although suitable habitats are present in the Appalachian Plateau of southwestern Pennsylvania, the snowshoe hare is rare there.

During summer, the snowshoe hare eats a varied diet of succulent plants including grasses, herbs, and shrubs. During winter, it browses on buds and twigs of deciduous vegetation and commonly girdles young trees, a practice which may cause the saplings to die. Unlike most lagomorphs, the snowshoe hare is fond of meat and is known to consume carrion. Its dietary preferences correspond closely to those of the white-tailed deer, and the two may compete for food when populations are high.

Lepus americanus forms an important link in the food chain and, when abundant, represents the staple in the diet of such predators as foxes, bobcats, red-tailed hawks, and barred and great horned owls. Weasels prey on young hares. External parasites of the snowshoe hare include ticks, mites, and fleas, whereas internal parasites are tapeworms and roundworms. The botfly also infects *L. americanus*, and it is susceptible to coccidiosis, tularemia, and lungworms.

In more northern latitudes, the snowshoe hare and its predators undergo cycles of abundance, reaching maximum densities every 10 or 11 years. During a peak year, hares may reach a density of up to 1,300 per square kilometer (3,380/sq. mi.) and will then suddenly decline to a low of only 1 per square kilometer (3/sq. mi.). The reasons for such great fluctuations are not fully known. Explanations range from the influence of sunspots on reproductive rates to a rare "shock disease" peculiar to *L. americanus*. At present, these dramatic fluctuations are best explained by a combination of factors including predator pressure, reduced food availability, disease, and social interactions.

Behavior and Reproduction

Like other leporids, the snowshoe hare does not hibernate but is active throughout the year. It is most active at night. During the daytime, *L. americanus* sits in a "form"—a small, scratched-out depression on the ground usually near a log or beneath a tree. If pursued, the snowshoe hare escapes in a circuitous route, predictably returning to its original site. It periodically seeks refuge in hol-

low logs or the burrows of woodchucks. The snowshoe hare is also known to take "dust baths" in areas of bare dirt. Such spots may act as congregating sites for small groups of hares.

Although somewhat secretive and shy during most of the year, the snowshoe hare exhibits elaborate courtship behavior during the breeding season. In late March, males (bucks) fight vigorously among one another, and females (does) are actively hostile toward bucks. Courtship rituals are characterized by both sexes employing much chasing, jumping, biting, and vocalizations in the form of guttural hissing. Further, each sex commonly urinates on its partner during courtship. At the height of the courtship display, the doe resigns from the chase and copulation occurs.

Following a gestation period of about 36 days, a litter of one to seven young (usually four) is born. At birth, young hares (leverets) weigh about 70 grams (2.5 oz.) and are precocial—that is, they have fur and open eyes. Leverets do not benefit from a well-insulated nest as do cottontails; instead, they are placed in a shallow, well-concealed "form."

Growth of the young is very rapid, and at one day old they begin to walk and hop. Before they are two weeks old, leverets have doubled their weight; soon thereafter they begin to consume solid food. Weaning occurs when the young are about five weeks old, at which time they weigh about nine times their birth weight. Because hares are polyestrous and exhibit postpartum heat, females may be pregnant while young are still in the nest. When this is the case, weaning may occur slightly earlier. At five months of age, the young attain their adult weight, but sexual maturity is not reached until the next year. Females may bear one to three litters per year, with the breeding season extending from March to August.

Status in Pennsylvania

Because the abundance and the geographic range of the snowshoe hare in Pennsylvania have undergone declines during the past century, *L. americanus* has been classified as "vulnerable" by the Pennsylvania Biological Survey in its report *Species of Special Concern in Pennsylvania* (Genoways and Brenner, 1985). Generally, this status has resulted from the maturation of Pennsylvania's forests and the high numbers of white-tailed deer, which compete with hares for browse and, thus, reduce cover and forage.

The Survey recommends that viable populations of the snowshoe hare in Pennsylvania be mapped, a habitat improvement plan be implemented, and hunting seasons be adjusted to reflect the dynamics of snowshoe hare populations in the state. Lastly, introductions of snowshoe hares into Pennsylvania should be curtailed, because new subspecies may destroy the biological integrity of endemic populations; these new subspecies also may introduce disease and parasites into resident populations.

GNAWING MAMMALS

Order Rodentia

Rodentia is one of the most successful orders of mammals, including approximately 40 percent of all living species. There are 30 modern families, with 1,620 species arranged in some 400 genera. Rodents are first known from fossils dating from the late Paleocene Epoch of North America, about 60 million years ago. Later, humans introduced the family Muridae (Old World Rats and Mice) to many parts of the world by bringing them along on explorations and during colonizations. Even without the aid of humankind, rodents were able to colonize Australia. Today, rodents are found throughout the world, occurring naturally on all continents except Antarctica and many oceanic islands. Their ecological distribution ranges from arctic tundra to lowland rain forest, from desert to aquatic habitats.

Rodents are best characterized by the presence of a single pair of ever-growing, chisel-like incisors on both upper and lower jaws. Because canine teeth are absent, a wide gap (diastema) occurs between the incisors and cheekteeth (premolars and molars). The cheekteeth show much variation in occlusal patterns as a result of adaptation to diverse foods ranging from plants to insects. The total number of teeth in rodents never exceeds 22.

Rodents have undergone an extensive adaptive radiation resulting in a diverse array of life-styles including terrestrial (mice, voles), arboreal (squirrels), fossorial (woodchucks), semiaquatic (beavers and muskrats), and volant (flying squirrels). Their sizes range from the tiny harvest mouse of Europe, weighing about 5 grams (0.2 oz.), to the pig-sized capybara of Central America, weighing up to 66 kilograms (146 lbs.).

A total of six families of rodents, comprising 24 species in 18 genera, reside in Pennsylvania.

Squirrels
Family Sciuridae

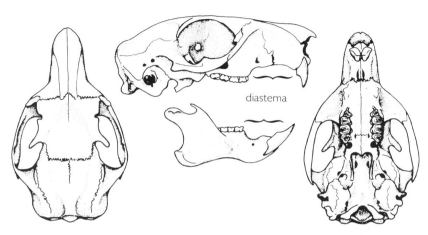

Skull of a sciurid (*Sciurus,* × ¾).

The family Sciuridae includes ground squirrels, woodchucks, chipmunks, tree squirrels, and flying squirrels. Sciurids are well known to humans because many inhabit residential areas and are commonly seen during daylight hours. This family dates from the Oligocene Epoch of Eurasia and North America, around 30 million years ago, and currently comprises about 50 genera with some 250 species. They are distributed throughout the world except in the Australasian region, southern South America, certain deserts of the Middle East, and the polar regions.

Squirrels can be separated into three basic types: the familiar tree squirrels, the rarely observed nocturnal flying squirrels, and the common ground-dwelling squirrels such as woodchucks and chipmunks. The family name, meaning "shade tail," alludes to the fact that some members of this family have a long, bushy tail. This characteristic is useful in recognizing the arboreal sciurids, since ground-dwelling squirrels have shorter and less bushy tails than the tree squirrels.

In Pennsylvania, five genera and seven species of sciurids are recognized. They inhabit many different plant communities ranging from montane coniferous forests to residential areas of large cities.

Eastern Chipmunk

SCIENTIFIC NAME
Tamias striatus (*Tamias* is a
Greek word for "steward" or
"treasurer"; *striatus* is Latin for
"striped.")

SUBSPECIES IN PENNSYLVANIA
*Tamias striatus fisheri; Tamias
striatus lysteri*

ALSO CALLED
Chippie, grinny, hackee, chipping
squirrel, striped ground squirrel

TOTAL LENGTH
225–268 mm (8.8–10.5 in.)

LENGTH OF TAIL
66–109 mm (2.6–4.3 in.)

WEIGHT
65–125 g (2.3–4.4 oz.)

MAMMAE
Four pairs

POPULATION DENSITY
15–75/ha (6–30/acre)

HOME RANGE
0.2–0.6 ha (0.5–1.5 acres)

LONGEVITY
4–6 yrs. in the wild

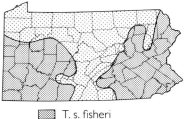

■ T. s. fisheri
⬚ T. s. lysteri

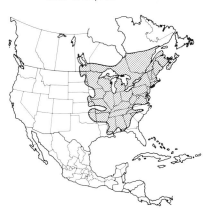

Description

The back of the eastern chipmunk
is agouti, or grayish; its belly is
white. It is easily recognized by
the combination of its highly vocal nature and distinctive stripes.
Five prominent brownish black
stripes run from shoulder to rump.
On each side, two of these stripes
sandwich in a cream-colored
stripe. The fifth brownish black
stripe is longer than the others
and runs along the midline. The
body stripes fade into a reddish
brown rump.

The eastern chipmunk has a
bushy, flat tail that is reddish below and brownish above. Its reddish brown head has a cream-
colored stripe above and below
each eye. Like other North American chipmunks, *T. striatus* has
internal cheek pouches. Adults
molt in late spring, early summer,
and late autumn. Sexes are equal
in size.

Eastern chipmunk (*Tamias striatus*).
See plate 4, following page 172.

Ecology

Tamias striatus, widespread and common in Pennsylvania, adapts to many different plant communities but is least common in coniferous forests and swamps. It often inhabits open deciduous woodlands with a well-developed understory and an abundance of stumps, logs, and rocks where it forages and nests. It is also conspicuous along country roads where it forages in brushy zones. Its practice of gathering nuts that have fallen on the roadway from overhanging trees commonly proves fatal, as evidenced by the many chipmunks killed on back roads, especially during spring and late summer when young are dispersing. Because of its diurnal activity pattern and tolerance of human activity, the chipmunk is frequently seen at bird feeders and around homes.

Like its habitat preference, the diet of the eastern chipmunk is quite varied. The bulk of its diet usually consists of nuts, fruits, and buds. As winter approaches, the chipmunk carries large amounts of food in its cheek pouches and caches the food in its burrow largely for winter use. These cheek pouches are well adapted for carrying food. An early biologist discovered a total of 32 beechnuts in the cheek pouches of one chipmunk (Allen, 1938). Preferred items in the winter diet of *T. striatus* include hickory nuts, beechnuts, maple seeds, acorns, and a long list of seeds of woody and herbaceous plants.

The chipmunk is also fond of mushrooms and consumes invertebrate prey such as insect larvae, earthworms, snails, slugs, and even butterflies. The irate gardener who attributes the demise of his sacred carrots and potatoes to the chipmunk is advised to credit the control of many insect pests to this rodent. The chipmunk also occasionally consumes vertebrate prey such as salamanders, birds, mice, and small snakes.

Major predators of *T. striatus* include hawks, weasels, foxes, and snakes. Humans and domestic dogs and cats also kill chipmunks residing near homes. Ticks, mites, chiggers, lice, and fleas are external parasites of the eastern chipmunk, whereas internal parasites include tapeworms, roundworms, and spiny-headed worms. Infestations by the larvae of the botfly are common in late summer and usually are isolated in the inguinal (groin) area of chipmunks. Although these large parasites appear to harm the chipmunk host, there is little direct evidence that botfly parasitism causes death or even lowered survival to *T. striatus.*

Behavior

Although the playful antics of the eastern chipmunk are commonly interpreted as being friendly and cute, this animal is actually highly territorial and unsocial. Except during the period of mother-offspring grouping, the chipmunk is solitary. Each individual normally occupies a separate burrow. The well-defined area around the burrow is vigorously defended, especially during the breeding season. Defense is directed toward other chipmunks, but true fights resulting in injuries rarely occur. Instead, the defense consists of threat displays, chasing, and much vocalization.

The vocal repertoire of *T. striatus* consists of four basic calls: a single, high-pitched "chip"; a loud chip followed by a trill; a series of chips close together (chipping); and a low-pitched "cuk" sound. In addition to serving as a part of its territorial display, these sounds may also function as alarm calls alerting individuals to the presence of a predator. The chip-trill call, accompanied by twitching of the tail, is commonly employed during escape from a predator, a hiker, or even a biologist!

The chipmunk is diurnal, with peak activity occurring during the middle of the day. In hot weather in late summer, activity decreases. During autumn, the chipmunk does not accumulate large quantities of fat as does a true hibernator. Instead, it subsists on provisions hoarded in its elaborate underground caches. The chipmunk also undergoes periodic bouts of torpor during winter in Pennsylvania. These periods of inactivity usually begin in late October and continue until early March when breeding commences. Unlike the hibernation of mammals such as woodchucks, the torpor of the chipmunk is quite variable in its duration and frequency, as shown by periodic arousals and foraging bouts that occur on sunny winter days.

Tamias striatus digs its own burrow under rocks, roots of trees, and stumps. The same chipmunk may occupy a given burrow system for its entire life. Entrance holes are rather inconspicuous, and each burrow system is composed of many branches, with storage and nest cavities located up to a meter (3 ft.) below the surface and measuring some 10 meters (33 ft.) long. Storage cavities may be quite large, some holding up to a bushel of food. Within this labyrinth of subterranean tunnels is also located a large cavity that houses the nest of *T. striatus.* The nest is made of chewed or crushed leaves.

Reproduction and Development

In Pennsylvania, the eastern chipmunk usually breeds twice each year, once in spring and again in late summer. The first litter is born between early April and early May, following a gestation period of 31 days. In mid- to late August, the second litter is produced. Litter size averages four or five.

At birth, the young weigh about 3 grams (0.1 oz.) and are hairless and blind. By the eighth day of life, their stripes begin to appear. By one month of age, they weigh 30 grams (1 oz.), their eyes open, and they are well furred. Weaning occurs at five to seven weeks of age, at which time they weigh about 35 to 40 grams (1.2 – 1.4 oz.). In Pennsylvania, young from the spring litter may appear above ground by early May and do not reproduce until the following spring.

Woodchuck

SCIENTIFIC NAME
Marmota monax (*Marmota* is
Latin for "marmot"; *monax* is
from the Greek word *monas*,
meaning "alone" or "solitary.")

SUBSPECIES IN PENNSYLVANIA
Marmota monax monax;
Marmota monax rufescens

ALSO CALLED
Groundhog, chuck, marmot,
whistle pig, whistler, red monk

TOTAL LENGTH
528–650 mm (20.6–25.4 in.)

LENGTH OF TAIL
100–170 mm (3.9–6.6 in.)

WEIGHT
2–5 kg (4.4–11 lbs.)

MAMMAE
Four pairs

POPULATION DENSITY
7–20/ha (3–8/acre)

HOME RANGE
0.5–3 ha (1.2–7.4 acres)

LONGEVITY
3–4 yrs. in the wild;
approximately 6 yrs. in captivity

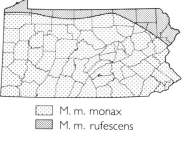

▦ M. m. monax
▦ M. m. rufescens

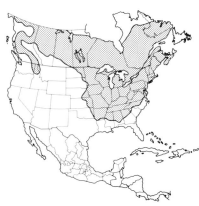

Description

The woodchuck is the largest
member of the squirrel family in
Pennsylvania. Its white front incisors also make the woodchuck
unique among Pennsylvania sciurids; the front incisors of other
members of the family are
yellowish.

The woodchuck has thick,
coarse fur. Its coat is yellowish
brown to brown on the back with
slightly paler underparts. Because
its reddish brown guard hairs have
white tips, the woodchuck appears grizzled or frosted. Albino
and melanistic (black) individuals
occur occasionally. Although
sexes are colored alike, males tend
to be slightly larger than females.
The annual adult molt extends
from May to August or September
and usually takes less than four
weeks to complete.

Woodchuck (*Marmota monax*).

The woodchuck shows many adaptations for fossorial (burrowing) life. It has short, powerful legs with forefeet equipped with four well-developed toes having long, curved claws. The thumb (pollex) is reduced to a short stump with a blunt claw. The head is blunt and flat with small eyes and small, round ear pinnae (flaps) that can be closed over the ear openings to keep out dirt.

Ecology

In Pennsylvania, the woodchuck prefers to live in open fields, fencerows, and forest edges supporting brushy cover. Mature forests of beech, maple, and poplar characterized by rocky outcrops as well as hayfields and pastureland provide suitable habitat. Because of its excavational tendencies, the woodchuck is generally disliked by farmers, gardeners, and golf-course groundkeepers. *Marmota monax* is actually beneficial, however, because its feces fertilize the soil and its digging loosens and aerates the soil. In the state of New York, woodchucks are reported to turn over 1,600,000 tons of soil each year (Whitaker, 1980).

The food habits of *M. monax* are as varied as its habitats. It feeds chiefly on cultivated alfalfa and clover, a variety of grasses, and succulent herbs such as dandelion, goldenrod, aster, daisy, wild mustard, and onions. Much to the dismay of gardeners, the woodchuck gladly feasts on vegetables such as beans, peas, carrots, and corn. In autumn, apples are consumed. Forest residents will even forage on leaves and buds of herbaceous plants such as *Clintonia*. Although principally a vegetarian, the woodchuck occasionally eats invertebrates such as grasshoppers, june beetles, and even snails. Unlike some other sciurids, such as chipmunks and tree squirrels, it does not cache food.

Predators of the woodchuck include dogs, foxes, minks, weasels, large hawks, and owls. Each year, humans kill many woodchucks—either for sport, because *M. monax* is a garden pest, or by accident when the woodchuck is "sunbathing" and foraging along the roadside. Also, *M. monax* occasionally suffers from malocclusion or improper growth of the incisor teeth. The failure of the upper and lower incisors to meet correctly may prevent proper wear of this rodent's continuously growing teeth and cause the incisors to grow in a circular pattern. As a result, the woodchuck may be unable to feed normally and may starve, or one of the teeth may curve until it eventually penetrates the skull and kills the animal.

The woodchuck is parasitized externally by ticks, lice, mites, chiggers, and fleas. Internally, it is infected by roundworms. It is also infested by the larvae of the botfly and is susceptible to tularemia, rabies, and arteriosclerosis.

Behavior

The woodchuck spends a great deal of time resting in its den. Principally diurnal, the animal can be seen during midmorning and afternoon sunbathing and foraging in pastures and fields. It is primarily terrestrial and can gallop up to speeds of 16 kilometers per hour (10 mi./hr.). It may also climb small trees searching for

food and, although not particularly fond of water, is an adept swimmer.

Marmota monax seldom ventures farther than about 100 meters (325 ft.) from its den entrance. Having good vision, the woodchuck is rarely taken by surprise. If alarmed, it rapidly retreats to the safety of its den. Nonetheless, *M. monax* is a strong, furious fighter; its incisors are formidable weapons most dogs avoid.

The woodchuck vocalizes in a unique, loud, shrill whistle—hence, the vernacular name *whistle pig*. Other calls include hissing, growling, and squealing sounds. When angered, the woodchuck chatters its teeth.

As the species name *monax* denotes, this rodent generally lives alone but may also reside in small family groups. It constructs extensive burrows. Entrances are marked by an elevated mound of soil where, when a burrow is active, fresh tracks can be seen. This "front porch" acts as a good site for sunbathing and as a lookout for intruders. Two dens may be established: one for summer and one for winter occupancy. The winter den is situated in brushy or wooded areas, whereas the summer den is found in flat, open country such as pastureland. The woodchuck also commonly uses the winter den as year-round quarters.

Burrows vary greatly, ranging from 0.6 to 1.8 meters (2–6 ft.) in depth, with tunnels reaching up to 15 meters (50 ft.) in length. Each burrow has a main entrance and one or more secondary entrances. The burrow system includes nest chambers, a hibernating chamber, and a "latrine"—all of which radiate off from the main tunnel. Nest and hibernating chambers, which are about 40 to 45 centimeters (16–18 in.) in diameter and some 25 centimeters (10 in.) high, are lined with dead leaves and grass.

The woodchuck is one of the few true hibernating mammals in Pennsylvania. In midsummer, it begins putting on essential fat for hibernation. Just prior to hibernation, its weight is about 30 percent greater than that in early summer. In autumn, after lining its hibernaculum with leaves and grasses, the obese woodchuck moves into its den, plugs the entrances, and curls up into a tight ball. The earthen plug is important in maintaining proper temperature and humidity in the den; the temperature remains about 13°C (56°F) during winter regardless of outside temperature changes. These plugs also ensure that unwelcome visitors such as skunks, opossums, and foxes do not interrupt the woodchuck's winter dormancy.

During the period of hibernation, which runs from about late October to early March, the woodchuck's body temperature remains about 4.4°C (40°F), some 32°C (57°F) below normal. At this time, the breathing rate slows and the heartbeat drops from over 100 beats per minute to only 4 beats per minute. In spring, arousal occurs with males emerging first. At this time, the woodchuck is rather skinny, having lost almost one-half the autumn weight. Females emerge in March, and mating occurs immediately.

Contrary to popular belief, the woodchuck is a poor "weatherman." No scientific evidence supports the postulate that each year, on February 2, "Punxsutawney Phil" will predictably emerge from his den and forecast the weather for the next six weeks. As one author/naturalist recently observed, "This is perfectly wholesome silliness, but its relation to natural history is about the same as that of the tooth fairy to dentistry" (Gilbert, 1985).

Reproduction and Development

From two to nine young (normally four or five) are born between mid-April and mid-May, following a gestation period of about 32 days. Pups are born naked, helpless, and wrinkled. They are a dark pink color, and their eyes are closed. Newborns weigh about 26 grams (1 oz.)—about the size of an adult red-backed vole—and measure some 105 millimeters (4 in.) long. At four weeks of age, their eyes open, a short pelage is apparent, and they are able to forage near the burrow entrance. Weaning occurs at about five to six weeks of age, and, when two months old, the young are on their own. Dispersal of juveniles from the natal burrow occurs at this time. Woodchucks produce only one litter per year, and young generally reach sexual maturity at one year of age but normally do not breed until two years old.

Gray Squirrel

SCIENTIFIC NAME
Sciurus carolinensis (*Sciurus* is Greek for "shadow tail" or "shade of tail" and alludes to this squirrel's habit of sitting in the shade of its tail; *carolinensis* is a Latinized adjective that means "belonging to Carolina.")

SUBSPECIES IN PENNSYLVANIA
Sciurus carolinensis pennsylvanicus

ALSO CALLED
Eastern gray squirrel, cat squirrel, black squirrel, bannertail, silvertail, timber squirrel

TOTAL LENGTH
419–538 mm (16.5–21.2 in.)

LENGTH OF TAIL
164–248 mm (6.5–9.8 in.)

WEIGHT
419–685 g (14.8–24.1 oz.)

MAMMAE
Four pairs

POPULATION DENSITY
5–50/ha (2–20/acre)

HOME RANGE
0.8–3 ha (2–7.4 acres)

LONGEVITY
9–13 yrs. in the wild; up to 15 yrs. in captivity

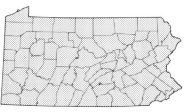

Description

Its color, large size, and flat, bushy tail distinguish *S. carolinensis* from all other Pennsylvania squirrels. As its common name "gray squirrel" denotes, *S. carolinensis* is predominantly gray in color. Rust red and black hairs often mingle with the gray to give this squirrel a brownish or tawny cast. The chin, throat, and belly of the gray squirrel are white—as is an eye ring—and its face ranges from clay color to cinnamon buff. The hairs of its distinguished tail are brown at the base, blackish near the middle, and tipped with white. After an autumn molt, which lasts from September through October, the pelage is paler. Its spring molt begins in March and ends by June. Interestingly, a melanistic (black) color phase commonly occurs, and

Gray squirrel (*Sciurus carolinensis*).
See plate 5, following page 172.

albino squirrels are occasionally observed in Pennsylvania. Sexes are equal in size.

Ecology

The gray squirrel inhabits hardwood and mixed coniferous-deciduous forests dominated by seed-producing trees. Not restricted to "wild" habitats, this squirrel can be found in urban parks. Its abundance is dictated by seed crop productivity rather than by a specific plant community. In Pennsylvania, habitats include tree species such as oak, hickory, beech, maple, poplar, and walnut. In northcentral Pennsylvania, large populations have been reported for mature sugar maple-beech-yellow birch communities and communities dominated by black oak and scarlet oak.

The mainstay of the gray squirrel is nuts—acorns, hickory nuts, beechnuts, walnuts, and hazelnuts. In spring, when nuts are unavailable, the squirrel feeds on buds, fruits, berries, flowers, roots, mushrooms, and insects. During autumn, the gray squirrel, like the fox squirrel, "scatter hoards" nuts, burying them singly about 2.5 centimeters (1 in.) below ground. These buried caches, relocated and consumed during winter, do not have a particular ownership; many different individual gray squirrels may share this community food source. Buried nuts are located both by keen smell and by a good memory. If nuts are not recovered, they become an important source of potential seedlings.

Like other tree squirrels, the gray squirrel may fall prey to a legion of predators such as hawks, barred and great horned owls, foxes, bobcats, weasels, and snakes. *Sciurus carolinensis* is also a popular game species, and millions are killed each year in Pennsylvania for sport. Fires, automobiles, and electrical wires also take their toll on this squirrel.

Ectoparasites of the gray squirrel include fleas, lice, mites, chiggers, and ticks. Among these external parasites, the scabies mite is particularly serious; it causes sarcoptic mange, which may become epidemic and lead to death. Roundworms, tapeworms, and flukes infect the gray squirrel internally. *Sciurus carolinensis* also harbors botflies and many different protozoan parasites and is known to contract tetanus and tularemia. Hunters should note that the most obvious sign of tularemia in an infected animal is the presence of small white spots on the surface of the liver. The rabies virus is also reported to occur in gray squirrels inhabiting Pennsylvania, but the incidence is very low.

Behavior

The gray squirrel is diurnal, with activity peaks occurring around dawn and shortly before dusk. Active year-round, *S. carolinensis* does not hibernate or undergo torpidity. During cold periods in the winter, it remains in its nest.

Foraging is primarily confined to the arboreal habitat, although the gray squirrel ventures to the ground to bury and collect nuts. It displays great agility in trees— aided by its long, flat, bushy tail. *Sciurus carolinensis* uses this tail as a counterbalance and as a sort of parachute when jumping from tree to tree or falling to the ground. On the ground, the chief mode of locomotion for the gray squirrel is hopping; it is reported to jump a distance of up to 3 meters (10 ft.). A slow, ambling gait is common when the gray squirrel is searching for buried nuts, but it is also reported to be able to run up to 17 kilometers per hour (10.5 mi./hr.).

The gray squirrel is usually solitary, does not form aggregations as does the flying squirrel, and is rather shy and nonaggressive. Nonetheless, *S. carolinensis*— though not as noisy as the red squirrel—is far from silent. When alarmed, its vocal repertoire may include barks, grunts, and possibly a song. These calls may be accom-

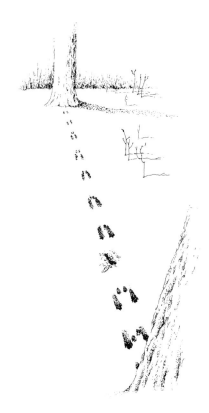

Gray squirrel tracks in snow.

panied by tail flicking to emphasize a point. Vocalizations and threat displays are directed to individuals of its own species as well as to other species. Contrary to popular belief, actual fights are rare.

The gray squirrel is rather sedentary and remains comparatively close to the home nest during most of its life. Tree cavities such as abandoned woodpecker holes are favored nest sites, although an outside nest lodged in the fork of a tree is quite common. This nest, slightly larger than that of the red squirrel, is composed of leaves and

Gray squirrel nest in tulip poplar tree.

twigs forming a water-resistant, globular mass. The squirrel lines the inner chamber with moss, grass, shredded bark, and other available vegetation and positions the single entrance to face the main tree trunk. These complex nests are situated as high as 21 meters (70 ft.) above the ground.

Reproduction and Development

In Pennsylvania, gray squirrels produce two litters each year; the first is born between February and April, and the second, in July or August. Males are promiscuous breeders, and several will chase a female in heat. The gestation period is approximately 40 to 45 days, and the litter size ranges from one to eight (usually two to four).

Pups are born naked, pink, and helpless. They are born with their eyes closed and weigh about 15 grams (0.5 oz.). At about one week of age, their eyes open, and, by four weeks, they have a coat of very fine fur. Pups may emerge briefly from the nest when they reach seven weeks old. By the time they are two months old, they are fully furred, have a bushy tail, and weaning is under way. The young usually remain with the mother until she has a second litter, and the summer litter will commonly remain with her during winter. Young squirrels will breed at one year of age.

Fox Squirrel

SCIENTIFIC NAME
Sciurus niger (*Sciurus* is Greek for
"shadow tail" or "shade tail" and
alludes to this squirrel's habit of
sitting in the shade of its tail;
niger is Latin for "dark" or
"black.")

SUBSPECIES IN PENNSYLVANIA
*Sciurus niger rufiventer; Sciurus
niger vulpinus*

ALSO CALLED
Black squirrel, eastern fox
squirrel, red squirrel

TOTAL LENGTH
510–592 mm (19.9–23.1 in.)

LENGTH OF TAIL
218–280 mm (8.5–10.9 in.)

WEIGHT
879–1,017 g (1.9–2.2 lbs.)

MAMMAE
Four pairs

POPULATION DENSITY
1–5/ha (less than 1–2/acre)

HOME RANGE
3–10 ha (7.4–24.7 acres)

LONGEVITY
4–7.5 yrs. in the wild; up to 15
yrs. in captivity

STATUS IN PENNSYLVANIA
Undetermined for *S. n. vulpinus*

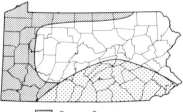

S. n. rufiventer
S. n. vulpinus

Description

The fox squirrel is the largest tree
squirrel in North America. Its
size—coupled with its dark head
and nose, general brownish orange
color, and long, bushy tail—distinguishes *S. niger* from all other
tree squirrels. The brownish
orange back and sides are grizzled
with gray and grade to yellowish
brown on the underside. The tail
is similar in color to the back, but
the hairs are tipped with brown,
not white as in the gray squirrel.
The feet are brownish orange, and
the eye ring is buff.

The bones of the fox squirrel
and gray squirrel can be distinguished by their color: The bones
of the former are pink, while those
of the latter are white. Also, the
fox squirrel has two fewer cheek
teeth than the gray squirrel.

Fox squirrel (*Sciurus niger*).
See plate 6, following page 172.

The annual molt of *Sciurus niger* usually occurs in April and May, although this molt may be delayed in breeding females until late August or September. The sexes are colored alike. Like the gray squirrel, the fox squirrel shows many color variations including albino and melanistic (black). The vernacular name *black squirrel* is derived from the black color phase, common in southern United States.

Ecology

Sciurus niger is uncommon in Pennsylvania. Like the gray squirrel, it resides in deciduous forests characterized by an abundance of seed-producing trees such as oak, hickory, walnut, beech, maple, and black cherry. The habitat preferences of the fox squirrel and the gray squirrel, however, show subtle differences: The gray squirrel is common in heavy forests with a well-developed understory, whereas *S. niger* prefers open woods or forest edges with a poorly developed understory. Small woodlots with park-like conditions adjacent to cultivated fields or orchards are favored habitats for the fox squirrel. In Pennsylvania, it may inhabit urban parks.

The fox squirrel feeds chiefly on the nuts of oak, maple, hickory, beech, walnut, and black cherry. Other foods include fruit, berries, flowers, roots, fungi, corn, insects, birds' eggs, and even young birds. The cambium layer beneath the bark of trees is also a favored food of *S. niger*, as is the sap of certain trees such as maple. In late summer and autumn, it "scatter hoards" nuts in shallow holes in the ground. The fox squirrel returns to these buried nuts during winter, guided principally by its keen sense of smell.

Because the fox squirrel spends a greater amount of time foraging on the ground than the gray squirrel, it is more susceptible to terrestrial predators. Chief among these are foxes, raccoons, and domestic cats. Long-tailed weasels, hawks, owls, and snakes also prey on *S. niger*, and many fox squirrels are killed each year on roads by automobiles.

The fox squirrel is parasitized externally by fleas, ticks, lice, mites, and chiggers. Among these, the scabies mite is noteworthy as causing sarcoptic mange. The botfly also infects *S. niger*. Endoparasites include roundworms, tapeworms, spiny-headed worms, and protozoans. Tularemia is also known to infect populations of the fox squirrel.

Behavior

Like other tree squirrels, *S. niger* is active year-round; it does not hibernate or undergo torpidity.

Seasonally, its greatest activity occurs during autumn, when much energy is spent on nest building and food hoarding. During winter months, the fox squirrel may hole up in its nest for long periods, as do other tree squirrels.

The daily activity of *S. niger* is diurnal—concentrating foraging between sunrise and sunset. Although most foraging occurs near the nest site, the fox squirrel has a larger home range than the gray squirrel. This fact is attributed, in part, to the habitat differences of the two species. The more open habitat of the fox squirrel has a lower density of nut-producing trees than the heavy forests where the gray squirrel resides; fewer trees necessitate a greater foraging radius.

Like the gray squirrel, the fox squirrel travels on the ground principally by hopping and is reported to move at a rate of up to 20 kilometers per hour (12 mi./hr.). A slow, ambling gait is common when *S. niger* is searching for buried nuts.

The fox squirrel is probably the least vocal of the three Pennsylvania tree squirrels. Like the gray squirrel, it vocalizes by employing barks, growls, and chattering. These calls are more guttural and of a slightly lower pitch than those of the gray squirrel and are commonly accompanied by tail wagging.

Like other tree squirrels, *S. niger* either dens in tree cavities or constructs nests among the branches. Old woodpecker cavities are often enlarged to accommodate the squirrels. When using tree cavities, the fox squirrel gnaws entrance holes of about 7.5 centimeters (3 in.) and establishes an inside chamber measuring about 15 centimeters (6 in.) wide and some 40 centimeters (16 in.) deep. In preparation for winter, the cavities are filled with leaves during autumn. Housecleaning occurs in spring.

Outside leaf nests vary greatly in size and architecture. They may be placed at a height of 3 to 15 meters (10–50 ft.) above ground and are made of leaves, grass, and roots with a framework of twigs. The nest size ranges from about 30 to 50 centimeters (12–20 in.) in outside diameter, with an inner cavity diameter of some 15 to 20 centimeters (6–8 in.). Squirrels enter by a hole in the side of the nest adjacent to the tree trunk. A fox squirrel can construct such nests in less than 12 hours, and the nests may last for several years if properly maintained.

Reproduction and Development

Generally, the fox squirrel lives a solitary life except during the breeding season, when pairs may reside in the same nest. The breeding pattern of the fox squirrel is similar to that of the gray squirrel, although the former is reported to breed slightly earlier. Mating occurs from mid-January to March and again from June to July. A mating ritual with several males chasing a female in heat is common. By late February or March, the first litter is born, following a gestation period of about 45 days. From two to six (usually three) young are born naked, blind, and helpless. These newborns weigh about 15 grams (0.5 oz.).

As with other tree squirrels, the development of the young is slow. The eyes do not open until the young are four weeks old, at which time a juvenile pelage is evident. When pups are 10 to 12 weeks old, they venture outside the natal nest, and weaning is under way. Although they begin fending for themselves at this time, they remain dependent on their mother until they reach three or four months of age. A second litter may be born in August or September, at which time the young from the spring litter generally disperse from the natal nest and establish their own nests nearby. Little information is available from Pennsylvania to document the occurrence of a second litter for fox squirrels.

Status in Pennsylvania

Two subspecies of fox squirrels reside in Pennsylvania. The western half of the state is home to *S. n. rufiventer,* an introduced race from the west. The southcentral counties of Juniata, Perry, Cumberland, and Franklin represent the northern tip of the range of the second subspecies, *S. n. vulpinus.* Both subspecies are uncommon in Pennsylvania and are difficult to distinguish from one another. *Sciurus n. vulpinus* is reported to have a generally grayer pelage on the back and sides than the more western *S. n. rufiventer.*

The eastern fox squirrel (*S. n. vulpinus*) has been classified as "undetermined" in the Pennsylvania Biological Survey's report *Species of Special Concern in Pennsylvania* (Genoways and Brenner, 1985). This status was assigned because of the lack of information on its distribution and life history in Pennsylvania. Research efforts aimed at defining its ecological status and distribution in the state are recommended.

Red Squirrel

SCIENTIFIC NAME
Tamiasciurus hudsonicus (*Tamiasciurus* is from the Greek words *tamias,* meaning "steward," and *sciurus,* meaning "shadetail"; *hudsonicus* refers to the site where the type specimen was obtained, on the coast of Hudson Bay, northern Ontario, Canada.)

SUBSPECIES IN PENNSYLVANIA
Tamiasciurus hudsonicus loquax

ALSO CALLED
Chickaree, pine squirrel, chatterbox, boomer, rusty squirrel, Bang's red squirrel, fairy diddle

TOTAL LENGTH
241−352 mm (9.4−13.7 in.)

LENGTH OF TAIL
100−165 mm (3.9−6.4 in.)

WEIGHT
126−234 g (4.4−8.2 oz.)

MAMMAE
Four pairs

POPULATION DENSITY
2.5−7.4/ha (1−3/acre)

HOME RANGE
0.08−1.2 ha (0.2−3 acres)

LONGEVITY
Up to 10 yrs. in the wild

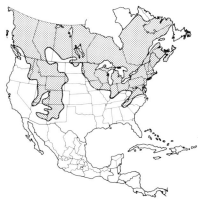

Description

The red squirrel is distinguished from all other tree squirrels by its red color, small size, and white eye ring. It is the smallest tree squirrel within its range in North America and the most vocal of the Pennsylvania squirrels. In fact, the red squirrel is usually heard before being seen.

The color of the red squirrel varies seasonally. In autumn it changes into its winter coat, and in spring it molts into summer pelage. In winter, *T. hudsonicus* sports a rust-colored broad band along its back extending from between the ears to the tip of the tail; its sides are olive gray, and its belly is grayish white. It also displays prominent tufts of hair on the tips of the ears—a unique characteristic of this squirrel. In summer, the ear tufts of the red squirrel are absent, a duller grayish pelage replaces its broad dorsal

Red squirrel (*Tamiasciurus hudsonicus*). See plate 7, following page 172.

red band, its belly becomes whitish in color, and a black stripe appears along its side. The sexes are about equal in size.

Ecology

Although the red squirrel reaches maximum abundance in mature, closed-canopy, coniferous forests of white pine and hemlock, it can also be found in mixed forests and pure deciduous woodlands. In northwestern Pennsylvania, for example, *T. hudsonicus* may inhabit plant communities typified by the presence of black cherry, hickory, black locust, and sassafras marked by tangles of wild grape. In southwestern Pennsylvania, it may reside in forests of beech, maple, poplar, and oak with periodic stands of hemlock interspersed. In these mixed forests, one may encounter both red and gray squirrels. In such instances, *T. hud-*

sonicus tends to be restricted to coniferous growth, while gray squirrels select deciduous areas in the same forest.

Coniferous seeds (from white pine, hemlock) and deciduous seeds (from oak, hickory, maple, walnut, beech, witch-hazel, poplar) make up the major food of the red squirrel. In addition, it feeds on nuts, fruits, buds, green twigs, and, occasionally, insects. It also is known to consume large quantities of mushrooms; even the poisonous fly agaric is eaten without harming the red squirrel.

Unlike the gray and fox squirrels, *T. hudsonicus* does not bury its food singly at random but, rather, establishes a well-defined food cache. The animal commonly harvests seeds shortly before ripening and takes them to a "midden" (a pile of seeds found on stumps, on logs, in hollows of trees, or even underground). One or more middens are included within the territory of each red squirrel. Over the course of several years, a squirrel may accumulate up to several bushels of cones and seeds. During winter months it feeds on the cache, and year-round it vigorously defends its hoards against intruders such as humans and other squirrels.

Predators of the red squirrel include humans, house cats, weasels, foxes, large hawks, owls, and snakes. Red squirrels residing in plantings of coniferous trees along Pennsylvania roads commonly are killed by automobiles. *Tamiasciurus hudsonicus* is parasitized externally by fleas, lice, mites, chiggers, and ticks and internally by tapeworms and roundworms.

Black walnuts opened by a red squirrel. Note the irregular hole made in each shell to remove the endosperm.

Behavior

The red squirrel is active, principally during daylight hours, year-round; it does not hibernate or undergo torpidity. In summer, this sciurid tends to forage in early morning and late afternoon. During winter, *T. hudsonicus* shifts its activity to midday. Unlike its larger relatives, the red squirrel does not confine its foraging to trees alone. It speds much of its time on the ground and may even tunnel in the soil. In winter, its tracks are commonly seen in the snow, and its tunnels can be traced to the subnivean environment.

Tamiasciurus hudsonicus prefers to locate its nests in tree cavities such as deserted woodpecker holes. If these cavities are unavailable, the red squirrel lives in abandoned nests of crows or hawks. The red squirrel also constructs outside nests in the upper canopy, sometimes as high as 20 meters (65 ft.) above ground. Here, the nest straddles several branches and is supported below by a platform of twigs. Built of leaves, grasses, shredded bark, and moss, the nest is about the size of a bas-ketball and has an inner chamber about 7.5 to 15 centimeters (3–6 in.) in diameter. Squirrels enter by way of a single entrance positioned close to the tree trunk. The nest of the red squirrel is distinguished from that of the gray squirrel by its slightly smaller size and its finer construction materials.

The reputation of the red squirrel as rather unsocial and aggressive is generally supported by fact. When disturbed, *T. hudsonicus* utters a long, rapid, staccato "cherr" sound. This territorial call may be accompanied by tail flicking and angry stomping of the feet. Encounters with gray squirrels may result in the red squirrel chasing off its larger rival. This conduct is not an instinctive mean streak; rather, it is normal territorial behavior probably associated with defending a nearby food cache from an intruder.

Reproduction and Development

Red squirrels are promiscuous. Pairing occurs only briefly for the purpose of copulation. Following this act, the animals become antagonistic to each other, and they separate. In Pennsylvania, the breeding season extends from February through September, with two litters born each year, in spring and in late summer. Following a gestation period of about 35 to 38 days, one to seven young (usually four or five) are born.

As in other tree squirrels, development is rather slow. At birth, the young are helpless, naked, and blind. They weigh about 7.5 grams (0.3 oz.) and measure approximately 11 centimeters (4 in.) long. When young red squirrels reach about 10 days of age, a coat of fine fur is discernible. Their eyes do not open until they are one month old, at which time they are fully furred. Although the young may venture from the nest at this time, weaning is prolonged until the mother establishes a nest for her young on the periphery of her territory. Once this is accomplished, young are weaned and disperse. At this time, they are usually between 9 and 11 weeks old. Females of the spring litter will not mate until the following spring, and young of the late summer litter will not become sexually mature until the next summer.

Southern Flying Squirrel

SCIENTIFIC NAME
Glaucomys volans (*Glaucomys* combines the Greek words *glaukos*, meaning "gray," and *mys*, meaning "mouse"; *volans* is Latin for "flying.")

SUBSPECIES IN PENNSYLVANIA
Glaucomys volans volans

ALSO CALLED
Eastern flying squirrel, white-furred flying squirrel, glider squirrel, fairy diddle

TOTAL LENGTH
210–253 mm (8.2–9.9 in.)

LENGTH OF TAIL
79–130 mm (3.1–5.1 in.)

WEIGHT
38–85 g (1.3–3 oz.)

MAMMAE
Four pairs

POPULATION DENSITY
2–26/ha (1–11/acre)

HOME RANGE
0.5–2 ha (1.2–4.9 acres)

LONGEVITY
Up to 5 yrs. in the wild; up to 10 yrs. in captivity

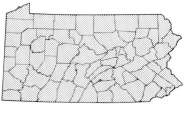

Description

The southern flying squirrel is easily recognized by the presence of its gliding membrane (patagium), which consists of a loose flap of skin extending from the wrist to the ankle on both sides of the body. The flattened, kite-like body surface and dorso-ventrally flattened tail are unique adaptations for its gliding form of locomotion.

The southern flying squirrel is also well adapted for its arboreal way of life by having sharp, curved claws, present on all four toes of the forefeet and on the five toes of the hindfeet. The feet vary in color from buffy white to brown. They blend well with the silky, dense pelage of this squirrel, which ranges from grayish brown on the back to creamy white on the belly. This color aids in distinguishing *G. volans* from the north-

Southern flying squirrel
(*Glaucomys volans*).
See plate 8, following page 172.

ern flying squirrel, which is darker with a reddish back and a lead color at the base of the hairs on the belly.

The eyes of the southern flying squirrel are very large. A brownish eye ring contrasts against a facial color of smoky gray. The tail is brownish above and pinkish buff below. The southern flying squirrel undergoes one molt each year. This molt begins in late September or early October and is completed usually by late November.

Like other sciurids, *G. volans* feeds mainly on fruits and seeds. Beechnuts and acorns are staples in its diet. During autumn, these items are cached in nest cavities and tree holes for consumption during winter. The nut-storing activity appears to be triggered photoperiodically, that is, by the decreased day length during autumn. More omnivorous than the gray squirrel, the southern flying squirrel is reported also to eat tree buds and blossoms, berries, maple sap, mushrooms, and even bark. It is the most carnivorous member of the squirrel family and readily eats insects, birds, eggs, nestlings, and even small mice and shrews. *Glaucomys volans* also consumes carrion if available.

Nocturnal avian predators such as barred and great horned owls are the principal consumers of the southern flying squirrel. Domestic cats and foxes may capture *G. volans* on the ground, whereas weasels, raccoons, and black rat snakes prey on this squirrel while it is in its tree nest. Ectoparasites include fleas, lice, mites, and chiggers. Internal parasites of the southern flying squirrel are tape-

Ecology

The optimal habitat in Pennsylvania for *G. volans* is a mature deciduous forest with an abundance of nut-producing trees such as oak, beech, and hickory. It can also be found in mixed deciduous and coniferous forests dominated by hemlock and in thickets of maple, black cherry, locust, and oak.

Hickory nuts opened by a southern flying squirrel. Note the circular openings characterized by fine tooth marks, resulting in a smooth edged hole.

worms, roundworms, and spiny-headed worms. Various protozoans also are known to infect *G. volans,* and it is reported to harbor the rabies virus.

Behavior

The southern flying squirrel is a beautiful, nocturnal animal with a shy, gentle disposition. If handled properly, *G. volans* seldom bites. Like the tree squirrels, the southern flying squirrel does not hibernate, although it is reported to undergo periodic bouts of torpor. Like the northern flying squirrel, *G. volans* also "huddles" to save energy during cold weather. These group huddles may be composed of up to 20 individuals, but groups of under 10 are more common.

The elaborate nest of the southern flying squirrel is helpful as a heat-conserving device. Commonly lined with plant fibers such as shredded bark, leaves, and grasses, the globular nests of *G. volans* are usually located about 4.5 to 6 meters (15–20 ft.) above ground in tree cavities such as abandoned woodpecker holes. The nests are of two types. The southern flying squirrel has a primary, frequently used nest and several secondary nests used intermittently as feeding stations or possibly as retreats if the primary nest is disturbed. The entrances to the nests usually measure from 40 to 50 millimeters (1.6–2 in.) in diameter. The small entrance size is critical; it prevents larger tree squirrels from using the nest. A meticulous "housekeeper," *G. volans* does not defecate in its nest.

The southern flying squirrel and its close relative the northern flying squirrel are the only two nocturnal tree squirrels in Pennsylvania. They travel principally by gliding from one tree to another with their patagia outstretched. They do not truly fly but volplane through the air as does a soaring glider.

In preparation for a glide, a flying squirrel climbs into a tree, assesses the glide distance and landing site, and lowers its head. A glide path of about 30 degrees from horizontal is common. Travel distances of 8 to 12 meters (26–40 ft.) are the norm, but *G. volans* is known to glide for distances up to 90 meters (300 ft.). During the glide, the squirrel uses its dorsoventrally flattened tail to steer, avoiding obstacles by rapid veering movements.

Because it is nocturnal, *G. volans* is rarely observed by humans. It may be located at night by its calls. The vocalizations vary and include a bird-like chirp, a high-pitched "tseet," a soft sneeze-like call, or a "chuck, chuck" note.

Reproduction and Development

In Pennsylvania, the southern flying squirrel bears two litters each year, one in spring and another in late summer. The first litter is born in late April or early May, following a gestation period of 40 days. The number of young per litter averages three or four.

Newborns are pink and hairless with closed eyes and ears. The folds of their patagia are evident.

At birth, they weigh about 4 grams (0.14 oz.) and are about 62 millimeters (2.5 in.) long. Growth is rapid, and, by seven days old, their weight has doubled. At four weeks of age, the young are fully furred. They almost reach adult size by the end of seven weeks. At this time, weaning is well under way, and they begin foraging and are capable of short glides. The young from the first litter may remain with the mother until the late summer litter is born. The young from both litters are capable of breeding within the next year.

Northern Flying Squirrel

SCIENTIFIC NAME
Glaucomys sabrinus (*Glaucomys*
combines the Greek words *glaukos*, meaning "gray," and *mys*,
meaning "mouse"; *sabrinus* is
from the Latin name for the Severn River in England. The type
specimen was collected at the
mouth of the Severn River in
northwestern Ontario, Canada.)

SUBSPECIES IN PENNSYLVANIA
Glaucomys sabrinus macrotis

ALSO CALLED
Mearn's flying squirrel, big flying
squirrel, Canadian flying squirrel

TOTAL LENGTH
246–279 mm (9.6–10.9 in.)

LENGTH OF TAIL
100–128 mm (3.9–5 in.)

WEIGHT
62–123 g (2.2–4.3 oz.)

MAMMAE
Four pairs

POPULATION DENSITY
1–10/ha (1–4/acre)

HOME RANGE
1–3 ha (2.5–7.4 acres)

LONGEVITY
4–6 yrs. in the wild

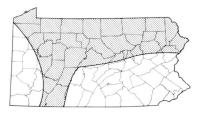

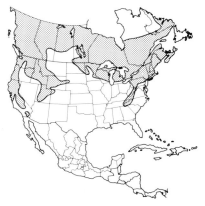

Description

Although the northern flying
squirrel is similar in overall appearance to the southern flying
squirrel, they can be distinguished
by subtle differences in body size
and coat color. First, *G. sabrinus*
is somewhat larger than the southern flying squirrel. Secondly, the
northern flying squirrel has hairs
on its belly that are grayish white
at the tip and lead gray at the base,
while the base of each belly hair
of the southern flying squirrel is
pure white. Finally, the back of *G.
sabrinus* is more reddish in color
than that of the southern flying
squirrel.

As with the southern flying
squirrel, the northern flying squirrel undergoes a single annual molt
in autumn. The sexes are equal in
size. (See the species account of
the southern flying squirrel for a

Northern flying squirrel
(*Glaucomys sabrinus*).
See plate 9, following page 172.
Photo by Nancy M. Wells.

description of the patagium and
other features associated with the
arboreal life-style of the flying
squirrel.)

Ecology

The northern flying squirrel favors
mixed deciduous and coniferous
forests of mountainous regions of
the northern part of Pennsylvania.
Although suitable habitat occurs
at higher elevations in the mountains of southwestern Pennsylvania, *G. sabrinus* has not been
found there. Within its range in
the Commonwealth, the northern
flying squirrel prefers habitats
characterized by a variety of seed-
producing trees such as oak, beech,
yellow birch, and sugar maple. In
northeastern Pennsylvania, *G.
sabrinus* was reported to co-
inhabit chestnut oak and hemlock
communities with the southern
flying squirrel.

Parts of the northern flying
squirrel's diet are unusual. Fungi
and lichens collected from trees or
from the ground are staples during
certain times of the year. Other
important foods are acorns, beechnuts, and conifer seeds. The omnivorous diet also includes fruits,
catkins, staminate cones of conifers, and buds, as well as arthropods, birds' eggs, and even
nestlings of birds. *Glaucomys
sabrinus* seems to be slightly less
carnivorous than its southern
relative, but this supposition may
represent, in part, a lack of research. Food-hoarding behavior is
also not as common in *G. sabrinus* as in the southern flying
squirrel.

Avian predators of the northern
flying squirrel include barn,
barred, and great horned owls, as
well as goshawks and red-tailed
hawks. Mammalian predators
are humans, foxes, bobcats, martens, weasels, and house cats. As
with the southern flying squirrel,
snakes are predators of nests of *G.
sabrinus*. External parasites include fleas, mites, lice, and ticks,
whereas endoparasites are roundworms and tapeworms.

Behavior

Glaucomys sabrinus is active primarily during evening hours, although it may emerge briefly
during the day. Active year-round,
it does not hibernate or undergo
torpidity. During winter, it forages
within the subnivean environment; tracks on the snow evidence its presence. During severe
cold, the gregarious northern flying squirrels form aggregations to
keep warm.

Tree cavities such as abandoned

woodpecker holes represent optimal nest sites for the northern flying squirrel. It also remodels old crows' nests or nests of red squirrels. Outside nests, located on sides of trees, are also built by using bark, twigs, roots, lichens, and grasses. These outside nests are used primarily during warmer seasons. Cavity nests are spherical, located from 1 to 18 meters (3–60 ft.) above ground, and composed of natural materials such as shredded bark, lichens, moss, grasses, pine needles, leaves, fur, and feathers. Both outside nests and cavity nests are used as feeding stations and, to a lesser degree, as hoarding sites.

Like its southern counterpart, *G. sabrinus* travels principally by gliding locomotion. Its gliding posture and aerodynamics are similar to that of the southern flying squirrel. The mean gliding distance is reported to be about 20 meters (66 ft.), ranging from 2 to 48 meters (7–158 ft.). *Glaucomys sabrinus* also spends considerable time foraging on the ground. It moves in a series of short jumps. Although its gait is rather ungainly and its progress is hampered by the formidable patagium, this squirrel has been clocked running at speeds of up to 13 kilometers per hour (8 mi./hr.).

The northern flying squirrel is slightly less vocal than the southern flying squirrel and emits a low, soft chip. When disturbed, it makes a chuckling sound.

Reproduction and Development

Glaucomys sabrinus usually produces two litters each year in Pennsylvania, but only one litter per year is typical in more northern parts of its range. In the state, young are born in late March and again in late August, following a gestation period of 37 to 42 days. Litters usually contain between two to six young, averaging four.

Pups are born blind and hairless. At birth, they weigh about 6 grams (0.2 oz.) and measure some 70 millimeters (3 in.) long. When they reach one week old, a thin coat of fine hair is evident. At two weeks of age, the hair becomes thicker and turns brownish on the back. When pups reach about one month of age, they are fully furred, their eyes are open, and they are able to walk. Young leave the nest for short periods when about six weeks old and eat solid foods at this time. At the age of two months, weaning begins. The first "test flight" occurs when the young reach about three months old. During winter, young may remain with the mother and be included in the wintering aggregation or "huddle" common to flying squirrels.

Beavers
Family Castoridae

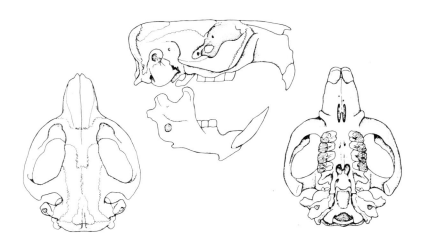

Skull of a castorid (*Castor*, × ⁹⁄₁₆).

This family contains the beavers, represented today by only one genus, *Castor*. This genus has two extant species: *Castor canadensis* inhabits most of North America, and *Castor fiber* resides in northern Europe and northern Asia. The fossil record of the family extends from the early Oligocene Epoch to the Recent Epoch in North America and from the late Oligocene to the Recent Epoch in Eurasia. Beavers are the second-largest rodent in the world, exceeded in size only by the capybara of South America. Distinguishing characteristics of the beaver are mentioned in the species account of *Castor canadensis*.

Beaver

SCIENTIFIC NAME
Castor canadensis (*Castor* is
Greek for "beaver"; *canadensis*
refers to Canada, where the type
specimen was collected.)

SUBSPECIES IN PENNSYLVANIA
Castor canadensis canadensis

ALSO CALLED
Canadian beaver, American
beaver, flat-tail, bank beaver,
castor, castor cat

TOTAL LENGTH
885–1,350 mm (35.4–53 in.)

LENGTH OF TAIL
240–450 mm (9.3–17.5 in.)

WEIGHT
12–27 kg (26–60 lbs.)

MAMMAE
Two pairs

POPULATION DENSITY
0.4–3 colonies/km² (1–8
colonies/mi.²) (One colony equals
4–8 individuals.)

HOME RANGE
Up to 200 meters (660 ft.) from
the lodge

LONGEVITY
Up to 11 yrs. in the wild; 15–21
yrs. in captivity

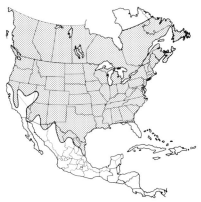

Description

The beaver, one of the largest
rodents in the world, is easily
identified by its size, rich color,
and unique tail. Both sexes sport
brownish black or yellowish brown
fur on the back and slightly paler
underparts. Immature beavers resemble adults in color, and only
one annual molt occurs. Melanistic (black) and albino individuals
have been reported.

Flat and covered with soft, black
scales, the tail of *C. canadensis* is
broadly oval in shape. Contrary
to popular belief, it is not employed as a trowel for carrying
mud. Rather, the tail is important
in temperature regulation, for fat
storage, and as a means of communication. In addition, the paddle-
like tail serves as a sort of rudder
for the semiaquatic beaver.

·The beaver shows many other
structural adaptations for aquatic

Beaver (*Castor canadensis*).
Photo by James F. Parnell.

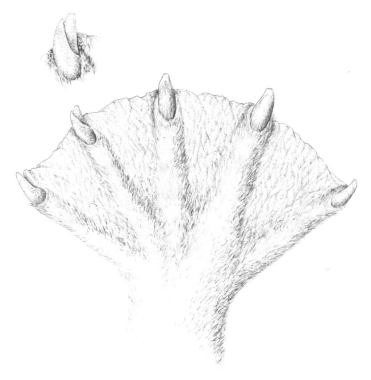

Upperside of the right hindfoot of a beaver, showing specialized double claws used for applying oil to the fur.

life. Its pelage is dense and heavy; the waterproof outer layer of guard hairs is underlaid by a dense layer of insulative underfur. *Castor canadensis* maintains the waterproof quality of its fur by using its specialized claws on its hindfeet to apply oil, taken from two abdominal glands. These double claws, located on the two inner toes, serve as a handy, comb-like device unique to beavers.

The eyes, ears, nose, and mouth of the beaver are also modified for aquatic life. A nictitating membrane covers the eyes of *C. canadensis*. This membrane acts as a transparent inner eyelid, covering the eye when underwater and, thus, permitting a clear field of vision. The ears, nose, and mouth, being valvular, can be closed voluntarily during submersion. The lips close behind chisel-like incisors to permit gnawing underwater.

The skull of the beaver is broad and flattened, with high-crowned cheekteeth and strong, large incisors well-suited for a herbivorous diet of bark, twigs, and leaves. Sexes are difficult to distinguish, unless the female is pregnant or lactating. Beavers have a cloaca-like chamber which contains both the anus and urogenital openings.

Ecology

The beaver played a major role in the settlement of North America. With prime pelts netting about $65 during colonial times, the beaver was the backbone of the North American fur trade. Economic incentive attracted trappers who were followed by settlers to the West. One author estimates the total number of beavers in North America in precolonial times to be as high as 400 million (Seton, 1929). In a relatively short time, because of overharvesting, the beaver was brought close to extinction.

In Pennsylvania, extensive trapping and logging during colonial times up to the early 20th century resulted in the extirpation of this once-common rodent. The last native beaver in the Commonwealth is reported to have been killed in Union County in 1912. As early as 1917, the beaver was reintroduced to Pennsylvania. Subsequent introductions and natural dispersal provided for an expanded distribution throughout those parts of the state with suitable habitat.

The beaver resides along rivers, streams, or in small lakes bordered by stands of trees. Many physical features of lake and stream areas influence the suitability of a given habitat for beaver occupation. The beaver, for instance, is rare in sandy areas, because mud is unavailable for lodge and dam construction.

A vegetarian, *C. canadensis* consumes bark, leaves, twigs, and roots of woody plants growing near water. Its food habits vary seasonally with plant forage availability. Aspen, poplar, birch, alder, willow, and maple—also used as building material—are the preferred plant forage species. Grasses, sedges, and rushes are also eaten, principally during summer months. During autumn, the beaver prepares for winter by building an underwater food cache. Green branches and small logs are partially buried in the mud on a pond bottom. This stockpile, lo-

Tree cut by a beaver.

cated near the lodge, measures about 1 to 3 meters (3 – 10 ft.) high by about 6 to 12 meters (20 – 40 ft.) in diameter; it often reaches to the surface of the water.

The beaver normally forages on small trees no more than about 90 meters (300 ft.) from water. Only one individual gnaws on a tree at a given time. Small trees are gnawed from one side, but larger ones are gnawed from all sides. This technique results in the characteristic hourglass shape of the cut. Although an excellent engineer, the beaver cannot predict the direction the tree will fall. Some trees, as a result, may fall against other trees, rendering them useless to the beaver. On occasion, the tree may fall on the beaver, resulting in death. Many trees do fall toward the water, however, because that is the usual direction of growth.

A felled tree serves as forage for several beavers. A team effort is employed to gnaw branches and sections of the trunk and to haul them to the feeding grounds or add them to the dam or lodge. On land, the beaver, with its head turned to one side, hauls the tree

or branch in its large incisors. In water, the beaver grasps the material in its forepaws while swimming. A complex system of canals, which may extend hundreds of meters from the pond, is often maintained for the purpose of floating logs to the dam or lodge site.

The beaver is a rather slow swimmer, yet very graceful. It normally swims at speeds of about 3 kilometers per hour (2 mi./hr.), and its large lungs and liver permit it to store enough air and oxygenated blood to remain submerged for up to 15 minutes. On land, *C. canadensis* walks slowly with a flat-footed gait. It is reported to gallop for short distances if alarmed.

Because of its large size, the beaver has few natural enemies, although humans still kill many of them. During 1982 and 1983, over 5,000 beavers were harvested in the Commonwealth for the pelts, which yielded a market value of nearly $14 each. In certain parts of its range, the beaver may face predation pressure from wolves, coyotes, lynx, fishers, wolverines, and, occasionally, bears. Minks, hawks, and owls periodically prey on unsuspecting kits.

The beaver is host to external parasites such as mites, ticks, lice, and a parasitic beetle. Endoparasites include roundworms and flukes. The beaver is also reported to contract lung fungus, lumpy jaw, and tularemia, spread directly by water or a tick. Although no incidence of rabies is reported for *C. canadensis* residing in Pennsylvania, the rabies virus is known to infect this species.

Beaver dam with lodge in the background.

Behavior

The beaver is active year-round. Although mainly nocturnal, it is occasionally seen on a summer day. Its greatest activity occurs during autumn when much energy is spent on dam and lodge repair and procurement of food for the underwater cache. The beaver remains in its lodge for much of the winter, periodically visiting its submerged food supply. In northern regions, this cache may prove insufficient to permit survival for the long, cold winter. The beaver may then conserve energy by reducing its activity, huddling, and subsisting on fat from both its body and large tail. A well-insulated lodge also aids energy conservation; the temperatures inside the lodge in winter rarely fall below 0°C (32°F) and, thus, are commonly warmer than outside winter temperatures.

The engineering ability of *C. canadensis* is exemplified by the construction of its elaborate dam and lodge. Initially, the beaver lays a barrier of logs, sticks, leaves, and mud across a small stream. Then, it places sticks on top of the dam in crisscross fashion. As the pond's water level rises, brush and sticks are added to the dam and secured with mud, leaves, and soggy vegetation.

Dams vary greatly in size, the largest being about 4.2 meters (14 ft.) high and some 900 meters (3,000 ft.) long. The impounded water may form ponds many hectares in area. Each pond serves as a transportation route for *C. canadensis* as well as a home for wildlife such as minks, muskrats, waterfowl, and fish. As a pond grows in size, its margins become favorable habitat for mesic-adapted plants such as willows, alders, cottonwood, and aspen—used by the beaver both for food and dam maintenance materials.

Beaver lodge and adjacent underwater food cache.

Lodges are large, hemispheric piles of mud, logs, and sticks customarily built on a bank or on small islands near the middle of a pond. They usually measure 1.5 to 1.8 meters (5–6 ft.) high and some 6 to 9 meters (20–30 ft.) in diameter. Beaver lodges have an inner chamber just above the waterline connected to the outside by one or more underwater tunnels. This chamber measures about 180 to 240 centimeters (6–8 ft.) wide by about 60 centimeters (2 ft.) high, is lined with grass and shredded bark, and is equipped with a ventilation hole to the surface.

Normally, a single family of beavers live together in a lodge, which is built and maintained by all family members except kits. Each autumn, the family adds a thick coating of sticks and mud to the lodge exterior. This coating provides insulation and prevents intruders from entering. During winter, the lodge may contain up to three generations of beavers, numbering between 8 to 10 individuals.

Although lodges typify the presence of beavers, not all beavers build them. Some construct bank burrows, especially in marginal habitats that do not support adequate forage or in which swift streams prohibit construction of dams.

Groups of related individuals constitute colonies that establish very strict territorial boundaries through scent marking. They build small mounds of mud and periodically smear them with "castoreum," an odorous yellowish brown oil produced from two large castor glands at the base of the tail. Oddly enough, this oily substance has been used as a base for perfumes!

To defend its domain against other colony members and intruders, a beaver employs various body postures and other tactics. By slapping its tail against water, a beaver effectively warns other colony members of approaching danger or frightens an enemy. Vocalization in the form of grunts, hisses, and teeth chattering is another common mode of communication. Kits are most vocal, producing soft whines and cries.

Reproduction and Development

The beaver is one of the few monogamous mammals; the female is reported to mate for life, although males are polygamous. In Pennsylvania, breeding begins about mid-January and extends to late February. Copulation commonly occurs in the water but may also take place in the lodge or burrow. Birth occurs in May or June, following a gestation period of about 107 days. A single annual litter is produced, ranging from one to nine kits (usually three or four).

At birth, kits are precocious. They are fully furred, and their eyes are open. Weighing between 350 and 650 grams (12–23 oz.) and measuring about 3 centimeters (1 in.) long, the newborn beaver is about the size of a walnut. Weaning begins when the young reach about two months of age, but lactation continues for another month. The family unit is composed typically of a pair of adults, yearlings, and kits, with the adult female being dominant. Two-year-olds are "kicked out" or disperse voluntarily before the birth of a second litter. This emigration occurs commonly in pairs; they will move between 16 and 110 kilometers (10–68 mi.) from the parental colony to establish their own household.

Beavers as an Ecological Force

The beaver exerts a major influence on the environment. As it constructs dams, the impounded water forms ponds and, thus, alters the area's soil chemistry. This change and the "selective lumbering" by the beaver alter the plant and animal life of the community: A diversity of aquatic animals find a new home, and mesic-adapted plants replace the original forest. Through time, however, the beaver pond fills with silt from upstream, or possibly the dam breaks and is not repaired. As a result, the beaver colony moves on, and the silt bed sets the stage for a new forest. Pioneer species of plants and animals colonize the silt plateau and streamside community. In time, the original forest is restored, followed by immigration of a terrestrial fauna. Such is the dynamic role of the beaver in the evolution of the North American landscape.

Native Rats, Mice, and Voles

Family Cricetidae

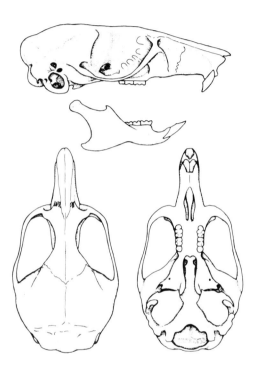

Skull of a cricetid (*Peromyscus*, × 2¼).

Comprising about 567 species arranged in some 97 genera, the family Cricetidae represents the most diverse family of rodents. It also accounts for about 14 percent of all living species of mammals and is the largest family of mammals in the world. Fossil remains of cricetids date back some 34 million years to the Oligocene Epoch of both Eurasia and North America.

Cricetids occur throughout the world except in Australia, Southeast Asia, and Antarctica. Representatives include spiny mice, harvest mice, pygmy mice, deer mice, grasshopper mice, woodrats, cotton rats, fish-eating rats, voles, lemmings, muskrats, and a legion of others. The gerbil and the hamster, two common household pets, are Old World members of Cricetidae.

Humans also know other members of this rodent family as carriers of disease, crop pests, and sources of meat or pelts, or possibly for their "explosive" population cycles. In Pennsylvania, the harmless "field" mouse is often an uninvited guest in homes. Sometimes only periodic rustling in the walls and attic or plentiful droppings on a countertop evidence its presence.

Highly adaptable and opportunistic, the cricetids are widespread. They reside in all habitat types, from salt marshes and deserts to high arctic tundra. Their food habits are as diverse as the habitats they occupy. The family includes specialists—such as those that consume primarily insects and those that subsist principally on underground fungi. Most members, however, are generalists, eating seeds, vegetation, invertebrates, and most any food seasonally available.

Modes of locomotion also vary. Some are terrestrial, others scansorial (capable of climbing), and still others semiaquatic or fossorial. Many cricetids nest communally and/or undergo torpidity during cold periods of the year, but hibernation is uncommon except for some hamsters of the Old World. Species occupying warm climates may undergo aestivation as an adjustment to periods of drought or heat.

Two subfamilies of cricetids occur in Pennsylvania: the cricetines (rice rat, woodrat, and mice) and the microtines (voles, bog lemming, and muskrat). Some zoologists merge the cricetids with the closely related Old World rats and mice, but this arrangement is not followed here. Pennsylvania is the home of 7 genera and 10 species of cricetids.

Plate 1. Silver-haired bat (*Lasionycteris noctivagans*).
See species account, page 97. Photo by Robert Wayne Van Devender.

Plate 2. Red bat (*Lasiurus borealis*).
See species account, page 107. Photo by Robert Wayne Van Devender.

Plate 3. Hoary bat (*Lasiurus cinereus*).
See species account, page 113. Photo by Robert Wayne Van Devender.

Plate 4. Eastern chipmunk (*Tamias striatus*).
See species account, page 136.

Plate 5. Gray squirrel (*Sciurus carolinensis*).
See species account, page 144.

Plate 6. Fox squirrel (*Sciurus niger*).
See species account, page 148.

Plate 7. Red squirrel (*Tamiasciurus hudsonicus*).
See species account, page 152.

Plate 8. Southern flying squirrel (*Glaucomys volans*).
See species account, page 156.

Plate 9. Northern flying squirrel (*Glaucomys sabrinus*).
See species account, page 160. Photo by Nancy M. Wells.

Plate 10. Southern red-backed vole (*Clethrionomys gapperi*).
See species account, page 191.

Plate 11. Meadow vole (*Microtus pennsylvanicus*).
See species account, page 195.

Plate 12. Woodland vole (*Microtus pinetorum*).
See species account, page 202. Photo by John R. MacGregor.

Plate 13. Meadow jumping mouse (*Zapus hudsonius*).
See species account, page 226.

Plate 14. Woodland jumping mouse (*Napaeozapus insignis*).
See species account, page 230.

Plate 15. Red fox (*Vulpes vulpes*).
See species account, page 250.

Plate 16. Gray fox (*Urocyon cinereoargenteus*).
See species account, page 254. Photo by James F. Parnell.

Plate 17. Black bear (*Ursus americanus*).
See species account, page 260.

Marsh Rice Rat

SCIENTIFIC NAME
Oryzomys palustris (*Oryzomys* combines the Greek words *oryza*, meaning "rice," and *mys*, meaning "mouse"; *palustris* is Latin for "marshy.")

SUBSPECIES IN PENNSYLVANIA
Oryzomys palustris palustris

ALSO CALLED
Rice rat

TOTAL LENGTH
217–260 mm (8.5–10.1 in.)

LENGTH OF TAIL
103–119 mm (4–4.6 in.)

WEIGHT
49–70 g (1.7–2.5 oz.)

MAMMAE
Eight pairs

POPULATION DENSITY
0.1–50/ha (1–20/acre)

HOME RANGE
0.23–0.37 ha (0.6–0.9 acre)

LONGEVITY
7–18 mos. in the wild

STATUS IN PENNSYLVANIA
Undetermined

Description

The marsh rice rat is a medium-sized rat that may be confused with a young Norway rat. The marsh rice rat has softer fur than the Norway rat, a slighter build, and its tail is more slender and slightly furred, in contrast to the naked tail of the Norway rat. The rice rat further distinguishes itself from the Norway rat by having two rather than three rows of cusps on its upper molar teeth.

The marsh rice rat is grayish brown on the back with a grayish white belly and feet that are white above. It has dense, soft, water-repellent underfur; well-furred, medium-sized ears; and small internal cheek pouches. Its tail is dark brown above and slightly paler below but not bicolored. There are four toes and a minute thumb on the forefeet and five toes on the hindfeet. The sexes are alike in size and color, and one an-

Marsh rice rat (*Oryzomys palustris*).
Photo by Richard K. LaVal.

nual molt occurs during summer months.

Ecology

As its vernacular name indicates, this amphibious rodent is a common resident of marshes, swamps, and other wetlands. Found in the eastern United States, especially along the Atlantic coast and Gulf of Mexico, it reaches the northern limit of its geographic range in southeastern Pennsylvania. There, it is reported from tidal flats along the Delaware River, near Tinicum, Delaware County. Because no actual specimens are available to document this, the present representation of *O. palustris* in this region is questionable; the marsh rice rat, however, is locally abundant in salt marshes of nearby New Jersey and Delaware. In optimum habitats, the rice rat may establish an extensive network of runways or may tunnel into banks. It often shares this habitat with the meadow vole and the muskrat.

Oryzomys palustris shows generalized and opportunistic feeding habits, which strongly correspond with seasonal availability of resources. It relies on seeds and succulent vegetation for most of the year. At certain times, the rice rat is highly carnivorous—eating insects, small crabs, snails, and even baby turtles. In the Georgia salt marshes, *O. palustris* is known as a major predator of the eggs and young of long-billed marsh wrens. The subterranean fungus *Endogone* is also an important food of the rice rat. Unlike some cricetids, this rodent is not known to establish large food caches. It has been shown to eat about one-quarter of its weight in food per day when in the laboratory.

The marsh rice rat serves as an important food for many predators. Based on the frequency of finding *O. palustris* remains in the pellets of barn owls, this avian predator seems to be the chief enemy of the marsh rice rat. Marsh hawks also feed on them, as do mammals such as raccoons, red foxes, minks, weasels, and skunks. Even certain watersnakes readily consume *O. palustris*.

Fleas, mites, ticks, and lice are common ectoparasites of the marsh rice rat. Internally, roundworms, flukes, several protozoans, and the parasitic larval stage of the tongue worm infest *O. palustris*.

Behavior

The marsh rice rat is active year-round and is principally nocturnal. An adept swimmer and diver, it is at home in the water; it commonly swims underwater for distances up to 10 meters (33 ft.), using its feet for propulsion. If surprised in its nest, *O. palustris* will retreat quickly to the safety of the water with a resounding "plop" and soon be gone. The rice rat tends to be rather intolerant of other rice rats, and fighting is common, sometimes resulting in the death of one of the combatants.

The spherical, grapefruit-sized nests of *O. palustris* are composed of shredded and woven grasses and sedges. They are located at bases of shrubs or, in tidal zones, may be situated in marsh vegetation slightly above water level. A fastidious housekeeper, this rat employs "latrine sites" outside the nest. It spends much time grooming, which aids in maintaining the water-repellent quality of its fur.

Reproduction and Development

No information is available on the reproductive biology of *O. palustris* in Pennsylvania. Studies conducted in Maryland, New Jersey, and Delaware, however, provide a realistic picture of this animal's habits in the Commonwealth. The breeding season probably extends from March to November; like many cricetids, the rice rat is polyestrous and exhibits a postpartum heat. The period of estrus is about one week long. Following a gestation period of about 25 days, females bear a litter of one to six young (usually four or five). Newborns are blind; have a light, fuzzy pelage; and weigh about 3 to 4 grams (0.11 – 0.14 oz.). They grow rapidly; by the eighth day their eyes open and they can eat solid food. Weaning occurs between 11 and 13 days of age, and young are soon on their own. They reach sexual maturity by two months and may breed during their first summer. By the age of four months, the rice rat is fully grown.

Status in Pennsylvania

The present occurrence of the marsh rice rat in Pennsylvania is questionable. Historically, *O. palustris* probably resided in the tidal marshes of the Delaware River. But formerly suitable habitat in the vicinity of Philadelphia and Chester has been extensively drained and reclaimed for industrial complexes. The Pennsylvania Biological Survey, in its report *Species of Special Concern in Pennsylvania* (Genoways and Brenner, 1985), has assigned the status of "undetermined" to the marsh rice rat in the Commonwealth. Research must be initiated to locate suitable habitats for the marsh rice rat; such areas may be found along the Delaware River of southeastern Pennsylvania. If appropriate areas are located, studies should be designed to determine if *O. palustris* resides there and, if it does, researchers must gather data on this rodent's life history and ecology.

Deer Mouse

SCIENTIFIC NAME
Peromyscus maniculatus
(*Peromyscus* is from the Greek
roots *pero*, meaning "defective,"
and *myskos*, meaning "mouse";
maniculatus is a diminutive
adjective from a Latin word for
"hand.")

SUBSPECIES IN PENNSYLVANIA
Peromyscus maniculatus bairdii
(prairie deer mouse); *Peromyscus
maniculatus gracilis* (woodland
deer mouse); *Peromyscus
maniculatus nubiterrae*
(cloudland deer mouse)

ALSO CALLED
Field mouse, vesper mouse

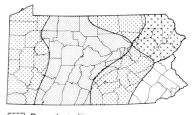

☐ P. m. bairdii
☐ P. m. bairdii *and* P. m. nubiterrae
☐ P. m. gracilis

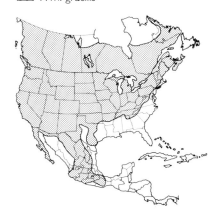

TOTAL LENGTH
P. m. bairdii: 121–160 mm
(4.7–6.2 in.); *P. m. gracilis:*
158–203 mm (6.2–7.9 in.);
P. m. nubiterrae: 179–205 mm
(6.9–8 in.)

LENGTH OF TAIL
P. m. bairdii: 50–70 mm (2–2.7
in.); *P. m. gracilis:* 70–107 mm
(2.7–4.2 in.); *P. m. nubiterrae:*
90–109 mm (3.5–4.3 in.)

WEIGHT
P. m. bairdii: 10–24 g (0.4–0.8
oz.); *P. m. gracilis:* 12–30 g
(0.4–1.1 oz.); *P. m. nubiterrae:*
11–23 g (0.4–0.8 oz.)

MAMMAE
Three pairs

POPULATION DENSITY
8–90/ha (3–36/acre)

HOME RANGE
0.01–1 ha (0.02–2.5 acres)

LONGEVITY
1 ½–2 yrs. in the wild; 5–8 yrs. in
captivity

Description

Although its generic name implies
that the deer mouse is a "defective
mouse," *P. maniculatus* is the
epitome of mouse-like architecture. It wears a brown coat with a
grayish brown middorsal stripe
and snowy white underparts and
feet. Its tail is dark brown above
and white below. The deer mouse
has two small internal cheek
pouches and medium-sized ears

Deer mouse (*Peromyscus maniculatus*).

that are scantily haired and dusky in color. As befits a creature of the night, its black eyes are large and luminous.

When identifying the deer mouse, it is important to know that the sexes are equal in size and colored alike and that two distinct developmental molts occur. A juvenile deer mouse is gray in color; when it reaches about four to six weeks of age, it begins to molt to a brownish subadult pelage. This molt takes about one month to complete. When about four months of age, the mouse undergoes a second molt, producing the brownish adult pelage. Thereafter, adult molts usually occur in spring and early summer.

Three subspecies of the deer mouse reside in Pennsylvania. These and the one species of the white-footed mouse in the Commonwealth are difficult to differentiate between.

The woodland deer mouse (*P. m. gracilis*) makes its home in northeastern Pennsylvania. It is slightly larger than the other two subspecies and is characterized by a long, sharply bicolored, tufted tail. It prefers cool, moist forests at high elevations such as the beech, birch, and maple forests of the Pocono Plateau.

· The cloudland deer mouse (*P. m. nubiterrae*) inhabits cool, moist forests and swamps within the Mountain and Plateau sections of Pennsylvania. This subspecies is the most common "mouse-like" rodent inhabiting the rocky forests of beech, maple, poplar, and hemlock at high elevations along Laurel Ridge in Westmoreland County, where it exhibits habitat overlap with the white-footed mouse. Like the woodland deer mouse, the cloudland deer mouse is characterized by its long, sharply bicolored, tufted tail.

The third subspecies, the prairie deer mouse (*P. m. bairdii*), is the most distinctive of the deer mice in Pennsylvania because of its small size and extremely short tail. In addition, recognition is facilitated by its distinctive habitat. The prairie deer mouse occurs in cultivated fields, grasslands, and most early successional habitats with sparse herbaceous cover. Although not found in Pennsylvania's forest habitats, it permeates the Mountain and Plateau sections of the state by following grassy and weedy berms of highways, thus colonizing various agricultural areas where no other *P. maniculatus* would care to live.

In Pennsylvania, identification of deer mice is complicated by the presence of the white-footed mouse, which closely resembles the woodland and cloudland deer mice and generally shares the same habitats. The species are best distinguished by differences in their skulls and teeth, but subtle differences in general appearance do exist. The deer mouse is best distinguished from the white-

footed mouse by the ratio of the length of the tail to the total length of the head and body. The tail of the deer mouse is usually as long or longer than the head and body, whereas in the white-footed mouse the tail is seldom as long as the head and body.

The total length of the tail alone is not a good diagnostic tool, because large white-footed mice may have longer tails than small deer mice. Other characteristics such as color are more variable but may be useful. For example, the deer mouse frequently exhibits a distinctly bicolored tail with a well-developed white tuft on the end. This tuft is lacking in the white-footed mouse, and its tail is indistinctly bicolored. The deer mouse also tends to have a soft, luxuriant grayish brown coat with a slight middorsal stripe; the white-footed mouse is more reddish with a less luxuriant pelage marked by a well-defined middorsal stripe.

Ecology

In Pennsylvania, nearly every terrestrial habitat—ranging from cultivated fields and weedy roadsides in the lowlands to mature, cool, moist hemlock forests at high elevations—has been colonized by the deer mouse. Its food habits vary with the habitat occupied and seasonal availability of food. The prairie deer mouse, for example, feasts principally on seeds of herbaceous vegetation such as sweet clover, ragweed, pokeweed, and various grasses. It also consumes cultivated grains, soybeans, and corn when available. The forest-dwelling deer mouse, on the other hand, consumes a wide variety of seeds, berries, buds, nuts, and fungi including mushrooms.

Although the teeth of the deer mouse are adapted to eating seeds and vegetation, insects are also a staple in its diet. In late summer, insects such as crickets, grasshoppers, and ground beetles are important dietary items for the prairie deer mouse. The deer mouse also is a principal predator of caterpillars and, thus, acts as an important biological control of insect pests such as the gypsy moth. Other invertebrates consumed by the deer mouse include earthworms, centipedes, millipedes, slugs, and spiders.

During autumn, the deer mouse transports seeds—either in its mouth or in its internal cheek pouches—to logs, stumps, hollow trees, and even abandoned birds' nests near the home site. An opportunist, this rodent may also establish these caches in old boots and dresser drawers in rural cottages. Because the deer mouse does not hibernate, these pantries function as a fairly predictable food depository during harsh winters.

Because of its abundance and omnipresence, the deer mouse forms an essential link in the complex food web. It represents the major herbivore component bridging the gap between producers (green plants) and meat-eating animals. Because of this ill-fated position, the deer mouse is faced with a legion of predators. In Pennsylvania, these include house cats, foxes, raccoons, skunks, weasels, hawks, owls, and snakes.

Northern short-tailed shrews are also known to prey on the young and, occasionally, on adult deer mice. In addition, *P. maniculatus* residing in homes in rural areas is subject to predation by humans in the form of mousetraps and poisons. Many deer mice are killed by fire and spring floods. High mortality may also occur during winter when snowcover is insufficient to insulate the ground from subfreezing temperatures.

Ectoparasites known to infest the deer mouse include fleas, lice, mites, chiggers, and ticks. During late August and September, the botfly larvae are common parasites. One deer mouse may be infected with up to four larvae, but they cause little permanent injury to their host. Internal parasites infesting the deer mouse are tapeworms and roundworms.

Behavior

In contrast to other small mammals such as shrews and voles, the deer mouse is principally nocturnal. During winter, it confines most activity to the comparatively warm subnivean environment, although periodic forays to the surface occur as evidenced by tracks on the snow. During extremely cold periods, the deer mouse undergoes torpidity as an energy-saving mechanism. In addition, it employs communal nesting; from two to five individuals may aggregate in a single nest during winter. This congregation usually includes only deer mice but may occasionally include a mixture of both deer mice and white-footed mice. Such "huddles" during winter confer the adaptive advantage of conserving body heat.

The deer mouse is an agile climber and commonly nests in a hollow tree or abandoned nest of a squirrel or bird as high as 15 meters (50 ft.) above ground. Its ball-shaped nests are frequently placed in fallen logs, stumps, or fence posts; beneath rocks; or in root channels below ground. They measure from 15 to 20 centimeters (6–8 in.) in diameter; are made of grasses, leaves, and various plant materials; and are lined with fur, feathers, and finely shredded plants. They function as sleeping quarters, as protection against predators and cold, and as maternity wards. Each nest has a single entrance, and an adjoining burrow is equipped with a "latrine" and a chamber of cached food.

Reproduction and Development

In Pennsylvania, the breeding season for the deer mouse commences in March and extends through October. The prairie deer mouse of southcentral Pennsylvania is an exception: It reportedly breeds year-round, under favorable weather conditions. Following a gestation period of about 23 days, three to seven young are born. Females ovulate immediately after parturition and commonly become pregnant while nursing the litter. This reproductive strategy permits the deer mouse to produce from three to four litters during the course of the breeding season. Thus, in a good year, a single female deer mouse may bear up to 28 young in less than eight months. Few females, however, live long enough to do so.

Young are born in an altricial state: pink, naked, blind, and helpless. They measure about 45 millimeters (2 in.) long and weigh approximately 1.5 grams (0.05 oz.). Pups are vocal, uttering high-pitched squeaking noises. Both parents may occupy the natal nests with the pups, and the male has an important role in caring for the young.

Growth of the young is rapid, and hair is evident within two to four days after birth. The eyes open by the time the pups are two weeks old. Weaning occurs rather abruptly at the age of three and one half weeks, because the mother usually gives birth to a new litter at this time. At weaning, the pups have a gray pelage. By two months of age, they are sexually mature, although only about half their adult weight. Young of spring litters are capable of breeding by autumn, and their young are an important contribution to the overwintering population.

White-footed Mouse

SCIENTIFIC NAME
Peromyscus leucopus
(*Peromyscus* is from the Greek
roots *pero,* meaning "defective,"
and *myskos,* meaning "mouse";
leucopus is from the Greek word
for "white-footed.")

SUBSPECIES IN PENNSYLVANIA
Peromyscus leucopus
noveboracensis

ALSO CALLED
Wood mouse, field mouse

TOTAL LENGTH
150–200 mm (5.9–7.8 in.)

LENGTH OF TAIL
60–95 mm (2.3–3.7 in.)

WEIGHT
13–27 g (0.5–1.1 oz.)

MAMMAE
Three pairs

POPULATION DENSITY
6–38/ha (2–15/acre)

HOME RANGE
0.04–1 ha (0.1–2.5 acres)

LONGEVITY
1½–2 yrs. in the wild; 5–8 yrs. in
captivity

Description

The white-footed mouse closely
resembles the two long-tailed subspecies of the deer mouse. Although best distinguished on the
basis of differences in the skulls
and teeth, the two species can be
identified through subtle differences in external appearance. The
white-footed mouse wears a reddish brown pelage marked by a
well-defined, broad middorsal
stripe. This stripe is less well defined in the deer mouse, and the
deer mouse is more grayish in
color. Further, the pelage is less
luxuriant in *P. leucopus* than in *P.*
maniculatus.

Probably the best way to distinguish live specimens of these two
mice is by comparing the propor-
tional length of their tails. The
tail of the white-footed mouse is
generally shorter than the total
length of its head and body,

White-footed mouse (*Peromyscus leucopus*).

whereas the tail of the deer mouse is equal to or longer than its head and body. Also, the tail of the white-footed mouse lacks a white tuft at the end and is indistinctly bicolored; that of the deer mouse is distinctly bicolored with a well-developed white tuft on the end.

Like the deer mouse, the white-footed mouse has a snowy white belly and feet. It has two small internal cheek pouches and medium-sized ears that are dusky in color with a narrow white edge. Juveniles are grayish in color and, as with the deer mouse, undergo two developmental molts. Adults are reported to molt in spring or early summer and again in autumn.

Ecology

The white-footed mouse is the most abundant and ubiquitous ro-

dent in Pennsylvania. It readily adapts to a broad spectrum of habitats—from cultivated fields and roadside ditches to mature rhododendron thickets and hemlock forests at high elevations. Fencerows, swampy areas, small thickets, and even outbuildings in rural areas are common homes for *P. leucopus*. It is also one of the first small mammals to colonize reclaimed strip mine sites and clearcuts. In the Allegheny Mountain Section of Westmoreland County, the white-footed mouse lives beside the deer mouse in riparian beech, maple, poplar forests marked by rocky outcrops and a lush understory of ferns and herbaceous cover. As with other mouse-like rodents, density tends to increase during summer, reaching peak numbers in late summer and early autumn. A gradual decline in abundance occurs through winter.

The diet of the white-footed mouse closely resembles that of the deer mouse and reflects the seasonal availability of forage. During late autumn and winter, about 75 percent of the diet of *P. leucopus* consists of arthropods such as beetles, centipedes, spiders, and miscellaneous insect pupae and larvae; the remainder of the diet includes nuts and seeds, green plant materials, and other items. During spring and summer, seeds and fruit constitute close to one half of the food intake of *P. leucopus*, but insects still predominate as a staple in the diet. Like the deer mouse, the white-footed mouse plays an important role in the control of insect pests such as the gypsy moth. Actually, the opportunistic white-footed mouse will eat almost anything including fungi, snails, small birds, and even other white-footed mice. It is reported to consume about 30 percent of its body weight in food per day.

Food hoarding is pronounced in *P. leucopus* during autumn. Its small internal cheek pouches facilitate transportation of tiny seeds from such plants as blueberries, raspberries, and jewelweed to nearby caches hidden under logs or stumps or in cavities of trees. Larger nuts such as acorns, hickory nuts, and beechnuts are commonly cached for future use.

Like the deer mouse, the white-footed mouse forms the base of the vertebrate food chain and thus serves as a food source for many other animals. In Pennsylvania, its predators include skunks, weasels, raccoons, foxes, and owls. Black rat snakes are known to kill *P. leucopus* residing in nests within tree cavities. Short-tailed shrews may occasionally kill young white-footed mice but are generally unable to capture adults because of their superior speed.

External parasites of the white-footed mouse include fleas, lice, chiggers, and ticks. A serious external parasite, the mange mite, may also infect the white-footed mouse, causing severe hair loss and scabby eruptions. Further, botfly larvae frequently parasitize populations of the white-footed mouse. Infestations may reach as high as 42 percent of the population in late summer. Other than slightly impairing locomotor ability because of their large size, botflies do not cause permanent or fatal harm to the white-footed mouse. Endoparasites that infest *P. leucopus* are tapeworms, roundworms, and various protozoans.

Behavior

The white-footed mouse is principally nocturnal, although it will be seen occasionally during the day, especially during winter. In Pennsylvania, some individuals exhibit daily torpor from mid-December to early February, whereas others may be active, foraging in the subnivean environment and leaving behind their tracks on the snow. Individuals may even alternate several days of torpor with several days without torpor. The white-footed mouse also conserves energy during cold periods by huddling in groups of two to six animals. These "huddles" may be composed of a mix of both *P. leucopus* and *P. maniculatus*.

Being semiarboreal, the white-footed mouse is at home in trees. Its nests can be found in tree hollows, among tree roots, and under stumps, logs, and rock piles. The white-footed mouse may even remodel abandoned nests of squirrels or birds or build nests in dresser drawers and old teapots in summer cabins. Although an adept climber, the white-footed mouse is reported to show less arboreal activity than the two long-tailed subspecies of the deer mouse.

The globular nest of *P. leucopus* is similar to that of the deer mouse. It measures from 15 to 25 centimeters (6–10 in.) in diameter and is composed of finely shredded leaves, vines, bark, grass, and other plant fibers. The entrance is usually near the bottom and is commonly covered by nest material. The white-footed mouse probably constructs more than one nest and may change nest sites often, especially when females with litters are disturbed.

Reproduction and Development

In Pennsylvania, the white-footed mouse breeds from early March through late October. It rarely breeds during winter. Like the deer mouse, the white-footed mouse is polyestrous and exhibits a postpartum heat. Males are generally promiscuous.

The gestation period is about 21 days for nonlactating females. The first litter is usually born between late March to mid-April, and litter size ranges from two to six young. In Pennsylvania, the female white-footed mouse may produce between three and four litters per year. The young are altricial—naked, pink, and blind—and weigh between 1.4 and 2.4 grams (0.05–0.08 oz.). By two weeks of age, their eyes open; one week later their gray juvenile pelage is evident. Weaning occurs between three and four weeks of age, but, if the mother bears another litter, her first litter will be weaned immediately. Young females can mate by two months of age, and spring-born mice commonly breed during their first summer.

Eastern Woodrat

SCIENTIFIC NAME
Neotoma floridana (*Neotoma* combines the Greek roots *Neo,* meaning "new," and *toma,* meaning "cut"; *floridana* refers to Florida, where the species was first found.)

SUBSPECIES IN PENNSYLVANIA
Neotoma floridana magister

ALSO CALLED
Woodrat, Allegheny woodrat, cave rat, cliff rat, pack rat, trade rat

TOTAL LENGTH
381–465 mm (14.9–18.1 in.)

LENGTH OF TAIL
162–215 mm (6.3–8.4 in.)

WEIGHT
273–447 g (9.6–15.6 oz.)

MAMMAE
Two pairs

POPULATION DENSITY
1–4/ha (1–2/acre)

HOME RANGE
0.17–0.26 ha (0.4–0.6 acre)

LONGEVITY
Up to 3 yrs. in the wild

STATUS IN PENNSYLVANIA
Threatened

Description

The eastern woodrat is the only member of the genus *Neotoma* residing in the eastern United States. Its head is gray, its feet and belly are white, its sides are light brown, and the hairs along its midline are a slightly darker brown. Because black hairs are mixed in with the brownish gray pelage, the eastern woodrat appears grizzled. In summer, adults are more brightly colored than in winter, tending toward bright cinnamon orange, whereas the winter pelage is slightly darker and longer. Young are grayer than adults, and sexes are colored alike. Albino woodrats have been reported, but melanistic (black) individuals are unknown.

Superficially, the eastern woodrat resembles the Norway rat; however, the woodrat has a blunter

Eastern woodrat (*Neotoma floridana*).

snout, larger ears, more prominent eyes, and a less coarse pelage than the Norway rat. The woodrat also has a densely haired, distinctly bicolored tail that lacks annulations (scaly rings). The tail is dark gray above, white below.

Ecology

The eastern woodrat is a resident of the Mountain and Plateau sections of Pennsylvania. Here, limestone caves, rocky cliffs, and accumulations of residual sandstone boulders marked by deep crevices with underground galleries represent favored habitat. Along Laurel Ridge, Westmoreland County, the woodrat inhabits cliffs and talus slopes in beech, poplar, maple forests at elevations ranging from about 400 to 850 meters (1,320–2,800 ft.).

Like other cricetids, *N. floridana* is opportunistic and may take up residence in deserted outbuildings. Caves, crevices, and cliff ledges with an overhanging rocky roof serve as ideal sites for placement of the woodrat's unique large, bulky house.

The eastern woodrat is principally vegetarian; its diet consists of leaves of herbaceous plants, berries (wild grape), and nuts such as acorns and beechnuts. This rodent does not show a preference for insects as do the deer mouse and white-footed mouse. In autumn, the woodrat caches a variety of food—such as leafy twigs, branches of trees or shrubs, and even puffballs and other mushrooms—and places it either on top of the house or within its interior. These materials may serve as a food source during winter.

The eastern woodrat has many natural predators such as foxes, weasels, skunks, raccoons, great horned and barred owls, and, occasionally, hawks. Large snakes such as the black rat snake also take a toll. Rather unexpectedly, timber rattlesnakes and copperheads residing in close proximity to the woodrat in Pennsylvania have not been found to consume this rodent. The woodrat residing in caves, however, is vulnerable to the activities of humans in the form of harassment and killing by spelunkers.

The woodrat supports a plentiful number of external parasites including fleas, mites, chiggers, ticks, and lice. A common parasite of *N. floridana* is the botfly or warble fly larva. Adult flies lay eggs at the entrance to the woodrat house; the eggs subsequently adhere to the woodrat's fur. Larvae penetrate the skin, lodging in the neck, chest, and inguinal area. Here, the pupae develop and reach about 18 millimeters (1 in.) long before the adult fly emerges in late summer. Botflies are reported to infest up to 16 percent of the woodrat population, yet the woodrat does not show any obvious signs of discomfort from this large larval parasite. Internal parasites include roundworms, tapeworms, and a variety of protozoans. In some states, the woodrat is known to carry fleas harboring the bacterium associated with bubonic plague.

Behavior

The eastern woodrat is nocturnal and active throughout the year. It does not hibernate or undergo torpidity. It leads a solitary existence, with each individual residing in its own house, except when pairing occurs during the breeding season and when raising young.

Woodrat houses provide escape from predators, offer protection from the elements, and have nest quarters for raising young. They are also depositories for the treasures of this legendary rodent, appropriately called a "pack rat." Items such as nails, bones, scraps of paper, old mammal skulls, feathers, eyeglasses, shotgun shells, rubber bands, flashlight batteries, eating utensils, bottle caps, and other debris found in the woods or confiscated from cabins or abandoned camp sites have been found along the perimeter and inside woodrat houses. In this cache can also be found food such as mushrooms and various berries and nuts. One scientist reports hearing about a woodrat that actually stole a half dollar from one poor soul and returned later with two quarters in change (Lowery, 1974)!

Not very selective about construction materials, *N. floridana* builds its houses of sticks, twigs, shredded bark, grass, and a variety of dried, woody vegetation—a good cross section of the surrounding environment. The houses range in architectural design from cone-shaped to rather flattened, depending on the location, and they vary greatly in size. They may be as large as 4 meters (13 ft.) long; 2 meters (6.5 ft.) wide, and

Eastern woodrat in nest.

up to 1 meter (3 ft.) high. In Pennsylvania, however, most woodrat houses are small, having an outside diameter of only about 50 centimeters (20 in.).

Woodrat houses typically contain two or more spherical nests measuring about 12 centimeters (5 in.) across and composed of dry grasses, shredded bark, fur, and, occasionally, feathers. The houses are used year-round and last for the life of the occupant; succeeding generations inherit the structure. Often the houses provide shelter for other animals such as eastern cottontails and white-footed mice, in addition to snakes, toads, salamanders, and many invertebrates such as insects and spiders. When one of the two or more entrances is covered with spider webs, the woodrat home is vacant.

Although the perimeter of the house is littered by a formidable midden of junk, the woodrat is a good housekeeper. This sanitary animal establishes "latrine" sites, to be used by several individuals, on nearby rock surfaces. Heaps of droppings can be found, sometimes measuring from 25 to 45 centimeters (10–18 in.) across and reaching depths of 5 centimeters (2 in.).

The woodrat is territorial and will defend its home from other woodrats. It accomplishes this by teeth chattering and thumping its hindfeet on the ground. Actual fights are uncommon, but, if they occur, the most common mode of defense is jabbing the opponent in the head with the forefeet while in a bipedal stance. Biting is unusual and used only as a last resort.

Reproduction and Development

Little is known about the reproductive activities of the woodrat in Pennsylvania. The breeding season probably begins in late winter and continues until late summer. Females are reported to breed while nursing. Not as prolific as most cricetids, the woodrat probably produces from two to three litters per year in Pennsylvania. The first litter is born in late April or early May, following a gestation period of about 35 days. The two to four young in each litter are blind and nearly helpless, weighing about 14 grams (0.5 oz.) and measuring some 88 millimeters (3.4 in.) long. The mother assists with the delivery by using her forepaws.

Development of the young is rapid, with an average weight gain of about 1.5 grams (0.05 oz.) per day during the first two months. The eyes open when the pups reach two and one-half weeks old, and they are weaned at about four weeks. Young born in spring may breed in the same year, but they normally do not attain sexual maturity until the next spring.

Status in Pennsylvania

Information on the life history and population dynamics of the eastern woodrat in the Commonwealth is greatly lacking. Recent field observations indicate that this large rodent is now absent from localities in eastern Pennsylvania where it was once quite abundant. Further, numbers throughout its present range in the state seem to be declining rapidly for unknown reasons. As a result of this rapid decline in numbers and dwindling geographic range, the Pennsylvania Biological Survey has assigned the status of "threatened" to the eastern woodrat in its publication *Species of Special Concern in Pennsylvania* (Genoways and Brenner, 1985). Extensive field studies are urgently required to document distributional patterns and ecological requirements of this species in the Commonwealth.

Southern Red-backed Vole

SCIENTIFIC NAME
Clethrionomys gapperi
(*Clethrionomys* is Greek for "kind
of dor-mouse"; *gapperi* refers to
Gapper, a zoologist.)

SUBSPECIES IN PENNSYLVANIA
Clethrionomys gapperi gapperi;
Clethrionomys gapperi
paludicola; Clethrionomys
gapperi rupicola

ALSO CALLED
Red-backed vole, Gapper's red-
backed mouse, boreal red-backed
vole, red-backed mouse

TOTAL LENGTH
120–158 mm (4.7–6.2 in.)

LENGTH OF TAIL
30–50 mm (1.2–2 in.)

WEIGHT
16–38 g (0.6–1.3 oz.)

MAMMAE
Four pairs

POPULATION DENSITY
2–38/ha (1–15/acre)

HOME RANGE
0.01–0.5 ha (0.2–1.2 acres)

LONGEVITY
1½–2 yrs. in the wild

STATUS IN PENNSYLVANIA
Undetermined for *C. g. paludicola*
and *C. g. rupicola*

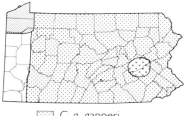

:::: C. g. gapperi
☐ .C. g. paludicola
∷ C. g. rupicola

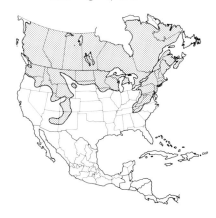

Description

With its black eyes, inconspicuous
ears, blunt face, and prominent
orange teeth, this rodent looks
much like other voles and lemmings. The southern red-backed
vole, however, is more brilliantly
colored and can be easily distinguished by a broad, reddish band
running from its forehead to its
rump. The nose, the sides of the
head, and the body of the southern red-backed vole are gray, often
with a yellowish cast. Its belly
ranges from silvery white to pale
yellow, and its tail is bicolored:
dark brown above, whitish below.

A juvenile vole is gray in color.
The postjuvenile molt begins at
about one month of age. The first
seasonal molt occurs in autumn
and results in winter pelage by

Southern red-backed vole
(*Clethrionomys gapperi*).
See plate 10, following page 172.

November. Summer pelage is attained by mid-May.

Ecology

The southern red-backed vole is most commonly found in coniferous, deciduous, and mixed forests with abundant mosses and ferns. In the mountains of southwestern Pennsylvania, this rodent prefers rocky outcrops in beech-maple-poplar forests where stumps, rotting logs, and exposed roots are abundant.

Being semifossorial, adapted to burrowing, *C. gapperi* travels in natural runways along and beneath logs, rocks, and roots of trees. Unlike such voles as the meadow vole that dwell in grasslands, the southern red-backed vole does not construct its own elaborate runways. Instead, it commonly uses the burrow systems of other small mammals such as the northern short-tailed shrew. These subterranean passageways permit the rodent to forage year-round, unhampered by snow or inclement weather.

Unlike most voles, the southern red-backed vole has cheekteeth that are rooted and, thus, not adapted for a steady diet of abrasive grasses. This vole, instead, is an omnivorous, opportunistic feeder. It takes advantage of whatever the forest has to offer in the way of food—including nuts, seeds, berries, mosses, lichens, ferns, fungi, the vegetative portions of plants, and arthropods. In contrast to some species of mice, the southern red-backed vole consumes few insects.

In the summer and autumn, various subterranean fungi are a staple for the southern red-backed vole. If it caches or stores food, which is uncommon, it does so during autumn. Winter foods include seeds, roots, bark, and miscellaneous plant parts. During midwinter, the southern red-backed vole usually forages under the snow, in the subnivean environment. Its home range in this environment is actually larger than the home range during the snow-free season. If snowcover is insufficient to insulate its foraging zone against cold temperature, high mortality may result.

The southern red-backed vole, like other small forest rodents, is preyed upon by a variety of birds, snakes, and mammals—in particular, the long-tailed weasel. External parasites of the vole include fleas, lice, ticks, mites, and chiggers. The southern red-backed vole also harbors a variety of internal parasites such as protozoans, tapeworms, and roundworms.

Behavior

No matter what the season, the southern red-backed vole is active. Although its activity peaks at dusk and during hours of darkness, *C. gapperi* may be active anytime. Like other voles, it does not hibernate or undergo torpidity.

The usual mode of locomotion for the southern red-backed vole is hopping, although it commonly runs under vegetation, logs, and debris. To surmount obstacles, *C. gapperi* can jump at least 15 to 20 centimeters (6–8 in.). It is also a good swimmer and readily enters water. When disturbed, the southern red-backed vole may exhibit "waltzing," a condition in which the animal makes rapid, circling movements from left to right and jerks its head.

The southern red-backed vole is a prolific breeder but, unlike its relative the meadow vole, does not undergo population explosions. During a given year, the density of the southern red-backed vole tends to increase in summer, reaching peak numbers in late summer and early autumn. A gradual decline in abundance occurs throughout winter.

It begins breeding in late March and continues through November. Unlike mice of the genus *Peromyscus,* the southern red-backed vole does not form large communal nesting groups. Instead a male, female, and their litter of pups usually occupy a single nest. The male moves from the nest as the young grow larger, and, although he does not care for the young, the male remains congenial with the family unit.

Nests of the southern red-backed vole are simple and globular, 75 to 100 millimeters (3–4 in.) in diameter and lined with grass, stems, dead leaves, moss, *Sphagnum,* or other litter. As a rule, nests are not located in trees, although the vole is an agile climber. Instead, it uses natural cavities, abandoned holes, and nests of other small mammals.

Reproduction and Development

The gestation period of *C. gapperi* ranges from 17 to 19 days, and two or three litters are produced annually, with four to five young making up the average litter. At birth, the southern red-backed vole is altricial—blind, toothless, hairless, and pink throughout. The newborn weighs about 1.9 grams (0.07 oz.). About 12 days after birth, when weaning begins, the eyes open; by this time the body is covered with short hair. Weanlings, weighing about 12 grams (0.4 oz.), begin to eat solid food at 14 days of age. By about 17 days of age, weaning is completed, and the young vole reaches sexual maturity within about three months.

Status in Pennsylvania

The southern red-backed vole is represented in Pennsylvania by three subspecies. *Clethrionomys g. gapperi* is the most widespread race, found in suitable habitats throughout the Mountain and Plateau sections of the Commonwealth. In the northwest corner of the state, *C. g. paludicola* is reported to reside only in the vicinity of Pymatuning Reservoir, Crawford County, where it occupies boggy, lakeside areas. The third subspecies, *C. g. rupicola*, like the latter, shows a very localized distribution in the state, being confined to the crest of the Kittatinny Ridge and mountains of southeastern Pennsylvania. There, it resides in mesic forests of black birch, yellow birch, and hemlock.

Because of the localized and restricted nature of *C. g. paludicola* in the northwest and *C. g. rupicola* in the southeast, little is known of their ecological requirements. As a result of this paucity of information, the Pennsylvania Biological Survey in its report *Species of Special Concern in Pennsylvania* (Genoways and Brenner, 1985) has assigned these two subspecies the status of "undetermined." Additional field research is recommended to delineate the distributional limits and specific habitat requirements of these two subspecies of southern red-backed vole in the Commonwealth.

Meadow Vole

SCIENTIFIC NAME
Microtus pennsylvanicus
(*Microtus* is Greek for "small
ear"; *pennsylvanicus* refers to
Pennsylvania, the state where the
species was first described.)

SUBSPECIES IN PENNSYLVANIA
*Microtus pennsylvanicus
pennsylvanicus*

ALSO CALLED
Field mouse, eastern meadow
mouse, meadow mouse, ground
vole, meadow mole, bull mouse

TOTAL LENGTH
130–190 mm (5.1–7.4 in.)

LENGTH OF TAIL
35–65 mm (1.4–2.5 in.)

WEIGHT
20–65 g (0.7–2.3 oz.)

MAMMAE
Four pairs

POPULATION DENSITY
5–665/ha (3–270/acre)

HOME RANGE
0.004–1.3 ha (0.01–3.2 acres)

LONGEVITY
1–1½ yrs. in the wild

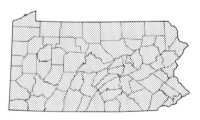

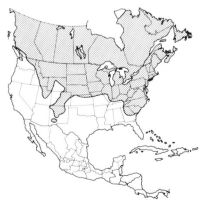

Description

The meadow vole is the most
common vole in eastern North
America. It is a shaggy rodent
with beady black eyes and short,
rounded ears concealed in the fur.
During summer, *M. pennsylvanicus* wears a short, dense,
chestnut brown coat peppered
with black. In winter, its back is
dark brown. Its belly fur is dark
gray, and its tail is indistinctly bicolored, dark brown above and
gray below. Juveniles are grayish
black in color. Whereas the sexes
are colored alike, males are slightly
larger than females. Colors such
as all white, albino, white spotted,
black, and cinnamon are known to
occur but are uncommon.

Although similar in appearance
to the woodland vole and the
southern bog lemming, *M. pennsylvanicus* is best distinguished
by its long tail. Its tail is twice the
length of its hindfoot, whereas the

Meadow vole (*Microtus pennsylvanicus*). See plate 11, following page 172.

tails of the woodland vole and southern bog lemming are bobbed. The woodland vole also has an auburn back and shorter ears than the brown meadow vole, and the southern bog lemming is further differentiated by its unique grooved upper incisors.

Ecology

The meadow vole is one of the most abundant and widespread mammals in Pennsylvania. It ranges from the low valleys of the Susquehanna and Delaware rivers to the Laurel Summit glade of southeastern Westmoreland County, an elevation of about 820 meters (2,700 ft.). Optimum habitat for the meadow vole includes moist, unpastured meadows and fields characterized by grasses, sedges, and rushes. Although *M. pennsylvanicus* is not found in forests on a permanent basis, it may inhabit grassy meadows, bogs, and small clearings bordered by forests. A low, protective cover of

dead grass and herbs appeals to this vole.

In favorable habitats, a meadow vole's presence may be detected by an intricate system of surface runways crisscrossing fields. These miniature highways are about 2.5 centimeters (1 in.) across, slightly wider than a garden hose. Products of the vole's feeding activities, these runways are clean and well manicured. The vole commonly establishes "latrine" sites for depositing its brownish green feces.

The meadow vole is herbivorous, feeding primarily on grasses, sedges, legumes, tubers, and roots. Beginning in midsummer, seeds constitute an important food of voles. Grass seeds are obtained by severing the plant at its base, then cutting it into short lengths. These cuttings can be found lining runways or cached in small piles, to be eaten later. At high population densities, *M. pennsylvanicus* may damage apple orchards and nursery plantings by girdling the trunks of young trees. Insects, underground fungi, and animal remains are also part of the meadow vole's diet. *Microtus pennsylvanicus* hoards food for winter consumption. Its caches are located above and below ground and may contain seeds, fruits, grasses, tubers, and roots.

Like the deer mouse and white-footed mouse of Pennsylvania's forests, the meadow vole forms an essential link in the grassland food web. The species bridges the gap between producers (green plants) and meat-eating animals. It is, thus, the misfortune of the meadow vole to be a food item of many of Pennsylvania's carnivorous mammals—including snakes, weasels, minks, raccoons, foxes, skunks, and opossums. Northern short-tailed shrews are known to kill young meadow voles in the nest. Humans and house cats also kill voles, especially those residing in farming areas. Avian predators include many hawks and owls, bluejays, crows, and shrikes. In addition, young voles in the nest are killed occasionally by fires and flooding.

The meadow vole is host to many different parasites. External parasites include fleas, ticks, mites, chiggers, and botflies. Tapeworms, flukes, roundworms, and spiny-headed worms infest the meadow vole internally. *Microtus pennsylvanicus* is also subject to various protozoan, bacterial, and viral infections.

Behavior

The meadow vole is active throughout the year, both day and night, with peak activity at dawn and dusk. During winter, the vole lives in surface runways within the subnivean environment. Subterranean burrows are also used, especially during winter to escape the cold.

The meadow vole builds elaborate nests to provide protection from predators and inclement weather and as a site for rearing young. These nests may be located 8 to 10 centimeters (3–4 in.) underground or situated on the ground surface, commonly in the center of a tussock of grass. They are globular and made of a wide

Nest of a meadow vole.

variety of grasses, sedges, or rushes and measure about 13 to 20 centimeters (5–8 in.) in diameter. The lining consists of finely shredded grasses or sedges. During winter, several meadow voles huddle together in a nest for warmth. During the breeding season, although females with young occupy a nest communally, males are solitary and occupy separate nests.

The meadow vole is rather pugnacious and commonly bickers with other meadow voles, especially during the breeding season. At this time, breeding females vigorously defend their territories against other breeding females. These unsocial encounters can be evidenced a posteriori by the chewed ears of many wild individuals. During autumn when breeding ceases, aggression subsides and communal nesting commences.

The meadow vole is an excellent swimmer and diver. In nature, it is known to swim 200 meters (660 ft.) with no ill effects. Because of the water-repellent and insulating qualities of its thick fur, it shows an ability to swim superior to that of the white-footed mouse. The meadow vole also displays a well-developed homing instinct. It has been shown to return successfully to its home when released up to a few hundred meters away.

Reproduction and Development

Without a doubt, the meadow vole is the most prolific of the mammals of Pennsylvania. In the southern parts of the Commonwealth, the species breeds year-round, weather permitting. Over most of its range in the state, however, its breeding season commences in late March and runs until late autumn.

Like other cricetids, the male meadow vole is a promiscuous breeder, and the females are polyestrous and exhibit a postpartum heat. Under field conditions, the meadow vole may produce up to eight or nine litters of from five to eight young each year. A single female meadow vole may potentially produce up to 72 offspring during the breeding season, but this is rare. One famous zoologist reported that a captive female vole produced 17 families in a single year. Further, one of her daughters produced 13 families before she reached the age of one year (Bailey, 1924).

Meadow voles are born following a gestation period of about 21 days. Newborn young are blind, pink, hairless, and helpless, weighing between 2 and 3 grams (0.07 – 0.1 oz.). Growth is rapid, and, by the time they reach a week old, they are fully furred and their eyes open. The young are weaned when two weeks old; a week later they are independent. Within a week or so, the mother is likely to bear another litter. Young females become sexually mature at the age of only four weeks, and males reach sexual maturity at five weeks of age.

The concept of population explosions is synonymous with voles and lemmings. Meadow vole populations undergo cyclic fluctuations in density, reaching their maximum about every four years. Populations of *M. pennsylvanicus* residing in southern Canada, for example, are reported to reach up to 665 voles per hectare (270/acre). Following this peak, the population abruptly "crashes," only to build again.

Scientists have proposed many possible "regulators" for these rather predictable cycles—including food quality, predation, climatic events, physiological stress, and behavioral and genetic factors. There are almost as many theories for this age-old phenomenon as there are scientists working on the mystery. But, alas, a satisfactory explanation has yet to be found for these perplexing microtine cycles, and it is unlikely that there is a single explanation.

Rock Vole

SCIENTIFIC NAME
Microtus chrotorrhinus (*Microtus* is Greek for "small ear"; *chrotorrhinus*, also Greek, means "yellow nose.")

SUBSPECIES IN PENNSYLVANIA
Microtus chrotorrhinus chrotorrhinus

ALSO CALLED
Yellow-nosed vole, fern vole

TOTAL LENGTH
142–169 mm (5.5–6.6 in.)

LENGTH OF TAIL
43–50 mm (1.7–2 in.)

WEIGHT
30–40 g (1.2–1.6 oz.)

MAMMAE
Four pairs

POPULATION DENSITY
Unknown

HOME RANGE
Unknown

LONGEVITY
1 ½-2 yrs. in the wild

STATUS IN PENNSYLVANIA
Vulnerable

Description

The rock vole closely resembles the meadow vole in overall appearance and size. These microtines are best separated by differences in their skulls and patterns of enamel in the second upper molar. Without the benefit of an examination of their skulls and teeth, the two voles can be differentiated by their color. The rock vole sports a yellowish orange snout and yellowish brown dorsal hair; the meadow vole is chestnut brown peppered with black. Further, the two species exhibit distinct ecological separation: The rock vole resides in forests, whereas the meadow vole lives in meadows or grasslands.

Like most other microtines, the eyes of the rock vole are small, and its ears protrude slightly beyond its body fur. The belly is silvery gray as are the tops of the feet. The rock vole's tail is indis-

Rock vole (*Microtus chrotorrhinus*).
Photo by Roger W. Barbour.

tinctly bicolored, dark above and light below. Some individuals have a dull, yellowish wash on their rump. Males may be slightly larger than females. *Microtus chrotorrhinus* exhibits three developmental molts, and juveniles are gray in color.

Ecology

The common name *rock vole* accurately describes the optimal habitat of this handsome microtine; it invariably is associated with rocky habitats. In Pennsylvania, the rock vole is known from only four northeastern counties. Here, it resides in cool, moist forests of yellow birch, maple, hemlock, and mountain ash where the forest floor is characterized by sandstone boulders and a lush, her-baceous understory frequently dominated by ferns. *Microtus chrotorrhinus* shares this habitat with southern red-backed voles, deer mice, woodland jumping mice, and assorted shrews. The rock vole may occur in localized colonies within the favored habitat.

Little is known about the food habits of the rock vole, but they probably correspond closely to those of the southern red-backed vole. In the northern part of its range, *M. chrotorrhinus* feeds primarily on green plants, namely bunchberry, mayflower, violet, goldenrod, and blueberry. Other foods include mosses, ferns, seeds, stems, leaves, subterranean fungi, and lepidopterous larvae. Forbs (herbs other than grass) are also harvested by the rock vole, and cut portions are cached in subsurface cavities. Like the southern red-backed vole, the rock vole exhibits a high water requirement, and the damp, moist environment of its subsurface retreats helps *M. chrotorrhinus* to fulfill this need.

Predators of the rock vole include weasels, foxes, northern short-tailed shrews, timber rattlesnakes, and copperheads, to mention a few. Predation by avian predators is probably minimized because of the inaccessibility of its foraging zone. External parasites reported for *M. chrotorrhinus* are ticks and fleas. The rock vole also shows a high incidence of parasitism by botflies, which may be attributed to its moist habitat. Internal parasites include tapeworms and roundworms.

Behavior and Reproduction

The behavior and reproductive biology of the rock vole is poorly documented. What is known about the rodent is that the species is active year-round and does not hibernate or undergo torpidity. Also, the rock vole is principally diurnal, with most activity occurring during morning hours. Studies indicate that this vole is difficult to maintain in the laboratory, but when handled it is docile.

In Pennsylvania, *M. chrotorrhinus* breeds from early spring to late autumn. It exhibits a postpartum heat and may produce two to three litters each year. Following a gestation period of about 19 to 21 days, a litter of one to seven young is born. This reproductive rate seems slightly lower than that of the meadow vole in the Commonwealth. No information is available on the development of young for this species of vole.

Status in Pennsylvania

In Pennsylvania, the rock vole is restricted to small, isolated populations in the northeast. The knowledge of the biology of this vole in Pennsylvania is derived primarily from field research conducted during the Pennsylvania Mammal Survey (1946–1951; see Grimm and Whitebread, 1952 in section III.A of "Selected References"). More recently, the Pennsylvania Biological Survey assigned the status of "vulnerable" to the rock vole in its publication *Species of Special Concern in Pennsylvania* (Genoways and Brenner, 1985). This report recommends that extensive field studies be undertaken to delimit the present distribution and habitat requirements of the rock vole in northeastern Pennsylvania. Suitable habitat for this vole must be preserved and protected from various commercial and recreational development interests surfacing in this part of the state.

Woodland Vole

SCIENTIFIC NAME
Microtus pinetorum (*Microtus* is Greek for "small ear"; although *pinetorum* is from the Latin word *pinetum*, meaning "of the pine grove," this species is rarely found in pine habitats.)

SUBSPECIES IN PENNSYLVANIA
Microtus pinetorum scalopsoides

ALSO CALLED
Pine vole, pine mouse, mole mouse, potato mouse, mole pine mouse, bluegrass pine mouse, woodland pine mouse

TOTAL LENGTH
110–140 mm (4.3–5.5 in.)

LENGTH OF TAIL
17–24 mm (0.7–1 in.)

WEIGHT
25–37 g (0.9–1.3 oz.)

MAMMAE
Two pairs

POPULATION DENSITY
2–124/ha (1–50/acre)

HOME RANGE
0.0014–0.2 ha (0.003–0.5 acre)

LONGEVITY
1–1½ yrs. in the wild

Description

The woodland vole is Pennsylvania's smallest vole, just slightly smaller than the southern bog lemming. The glossy fur of *M. pinetorum* is chestnut brown on the back, and the belly is silvery gray. Its short tail—slightly longer than its hindfoot—is faintly bicolored, brownish above and pale below. The combination of small size, mole-like fur, brown back, and short tail distinguishes the woodland vole from all other Pennsylvania microtines.

Being highly fossorial, the woodland vole has several physical features that suit it for burrowing: short ears, small eyes, strong forefeet, and velvety fur that sheds dirt. Its mouth is small, and its upper lip closes tightly behind the upper incisors—an adaptation for gnawing through soil.

Woodland vole (*Microtus pinetorum*).
See plate 12, following page 172.
Photo by John R. MacGregor.

The sexes of *M. pinetorum* are colored alike and equal in size. Juveniles are more grayish than adults. The species undergoes two annual molts: A spring molt occurs in May and June, producing the summer coat; the autumn molt begins in early November and yields the winter coat by December.

Ecology

The woodland vole occupies a diverse array of habitats in Pennsylvania. In the west, it resides in sandy soil along woodland creeks where the forest communities are typified by black walnut, black cherry, and basswood in the north and beech, maple, and oak in the south. A dense understory of herbaceous growth and a well-developed layer of litter provide optimal conditions for this rodent. On the Pocono Plateau, the distribution of *M. pinetorum* is spotty and localized. There, the woodland vole is reported to inhabit cool hemlock and northern hardwood forests marked by rocky terrain and an abundance of mosses and ferns. The lowlands of southern and eastern Pennsylvania, however, are the stronghold of the woodland vole's distribution in the state. There, the species is common in loose, sandy soil of old fields, thickets, and edges of agricultural land; along fencerows; and in gardens and orchards. Common co-inhabitants are the southern red-backed vole, woodland jumping mouse, and other mesic-adapted small mammals.

The woodland vole exhibits small home ranges and concentrates foraging in its underground subways, where its food consists of roots, tubers, stems, leaves, seeds, and fruits. Subterranean fungi, insects, and other invertebrates are also consumed, as are hickory nuts, acorns, and beech-nuts. During winter, the woodland vole relies on roots and bark for sustenance, and this diet places the species in disfavor with orchardists, especially in the Cumberland Valley, where it is capable of girdling apple trees by feeding on their bark. The vole is also unpopular with gardeners because of its affinity for potatoes, peanuts, lily bulbs, and freshly planted seeds.

Like many other small mammals, the woodland vole hoards food, an activity occupying much time during autumn. Underground caches, which may reach up to a gallon in volume, radiate off the main burrow and may be as deep as 45 centimeters (18 in.) below ground.

Although its elaborate network of subterranean tunnels affords some immunity from predators, the woodland vole still has its fair share of enemies. In Pennsylvania, screech, barred, and great horned owls and many hawks feed on *M. pinetorum*. Foxes, opossums, skunks, raccoons, weasels, northern short-tailed shrews, and house cats also take a toll, as do snakes such as the copperhead and the black rat snake. Flooding of burrow systems also kills many woodland voles, especially nesting pups.

The moist environment of the woodland vole's underground abode also seems to attract a sizable number of parasites. Fleas, lice, mites, chiggers, and ticks commonly infect the woodland vole externally. Internal parasites include tapeworms, roundworms, and spiny-headed worms.

Behavior

The woodland vole is active day and night year-round. During winter, this rodent does not hibernate or undergo torpidity but forages principally in its burrows and beneath leaf litter and humus within the subnivean environment. Pennsylvania's most fossorial microtine, *M. pinetorum* establishes elaborate burrow systems in loose, light, easily crumbled soil. Its tunnels are usually shallow, weave slightly below leaf litter, measure about 20 to 25 millimeters (0.8–1 in.) in diameter, and are commonly used by meadow voles, hairy-tailed moles, and assorted shrews.

To construct its tunnels, the woodland vole loosens dirt with its head, neck, and forefeet and pushes it to the rear with its hindfeet. Occasionally, it turns around and pushes accumulated debris out of its tunnel, an action resulting in small conical piles of soil measuring about 10 centimeters (4 in.) across and some 6 centimeters (2.5 in.) high.

Globular nests made of dry, shredded grasses, leaves, and roots are placed at the terminus of a burrow under the protection of rocks, logs, or stumps. In orchards, nests tend to be located close to tree trunks or nestled within a tangle of roots. Nests measure about 15 to 18 centimeters (6–7 in.) in diameter.

In contrast to meadow voles, the woodland vole is not territorial. Social groups contain numerous adults of both sexes, and their young may occupy a single burrow and nest. One investigator reported finding a nest containing 11 individuals, although a more usual communal group number is about four or five (Raynor, 1960).

Reproduction and Development

In Pennsylvania, the woodland vole breeds from late February through late autumn. Although year-round breeding is not reported for the woodland vole in Pennsylvania, it may occur in the South, weather permitting. During courtship, the female assumes an aggressive role, in which she initiates copulation by seizing a male on his side with her teeth. Sometimes she may even drag the male.

Following a gestation period of about 24 days, a litter of three to six young (usually four) is born. Newborns weigh about 2.3 grams (0.08 oz.) and are naked, blind, and helpless. Development is rapid, and pups have a covering of grayish brown fur by the end of one week of life. Their eyes open by about day 12, and, by the time they are three weeks old, weaning is under way and the young can eat solid food. Juveniles reach sexual maturity at about two months of age.

The woodland vole is less prolific than the meadow vole, and in Pennsylvania probably produces a maximum of only two litters each year. Its litter size is also smaller than most other species of *Micro-* *tus.* The fact that *M. pinetorum* has only four mammae limits the number of young the woodland vole can rear successfully. In addition, this microtine does not display cyclic population fluctuations as meadow voles do. The species can, however, become quite numerous at times; a density of up to 700 voles per hectare (300/acre) was recorded from one New York orchard (Hamilton, 1938).

Southern Bog Lemming

SCIENTIFIC NAME
Synaptomys cooperi (*Synaptomys* combines the Greek words *synaptein*, meaning "to unite," and *mys*, meaning "mouse"; *cooperi* alludes to William Cooper, the zoologist who collected the first specimen.)

SUBSPECIES IN PENNSYLVANIA
Synaptomys cooperi cooperi; *Synaptomys cooperi stonei*

ALSO CALLED
Lemming mouse, lemming vole, bog mouse

TOTAL LENGTH
115−145 mm (4.5−5.7 in.)

LENGTH OF TAIL
15−24 mm (0.6−1 in.)

WEIGHT
25−45 g (0.9−1.6 oz.)

MAMMAE
Three pairs

POPULATION DENSITY
4−12/ha (2−5/acre)

HOME RANGE
0.04−0.32 ha (0.1−0.8 acre)

LONGEVITY
1−1½ yrs. in the wild; up to 3 yrs. in captivity

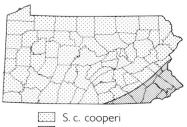

S. c. cooperi
S. c. stonei

Description

The southern bog lemming is one of Pennsylvania's smallest microtine rodents, second only to the woodland vole. Its long fur is grizzled brown on the back and grades to silverish gray on the underside. Its eyes are small, and its ears are well hidden in thick fur. Someone glancing quickly at *S. cooperi* might confuse the species with the meadow vole or woodland vole, but the southern bog lemming is distinguishable by the combination of its short tail (only slightly longer than its hindfoot) and grooved upper incisors. These longitudinal grooves are easily observed in live animals by pushing back the upper lip and carefully looking along the side of the incisor. Because no other rodent in

Southern bog lemming (*Synaptomys cooperi*).
Photo by L. Master (ASM Mammal Slide Library).

Pennsylvania has these unique grooves except the jumping mice, the grooves are the single best criterion separating *S. cooperi* from all other microtines.

When the southern bog lemming gnaws, its lips close behind orange incisors. The animal has four toes on the forefeet and five on the hindfeet. Sexes are colored alike and are the same size. Juveniles are gray in color, and a single annual molt occurs from spring to autumn. Albino and melanistic (black) individuals are rare.

Ecology

In Pennsylvania, the common name *bog lemming* is misleading when attempting to locate the favored habitat of this elusive microtine. *S. cooperi* occurs at low densities primarily in old field communities of poverty grass,

timothy, and broom sedge interspersed with scattered woody vegetation such as young hawthorn, crabapple, locust, and sassafras. A lush understory of ground pine, mosses, and liverworts commonly forms part of the optimal habitat profile for the southern bog lemming in the state. Other suitable habitats in Pennsylvania include damp, grassy clearings in forests; dry, postfire successional communities; and margins of permanent springs.

A thick mat of dead grass covering the ground provides an ideal site for constructing surface runways. These bog lemming "freeways"—built by the cutting and trimming activities of foraging individuals—measure about 2 centimeters (0.75 in.) in width. Not as tidy as the meadow vole, *S. cooperi* commonly litters its runways with cuttings of grass and bright green, oval scats. The color of this excrement is another indication that the southern bog lemming is around; other voles tend to void darker feces.

In Pennsylvania, the southern bog lemming may seem to occur occasionally in the same habitat as the meadow vole and to share its runways. Close inspection reveals, however, that these two species show distinct habitat separation, usually occupying different parts of the same general habitat. This habitat separation is maintained, in part, by competitive exclusion by the larger, more aggressive meadow vole.

The southern bog lemming feeds on succulent stems, leaves, and seeds of grasses and sedges, namely poverty grass, timothy, and blue grass. In addition, ferns, mosses, liverworts, fungi, and insects are consumed. *Synaptomys cooperi* has many predators including foxes, skunks, weasels, house cats, and raccoons. Several species of owls, hawks, and snakes also take a toll on the southern bog lemming. Fleas, ticks, lice, mites, and chiggers infest the southern bog lemming externally, and it harbors internal parasites such as tapeworms, flukes, and roundworms.

Behavior

The southern bog lemming is active year-round. Studies of its daily activity indicate it is active both day and night. It is reported to live in small colonies but is not known to show communal nesting habits as do the meadow vole, deer mouse, and white-footed mouse. *Synaptomys cooperi* places its nests of grass and shredded leaves in an enlarged section of its burrow system, either above or below ground. The nests are globular, measure about 10 to 20 centimeters (4–8 in.) in diameter, and are lined with dried grasses, sedges, fur, and feathers. During winter nests are commonly located several centimeters below ground, whereas in summer they can be found on the ground surface, well hidden in a dense clump of grass.

Reproduction and Development

In Pennsylvania, the southern bog lemming breeds from early spring to late autumn. Like many other cricetids, this species is polyestrous and exhibits a postpartum heat. Following a gestation period of between 23 to 26 days, three to five young are born pink in color. Their eyes are closed and their ear flaps (pinnae) are folded over. At birth, their average weight is about 4 grams (0.14 oz.). Growth is rapid, and hair is evident when pups are about one week old. Their eyes open when they reach 10 to 12 days of age, and weaning is completed by the end of their third week of life.

Muskrat

SCIENTIFIC NAME
Ondatra zibethicus (*Ondatra* is a Huron Indian word meaning "muskrat"; *zibethicus* is Latin for "musky odor.")

SUBSPECIES IN PENNSYLVANIA
Ondatra zibethicus macrodon;
Ondatra zibethicus zibethicus

ALSO CALLED
Musk beaver, mudcat

TOTAL LENGTH
484–640 mm (19–25 in.)

LENGTH OF TAIL
221–315 mm (8.6–12.3 in.)

WEIGHT
728–1,614 g (1.6–3.5 lbs.)

MAMMAE
Three pairs

POPULATION DENSITY
12–62/ha (5–25/acre)

HOME RANGE
10–180 m (33–600 ft.)

LONGEVITY
3–4 yrs. in the wild

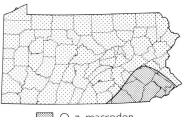

☒ O. z. macrodon
⬚ O. z. zibethicus

Description

The muskrat is the largest cricetid rodent in North America. Structurally, it resembles a giant meadow vole adapted to a semiaquatic lifestyle, but it looks and behaves more like a small beaver with a long, scaly, sparsely haired tail flattened side to side. Its general color is dark brown on the back, varying from chestnut to almost pure black. Individual muskrats sometimes exhibit different color variations such as black, albino, and pale tan. The belly color ranges from pale gray to bright cinnamon. Its waterproof coat consists of an outer layer of stiff, glossy, long guard hairs and a soft, wooly, grayish underfur.

Like the beaver, *O. zibethicus* shows many structural specializations for semiaquatic life. In addition to its waterproof coat, it has a valvular mouth with lips that close behind the incisors, allow-

Muskrat (*Ondatra zibethicus*).

ing the muskrat to secure food underwater. Its long, laterally flattened tail functions as a sort of rudder, and its hindfeet are partially webbed to serve as paddles. Stiff bristles lining its rear toes form swimming fringes, an adaptation also seen in water shrews, and its ankles are capable of a sideward twist which augments its "paddling power." An adept swimmer, the muskrat usually progresses at a rate of 1.5 to 5 kilometers per hour (1 – 3 mi./hr.). It can even swim backwards for short distances and remain submerged for 15 minutes or more.

The muskrat has tiny, beady black eyes, and its small ears are nearly concealed in thick fur. Juveniles are gray and duller in color than adults. The sexes, colored alike, are quite similar externally. Although males are slightly larger than females, the best way to tell them apart is by the presence of three pairs of mammae (one pectoral, two inguinal) in the female.

The muskrat undergoes a single annual molt occurring during summer months. In August, the density of the hair is at its minimum. Renewed growth begins in autumn, and the fur is prime when winter pelage is of maximum density, usually in February. The characteristic luster of the winter pelage is due to the increase in the number of dark, glossy guard hairs.

Ecology

The muskrat inhabits marshes, ponds, lakes, and slow-flowing creeks, where suitable herbaceous food plants are present. In Pennsylvania, *O. zibethicus* commonly resïdes in shoreline margins of farm ponds.

Although the muskrat mimics beavers in its general life-style, its diet is much more varied. *Ondatra zibethicus* consumes roots, shoots, stems, and leaves of most aquatic plants, preferring cattails, bur reeds, bulrushes, pond weed, arrowhead, and plantain. Although primarily a vegetarian, the muskrat is an opportunist and also eats insects, freshwater shellfish, crayfish, frogs, snails, and even carrion. It eats about one-third of its weight per day. Like other microtines, the muskrat hoards food and during winter may even consume parts of its home.

The muskrat has many predators, and humans are number one on the long list. With the average price of a muskrat pelt at about three dollars, the muskrat would not appear to be as valuable as other furbearers such as the luxurious mink. Nonetheless, *O. zibethicus* is the most valuable furbearing mammal in North America because of the total number harvested. In Pennsylvania alone, over 200,000 are harvested and sold annually.

In addition to this economic incentive, the muskrat is killed because its burrowing activities weaken dikes and dams, resulting in leaks and subsequent drainage of farm ponds. The muskrat also succumbs to fires, floods, and freezing weather; and automobiles take a toll, especially on those animals residing in cattail marshes along roadsides. Other predators include raccoons, foxes, river otters, large hawks and owls, and, most notably, minks. Young muskrats occasionally fall prey to snapping turtles and large predatory fish.

External parasites of the muskrat include fleas, ticks, mites, and chiggers. Internal parasites are flukes, tapeworms, roundworms, spiny-headed worms, and several protozoans. Many muskrats die of infectious hemorrhagic fever and are susceptible to tularemia, yellow-fat disease, porocephaliasis, and leptospirosis. *Ondatra zibethicus* in Pennsylvania is also known to harbor the rabies virus.

Behavior

The muskrat is active throughout the year. It is principally nocturnal, with activity peaks shortly after dark and again around midnight. On rainy or overcast days, this rodent may emerge during daylight hours and can be detected by V-shaped ripples in the water.

This industrious rodent constructs two types of living quarters as dictated by the physical makeup of the environment, either bank dens or houses. Throughout most of the Commonwealth, the muskrat tunnels into dams and banks of streams to construct the bank den. Entrances are usually underwater and penetrate the bank, sloping upward inside the den to a chamber where a bulky nest of dried vegetation is placed. Canal systems may be constructed between the nest burrow and foraging areas.

In northeastern Pennsylvania, because of the prevalence of suitable habitat in the form of shallow marshes and lakes, the muskrat constructs nesting and feeding houses. These dwellings are composed of plants and mud and are located in marshes or swamps where the water level is about 60 centimeters (2 ft.) deep.

The hemisphere-shaped nesting houses resemble beaver lodges except they are smaller. They range in height from about 0.5 to 1.5 meters (2 – 5 ft.) and measure some 2 to 3 meters (6.5 – 10 ft.) across. These houses have a central chamber located several centimeters above water level and lined with shredded herbaceous material. Muskrats enter this chamber by way of several underwater "plunge holes." The walls of the house, measuring about 0.3 meters (1 ft.) thick, provide protection from predators and inclement weather. Since muskrats commonly huddle together in the house to enhance survival in winter, the temperature inside is consistently higher than outside air temperature.

In addition to the primary nesting house, the muskrat builds several feeding huts or "feeders" close to the main house. These are roofed platforms, circular in shape, and smaller than the main house. They act as a site for muskrats to feed without interference from predators. As with the primary dwelling, several tunnels lead into the feeding hut from below the water's surface.

During winter, as a muskrat forages below ice, it creates small holes in the ice some distance from the main house. Each of these openings, which it makes by digging with its forearms and pushing up a mass of roots and submerged vegetation, may form a sizable pile of vegetation that serves as both a temporary feeding shelter and a breathing hole. During winter, when marshes and

ponds freeze over, the activity of the muskrat can be tracked by noting these "push ups." These holes are also a useful indicator of the muskrat's winter home range; this rodent can swim up to about 55 meters (180 ft.) underwater without breathing.

Although it normally forages close to its house or bank den, the muskrat has a well-developed homing instinct; tests demonstrate that individuals can locate their dens when displaced up to 4 kilometers (2.5 mi.) away! Rather territorial and not very social, *O. zibethicus* lives alone or with a mate except during winter, when several muskrats may share a home.

Although rather quiet, the muskrat is known to emit several sounds such as squeaks, whining growls, and teeth chattering. Like beavers, it commonly slaps the water with its tail as a form of communication and uses scent marking to attract members of the opposite sex and to communicate territorial boundaries. The muskrat scent is emitted by a pair of musk glands located under the skin near the anus (hence, the common name *muskrat*). Present in both sexes, these well-developed glands enlarge during the breeding season, especially in the males. Muskrats deposit the yellow, sweet-smelling secretion of the glands on feeding platforms, logs, and houses.

Reproduction and Development

Unlike its close relative the meadow vole, the muskrat does not undergo population explosions and crashes, although its populations follow a 10-year cycle of abundance. In Pennsylvania, *O. zibethicus* breeds from March through October. Copulation, initiated by the male, occurs in the water. Females produce about two litters each year, the first in May and the second in July or August. Like most other microtines, female muskrats exhibit a postpartum heat.

Following a gestation period of about 25 to 30 days, a litter of four to eight (usually six or seven) kits are born. At birth, the young are blind, almost hairless, and pinkish in color. Newborns measure about 102 millimeters (4 in.) long and weigh around 22 grams (0.8 oz.);

they are about the size of a northern short-tailed shrew. Growth is rapid, and in one week hair appears. Young are able to swim even before their eyes open at two weeks. By the time kits are one month old, they are nibbling on vegetation, are relatively independent, and resemble oversized meadow voles. In Pennsylvania, young do not breed during their first summer. In autumn, kits disperse from the natal home area to colonize new territories. This phenomenon, called the "fall shuffle," is a period of high mortality for muskrats because of predation and the trauma of venturing into new, unfamiliar areas.

Old World Rats and Mice

Family Muridae

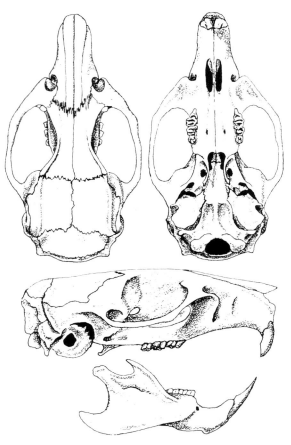

Skull of a murid (*Rattus*, × 1½).

With about 457 species arranged in some 98 genera, the family
Muridae is the second largest family of rodents in the world,
exceeded only in size and diversity by the family Cricetidae.
Murids are first known from the late Miocene Epoch, around
10 million years ago. Although native to the Old World, they are
today nearly cosmopolitan as a result of introduction by humans. Murids are structurally mouse- or rat-like in form, with
long, naked, scaly tails and three molar teeth on each side of

both jaws. Old World rats and mice have three longitudinal rows of cusps on their cheekteeth rather than two as in cricetids.

The family shows a great deal of evolutionary diversity, and living murids include semiaquatic, terrestrial, semifossorial, arboreal, and even saltatorial (hopping) species. Regarding overall diet, Old World rats and mice are opportunistic, feeding on a variety of plant and animal matter. They are highly prolific; feral house mice, for instance, are known to reach densities of nearly 500 per hectare (200/acre).

Murids are most abundant in tropical and subtropical areas of the world and occupy a broad spectrum of habitats. Some murids—namely the Polynesian rat, black rat, Norway rat, and house mouse—are especially adapted for life with humans and are economically significant. In negative terms, they are responsible for spreading serious diseases such as bubonic plague and typhus. Further, they are known to damage crops and despoil large quantities of stored grains and other foods. Although their reputation is marred by negative qualities, murids do have a beneficial side. Today, the laboratory white rat and the white mouse (bred from the Norway rat and house mouse, respectively) are used for biological and medical research.

Currently, only two representatives of the family Muridae reside in Pennsylvania: the Norway rat and the house mouse. A third member of this "introduced" family, the black rat, has a rather intriguing history in the Commonwealth.

The black rat (*Rattus rattus*), a native of Asia, was a "passenger" to Central America with the Spanish conquistadores in the early 16th century. It first appeared in North America with the early English colonists in 1607, some 168 years before the arrival of the Norway rat. The black rat quickly spread across the continent and was reportedly quite common throughout Pennsylvania before the late 18th century. With the arrival in North America around 1775 of the larger and more aggressive Norway rat, however, the numbers of black rats have declined drastically in the Commonwealth. This trend is also apparent in New England and other mid-Atlantic states. Consequently, the present distribution of the black rat is restricted primarily to the coasts of the south Atlantic Ocean, Gulf of Mexico, and Pacific Ocean.

Today, the black rat may appear infrequently in the vicinity of mid-Atlantic seaports such as Baltimore, Philadelphia, and New York, because they are more common on ships than Norway rats. It is unlikely, however, that their populations will become reestablished on the mainland because of the competitive superiority of resident Norway rats.

Norway Rat
Introduced Species

SCIENTIFIC NAME
Rattus norvegicus (*Rattus* is from the Latin word for "rat"; *norvegicus* is Latin for "of Norway," the country where the first specimen was named.)

SUBSPECIES IN PENNSYLVANIA
Rattus norvegicus norvegicus

ALSO CALLED
Brown rat, wharf rat, house rat, sewer rat, common rat, water rat, barn rat, alley rat

TOTAL LENGTH
320–450 mm (12.5–17.5 in.)

LENGTH OF TAIL
125–200 mm (4.9–7.8 in.)

WEIGHT
200–475 g (7–16.6 oz.)

MAMMAE
Six pairs

POPULATION DENSITY
25–100/city block; 50–300/ country farm

HOME RANGE
0.05–0.1 ha (0.12–0.25 acre)

LONGEVITY
2–3 yrs. in the wild; 3–4 yrs. in captivity

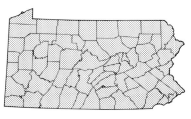

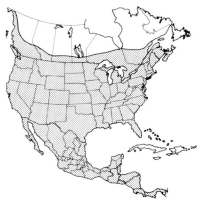

Description

The very common Norway rat has coarse grayish brown fur peppered with black on its back and grading to pale gray on the belly. Its large ears are naked, and its tail is scaly, annulated, and nearly hairless. The grayish forefeet of *R. norvegicus* are equipped with four clawed toes and a minute, clawless thumb; the hindfeet have five clawed toes.

Although it is unlikely that a Pennsylvanian would encounter the now scarce black rat, the Norway rat does resemble this relative but is larger and has a more robust build. Its tail is more scaly and slightly shorter than its head and body rather than longer than the head and body as in the black rat. The other two species which may be confused with the Norway rat

Norway rat (*Rattus norvegicus*).

are the marsh rice rat and the eastern woodrat. Although a young Norway rat looks similar to a marsh rice rat, the Norway rat has a heavier build, larger hindfeet, and a thicker tail which is only slightly bicolored. The eastern woodrat is easily distinguished from the Norway rat by its well-furred, bicolored tail and the sharp line of separation between its brownish gray back and white belly. Also, the skull of the Norway rat has three longitudinal rows of cusps on the cheekteeth rather than two rows, as in the rice rat, the woodrat, and other cricetids.

Male and female Norway rats are colored alike, while juveniles are paler than adults. The species has many color variations, including black, blotched gray blacks, and the familiar laboratory and pet store albino. Males are slightly larger than females.

Ecology

The Norway rat is actually a native of China. After spreading into western Europe, it arrived in North America aboard British vessels during the Revolutionary War era, around 1775. During the gold rush days of the 1850s, this rat colonized the Pacific coast of the United States. An avid "hitchhiker" aboard oceangoing ships, *R. norvegicus* has followed humans around the world, and today the species invariably resides in close proximity to human habitation.

In urban centers, this rat lives in sewers, garbage dumps, trash-filled alleys, and under and in buildings. A good swimmer, climber, and jumper, the amphibious Norway rat is even reported to surface occasionally inside toilet bowls of occupied homes! In rural areas, barns housing grain bins and stock feeding platforms represent optimal "habitat." Open fields near farmlands are also colonized by the Norway rat, but populations in the wild of the Norway rat in North America are rare.

The diet of *R. norvegicus* includes animal food such as invertebrates, fish, reptiles, barnyard poultry and young livestock, eggs, black rats, other small mammals, and even young, unprotected Norway rats. Carrion is also readily consumed. Although its teeth are poorly designed for a diet of coarse, fibrous plants, the Norway rat readily eats vegetation. In farming areas, grains such as wheat, corn, oats, and soybeans are a staple. The Norway rat eats as much as one-third of its weight in food per day. It has a high water requirement and is reported to gnaw through lead pipes to obtain moisture. It does not establish large food caches but, rather, feeds directly at the source. Unlike native species of rodents, this exotic rat is wasteful and frequently kills excess prey and leaves some to spoil.

The Norway rat has many enemies, and humankind is rated number one. Others include large owls and hawks, foxes, minks, weasels, and large snakes. Both cats and dogs are effective predators of Norway rats, but large rats are fierce fighters and not easily subdued.

A great number of parasites are associated with the Norway rat. External parasites include fleas, lice, mites, chiggers, ticks, and parasitic beetles. Internally, *R. norvegicus* is parasitized by tapeworms, roundworms, flukes, spiny-headed worms, and many protozoans. The Norway rat in Pennsylvania is also known to harbor the rabies virus.

Behavior

The Norway rat is active throughout the year; it is chiefly nocturnal but may be seen during daylight hours. A good digger, this rat excavates subterranean tunnels that reach depths of 45 centimeters (1.5 ft.). The passageways are about 7.5 centimeters (3 in.) in diameter and vary in length from 60 to 180 centimeters (2–6 ft.). *Rattus norvegicus* equips its burrow system with one or more entrances hidden under boards or debris and lightly plugs them with weeds or soil. Within the burrow, the rat builds a nest of shredded plants, cloth, paper, rags, and other materials.

The Norway rat is gregarious and forms colonies composed of several families totaling 10 to 12 individuals. These colonies commonly share nesting and feeding areas but have a strict social hierarchy "ruled" by a dominant individual, usually the largest and oldest male. Colonies vigorously defend their food supply and shelter against neighboring colonies. The best-known vocalization of the Norway rat is the alarm call, a high-pitched squeal. Other calls include squeaks, chirps, whistles, hisses, and teeth chattering.

Reproduction and Development

The Norway rat is extremely prolific and commonly breeds year-round in Pennsylvania. The female is polyestrous and exhibits a postpartum heat; she can mate with several males within a day after parturition. In Pennsylvania, females may produce from three to six litters per year. The gestation period is about 21 days, and the number of young per litter varies from 6 to 22, but 7 or 8 is the norm. One female Norway rat may wean 20 to 30 young per year.

Young are born in an altricial state—naked, pink, blind, and helpless. They measure about 51 millimeters (2 in.) in length and weigh about 6 grams (0.2 oz.). Growth is very rapid, and at the age of two weeks, the eyes open. Young are weaned at about three weeks of age, at which time the mother bears a new litter. Young females are capable of reproducing when they are 11- to 12-weeks old.

Relationship to People

In destroying or spoiling cereal grains, the Norway rat causes great economic loss to humans. Also, the species is a vector for many serious diseases and may attack small livestock and even people. *Rattus norvegicus* is truly a "pest" in Pennsylvania, and its numbers should be controlled.

The best control for these rodents is to maintain an environment free of trash, and buildings should be made rat-proof. For small populations, trapping is a possible method of control, but the Norway rat is trap shy. Poisoning is generally successful in eliminating the pest, but recent research indicates that this species is developing immunity to certain poisons. In regard to poisoning, it should be done with caution and in moderation, because most poisons are broad-spectrum and, therefore, may kill beneficial wildlife or pets.

House Mouse
Introduced Species

SCIENTIFIC NAME
Mus musculus (*Mus* is from the Latin word for "mouse"; *musculus* is Latin for "small mouse.")

SUBSPECIES IN PENNSYLVANIA
Mus musculus musculus

ALSO CALLED
Domestic mouse, common mouse, gray mouse, feral mouse

TOTAL LENGTH
140–190 mm (5.5–7.4 in.)

LENGTH OF TAIL
65–95 mm (2.5–3.7 in.)

WEIGHT
15–23 g (0.5–0.8 oz.)

MAMMAE
Five pairs

POPULATION DENSITY
3–1,250/ha (1–506/acre)

HOME RANGE
0.01–0.2 ha (0.02–0.5 acre)

LONGEVITY
1–2 yrs. in the wild; 3–6 yrs. in captivity

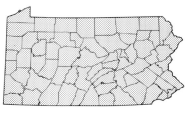

Description

The house mouse, undoubtedly the best known and most widely distributed rodent in the world, is a small mouse. It is easily recognized by its long, pointed nose; large, naked ears; and naked, scaly, indistinctly bicolored tail. This mouse has small, slightly protruding, beady eyes, and its fur is short and may be glossy in appearance.

The only two mice that *M. musculus* might be confused with are the native deer mouse and white-footed mouse. There is, however, a sharp contrast in color between the back and belly of these two *Peromyscus* species, whereas the house mouse wears an overall grayish brown color. Also, in *Peromyscus* species the molars have only two longitudinal rows of cusps, whereas the molars of the house mouse have three longitudinal rows of cusps like those of the Norway rat. The house mouse

House mouse (*Mus musculus*).

is further separated from all native mice by its sharp, musky odor, produced by paired anal scent glands.

Sexes of the house mouse are colored alike and are of equal size. Juveniles are grayer and have softer fur than adults. The house mouse shows much variation in color, including white and melanistic (black). In fact, the common white mouse of pet stores and research laboratories is an albino bred from *M. musculus*.

Ecology

Like the Norway rat, the house mouse is a native of central Asia. Following its invasion of Europe, *M. musculus* arrived in Latin America and Florida on ships of Spanish explorers in the early 16th century. The house mouse established a foothold in North America probably as a "passenger" with the first colonists and is now widespread throughout North America.

The house mouse lives in close association with humans. In Pennsylvania, it occupies houses, barns, outbuildings, granaries, warehouses, and other man-made structures. Wild populations reside in wheat and corn fields, abandoned fields, and weedy fencerows. In the Commonwealth, the house mouse may also occur in wooded areas near human habitation, especially during warm months.

Like the Norway rat, the house mouse is notably omnivorous and will eat practically everything organic. It prefers grains and seeds but will consume insects, their larvae and pupae, vegetable matter, many weedy species of plants, roots, subterranean fungi, and meat. The house mouse chews on paper and will feed on the glue of bookbindings. Gnaw marks on a bar of soap accompanied by many dark, spindle-shaped fecal droppings are other sure signs of a busy house mouse! Like the Norway rat, the house mouse usually wastes more food than it eats. It is known, however, to cache food.

The house mouse has many predators. Humans are a perpetual threat to this rodent, yet *M. musculus* is not as easily trapped as are the native deer mouse and white-footed mouse. The most efficient household predator is the domestic cat; it can kill its fair share of house mice both inside homes and in barns and outbuildings. Wild predators such as barn owls, various hawks, foxes, weasels, skunks, Norway rats, and snakes also prey on *M. musculus*.

The house mouse harbors numerous parasites and transmits serious bacterial and viral diseases. It is also known to host organisms responsible for murine typhus, leptospirosis, food poisoning (*Salmonella*), rickettsial pox, tularemia, and bubonic plague. Ectoparasites of the house mouse include fleas, lice, mites, chiggers, ticks, and the warble fly or botfly. *Mus musculus* internally hosts tapeworms and roundworms; some individuals are known to be infested with up to 100 intestinal roundworms!

Behavior

The house mouse is active throughout the year. Those individuals residing outdoors are active principally during hours of darkness, but mice living in homes are active both day and night. In the wild, this animal may use runways of the meadow vole but does not make its own surface tunnels. A speedy rodent, the house mouse travels at rates of up to about 13 kilometers per hour (8 mi./hr.).

Mus musculus is high-strung and rather curious. Like its close relative the Norway rat, the gregarious house mouse forms small colonies, both in buildings and in the wild. These colonies consist of a dominant male, several females, and their young. The house mouse is aggressive, and family groups tend to defend their territory against outsiders. This defense manifests itself in overt fights, defensive body postures, and vocalizations including squeaks and chattering. The house mouse also emits a high-pitched "song," similar to that of a canary, that can be heard up to about 7.5 meters (25 ft.) away.

Nests of the house mouse are globular in shape and composed of shredded paper, rags, grass, or other soft material. In homes, these nests may be found in walls, attics, or imaginative places such as dresser drawers, cupboards, old teapots, and even under the cushion of a seldom-used easy chair. A person usually smells an active nest before seeing it, because of the rather musky, pervasive odor of *M. musculus*. In the wild, the house mouse places its nests under logs or stones, in burrows, or in other protected places. A single nest may be used by several members of the same family and offers a site for rearing young as well as protection from predators and inclement weather.

Reproduction and Development

A prolific species, *M. musculus* may reach tremendous densities. In the Central Valley of California during the mid–1920s, there were estimates of over 200,000 per hectare (83,000/acre) (Hall, 1927). It reproduces from early spring to late autumn in Pennsylvania. As with many rodents, females may breed soon after giving birth to a litter. The gestation period is about 19 to 21 days. Females are capable of producing up to 14 litters each year, but, in Pennsylvania, five litters are usual. Litter size varies from 3 to 10 (usually 6). The young are born naked, pink, blind, and helpless. They develop a fur coat after 10 days, and their eyes open when they reach two weeks old. Pups are weaned at three weeks and are capable of reproducing at the young age of six to eight weeks.

Relationship to People

The house mouse is second only to the Norway rat in its ability to pilfer granaries. This age-old tendency is well documented and recalled in the Sanskrit name for this mouse, *musha*, meaning "thief." In addition to simply consuming vast amounts of grain, the house mouse despoils large quantities with its urine and feces. Its omnipresence, high reproductive rate, and adaptability place it as a major candidate for control measures.

Numbers usually can be kept in check through the use of commercial mousetraps baited with peanut butter, rolled oats, or bacon. Poisons, available in most hardware stores, should be used as a last resort, with caution and in moderation.

In defense of this exotic mouse, it is noteworthy that albino strains are used extensively in medical research and have added greatly to medical and genetic knowledge. Pet store "white mice" also make nice pets and seldom bite. Further, cooked house mouse meat is an age-old folk remedy for colds, fever, and coughs; its medicinal merits, if any, are compromised only by its distastefulness!

Jumping Mice
Family Zapodidae

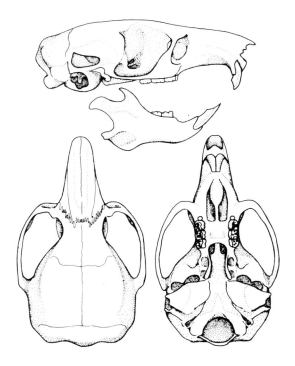

Skull of a zapodid (*Zapus*, × 2½).

The family Zapodidae is a very small and specialized family of rodents comprising only 4 genera with 11 species. Members of this family include the meadow jumping mouse (*Zapus*) and the woodland jumping mouse (*Napaeozapus*) of North America, the Chinese jumping mouse (*Eozapus*) of Central China, and the tiny birch mouse (*Sicista*) of northern Europe, Russia, Mongolia, and China. The fossil record of the family dates back some 30 million years ago to the Oligocene Epoch in Europe and about 38 million years ago to the late Eocene Epoch in North America.

Zapodids reside primarily in moist forests, grassy meadows, swamps, and thickets. They are small, delicate mice ranging in weight from about 6 to 25 grams (0.2–0.9 oz.). Most are distinctively colored; their reddish brown or bright orange backs contrast with snowy white bellies. Except for the birch mouse, all zapodids have long tails and elongated hindlimbs. Although well adapted for saltatorial (jumping) locomotion, they typically progress by scampering or running interrupted by intermittent long leaps. Several members of the family also undergo true hibernation, generally entering dormancy by early autumn and emerging in late spring.

Two genera of this remarkable and intriguing family reside in Pennsylvania: the meadow jumping mouse and the woodland jumping mouse.

Meadow Jumping Mouse

SCIENTIFIC NAME
Zapus hudsonius (*Zapus* is from
the Greek roots *za,* meaning "very,"
and *pus,* meaning "foot," which,
liberally translated, means "very
large hindfoot"; *hudsonius* refers
to Hudson Bay, the site where the
first specimen was captured.)

SUBSPECIES IN PENNSYLVANIA
Zapus hudsonius americanus

ALSO CALLED
Hudson Bay jumping mouse, jumping mouse, kangaroo mouse

TOTAL LENGTH
185–220 mm (7.2–8.6 in.)

LENGTH OF TAIL
110–140 mm (4.3–5.5 in.)

WEIGHT
15–21 g (0.5–0.7 oz.)

MAMMAE
Four pairs

POPULATION DENSITY
4–45/ha (2–18/acre)

HOME RANGE
0.04–1.1 ha (0.1–2.7 acres)

LONGEVITY
1½–2 yrs. in the wild

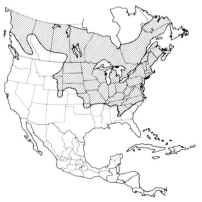

Description

The meadow jumping mouse is a
handsome little mouse, easily recognized by its huge hindfeet, brilliant color, and long, slender, scaly
tail. The tail—brownish above and
white below—is longer than the
total length of its head and body.
The pelage is yellowish brown
with a distinctly darker dorsal
stripe and yellowish orange sides.
Its contrasting belly and feet are
white, sometimes suffused with
yellowish orange. The large, scantily haired ears of this rodent are
rimmed with orange or yellow.

The meadow jumping mouse is
similar in appearance to its close
relative the woodland jumping
mouse, but the meadow jumping
mouse is slightly duller and more
yellowish in color and its tail has
a dark tuft at the tip rather than a
white tuft. Further, the meadow
jumping mouse has four upper
cheekteeth on each side of the jaw

Meadow jumping mouse
(*Zapus hudsonius*).
See plate 13, following page 172.

rather than three as in the woodland jumping mouse. As an additional distinguishing factor, *Z. hudsonius* is the only mammal in Pennsylvania that has a total of 18 teeth. Like the woodland jumping mouse, its deeply grooved upper incisors are orange on their anterior surface.

The sexes of the meadow jumping mouse are colored alike, but juveniles are duller in color than adults and have a less well-defined dorsal stripe. One annual molt occurs during summer. Females are slightly larger than males. The species does not have internal cheek pouches.

Ecology

Requiring moist conditions and adequate ground cover, the meadow jumping mouse resides in a variety of habitats such as abandoned grassy fields, thickets bordering ponds and streams, grainfields, and edges of woodlands. Optimal habitat in Pennsylvania is damp meadows with a lush ground cover of grasses, sedges, and herbaceous vegetation.

The food habits of the meadow jumping mouse strongly reflect seasonal availability. In spring, following emergence from hibernation, the jumping mouse consumes large quantities of animal matter such as caterpillars and beetles. Seeds of grasses and herbs are a staple eaten throughout the summer and early autumn. Other foods include berries, roots, nuts, and invertebrates. During late summer, fleshy fruit and subterranean fungus form a major part of the diet of this mouse. *Zapus hudsonius* also has a high water requirement but can live without actually drinking water if moisture in the form of dew and succulent foods is available. The meadow jumping mouse eats about one-half of its weight daily. Like its close relative the woodland jumping mouse, it does not store food for winter use.

Although the jumping mouse is active for only half of the year, it has many predators. These include owls, hawks, weasels, foxes, skunks, and snakes. Domestic cats may take a toll on jumping mice residing in meadows and grasslands near farms. Perhaps the most important single cause of death to *Z. hudsonius* is winter mortality. Its seems that mice born in early autumn are likely to die during hibernation because they are unable to accumulate adequate fat reserves to endure the long winter.

The meadow jumping mouse hosts fewer parasites than most small mammals, perhaps because of its solitary nesting habits. Externally, the jumping mouse is infested with fleas, lice, mites, chiggers, ticks, and the larval stage of the botfly. Internally, this mouse is parasitized by flukes, tapeworms, roundworms, and a variety of protozoans.

Behavior

In Pennsylvania, only three terrestrial mammals exhibit true hibernation: the woodchuck, the woodland jumping mouse, and, the smallest of the three, the meadow jumping mouse. In response to shortening day lengths of autumn, the meadow jumping mouse increases food consumption and rapidly accumulates fat. During a short two-week period, it may acquire some 6 grams (0.2 oz.) of fat in preparation for winter. Between late October and mid–November, the meadow jumping mouse enters hibernation.

This jumping mouse hibernates in a grapefruit-sized nest of grass and leaves, located in well-drained areas and situated up to 0.9 meters (3 ft.) below ground. Here—either singly or in small, closely huddled groups—*Z. hudsonius* assumes the characteristic hibernation posture. It curls into a tight ball with its nose placed between its hindlegs and its long tail coiled around its body. During the hibernation period, which may last up to six months, the body temperature of the mouse hovers between 2° to 4°C (35°–40°F), and the heart and breathing rate are drastically reduced. Except for brief interruptions for urinating, hibernation usually continues until late April or early May. When the jumping mouse emerges, it is rather thin, having depleted its fat supply. Males are first to emerge and begin foraging on the lush spring plant growth.

Zapus hudsonius is principally nocturnal and does not forage in burrows or runways as do some small mammals. Instead, this secretive mouse maneuvers through dense foliage. Contradictory to the common name, *jumping mouse, Z. hudsonius* does not jump but usually travels in a series of little hops measuring 2.5 to 15 centimeters (1–6 in.). When startled, the mouse may take several long leaps of about 0.3 meters (1 ft.) each. It commonly eludes a predator (or biologist) by employing several rapid hops and, to avoid detection, remains motionless, relying on its protective coloration which blends with the grassy environment. The meadow jumping mouse is also a topnotch swimmer, both on the surface and underwater, and adeptly climbs small shrubs and grass stems.

Although a solitary animal, the meadow jumping mouse is not antagonistic or belligerent to other members of its species. It is rather docile and seldom attempts to bite when handled. Except for emitting clucking noises and chirping sounds when excited, this rodent is usually silent. It may produce a drumming noise by vibrating its tail rapidly against the ground.

Reproduction and Development

Breeding for *Z. hudsonius* begins shortly after emergence from hibernation in spring. Unlike many small rodents, the meadow jumping mouse is not known to exhibit an immediate postpartum heat; females probably do not mate until a few weeks after giving birth. In

Pennsylvania, most female meadow jumping mice probably produce only two litters each year, the first in June and the second in late August or early September. The summer nests, used for rearing young, are little balls of grass and leaves with a soft, internal chamber. The nest may be hidden in a tuft of grass, under a hollow log, or in a burrow, usually less than 15 centimeters (6 in.) below ground.

Following a gestation period of about 18 to 21 days, a litter of two to eight young (usually five) is produced. Newborns are naked, blind, and helpless. They weigh about 0.8 grams (0.03 oz.) and measure between 30 to 39 millimeters (1.2 – 1.5 in.) long. The young are clothed in a fuzzy coat by the time they reach nine days old. At about 14 days of age, they are able to walk and make short hops. By the time they are three weeks old, their eyes open, weaning commences, they are fully furred, and even their distinctive dorsal stripe is apparent. Although meadow jumping mice born in spring will mate the same year, those individuals born in late summer will not breed until the next spring.

Woodland Jumping Mouse

SCIENTIFIC NAME
Napaeozapus insignis
(*Napaeozapus* is from three Latin
roots and is liberally translated "a
woodland nymph with very large
hindfeet"; *insignis* is Latin for
"insignia," referring to the distinguishing dark dorsal stripe of this
mouse.)

SUBSPECIES IN PENNSYLVANIA
Napaeozapus insignis insignis;
Napaeozapus insignis roanensis

ALSO CALLED
Kangaroo mouse

TOTAL LENGTH
215–250 mm (8.4–9.8 in.)

LENGTH OF TAIL
130–150 mm (5.1–5.9 in.)

WEIGHT
20–25 g (0.7–0.9 oz.)

MAMMAE
Four pairs

POPULATION DENSITY
0.7–59/ha (1–24/acre)

HOME RANGE
0.2–3.6 ha (0.5–8.9 acres)

LONGEVITY
1–2 yrs. in the wild

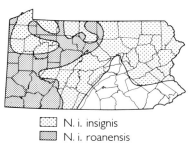

N. i. insignis
N. i. roanensis

Description

The woodland jumping mouse is
Pennsylvania's most strikingly colored forest-dwelling small mammal. It resembles the meadow
jumping mouse by having oversized hindfeet, radiant coloration,
and a slender, scaly tail. It is distinguished from the slightly smaller
meadow jumping mouse by its
larger ears, more brilliant yellowish brown pelage, and the white
rather than dark tip on its tail.
The woodland jumping mouse
also has three upper cheekteeth
on each side of the jaw rather than
four as in the meadow jumping
mouse. In addition, *N. insignis*
has a total of 16 teeth, like the
cricetid and murid rodents, not 18
like the meadow jumping mouse.

The back of the woodland jumping mouse is yellowish brown
peppered with black. A distinct,

Woodland jumping mouse
(*Napaeozapus insignis*).
See plate 14, following page 172.

broad middorsal stripe runs down its midline. Its sides are yellowish orange, its belly is snowy white, and its tail is distinctly bicolored, grayish brown above and white below, with a decided white tuft at the end. Like the meadow jumping mouse, the woodland jumping mouse lacks cheek pouches and has orange-faced incisors; the upper incisors are marked by deep, longitudinal grooves. The sexes are colored alike, and females are slightly larger than males. Adults molt once each year, usually between mid-June and late August.

Ecology

In Pennsylvania, the woodland jumping mouse is most abundant in cool, moist hemlock-hardwood forests of mountainous regions. Here, the species resides in rocky areas near streams that support a lush, low, woody vegetation. In northeastern Pennsylvania, for instance, *N. insignis* is encountered in the vicinity of mountain streams marked by rhododendron thickets and a canopy of birches, maples, and hemlocks. Within the

Commonwealth, the mouse also resides in bogs, swamps, damp rocky ravines, and thickets but rarely occurs in open fields or meadows that lack woody vegetation. This jumping mouse lives in cool forests side by side with the southern red-backed vole and other mesic-adapted small mammals. The woodland jumping mouse occasionally exhibits habitat overlap with the meadow jumping mouse along forest edges or in thickets bordering meadows.

The woodland jumping mouse is omnivorous but exhibits a distinct preference for seeds. In some instances, this energy-packed food may constitute 75 percent of its diet. Insects, especially caterpillars and adult beetles, are also favored foods. In light of the preference for larval Lepidoptera, the woodland jumping mouse may act as an important predator in the control of the gypsy moth in Pennsylvania. The woodland jumping mouse residing in New York state is known to consume large quantities of *Endogone*, a subterranean fungus widely used by many small rodents. Other foods such as blueberries, raspberries, nuts, mayapples, ferns, leaves, roots, mushrooms, and invertebrates attest to the omnivorous diet of this forest denizen. Like its close relative the meadow jumping mouse, the woodland jumping mouse does not establish food caches.

The jumping mouse has many predators such as screech owls, weasels, striped skunks, minks, bobcats, and, occasionally, house cats, rattlesnakes, and copperheads. Also, mortality during hibernation is high; up to 75 percent of those individuals entering hibernation will not emerge in the spring! Many mice lack sufficient fat reserves to subsist for the long winter and, without food in the hibernaculum, die. Other factors contributing to this grim statistic include the rigors of hibernation, spring flooding, and severe cold stress.

The woodland jumping mouse has comparatively few parasites, principally because of its solitary life. Externally, the species hosts fleas, mites, chiggers, and ticks, but not in great numbers. *N. insignis* is also parasitized by the larval form of the botfly. Internally, this mouse hosts tapeworms, roundworms, and a few protozoans.

Behavior

The woodland jumping mouse is a true hibernator. Shortening day lengths of autumn probably signal this animal to eat more to build up large fat reserves. In two short weeks, the woodland jumping mouse may put on fat equaling one-third of its body weight! In Pennsylvania, *N. insignis* begins hibernation during October. Either singly or in pairs, the animal retreats to its underground hibernation nest composed of dry leaves and grass on a well-drained hillside. Here, the woodland jumping mouse buries its nose in its belly fur and draws up its hindlegs along the face to form a tight ball. The long tail encircles the mouse.

During the hibernation period, the body temperature of *N. insignis* drops to nearly freezing, and all life processes are reduced to a minimum. For half of the year, the woodland jumping mouse remains in this state. In the Commonwealth, males emerge in late April and females arise about two to three weeks later. At this time, *N. insignis* is rather skinny, having lost up to about 30 percent of its autumn weight. The woodland jumping mouse regains its weight quickly, however, because of the plentiful insect supply and abundance of spring vegetation.

The woodland jumping mouse can be seen at dawn and dusk, but the animal is principally nocturnal, with most of its activity occurring on rainy or cloudy nights. It travels through the underbrush on "all fours" with a rather slow, methodical gait that may be interrupted by periodic hopping or even several giant leaps of up to 1.8 meters (6 ft.), especially if startled. When faced with predators, *N. insignis* may remain motionless for long periods, blending with the habitat and, thus, avoiding detection. The woodland jumping mouse is also an excellent swimmer but lacks the endurance of other rodents such as the meadow vole; it can swim only short distances. Further, it climbs small bushes with agility but does not ascend trees.

This species of jumping mouse is extremely nervous when handled in the field but will become rather docile if held in captivity and can be easily tamed. Although solitary in the wild, *N. insignis* is tolerant of other members of its species. It is not highly vocal but occasionally utters soft clucking sounds, exhibits tail drumming, and squeals if disturbed while sleeping.

The woodland jumping mouse digs its own burrows but is not opposed to using those of other small mammals. Its globular nest of dried grass and leaves measures about 12.5 to 15 centimeters (5–6 in.) in diameter and is placed in brush piles, under rotting logs or boulders, or in shallow underground burrows.

Reproduction and Development

In Pennsylvania, *N. insignis* begins breeding following hibernation, usually in mid-May. Following a gestation period of 21 to 29 days, females bear their first litter in June. Unlike many small mammals, the woodland jumping mouse does not undergo an immediate postpartum heat but may wait until the first litter is weaned before mating again. A second litter is produced in August.

Litter size varies from two to seven young (usually five). Newborns are naked, blind, and helpless; weigh about 1 gram (0.04 oz.); and measure 35 to 44 millimeters (1.4–1.7 in.) long. By the time they reach two weeks old, they have developed a fuzzy coat; a week later they have their distinctive dark dorsal band. Pups open their eyes by the age of 26 days, and weaning is under way by this time. The woodland jumping mouse becomes sexually mature at 38 days of age. Young born in the June litter may reproduce for the first time by late summer.

New World Porcupines

Family Erethizontidae

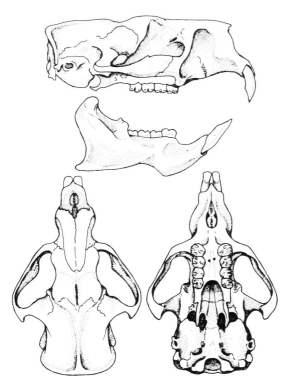

Skull of an erethizontid (*Erethizon*, × ½).

This small but easily recognized family consists of eight living species arranged in four genera. One species of the family (*Erethizon dorsatum*) resides in forests of the United States and most of Canada. Another member, *Coendou*, occurs from Sonora, Mexico, into South America. The remaining species are inhabitants of South America.

Erethizontids, commonly known as porcupines, are first known from fossils dating back some 34 million years ago to the Oligocene Epoch of South America and are not known in North America until three million years ago in the late Pliocene Epoch. Based on this fossil history, scientists believe this family is native to

South America and became established in North America following the rise of the previously inundated Isthmus of Panama during the Pliocene Epoch.

The porcupine is characterized by hair that is modified into sharp, short spines with minute, inwardly directed barbs. Large and robust, this rodent may weigh up to 16 kilograms (35 lbs.). Its massive skull is well adapted to support its large jaw muscles, its incisors are ever growing, and its cheekteeth are rooted.

Flat-footed (plantigrade), the porcupine travels on land with a rather slow, clumsy, deliberate gait. When in trees, however, it is agile and has superb balance. It is well adapted to an arboreal life because it has large feet with broad soles that have many small tubercles for traction; a modified big toe (hallux) consisting of a large, movable pad; and toes with elongated, curved claws. (It has four toes on its forefeet, five on its hindfeet.) In addition, the Neotropical porcupine (*Coendou*) has a prehensile tail used to grasp branches while climbing.

Erethizontids are primarily herbivorous. *Erethizon dorsatum* of North America prefers conifer needles and the bark of a variety of trees, while South American porcupines feed on leaves, stems, fruits, seeds, and even insects and small reptiles. Most porcupines take shelter in rock piles, hollow logs, and under the bases of trees, and generally do not dig burrows. With their elaborate courtship behavior, the erethizontids are a fascinating group of mammals. Only one species represents the family in Pennsylvania, *Erethizon dorsatum*.

Porcupine

SCIENTIFIC NAME
Erethizon dorsatum (*Erethizon* is from the Greek roots *erethi*, meaning "irritate," and *zon*, meaning "animal"; *dorsatum* is Latin for "back.")

SUBSPECIES IN PENNSYLVANIA
Erethizon dorsatum dorsatum

ALSO CALLED
Quill pig, porky, prickle pig, Canada porcupine, hedgehog

TOTAL LENGTH
568–780 mm (22.2–30.4 in.)

LENGTH OF TAIL
165–225 mm (6.4–8.8 in.)

WEIGHT
2–7.6 kg (4.4–16.8 lbs.)

MAMMAE
Two pairs

POPULATION DENSITY
0.8–9.5/km² (2–25/mi.²)

HOME RANGE
2.4–14.5 ha (6–36 acres)

LONGEVITY
Up to 12 yrs. in the wild; up to 10 yrs. in captivity

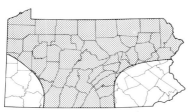

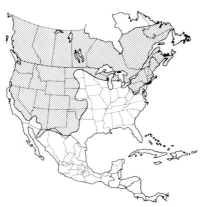

Description

The porcupine is one of the largest rodents in North America, second only to the beaver. This robust, rather awkward-looking rodent is best known for its arsenal of spines. Its head is comparatively small, equipped with a blunt snout, hairy lips, and small, beady eyes. It has short, bowed legs, and its toes—four on the forefeet and five on the hindfeet—all are equipped wih strong, curved claws. The soles of the animal's large, flat feet have many small, fleshy tubercles that enhance traction.

Ranging in color from glossy black to brownish black, the porcupine wears a unique coat of hair. Its pelage consists of three kinds of hair: thick, wooly underfur overlaid by long, coarse guard hairs mixed with the infamous sharp-pointed, hollow quills. These modified hairs—measuring

Porcupine (*Erethizon dorsatum*).

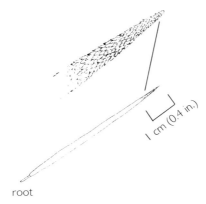

root

Porcupine quill with enlargement of tip showing barbs that slant backward.

6 to 8 centimeters (2–3 in.) long—are present on the back, sides, limbs, and tail; they do not occur on the belly. The quills are yellowish white at the base with brownish black tips that have numerous barbs that slant backwards. Loosely attached to the skin, they may dislodge easily and are replaced after being lost or pulled out. A single porcupine may bear 30,000 or more quills which, contrary to popular belief, cannot be thrown.

The porcupine usually undergoes one annual molt, during summer. Color variations range from coal black to albino. The sexes are colored alike, and males are slightly heavier than females. Juveniles are darker in color than adults.

Ecology

In Pennsylvania, the porcupine resides primarily in the Mountain and Plateau sections of the state. There, it prefers forests typified by stands of white pine, hemlock, and various hardwoods such as sugar maple, black cherry, and aspen. In these habitats, the porcupine selects cliffs and rocky slopes where suitable den sites are available.

During summer, the diet of *E. dorsatum* is quite varied and includes stems, roots, leaves, berries, seeds, nuts, flowers, and grass. During winter, the porcupine feeds on the succulent inner bark (cambium) of trees. It prefers coniferous trees such as pine and hemlock but readily girdles hardwoods including maple, oak, beech, birch, aspen, and cherry. Because porcupines can kill trees by stripping away the bark, some people view them as pests. This reputation is probably not deserved; since their damage is usually minor, it does not warrant intensive control programs. Damage estimates range from about $0.87 per hectare ($0.35/acre) in the Adirondack Mountains to a maximum of $2.72 per hectare ($1.10/acre) in Colorado.

This rodent also eats some rather bizarre foods. Being quite fond of salt, the porcupine can be seen along roadsides licking up residual salt deposits left from winter road maintenance. It is also known to gnaw on ax handles, supposedly to obtain salts left from human perspiration. In addition, reports claim the porcupine eats aluminum kettles, bottles, plastic tubing used to collect maple sap, and petrochemical products such as automobile tires and radiator hoses. One avid naturalist ventured many miles in subfreezing temperatures to photograph a porcupine "in the wild," only to

Forest Service sign chewed by porcupine.

return to his automobile to find the subject peacefully munching on his new radial tires!

Although its coat of quills is a strong deterrent to predators, the procupine does have enemies. Humans and fishers are the chief predators of this large rodent. Coyotes, bobcats, red and gray foxes, and martens also kill porcupines by flipping them over and attacking the unprotected belly. Killing a porcupine is not an easy task, and predators commonly pay the price of poor timing; an unlucky great horned owl is occasionally found dead with quills penetrating its face and chest. The porcupine also faces mortality due to fire, automobiles, and falling out of trees.

Externally, fleas, lice, mites, and chiggers parasitize the porcupine, and mange caused by the mite *Sarcoptes scabei* is common. Internally, *E. dorsatum* is infested by roundworms, flatworms, and larval tongue worms. The porcupine is also known to transmit tularemia and tick fever.

Behavior

The porcupine is active throughout the year; it does not hibernate or undergo torpidity. Although it may be seen resting during the day high in a tree, the animal is principally nocturnal. During severe cold spells, it retires to its den.

Dens are located in hollow logs, beneath rock piles, and in abandoned outbuildings. They are easily identified by large deposits of brown, crescent-shaped fecal droppings usually placed outside the entrance. If dens are unavailable, the porcupine will not construct an elaborate nest but, instead, spends the winter in a "station tree." These trees, commonly hemlock or spruce, are easily recognized by gnawed bark and a pervasive odor of urine. Several porcupines may den together in winter, but for most of the year the porcupine is solitary.

On the ground, *E. dorsatum* walks with a waddle or, if frightened, may travel with a clumsy gallop. Extremely agile in trees, it relies on its strong, curved claws and uses its stout tail as a sort of "fifth foot." It is not particularly fond of water, yet it will swim short distances to procure food which it locates using its keen sense of smell.

The porcupine is generally peaceful and good-natured; when molested, it usually retreats to the nearest tree. If cornered, however, it turns its back to the enemy and raises its quills. As a last resort, the porcupine lashes its tail from side to side in defense. It does not throw its quills, but the quills detach easily and become embedded in the flesh of the attacker. Being hollow, the quills readily expand when exposed to moisture and body heat. Thus, as a victim's muscles contract, the quills penetrate deeper and deeper at a rate of about 2.5 centimeters (1 in.) per day, causing great pain. If the quills reach the heart, arteries, lungs, or other vital organs, death may result. Dogs getting too close to porcupines commonly sustain a barrage of quills in their faces which may cause blindness or prevent them from eating. Although quills are difficult to remove, cutting off the end releases air pressure and, thus, facilitates removal.

Although myopic, the porcupine has acute hearing. It also has a diverse vocal repertoire including grunts, coughs, moans, whines, snorts, screeches, and chatters. When hurt or frightened, it cries or sobs like a child. The porcupine also emits a loud and penetrating scream similar to that of a mountain lion. Its vocalizations may be heard up to 0.4 kilometer (0.25 mi.) away.

Reproduction and Development

In Pennsylvania, the breeding season of the porcupine occurs during October and November and is marked by an elaborate courtship display. A male in rut performs a "three-legged dance" accompanied by a whining serenade for his chosen mate. As he dances, he commonly holds his genitals with his forepaw or rubs them with a stick. Just before mating, he showers his mate with urine.

Copulation in the porcupine is understandably complex and rather precarious. The female remains on all fours and moves her tail to the side, keeping her quills tightly appressed to her body. The male *carefully* hunches over his mate in the typical rear mount position of rodents, and they copulate. Although males and females usually pair for the mating period, a male may mate with more than one female in a given season.

The porcupine exhibits a lengthy gestation period of about seven months. Only one young is born each year, usually in May or June. Maternity nests are well padded with vegetation and usually located in a ground den. Like the beaver, the porcupine has precocial young. At birth, porcupettes weigh between 340 and 640 grams (12–22 oz.) and measure some 305 millimeters (12 in.) long. Their eyes are open, their teeth are well formed, and their pelage is well developed. Although at birth their quills are soft and measure about 25.4 millimeters (1 in.) long, within one-half hour they become stiff and functional.

Young are able to ascend trees a few hours after birth. Porcupettes feed on green plants by the second week and are quite independent, although they still nurse occasionally. Young are not fully weaned until about three months of age. They grow rapidly and weigh between 1.4 and 1.8 kilograms (3–4 lbs.) when they reach four to five months of age. By about six months, the mother and young drift apart. Sexual maturity is attained at the age of about one and one-half years.

CARNIVORES

Order Carnivora

The order Carnivora is a diverse group of mammals. Its members range from the tiny least weasel, weighing scarcely more than 28 grams (1 oz.), to the gigantic polar bear, weighing over 800 kilograms (1,760 lbs.). Living carnivores are represented by 7 families, comprising some 92 genera and 238 species. Scientists do not agree on the taxonomic arrangement of the order Carnivora. Some include the pinnipeds (sea lions, seals, and walruses) in this order, whereas others choose to place these marine mammals in the separate order Pinnipedia.

Carnivores are first known from the early Paleocene Epoch about 65 million years ago. Today, this order occurs on all continents except Antarctica, although the wild dog of Australia (the dingo) was probably introduced by early humans. If one chooses to include the marine mammals with the order Carnivora, then this group is truly cosmopolitan.

As the ordinal name suggests, Carnivora is composed of the flesh-eaters of the Class Mammalia. But not all members eat meat. Although the cats (Felidae) and weasels (Mustelidae) are principally carnivorous, the raccoons (Procyonidae) and bears (Ursidae) are notably omnivorous. Scavengers, insectivores, and vegetarians are also included in this diverse order.

In general, the dentition of carnivores is well adapted to a diet of meat. They can capture prey by using their large, strong, pointed canine teeth. Also, most carnivores have a "carnassial pair" of teeth—a combination in which the last upper premolar and the first lower molar teeth form a shearing surface when the mouth is closed. The carnassial pair is most highly developed in the cat family and least developed in the more omnivorous families of the bear and raccoon.

The feet of carnivores are five-toed or four-toed and bear sharp, curved claws that may or may not be retracted. Their stance varies from plantigrade (flat-footed) such as in raccoons and skunks to digitigrade (walking on the digits with the wrist and heel bones raised off the ground) as in cats and dogs. Although principally terrestrial, many carnivores are well adapted to life in trees; two species even have prehensile tails used for grasping branches while climbing. Further, all carnivores can swim. In fact, two members of the order, the polar bear and river otter, are semi-aquatic, and one carnivore, the sea otter, spends its entire life in the water.

Economically, the carnivores are one of the most important orders of mammals. Many members of the family Mustelidae, such as the mink, ermine, sable, and sea otter, are harvested for their valuable fur. Other members of the order are important game animals. Still other carnivores, the domestic dog (one of the first animals to be tamed) and cat are certainly the two most popular pets of modern humans. Carnivores also act as essential components of natural ecosystems, functioning as principal predators of small mammals.

Some North American carnivores, such as the coyote, are remarkably resilient despite persecution by humans; others such as the black-footed ferret, red and gray wolves, mountain lion, and ocelot are highly sensitive to direct or indirect disturbance and, as a result, are endangered or threatened in North America. Five families comprising 10 genera and 13 species of carnivores reside in Pennsylvania.

Dogs and Foxes
Family Canidae

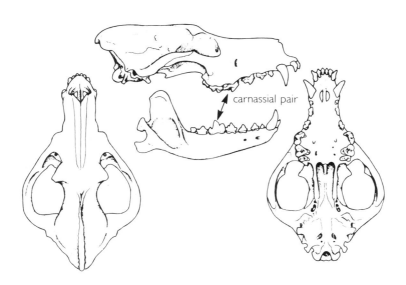

carnassial pair

Skull of a canid (*Canis,* × ³⁄₁₆).

The family Canidae includes dogs, wolves, foxes, and jackals.
Wild canids range in size from the tiny fennec, a fox of the Sa-
hara Desert about the size of a Chihuahua dog, to the massive
gray wolf of North America and Asia, which reaches a weight of
80 kilograms (176 lbs.). This family is first known from the late
Eocene Epoch in North America and Europe, some 38 million
years ago, and comprises about 16 living genera and some 36 species. Today, the canids are found throughout the world except in
Antarctica and some oceanic islands. They are highly adaptable
and range from the hot deserts of Africa to the arctic ice fields.

Structurally, wild canids are dog-like in appearance, with elongated muzzles, long legs, and bushy tails. The long nose of canids houses complex turbinal bones responsible for their keen
sense of smell. Their canine teeth are strong, sharp, and re-
curved. The carnassial teeth are well developed and produce an
effective cutting or shearing edge. Their molar teeth have crushing surfaces, an adaptation that allows them to eat almost any-

thing. (See the explanation of *carnassial pair* in "Carnivores: Order Carnivora.")

Canids have a digitigrade stance. Most species have four toes on the hindfoot and five on the forefoot. The thumb (pollex) of the forefoot is reduced and elevated. Their claws are blunt and not retractile as in the felids. Highly adapted for running (cursorial), members of the family—the coyote, for instance—can run at speeds of up to 65 kilometers per hour (41 mi./hr.).

In addition to their keen sense of smell, canids exhibit acute hearing and sight. They are intelligent and alert and hunt singly or in packs of up to 30 members. They are active throughout the year both day and night. Opportunistic, canids will eat all kinds of vertebrates, mollusks, crustaceans, insects, vegetable matter, and carrion. They capture prey by pouncing from an ambush or by open chase. In Pennsylvania, this family is represented by three genera and three species.

ZZZ

Coyote

SCIENTIFIC NAME
Canis latrans (*Canis* is Latin for "dog"; the Latin word *latrans*, meaning "a barker," refers to this animal's barking habit. Interestingly, the common name *coyote* is derived from the Aztec Indian word *coyotl* and is pronounced correctly "ki-O-tee" rather than the corrupted form "KI-ot.")

SUBSPECIES IN PENNSYLVANIA
Canis latrans latrans

ALSO CALLED
Eastern coyote, brush wolf, little wolf, prairie wolf, American jackal

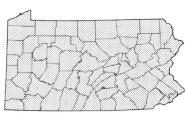

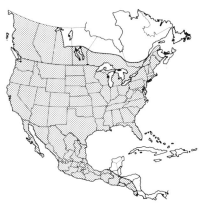

TOTAL LENGTH
1,180–1,400 mm (46–54.6 in.)

LENGTH OF TAIL
325–406 mm (12.7–15.8 in.)

WEIGHT
11.4–22.7 kg (25–50 lbs.)

MAMMAE
Four pairs

POPULATION DENSITY
0.2–0.8/km² (1–2/mi.²)

HOME RANGE
800–8,000 ha (1,976–19,760 acres)

LONGEVITY
6–8 yrs. in the wild; up to 18 yrs. in captivity

STATUS IN PENNSYLVANIA
Undetermined

Description

Although the coyote resembles a small German shepherd, this elusive canid has many distinctive characteristics. It has a long, narrow, pointed nose; erect, pointed ears; and round pupils that shine greenish gold at night. The dense, long pelage of *C. latrans* ranges from gray to yellow gray, and a middorsal dark band of long, black-tipped guard hairs extends to the base of its bushy, black-tipped tail. The head is grizzled gray, with a rusty or yellowish tint running along the neck and sides. The throat and belly, back of the ears, top of the nose, legs, and feet vary

Coyote (*Canis latrans*).
Photo courtesy of the U.S. Fish and Wildlife Service, photo by E. P. Haddon.

from orangish red to cinnamon in color.

Molting for the coyote begins in late spring and is completed during summer; its pelage becomes prime between early December and February. *Canis latrans* shows much variation in color, and individuals range from black to nearly white. Although both sexes are colored alike, adult males are slightly larger than females. The largest coyotes in North America reside in northeastern United States, where hybridization has occurred with the gray wolf.

Certain strains of domestic dogs and hybrids of the coyote and dog (coydogs) are extremely difficult to distinguish from the true coyote. The differences between the skulls of dogs, coyotes, and coydogs are well treated by Godin (1977), Schwartz and Schwartz (1981), and Bekoff (1982). Coydogs typically have darker fur than the true coyote.

Ecology

Canis latrans has only recently invaded the Commonwealth from New York and possibly Ohio. Present in Pennsylvania only in low numbers, the coyote is rarely seen in the wild by Pennsylvanians. There is no question, however, that this secretive canid currently resides in the state.

A highly adaptable animal, the coyote can be found in a wide variety of habitats ranging from marshlands and open grasslands to dense hardwood forests. Like the red fox, the coyote prefers brushy, disturbed edges of woodlands. It commonly finds shelter in brushy growth that invades forests after a cutting or burning.

Although *C. latrans* is notably omnivorous, the flesh of mammals accounts for over 90 percent of its diet. Chief among prey species are rabbits and rodents, followed by other wild mammals, wild birds, livestock and poultry, reptiles, amphibians, and fish. The coyote also eats fruit, insects, and plants. During winter, carrion of deer, sheep, cattle, and poultry are important items in the diet of this canid. Like the fox, *C. latrans* caches excess food in earthen holes it digs with its forefeet. The food is covered with soil by tamping with the nose and frequently marked by urination.

The coyote is accused of killing large numbers of domestic livestock, especially in the West. Its predation on livestock is difficult to evaluate, however, since it is impossible to determine if a food item was secured as a kill or eaten as carrion. Most diet analyses of the coyote indicate that the bulk of its food includes young, old, and sick animals, and that coyote predation is not limited primarily to big game or domestic livestock. Many times, the coyote is credited with killing livestock that, in fact, was killed by its tame relative, the domestic dog.

Many factors—namely climatic extremes, parasites and disease, food shortage, predation, and accidents—cause the mortality in *C. latrans*. But humans kill the largest number of coyotes. Because of its alleged depredation on poultry and livestock, *C. latrans* is thoroughly disliked by farmers and ranchers. As a result, bounties were set against the coyote in the United States beginning in 1825 and are still paid in some areas today. Control methods include poisoning, trapping, shooting from aircraft and snowmobiles, destroying young in the den, and using antifertility agents. Some contend

that, as a species, *C. latrans* can easily sustain human-inflicted mortality because of its adaptability; cunning, secretive nature; and high reproductive potential. This is not entirely true; intensive control programs have eliminated this species from many parts of its former range.

The pronounced social tendencies of the coyote foster a large and varied assortment of parasites and diseases. Fleas are the most abundant ectoparasites, followed by ticks, lice, and chiggers. Mange mites commonly infect the coyote even to the point of causing an almost complete loss of hair. Internally, *C. latrans* hosts tapeworms, roundworms, hookworms, whipworms, pinworms, heartworms, lungworms, flukes, and spiny-headed worms. The coyote is also susceptible to microbial diseases such as tularemia, canine distemper, rabies, Q fever, and bubonic plague.

Behavior

The coyote is active throughout the year. It is principally nocturnal with peak activity in the early evening. During summer, it may occasionally be seen foraging during daylight hours.

Coyotes hunt singly, in pairs, or in packs of three to eight individuals. They frequently travel—single file if hunting in pairs—along well-packed game trails and road cuts that may be used by the same individual for its entire life as long as prey is abundant. When hunting alone, the coyote takes small mammals systematically: An individual stalks its prey, freezes momentarily like a pointer dog, and then suddenly pounces on the victim. Packs may employ a team effort to hunt large game such as deer or elk. When hunting together, two or more coyotes may chase a large animal for up to 400 meters (1,300 ft.).

Canis latrans is the fastest of the canids, reaching speeds of up to 65 kilometers per hour (40 mi./hr.) and leaping some 4.3 meters (14 ft.) in the air. When running, the coyote distinguishes itself by holding its tail between its hindlegs; other canids such as foxes, domestic dogs, and wolves hold their tails parallel or curled over the back. A strong swimmer, the coyote is known to cross rivers up to 0.8 kilometer (0.5 mi.) wide.

A territorial animal, the coyote communicates its presence to other members of its species by a complex series of body postures and facial expressions as well as by scent marking and vocalizations. This canid sprinkles its strongly scented urine on rocks, bushes, stumps, and bases of trees, thus, delimiting the boundaries of its domain. The coyote also commonly defecates on small ridges and elevated sites along its habitually used hunting trails. In addition, both sexes have a scent gland located on top of the tail about 5 centimeters (2 in.) from the base. The coyote rubs the secretion of this gland on trees and bushes; the secretion's odor provides a means of individual recognition when coyotes sniff the natural objects or meet in the wild and sniff each other.

The rich vocal repertoire of *C. latrans* also functions to define its territory and strengthen social bonds. Vocalizations include barks, yelps, yips, and howls. The coyote may bark alone or in groups. Often one will start; then others will take up the call until a full-fledged chorus results! Howling occurs at any time of the year but is most common during the mating season. These evening serenades, symbolic of the western prairies of the United States, are unforgettable. Unfortunately, they are seldom heard in the East.

During most of the year, the coyote is not very choosey about its sleeping quarters and commonly rests in a concealed spot on a brushy hillside. During the breeding season, dens are used for rearing young. The coyote establishes natal dens in brush-covered slopes, rocky ledges, or sometimes in hollow logs. It is not opposed to excavating its own den but more frequently renovates an abandoned woodchuck, fox, or skunk den, if available.

Dens vary greatly in size and architecture. They are well concealed by brush and have one to several entrances measuring about 30 centimeters (1 ft.) in diameter. Tunnels range in length from 1.5 to 9 meters (5–30 ft.) and terminate at the nest chamber, which measures about 1 meter (3 ft.) in diameter. This chamber usually lacks nesting material.

Reproduction and Development

The coyote, as a rule, does not mate for life, but some pairs may stay together for several years. Unlike the domestic dog, the coyote is monestrous; it breeds only once per year, usually in February, with a four- to five-day period of estrus (heat). The gestation period ranges from 58 to 65 days, and five to seven pups (whelps) are born in April or early May.

At birth, whelps are blind, helpless, and covered by a brownish gray, wooly fur. They weigh about 250 grams (9 oz.). Growth is rapid, and the young gain some 300 grams (10.5 oz.) per week until weaning occurs. Both parents care for the young, with the male assisting by bringing food for the nursing female. Whelps are able to crawl when they are two to three days old and can walk at eight to ten days of age. Their eyes open by the time they reach two weeks old, and one week later they venture outside of the den. At this time, parents commonly provide the young with partly digested food regurgitated from their stomachs. Weaning occurs at about eight to nine weeks of age, at which time the family abandons the den and the young are taught to hunt.

The family group disbands in autumn, with young coyotes dispersing up to 200 kilometers (120 mi.) from the natal den. Young hunt alone from autumn until winter, when they may pair and breed; most coyotes will wait, however, until they are two years old before they breed. The coyote usually achieves adult weight when it reaches nine months of age.

Status in Pennsylvania

Very little is known about the life history and ecology of the coyote in Pennsylvania. Since this canid only recently invaded the Commonwealth from the north and west, its numbers are still low, and researchers have not had time to examine the new resident in detail. As a result, the classification of "undetermined" was assigned by the Pennsylvania Biological Survey in its report *Species of Special Concern in Pennsylvania* (Genoways and Brenner, 1985). To identify the coyote's geographic range, the Survey recommends that a state-wide communication network be established to report sightings of this mammal in the Commonwealth. Further, a livetrapping program combined with radio-telemetry techniques may enhance the knowledge of the population structure and ecology of *C. latrans* in Pennsylvania.

Red Fox

SCIENTIFIC NAME
Vulpes vulpes (*Vulpes* is Latin for "fox.")

SUBSPECIES IN PENNSYLVANIA
Vulpes vulpes fulva

ALSO CALLED
Silver fox, cross fox, black fox, Reynard, bastard fox

TOTAL LENGTH
955−1,080 mm (37.2−42.1 in.)

LENGTH OF TAIL
318−460 mm (12.4−17.9 in.)

WEIGHT
3.2−5.2 kg (7.1−11.5 lbs.)

MAMMAE
Four pairs

POPULATION DENSITY
1−4/km² (3−10/mi.²)

HOME RANGE
100−500 ha (245−1,235 acres)

LONGEVITY
3−5 yrs. in the wild

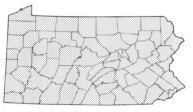

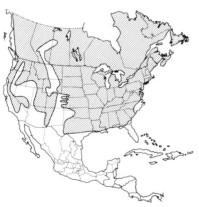

Description

This handsome canid—about the size of a small dog—has large, prominent ears, a pointed nose, vertically elliptical pupils, and a long, luxurious, white-tipped, bushy tail. Its coat is commonly red or yellowish red mixed—especially along the midline—with black-tipped hairs. In contrast to the reddish color of its coat, the throat, sides of the cheeks, and belly are white. Its dusky face and neck and black "stockings" provide further contrast.

Many color variations occur in the red fox; for example, some individuals are reddish brown with a dark cross on the shoulders (cross fox); others have black frosted hairs interspersed with white (silver fox); still others are melanistic (black fox). Although albinos are very rare, they do occur. The sexes are colored alike.

One molt occurs annually, during spring and early summer. In autumn, the coat is supplemented by additional underfur and becomes

Red fox (*Vulpes vulpes*).
See plate 15, following page 172.

prime from January to February. Because of the density of its pelage, the red fox appears considerably larger than it is, especially when it is wearing its prime coat. Males are generally larger than females.

Ecology

Excavation of pre-Columbian Indian villages in Pennsylvania has yielded no remains of the red fox, yet evidence of the gray fox is common in such sites. In light of these findings, most scientists believe that the present-day red fox residing in the Commonwealth is descended from the European red fox introduced into the eastern seaboard area around 1750 for the purpose of sport hunting by the colonial aristocracy.

The red fox in Pennsylvania is today an animal of brushy, successional areas such as old fields, borders of pastures, and rolling farmlands usually close to water. Unlike its close relative the gray fox, the red fox is not fond of mature, dense forests. Instead, this canid prospers in areas altered by human activities.

Vulpes vulpes is a valuable component of the natural eco-system and preys upon small mammals such as rabbits, meadow voles, and white-footed mice. An opportunist, the red fox will also eat anything else available. It consumes birds and their eggs, invertebrates, frogs, snakes, vegetable matter, and carrion. Seasonal preferences reflect availability, and during autumn berries and fruits—such as grapes and wild cherries—insects, and spiders are common food items. During winter, the red fox employs its hunting skills to capture rabbits and small mammals, many of which are stored in shallow depressions in the ground and covered with grass and leaves. These caches are marked by their owner with a sprinkling of urine and are eaten at a later time. On an average day, a red fox will consume between 0.5 and 1 kilogram (1–2 lbs.) of food.

Humans and their dogs represent the principal predators of *V. vulpes*. In Pennsylvania, the red fox is trapped for its pelt, worth an average of about $30, depending on the widely fluctuating fashion market. Many are hunted for sport, an activity justified on the basis of the fox's imagined depredation on poultry, game birds, and mammals. Recent studies show, however, that the red fox has little effect on wild populations of game birds and mammals such as pheasants, grouse, and rabbits. Further, modern poultry facilities, if properly maintained, are virtually impenetrable to even the cunning fox. Many red foxes are also killed on Pennsylvania highways by automobiles and in agricultural areas by farm machinery.

Natural enemies of this canid are few and include primarily

large hawks and owls. Foxes are subject, however, to many diseases such as canine distemper, tularemia, coccidiosis, sarcoptic mange, and septicemia. In Pennsylvania, the red fox acts as a vector for the rabies virus, and many die from the disease each year. Endoparasites are roundworms, heartworms, tapeworms, and flukes.

Behavior

The red fox is shy and nervous; its presence is first told by its tracks or by its long howls, screeches, and yells heard at night. Although chiefly nocturnal, the canid also forages at dawn and dusk.

Vulpes vulpes is a solitary hunter except during the breeding season at which time mates hunt side by side. They establish parallel tracks, which commonly encircle brush piles, logs, or boulders where a potential prey may be lurking. Once the quarry is isolated, the fox stands motionless, listening and watching intently. When the prey emerges, the fox instantaneously pounces on it, pinning it down with its front paws. Surprise is the key to its success, and, although the fox can reach speeds of up to 48 kilometers per hour (30 mi./hr.) and leap fences 2 meters (6.6 ft.) high, it rarely pursues its quarry for lengthy periods.

The red fox makes its home in a variety of locations and defines its territory by scent marking with a rather pungent odor emitted from scent glands near its anus. It nests in hollow logs, rocky caverns, and even deserted outbuildings. Most commonly, however, *V. vulpes*

nests in earthen dens situated on sunny, well-drained slopes. These dens may be newly excavated, or an abandoned woodchuck den may be remodeled. The dens are used mainly as shelter during inclement weather and as maternity wards. They commonly have two or more entrances, connected to the nest site by burrows measuring some 15 to 31 centimeters (6–12 in.) in diameter and about 1 to 1.2 meters (3–4 ft.) long. The red fox usually establishes more than one den in close proximity to another, and young are commonly shuffled back and forth.

In winter, adults rarely den up but, rather, rest in the open beneath brush of downed timber. There, an individual curls into a tight ball with its bushy tail covering its nose and feet. Additional protection from the cold may be provided by an insulating blanket of snow.

Reproduction and Development

Male and female red foxes pair for life. They remain together from midwinter through summer. In autumn, the foxes are solitary but reunite in winter for mating in January or February. Females bear only one litter per year.

Following a gestation period of about 51 days, four to six young are born in late March or early April. Pups are born blind with dark grayish brown fur and white-tipped tails and weight about 100 grams (3.5 oz.). When the young reach about one week old, their eyes open. Adult males are good providers and aid the female (vixen) in caring for the active litter of young. Until the pups can be left alone, the male brings food to the den for the mother and her litter. When the pups reach five weeks old, they emerge from the den and commonly play with each other or with bits of bone or twigs near the den entrance. At eight weeks of age, pups are weaned and join their parents on foraging trips, busily catching and eating mice at this time. In early autumn, the family unit disbands, and the pups disperse from the natal den and become independent. Both males and females are sexually mature by their first winter.

Gray Fox

SCIENTIFIC NAME
Urocyon cinereoargenteus
(*Urocyon* is from the Greek words
uro and *cyon,* meaning "tailed
dog"; *cinereoargenteus* combines
the Latin adjectives *cinereus,*
meaning "gray," and *argenteus,*
meaning "silver.")

SUBSPECIES IN PENNSYLVANIA
*Urocyon cinereoargenteus
cinereoargenteus*

ALSO CALLED
Tree fox, woodfox, grayback, cat
fox, mane-tailed fox, eastern gray
fox

TOTAL LENGTH
870–1,041 mm (34–40.6 in.)

LENGTH OF TAIL
305–382 mm (12–15 in.)

WEIGHT
4.1–5 kg (9–11 lbs.)

MAMMAE
Four pairs

POPULATION DENSITY
1–4/km^2 (3–10/mi.^{2})

HOME RANGE
75–650 ha (185–1,600 acres)

LONGEVITY
5–6 yrs. in the wild; up to 15 yrs.
in captivity

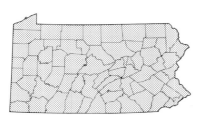

Description

The gray fox, well known for its
climbing ability, is easily identified. It wears a coarse gray coat
that appears grizzled because of a
mixture of black and white bands
in its black-tipped guard hairs.
This "salt-and-pepper" effect is interrupted by a dark, longitudinal
stripe along the midline extending
as a conspicuous black mane
along the top of its reddish brown
tail. The cheeks, lower jaw, throat,
and belly are white. When the
gray fox is seen at a distance, reddish patches on its neck, flanks,
legs, and underside of the tail momentarily fool an inexperienced
observer into misidentifying this
fox as a red fox.

The gray fox, however, should
be quickly separated from its
more flamboyant cousin by its
slightly smaller size, shorter
muzzle and ears, black-tipped tail,

Gray fox (*Urocyon cinereoargenteus*). See plate 16, following page 172. Photo by James F. Parnell.

and distinctive coloration. In addition, the pelage of *U. cinereoargenteus* is coarse, in contrast to the long, luxuriant coat of the red fox. Further, its feet have rusty brown or buff "stockings" rather than the black "stockings" of the red fox, and its forefeet claws are distinctly more curved than those of the red fox, an adaptation for climbing.

The sexes of *U. cinereoargenteus* are colored alike, and no seasonal change occurs in coloration. A single annual molt extends from summer through autumn. The sexes are about equal in size. Color variations are uncommon, but melanistic (black) and albino individuals are known to occur in the wild.

Ecology

Of the North American carnivores, none is more closely affiliated with deciduous forests than the gray fox. In contrast with the red fox, *U. cinereoargenteus* prefers hardwood forests typified by rocky terrain and abundant, brushy cover. Here, the tree-climbing gray fox finds many ideal sites for rest-

ing, foraging, and escaping predators. Although it prefers forests, the gray fox frequents a variety of other habitats such as meadows, grasslands, swamps, and abandoned fields, but rarely on a permanent basis.

The gray fox eats basically the same foods as the red fox—with rabbits, mice, rats, and other wild mammals contributing up to 75 percent of its menu. Other food items include birds and their eggs, invertebrates, frogs, and carrion. During late summer and autumn, plant material such as persimmons, wild grapes, acorns, hickory nuts, apples, grasses, and corn compose about one-third of the diet of *U. cinereoargenteus*. Insects are also a staple at this time of year. During winter, rabbits, small mammals, and plant material form the bulk of the sustenance of the gray fox. It not only eats more berries than the red fox but is known to eat greater numbers of passerine birds, possibly reflecting its readiness to ascend trees in search of food. *Urocyon cinereoargenteus* is also known to cache prey in shallow holes which it covers with dirt, leaves, and debris. The gray fox returns to the site, digs up its caches, and consumes the food at a later date.

Undoubtedly, the most important predator of the gray fox is humankind. As with the red fox, the incentive for killing this canid is the sale of its pelt, which today sells for about $28 in Pennsylvania. Because of the rather coarse, short fur, the gray fox pelt is not as desirable to furriers as that of the red fox and, thus, is used only for collars and trimming on inexpensive coats. Nevertheless, close to

27,000 pelts were harvested and sold during 1982 to 1983 in Pennsylvania alone. *Urocyon* is also hunted for sport, but most hunters become frustrated when pursuing this canid because of its habit of climbing trees and "holing up."

Natural predators of the gray fox include raptorial birds such as great horned owls and red-tailed hawks, in addition to domestic dogs and, occasionally, coyotes and bobcats. Parasites and diseases such as rabies, canine distemper, tularemia, leptospirosis, and a legion of others cause high mortality in the gray fox. Its ectoparasites are also numerous and include fleas, lice, ticks, mites, and chiggers. Unlike the red fox, *U. cinereoargenteus* is highly resistant to infestation by sarcoptic mange mites. Internally, the gray fox hosts flukes, tapeworms, roundworms, and spiny-headed worms.

Behavior

The gray fox is principally nocturnal but also exhibits crepuscular (dawn and dusk) foraging periods. It is more secretive and shy than the red fox and less tolerant of civilization.

Sometimes called the "tree fox," *U. cinereoargenteus* is reported to climb vertical, branchless tree trunks up to 18 meters (59 ft.) high. In a rather unorthodox canid behavior, the gray fox actually shinnies up a tree and jumps from branch to branch. Its agility is enhanced by the long, sharp, curved claws on its forefeet. When on the ground, the gray fox can run about 45 kilometers per hour (28 mi./hr.)

for short distances; it is not as proficient a runner as the red fox and lacks stamina and endurance.

The gray fox communicates by emitting a yapping bark louder and harsher than that of the red fox. Other vocalizations include growls, snarls, squeals, and chuckles. Like the domestic dog, *U. cinereoargenteus* communicates its presence to other foxes by scent marking trees and other objects with urine. During winter, one can follow the trail of this fox and observe spattered urine stains on the snow at bases of trees and brush piles.

The dens of *U. cinereoargenteus* are located in densely wooded habitats near permanent water. Suitable den sites include hollow logs, rocky outcrops, brush piles, and abandoned outbuildings as well as hollow trees in which the fox locates its den at heights of up to 9 meters (30 ft.) above ground. Occasionally, the gray fox dens in burrows in the ground and will appropriate woodchuck burrows for its home. Only as a last resort will *U. cinereoargenteus* excavate its own earthen den.

The den of a gray fox lacks a mound of dirt at its entrance and, thus, is somewhat less conspicuous than the red fox's den. The retreat is filled with grass, leaves, and shredded bark but lacks a formal nest. Several dens may be used by a family of foxes.

Reproduction and Development

The gray fox is monogamous and pairs for life. Like the red fox, *U. cinereoargenteus* breeds only once each year. Mating occurs in February and early March in Pennsylvania, with the gestation period ranging from 50 to 60 days, slightly longer than that of the red fox. In the home den, the female (vixen) gives birth to a litter averaging four to six young between mid-April and early May. As with the red fox, the male gray fox is highly solicitous and helps to raise the litter. He remains with the family group until it breaks up in late autumn.

At birth, the pups are scantily furred, black in color, blind, and helpless, and weigh about 75 grams (2.6 oz.). Growth is rapid, and their eyes open between the ninth and twelfth day after birth. At four weeks of age, the young venture out of the den, and weaning takes place when they are eight to twelve weeks old. Shortly after weaning, the pups accompany their parents on hunting trips. The family breaks up and the young disperse by autumn, at which time the young have attained their adult weight. Juvenile gray foxes are reported to have dispersed as far as 84 kilometers (52 mi.) from their natal den and are capable of breeding during their first winter.

Bears
Family Ursidae

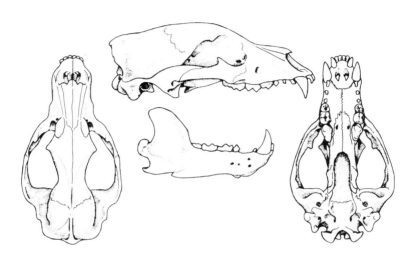

Skull of an ursid (*Ursus*, × ⅛).

The family Ursidae includes the largest terrestrial carnivore, the polar bear, which measures up to 3 meters (10 ft.) tall and weighs over 800 kilograms (1,760 lbs.). In contrast, the family also includes the small Malayan sun bear, which reaches a height of only about 70 centimeters (28 in.) and weighs between 27 to 65 kilograms (60–143 lbs.). Other members of the Ursidae include the familiar black bear and grizzly bear and the not-so-familiar Old World sloth bear, Asian black bear, and giant panda. In total, the ursids are represented today by four genera and eight species occurring throughout North America and Eurasia, in the Andes Mountains of South America, and in the Atlas Mountains of north Africa. True ursids can be traced to the Eocene Epoch, but they are an offshoot from the canid evolutionary line, first known from the middle Miocene Epoch of Europe, about 15 million years ago.

Ursids are typified by their robust build; rudimentary tail; small eyes; short, powerful limbs; and small, rounded, erect ears. The coat is shaggy and predominantly one color—either black, brown, or white. The few exceptions to this generalization are the four small Eurasian bears with their white or buffy colored chest markings and the giant panda with its striking black-and-white color pattern. The skulls of bears are massive with elongate canines, weakly developed carnassials, and broad, flat, crushing molars. Bears employ a plantigrade stance; that is, they walk on the soles of their broad, flat feet. Their feet are equipped with five long, curved, nonretractile claws adapted for tearing, digging, and climbing. Except for the polar bear and grizzly bear, all bears are adept climbers.

Bears have an acute sense of smell but do not hear or see very well. They are rather solitary and, unlike the canids, are quiet except for emitting occasional growls or grunts. Bears inhabiting colder regions undergo a period of winter dormancy or lethargy, during which time cubs are born. This behavior is not true hibernation, because body temperature and heart rate do not drop appreciably. Although bears mate in the spring, pregnancy is often extended by six to nine months by delayed implantation of the fertilized egg.

The ursids are notably omnivorous, eating insects, fruits, berries, or whatever is available. Two exceptions are the highly carnivorous polar bear, which prefers seals, and the herbivorous giant panda, which feasts principally on bamboo stems.

The family Ursidae is represented by one species in Pennsylvania, the black bear (*Ursus americanus*).

Black Bear

SCIENTIFIC NAME
Ursus americanus (*Ursus* is Latin
for "bear"; *americanus*, Latin for
"of America," alludes to eastern
North America, the locality cited
in the first description.)

SUBSPECIES IN PENNSYLVANIA
Ursus americanus americanus

ALSO CALLED
Brown bear, bruin, cinnamon bear

TOTAL LENGTH
127–178 cm (50–70 in.)

LENGTH OF TAIL
8–13 cm (3–5 in.)

WEIGHT
91–272 kg (200–600 lbs.)

MAMMAE
Three pairs

POPULATION DENSITY
0.03–1.5/km² (1–4/mi.²)

HOME RANGE
230–19,600 ha (570–48,400 acres)

LONGEVITY
5–8 yrs. in the wild; up to 30 yrs
in captivity

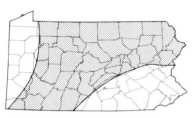

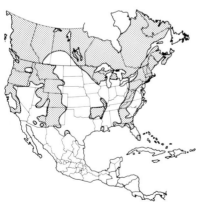

Description

The black bear is familiar to most
people, even if only from its promi-
nence in folk literature and zoos.
Interestingly, the black bear has
even been immortalized in the
form of a doll. In 1902, President
Theodore (Teddy) Roosevelt, a distinguished hunter and naturalist,
captured a black bear cub and
took it home with him. A re-
sourceful New York doll maker
fashioned a small fabric bear after
this "catch." Since then, "teddy
bears" have been a joy to children
and adults worldwide.

With its large size; flat-footed
stance; bobbed tail; short, stout
legs; and short, rounded, erect
ears—the black bear can be confused with no other Pennsylvania
mammal. Its normal color varies
from glossy black to brownish
black. Its face and long muzzle are
usually tinged with tan, and a

Black bear (*Ursus americanus*).
See plate 17, following page 172.

white spot occasionally appears on the breast. Variations in color such as cinnamon, chocolate, blue, and albino occur at different frequencies in the wild. Although no difference in color exists between the sexes, the male black bear (boar) is slightly larger than the female (sow).

The fur of *U. americanus* is longest and glossiest in autumn, whereas in summer the bear takes on a ragged, dull appearance because of wear. Molting usually begins in April or May and is completed in autumn.

Ecology

The Pennsylvania Game Commission calculates that about 7,000 black bears currently reside in the Commonwealth. The species prefers to live in Pennsylvania's heavily forested areas. Here, mixed stands of conifers and hardwoods supporting a dense, brushy understory in close proximity to a mountain stream represent optimal habitat for *U. americanus*. The bear selects prime habitats on the basis of availability of food and den sites and inaccessibility to humans.

The black bear is a first-rate omnivore, and its diet is dictated by seasonal availability and abundance of food. For such a large mammal, the black bear seems to spend an inordinate amount of time eating small items. Plant foods—fruits, nuts, acorns, berries, seeds, and roots—may make up as much as 75 percent of its diet. In many areas, carrion also provides a major portion of the bear's food. Its animal menu consists of small mammals, birds' eggs, frogs, fish, and adult and larval insects such as ants, bees, grasshoppers, crickets, and beetles. Being extremely fond of bees and their honey, the black bear is strongly disliked by Pennsylvania beekeepers. Moreover, the bear's infatuation with the foods of humans accounts for its presence at garbage dumps and its legendary role as an efficient raider of campers' food stores.

A bear's feeding habits result in obvious evidence of its recent presence. In search of insects, it rips open rotten stumps and turns over logs and boulders. Nearby, its large, dark brown, cylindrical droppings may be found, often containing berry seeds, insect parts, animal hair, and fragments of nutshells.

Except for humans and their dogs, the black bear has few enemies. During 1985, some 1,029 bears were killed by hunters in Pennsylvania. In 1984, over 200 were killed by automobiles in the state. Forest fires also take a toll on the black bear, and adult males are known to kill cubs occasionally.

The black bear seems to harbor comparatively heavy parasite loads. Externally, the species is infected by fleas, ticks, lice, and mites. Internal parasites include tapeworms, flukes, roundworms, spiny-headed worms, and several protozoans. The nematode *Trichinella spiralis* is also prevalent in the black bear; its meat, therefore, should be well cooked before eating to avoid danger of contracting trichinosis. The black bear is also known to be infected by various rickettsial and bacterial diseases.

Behavior

Although primarily nocturnal, the black bear may be seen wandering about during daylight hours. It forages along well-worn trails used by generations of bears. Along these paths, certain shaggy-barked trees may act as shedding posts, where the bear relieves itching and rubs away loose hair. Such trees are evidenced by rub marks and clumps of snagged hair clinging to the trunk. The domain of the black bear is further delimited by the presence of "bear trees," conspicuous by having scars of claw marks and even tooth marks as high as a bear can reach standing on its hindlegs. Whether this behavior sharpens claws or denotes territorial rights is unknown.

An adept climber, the black bear actually shinnies up trees. It employs its hindfeet, first by bringing them forward beneath the belly and then by extending them backward. The forefeet aid in grasping the trunk of the tree during the climb. A bear descends a tree rump first.

Like humans, the bear walks with a flat-footed stance. Its gait is usually a slow, lumbering walk. If

Yellow birch tree showing scratch marks of a black bear.

provoked or frightened, it may break into a rolling gallop, reaching speeds of up to 48 kilometers per hour (30 mi./hr.) for short distances. The black bear is also an excellent and powerful swimmer and does not hesitate to ford rivers.

The black bear is essentially a solitary animal and generally mild tempered. If encountered in the wild, it may rise on its hindfeet, inspect the intruder, and ramble off into the forest. Although usually silent, the bear may emit a growl, "woof," or snort if surprised. An injured bear is known to cry or sob like a human, and cubs whimper or squall if frightened or hungry. Although *U. americanus* is nearsighted (myopic), it has an excellent sense of smell and acute hearing.

The black bear has a novel way of coping with food shortages and the severe cold imposed by Pennsylvania winters. It simply sleeps through the difficult times. The black bear does not undergo true hibernation, as do woodchucks and jumping mice. Instead, it spends its winter in a deep sleep or dormancy in which respiration, heart rate, and body temperature are only slightly reduced. During autumn, the bear eats heavily and accumulates a layer of fat under its skin. This fatty layer may measure up to 10 centimeters (4 in.) in thickness and not only provides insulation and nourishment but also sustains developing and newborn young.

Ursus americanus usually dens alone, and females enter dormancy earlier than males. Dens can be found in sheltered sites such as under the roots of a large tree or in a crevice, cave, or hollow tree. There, the bear makes its bed of stripped bark, leaves, grasses, and moss. Females are more selective about den sites than males, perhaps because they may bear their young during dormancy.

The bear's winter sleep commences in late autumn and ends in spring, usually in March or April. A sleeping bear cannot defecate in winter because its rectum is blocked by a "fecal plug." This plug measures up to 30 centimeters (1 ft.) long and is composed of dry leaves, pine needles, and bits of hair mixed with intestinal mucus. When the bear emerges in spring, this plug is expelled. Rather thin with a ragged appearance because of its molting pelage,

the bear spends most of its springtime searching for food.

Reproduction and Development

In Pennsylvania, the black bear mates between early June and mid-July. After the ova are fertilized, they undergo a period of arrested development and are not actually implanted in the uterus until after the female enters hibernation in autumn. Cubs are born during January, following a gestation period of about seven months. The female usually gives birth to two or three young every other year.

Newborns are blind, helpless, and have a fuzzy coat of mottled gray hair. At birth, they are about the size of a guinea pig, weighing 200 to 340 grams (7–12 oz.). When they reach about six weeks of age, their eyes open, they are well furred, and they weigh about 1 kilogram (2 lbs.). At the age of two months, cubs may venture outside of the den with their mother. They now weigh about 2.5 kilograms (5.5 lbs.), are still nursing, but will eat some solid food. Cubs remain with the mother through the summer and autumn. Highly concerned about her cubs, the sow disciplines them strictly during their summer together. Weaning usually commences in August or September, when the cubs are about seven months old. Young may den with their mother or nearby during the first winter, but, thereafter, they are on their own. Females reach sexual maturity at three to four years of age, and males, about one year later.

Raccoons
Family Procyonidae

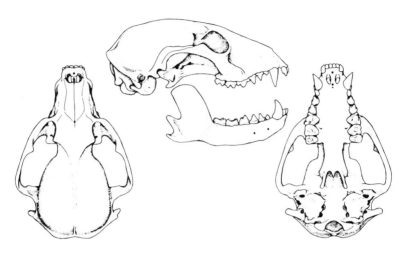

Skull of a procyonid (*Procyon*, × ⅜).

The family Procyonidae includes raccoons, coatis, kinkajous, olingos, ringtails, cacomistles, and the lesser panda of Asia. Members of this diverse family range in size from the ringtail, slightly larger than a fox squirrel, to the familiar raccoon, weighing up to 22 kilograms (49 lbs.). Procyonids have a common ancestry with the dog family (Canidae), and its earliest-known fossils date back to the late Oligocene Epoch of North America, some 28 million years ago. Today, the family is represented by 7 genera and 18 species. Except for the lesser panda of southeastern Asia, procyonids are exclusively American, occurring from southern Canada through Central America and most of South America.

The medium-sized, long-bodied procyonids are usually distinguished by their long tails with alternating light and dark bands. The body is variable in color, with contrasting combinations of white with gray, brown with black, or a uniform rich reddish brown as in the lesser panda. Being plantigrades, procyonids walk partly or wholly on the soles of their feet. They also have five clawed toes; except for the ringtail and lesser panda, which have semiretractile claws on the forepaws, the procyonids have nonretractile claws. Family members usually have pointed muzzles, although the kinkajou has a short nose and the coati has a long, flexible snout well suited for rooting out insects hiding in forest floor litter. Procyonids are largely omnivorous; their teeth, with broad, low-crowned molars and poorly developed carnassials, reflect this fact.

The raccoon and its allies occupy a wide variety of ecological settings, ranging from cool temperate and tropical rain forests to dry mesquite grasslands. A common resident of urban and agricultural areas, the raccoon is the only procyonid in Pennsylvania.

Raccoon

SCIENTIFIC NAME
Procyon lotor (*Procyon* is Greek for "before the dog"; *lotor*, a Latin word meaning "a washer," refers to this animal's habit of washing its food before eating.)

SUBSPECIES IN PENNSYLVANIA
Procyon lotor lotor

ALSO CALLED
Coon, ringtail

TOTAL LENGTH
720–915 mm (28.1–35.7 in.)

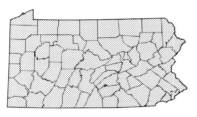

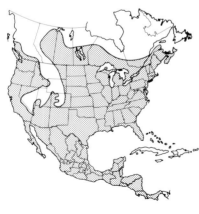

LENGTH OF TAIL
196–279 mm (7.6–10.9 in.)

WEIGHT
4–15 kg (8.8–33 lbs.)

MAMMAE
Three pairs

POPULATION DENSITY
2–20/km² (5–52/mi.²)

HOME RANGE
5–5,000 ha (12–12,350 acres)

LONGEVITY
4–6 yrs. in the wild; up to 17 yrs. in captivity

Description

Procyon lotor is stocky, about the size of a Boston bulldog. Although some individuals have variable amounts of yellow or brown fur, most members of the species have grizzled gray pelage composed of long, coarse guard hairs and short, soft underfur. What makes the raccoon unique among Pennsylvania mammals is its face and tail. The raccoon's broad face is covered with a black "bandit" mask. It has a pointed muzzle; black, medium-sized eyes; and prominent, erect, white-rimmed ears. The raccoon's heavily furred tail is distinguished by four to six alternating blackish and yellowish rings; the tip is black.

The sexes are colored alike and juveniles resemble adults. Males are slightly larger than females. The annual molt begins in spring and lasts through most of summer.

Raccoon (*Procyon lotor*).

The pelts of most adult raccoons become prime by late November. Albino, white, "red," chestnut, and melanistic (black) raccoons occur infrequently in the wild.

Ecology

In Pennsylvania, the raccoon prefers to reside in woodlands close to streams, ponds, or lakes, where den site availability in the form of hollow trees or crevices within rocky outcrops is important. Highly adaptable, *P. lotor* also lives in grasslands and farmlands, where it finds shelter in woodchuck dens or attics of old houses. Urban parks are even colonized by the "homesteading" raccoon, which becomes a frequent evening visitor to backyard garbage cans. Its dexterous fingers enable the animal to open trash can lids easily!

Like many other carnivores, the raccoon is highly omnivorous. Although it exhibits distinct food preferences, availability largely dictates its menu. During spring and summer, *P. lotor* feeds mainly on animal matter including insects, earthworms, snails, spiders, birds and their eggs, and many small mammals. *Procyon lotor* also consumes carrion and commonly visits creek edges to search for crayfish, frogs, fish, and other aquatic prey. True to legend, the raccoon may "wash" its food before eating, but this is not an invariable trait because much food is secured in waterless regions. During late summer, autumn, and winter, *P. lotor* mainly eats plant foods such as fleshy fruits and seeds. At this time, wild grape, acorns, beechnuts, blackberries, elderberries, pokeberries, wild cherries, apples, and corn constitute the bulk of the diet. Well known for its ability to damage standing corn, the raccoon seems to raid the fields just before harvest. For the small-scale gardener, a good dose of cayenne pepper on each ear of corn should deter such thievery.

Diseases and a few natural predators such as large raptorial birds take their toll on the raccoon, but humans are its worst enemy. In Pennsylvania, humans pursue *P. lotor* for sport, food, and fur—with a market value of $13 per pelt. "Coon hunting," popular during late autumn in Pennsylvania, involves specially bred hounds trailing and ultimately treeing a raccoon which is then usually shot. As a result of hunting and trapping, an estimated 846,000 raccoons were killed in Pennsylvania in 1981. Large numbers of raccoons also meet their demise each year on highways.

The raccoon is known to harbor externally a variety of fleas, lice, mites, chiggers, and ticks. The larvae of the botfly also infect *P. lotor.* Internal parasites include roundworms, tapeworms, flukes, and spiny-headed worms. Raccoon populations are highly susceptible to canine distemper and rabies. Other viral diseases of *P. lotor* include eastern equine encephalitis, fox encephalitis, and St. Louis encephalitis. Trypanosomiasis, coccidiosis, and toxoplasmosis are protozoan diseases the raccoon harbors, and its bacterial diseases include tularemia, tuberculosis, leptospirosis, and listeriosis.

Behavior

Although essentially nocturnal, *P. lotor* exhibits bouts of activity at dawn and dusk. It is not a true hibernator but will "den up" for extended periods during very cold weather, emerging occasionally on warm days to forage. Like the black bear, the raccoon builds up in autumn a heavy layer of fat which sustains it during winter when food is scarce. *Procyon lotor* emerges from its winter "sleep" in early spring in a rather emaciated state, having lost up to half its body weight.

The raccoon optimizes winter survival by communal nesting; communal "piles" are reported to include up to 23 individuals in a single den. Hollow trees are preferred den sites, but the raccoon also uses cavities under tree roots, crevices within rocky ledges, or even muskrat houses. It also remodels woodchuck, opossum, fox, or even skunk burrows. The most common tree dens are located at heights ranging between 6 to 12 meters (20–40 ft.) above ground, and the nesting cavity averages about 30 centimeters (1 ft.) in diameter by 90 centimeters (3 ft.) in depth. The raccoon does not construct actual nests within cavities, and it may have several den sites used for several days at a time.

Although flat-footed, the raccoon is a swift runner and can reach speeds of up to 25 kilometers per hour (15.5 mi./hr.) for short distances. It is a superb climber and readily ascends trees to forage and seek shelter. The raccoon is one of the few mammals capable of descending trees head first, a feat that requires a 180-degree rotation of the hindfeet. The animal is also at home in water; it swims "dog-paddle" style and can easily cross rivers and lakes up to 300 meters (985 ft.) wide.

Procyon lotor is rather sociable and, unlike canids, generally does not establish territories. Although nonaggressive, if agitated or cornered, the raccoon is a strong, fierce fighter able to subdue a dog its own size. As proclaimed in Indian folklore, it is curious, rather clever, and exhibits a high degree of intelligence. It is endowed with keen senses of sight and hearing, and its manual dexterity rivals that of primates. With a strong, tenacious grasp, the raccoon can easily turn doorknobs or catch flying insects. *Procyon lotor* also has a diverse vocal repertoire, ranging from snarls, growls, hisses, and screams signifying anger, to soft purring indicating contentment.

Reproduction and Development

In Pennsylvania, the raccoon normally breeds only once per year, usually in January or February. During this time, males wander widely in search of receptive females. Unlike foxes, the raccoon probably does not mate for life, but males may remain with "expectant" females until the young are born and occasionally help to care for pups.

Young are usually born in late March or April, following a gestation period of about 63 days. Litter size varies from three to six, averaging about four. Newborns are blind and well haired, with both the "bandit" mask and tail rings discernible. At birth, they weigh about 85 grams (3 oz.). At about three weeks of age, their eyes open. The pups grow rapidly, eat solid food when nine weeks old, and are weaned by 16 weeks, at which time they commonly travel with the mother. Females are devoted parents, aggressively defending their young and teaching them to climb and hunt during summer. In autumn, the family selects its winter denning sites. Cubs may den in the same tree cavity or in different cavities in trees close together. By early winter, the cubs weigh between 3 and 5.5 kilograms (7–12 lbs.) each; they do not achieve adult weight until they are nearly two years old. Females typically breed as yearlings, but males wait until their second winter.

Weasels and Allies

Family Mustelidae

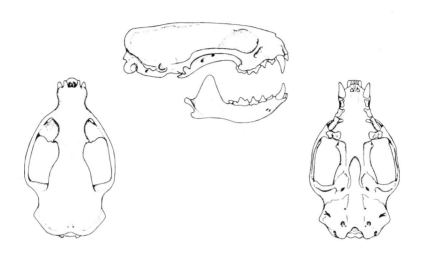

Skull of a mustelid (*Mustela*, × ⅝).

Weasels, skunks, minks, otters, and badgers make up the large, diverse family Mustelidae. The world's smallest carnivore—the least weasel—is a mustelid. The largest member of the family is the sea otter, which measures slightly over 1 meter (3.3 ft.) in length and can weigh as much as a large German shepherd, about 45 kilograms (100 lbs.).

The family Mustelidae is first known from the early Oligocene Epoch of North America, Europe, and Asia, about 34 million years ago. It is represented today by 25 genera and 70 species occurring worldwide except for Australia, Antarctica, and most oceanic islands. Highly adaptable, mustelids occur in many different habitats ranging from arctic tundra to tropical rain forests and from open seas to inland lakes. Within such habitats, their diverse life-styles include strictly terrestrial (weasels), arboreal (martens, fishers), semifossorial (badgers), semiaquatic (mink), and amphibious (otters) forms.

Mustelids typically have long, slender bodies with short limbs and "pushed-in" faces. The wolverine and badgers, being quite stocky, are exceptions. Some mustelids are plantigrade (flat-footed), whereas others are digitigrade since they walk on their toes with their wrists and heels raised. All species have five digits on each foot; most are equipped with curved, nonretractile claws, especially well developed in the badgers. The otter's digits are usually webbed, an adaptation that enhances swimming ability.

Color patterns of the mustelids are quite variable, ranging from the pine marten's uniform brown coat to the skunk's contrasting black-and-white pelage. Some forms have thick, silky coats making them valuable fur bearers. Various species living in north temperate regions produce a white winter coat. Unlike most mammals, a strong dimorphism between the sexes occurs in some of the smaller mustelids, with males often being up to 50 percent larger than females.

Mustelids are active, fierce hunters, with specialized methods of killing prey; but many are opportunistic, eating fruit and nuts, insects, or even honey as does the honey badger of the Old World. The sea otter has a predilection for sea urchins and abalone; it first dislodges this prey and then breaks its shell by using a rock tool. This is the only mammal other than primates which uses a tool while foraging. The dentition of mustelids is well suited for their predaceous habits. Most have conspicuous carnassial teeth; long, sharp canines; and well-developed crushing and shearing cheekteeth. Most also have well-developed anal scent glands used for species identification and defense. Skunks are especially well known for their odorous secretion which can be sprayed up to 4.5 meters (15 ft.) with great accuracy.

In Pennsylvania, the family Mustelidae is represented by four genera and seven species.

Ermine

SCIENTIFIC NAME
Mustela erminea (*Mustela* is
Latin for "weasel"; *erminea* is a
Latinized Old French word for the
white winter color of this animal.)

SUBSPECIES IN PENNSYLVANIA
Mustela erminea cicognanii

ALSO CALLED
Short-tailed weasel, Bonaparte's
weasel, small brown weasel, stoat

TOTAL LENGTH
230–295 mm (9–11.5 in.)

LENGTH OF TAIL
58–81 mm (2.3–3.2 in.)

WEIGHT
58–100 g (2–3.5 oz.)

MAMMAE
Four pairs

POPULATION DENSITY
2–10/km² (5–26/mi.²)

HOME RANGE
2–30 ha (5–74 acres)

LONGEVITY
4–7 yrs. in the wild

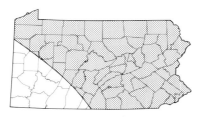

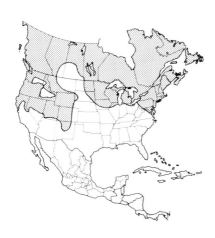

Description

The ermine, slightly larger than
an eastern chipmunk, is characterized by its slender, long neck
and body; short, stubby legs; and
triangular head. Its pelage is composed of glossy guard hairs underlaid by short, wooly underfur.
During most of the year, *M. erminea* is uniformly chocolate
brown above with a cream white
belly. During winter, the ermine
dons a pure white coat, except for
the tip of the tail which is black
throughout the year. Sexes are colored alike.

The molt from brown to pure
white begins in October and is
completed by mid-November.
This dramatic pelage change, mediated by the pituitary gland, is
triggered by shortening day lengths
in concert with colder temperatures. The spring molt from white
to brown usually takes place from
March through April; it occurs

Ermine (*Mustela erminea*).
Photo by Paul K. Anderson.

primarily in response to increased day length.

The ermine closely resembles the long-tailed weasel, but can be distinguished from this cousin by its smaller size, shorter tail (usually less than one-third of its total length), and white fur on the inside of its hindfeet. In addition, the soles of the ermine's feet are densely furred during both summer and winter, whereas those of the long-tailed weasel are concealed by fur during winter but are somewhat naked the rest of the year. When comparing these two species with respect to size, their sex should be taken into account: Male ermines are much larger than female ermines, but large male ermines are often about the same size as small female long-tailed weasels.

Ecology

The ermine occurs throughout Pennsylvania except for the southwest. It is less common in the Commonwealth than its larger cousin the long-tailed weasel and resides in open woodlands, brushy thickets, and hedgerows, usually close to water. In such habitats, it constructs dens beneath rock piles, under stone walls, in hollow logs, among tree roots, or even in abandoned chipmunk burrows. Its nest is usually lined with dry vegetation and fur or feathers of its victims.

A rather strict carnivore, *M. erminea* feeds mainly on mice, voles, shrews, chipmunks, young rabbits, birds, and, occasionally, invertebrates. This efficient predator will even tackle prey considerably larger than itself; cottontail rabbits and gray squirrels are frequently on the ermine's menu.

Predators of the ermine are quite numerous. Its principal avian enemies include great horned and barred owls and rough-legged, broad-winged, and red-tailed hawks. Red and gray foxes, domestic cats, and long-tailed weasels also prey on *M. erminea*, as do snakes such as the rattle-snake, copperhead, and black rat snake. Ermines also meet their demise on highways. Although valued by trappers for its white winter fur, the ermine is not commonly trapped in Pennsylvania because of its low numbers.

External parasites include fleas, ticks, lice, and mites. Internally, the animal hosts tapeworms, flukes, and roundworms. The nasal roundworm is the most frequently encountered nematode parasite of the ermine. It invades the nasal sinuses, causing pressure on the brain, commonly resulting in seizures and ultimately death. The ermine is also highly susceptible to canine distemper and tularemia.

Behavior

Mustela erminea is chiefly nocturnal but also hunts during the day. During winter, it commonly forages for small mammals under the snow, finding cover in the subnivean environment. Its tracks can be seen on the surface of the snow where it investigates its surroundings by standing on its hindlegs.

The gait of the ermine, similar to that of the long-tailed weasel, is a series of small bounds or lopes with the back greatly arched (inchworm style). It may exhibit leaps of up to 1.8 meters (6 ft.) in length and can reach speeds of 13 kilometers per hour (8 mi./hr.) for short distances. It is able to climb trees in search of prey and even swims well but spends most of its time on the ground.

The ermine generally leads a solitary life except during the breeding season or when young are being reared. According to their social hierarchy, adult males are dominant over females and young at this time.

Like other mustelids, *M. erminea* uses secretions from anal scent glands to define its territory, which it regularly patrols and scent marks.

The ermine has keen senses of smell, hearing, and sight. It vocalizes while hunting, playing, and mating—emitting many sounds such as trills, hisses, purrs, chatters, grunts, and screeches. When agitated or in pain, *M. erminea* emits a high-pitched squeal.

Reproduction and Development

Females produce only one litter per year. In Pennsylvania, mating takes place in early summer and is followed by a period of delayed implantation which produces an exceedingly long gestation period of about 10 months. Finally, during April or May, four to eight young are born.

Newborns are blind and helpless, covered with soft, fine white hair, and weigh about 1.7 grams (0.6 oz.). The pups soon develop a prominent brown mane on the neck, a nifty "handle" for the mother to use in transporting them around the nest. Growth is rapid; their eyes open at about five to six weeks of age, at which time brown dorsal pelage has developed, obscuring the mane. Soon the characteristic black tip appears on the tail. At this stage of development, the young become quite independent and actively play among themselves within the nest. Unlike most mustelids, the adult male ermine aids the mother by providing food for the growing young. Weaning is usually completed by six weeks of age, although lactation continues for another six weeks. By autumn, pups are nearly full grown and may be seen hunting alongside the female. Most adult males depart from the family group in autumn, although evidence suggests that some remain with the female throughout the year. Females are known to breed at three months of age, whereas males do not reach sexual maturity until their second year of life.

Least Weasel

SCIENTIFIC NAME
Mustela nivalis (*Mustela* is Latin
for "weasel"; *nivalis* is from the
Latin adjective *nix*, meaning
"snowy.")

SUBSPECIES IN PENNSYLVANIA
Mustela nivalis allegheniensis

ALSO CALLED
Mouse weasel

TOTAL LENGTH
181–206 mm (7.1–8.0 in.)

LENGTH OF TAIL
31–44 mm (1.2–1.7 in.)

WEIGHT
38–59 g (1.3–2.1 oz.)

MAMMAE
Three pairs

POPULATION DENSITY
2–25/km² (5–65/mi.²)

HOME RANGE
0.8–26 ha (2–64 acres)

LONGEVITY
Up to 3 yrs. in the wild; up to 10
yrs. in captivity

STATUS IN PENNSYLVANIA
Undetermined

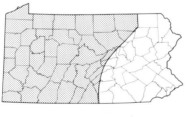

Description

The least weasel, the smallest carnivore, is only slightly larger than
a meadow vole, its principal prey.
It has a small, flat head with short,
rounded ears and prominent whiskers (vibrissae). Its beady eyes are
small and black. *Mustela nivalis*
is distinguished from all other
weasels by its diminutive size,
slender body (about the thickness
of a man's thumb), stubby legs, and
the lack of a black tip on its short
tail. Like other weasels, males are
larger than females.

The least weasel is rich chocolate brown above with white on
the chin, throat, chest, and belly.
Its pelage consists of soft, wooly
underfur overlaid by long guard
hairs. The tail is entirely brown.
In autumn, in response to shortening day lengths, the least weasel
in northern Pennsylvania may
produce a white winter coat, ac-

Least weasel (*Mustela nivalis*).
Photo by James F. Parnell.

counting for its specific name, *nivalis*. Throughout most of the state, however, *M. nivalis* acquires a pale brown coat following its autumn molt. The increased day lengths of spring act as the stimulus for color change to the brown summer pelage. Both molts take about three weeks and are mediated by the pituitary gland. The soles of the feet are heavily furred in winter but naked in summer.

Ecology

Because of its nocturnal habits, small size, and secretive nature, the least weasel is perceived to be rare in Pennsylvania. Actually, it is probably fairly common in the state. It is most abundant in brushy areas, open woodlands, old fields, pastureland, and fencerows supporting prey species such as the meadow vole and the white-

footed mouse. In Pennsylvania, *M. nivalis* also occurs in mature oak, hickory, and hemlock forests.

The favorite foods of the least weasel are voles and mice, but this ferocious hunter is also fond of shrews, insects and other invertebrates, ground-nesting birds, and carrion. It consumes up to half its body weight in food each day and, thus, can significantly affect a population of small mammals.

The slender, tiny body of this efficient killer permits it access to vole runways in order to stalk its quarry. Its killing technique is typified by seizing the victim by the head and neck and wrapping its limbs around the prey, which is most likely larger than the weasel. A series of rapid bites to the base of the skull cause instantaneous death to the victim. Next, the least weasel may lap blood from the wound and consume the head and brain, followed by the rest of the body. Prey is commonly devoured on the spot but occasionally may be cached near the den or taken to the nest to feed young.

Predators of the least weasel are numerous. The owls most efficient at capturing the tiny and elusive least weasel are the barn, barred, and great horned owls. Other raptors include broad-winged and rough-legged hawks. Foxes, minks, ermines, long-tailed weasels, and house cats are known to take a toll on *M. nivalis,* as are several snakes such as the black rat snake and copperhead.

Little is known of the influence of disease and parasites infecting the least weasel. It is reported to host externally lice, mites, chiggers, and ticks. Tapeworms and several species of roundworms including the nasal nematode are known to parasitize *M. nivalis* internally.

Behavior

The least weasel is active throughout the year; it does not hibernate or undergo torpidity. Like other weasels, it is principally nocturnal with peak activity occurring shortly after dusk. During winter, its presence is known by tracks in the snow—a series of jumps or bounds in which the prints of the hindfeet come down nearly in the tracks left by the forefeet.

Like other weasels, *M. nivalis* has anal scent glands and probably defines its domain by scent marking with the strongly odorous fluid secreted by these glands. It has keen senses of smell, sight, and hearing and communicates by use of a diverse vocal repertoire.

When disturbed, *M. nivalis* emits a chirp or screech, whereas it hisses or squeals when threatened. A trill is emitted when weasels are playing, mating, or investigating surroundings.

The least weasel generally nests below ground, usurping the burrows of its victims such as chipmunks, mice, or voles. The burrow entrance measures about 2.5 centimeters (1 in.) across and leads to the nest chamber located up to 15 centimeters (6 in.) below ground. The chamber is some 10 centimeters (4 in.) in diameter and lined with dried vegetation and the fur of prey—usually the former tenant. This nest is used for sleeping, rearing young, and as a cache for food. Each weasel may have more than one home.

Reproduction and Development

Mustela nivalis employs a different breeding strategy from other weasels in Pennsylvania. It is polyestrous and may breed anytime of the year, even during midwinter. It typically produces two to three litters per year. Further, since delayed implantation does not occur, the gestation period is quite brief, only 35 to 37 days. Litter size varies from three to six young, averaging about five. The least weasel produces more litters and more young per year than any other North American weasel.

At birth, the young are wrinkled, pink, hairless, and blind and weigh about 1.5 grams (0.05 oz.) each. Growth is rapid. At four days of age, they have tripled their weight and have a fine, thin white coat of fur. Pups are quite vocal, frequently emitting high-pitched squeaks. Between two and three weeks of age, brown summer pelage begins to develop, and the young begin eating solid food. Their eyes open at four weeks of age, at which time weaning commences and the pups venture outside the nest with the mother, who teaches them to kill prey. By the time they are six or seven weeks old, least weasels are proficient hunters. Young reach adult size between 12 and 14 weeks of age and soon thereafter disperse from the natal nest. Females are able to breed at the age of four months; some are reported to bear two litters before their first birthday. Males are slower to mature and are capable of breeding at the age of eight months.

Status in Pennsylvania

The least weasel occurs in most counties of the western half of Pennsylvania. There, it is probably fairly common in suitable habitat. Few people, however, observe this tiny carnivore, because it forages under the cover of darkness and is highly secretive.

A long time has elapsed since the status of *M. nivalis* was evaluated in Pennsylvania (Richmond and McDowell, 1952). As a result, the status of "undetermined" was assigned to the least weasel by the Pennsylvania Biological Survey in its report *Species of Special Concern in Pennsylvania* (Genoways and Brenner, 1985). The recommendation of the Survey includes a reevaluation of the distribution and abundance of *M. nivalis* in the Commonwealth. This study is critical because much of its range in the state since the 1950s has been disturbed by mining activities, agricultural practices, and construction of industrial and recreational facilities.

Long-tailed Weasel

SCIENTIFIC NAME
Mustela frenata (*Mustela* is Latin
for "weasel"; *frenata* is from the
Latin word *frenum,* meaning
"bridled," and pertains to the
facial "mask" found in some
southern subspecies.)

SUBSPECIES IN PENNSYLVANIA
Mustela frenata noveboracensis

ALSO CALLED
New York weasel, ermine, big
stoat, northern long-tailed weasel

TOTAL LENGTH
291–450 mm (11.3–17.6 in.)

LENGTH OF TAIL
84–164 mm (3.3–6.4 in.)

WEIGHT
67–312 g (2.3–10.9 oz.)

MAMMAE
Four pairs

POPULATION DENSITY
5–37/km² (13–96/mi.²)

HOME RANGE
4–120 ha (10–296 acres)

LONGEVITY
2–5 yrs. in the wild; 5–8 yrs. in
captivity

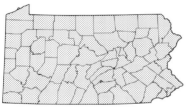

Description

The long-tailed weasel is the
largest, most common weasel in
Pennsylvania. It is identified by its
stubby legs; small, triangular
head; long, slender body and neck;
and long, black-tipped, bushy tail.
It has short, rounded ears; prominent whiskers; and small, beady,
black eyes that reflect a brilliant
emerald green when illuminated
by a spotlight or car headlight.

The pelage of the long-tailed
weasel consists of soft, wooly underfur overlaid by long, glistening
guard hairs. During most of the
year, *M. frenata* is rich brown
with a white chin, yellowish or
buffy brown belly, and brown feet.
In winter, long-tailed weasels in
northern Pennsylvania—about 30
percent of the state's population—
turn white; the other 70 percent
don a pale brown coat at that
time. The tip of the tail remains

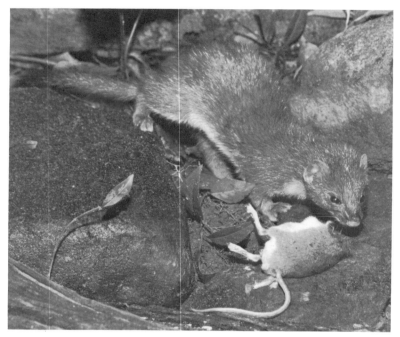

Long-tailed weasel (*Mustela frenata*).

black for all. Sexes are colored alike.

For all the long-tailed weasels, the autumn molt occurs from October to mid-November. The spring change usually takes place from March to April. Each molt, taking about three to four weeks, is governed by day lengths and mediated by the pituitary gland.

The long-tailed weasel resembles the ermine. *Mustela frenata* is distinguished from this cousin by its larger size, longer tail (over one-third of its total length), and lack of white fur on the inside of the hindlegs. Also, in *M. frenata*, the soles of the feet are concealed by fur in winter but are somewhat naked in summer, whereas the soles of the ermine are densely furred during both summer and winter. When comparing the size of the two species, their sexes must be taken into account; the female *M. frenata*, an average of 25 percent smaller than the male, is about the same size as a large male ermine.

Ecology

The long-tailed weasel is widespread in Pennsylvania, living in a diversity of habitats ranging from mature forests and woodlands to marshes and farmlands. In the state, *M. frenata* is most abundant along forest edges and farm woodlands that support a dense cover of briars and thickets close to streams or ponds. This adaptable mustelid will live near human habitation as long as abundant prey and suitable den sites are available.

Like the ermine, the long-tailed weasel is highly carnivorous and shows a distinct preference for small mammals, which make up about 95 percent of its diet. Meadow voles, white-footed mice, cottontail rabbits, chipmunks, shrews, squirrels, and moles are a few items on its menu. This mustelid also eats birds, reptiles, insects, and carrion. It is reported to consume 40 percent or more of its weight in food per day.

A swift, agile hunter, the long-tailed weasel uses its feet and sinuous body to hold down its prey. It then kills the victim by inflicting a rapid bite to the base of the skull or by severing the jugular vein with its sharp teeth. It first consumes the brain, then moves on to the heart, lungs, and, ultimately, the entire body, including most bones and fur. *Mustela frenata* does not suck blood but commonly laps fresh blood seeping from the rear of the victim's skull. During feeding, drowsiness may set in, and the weasel may take a brief midmeal snooze.

Mustela frenata allegedly kills more prey than it can eat at a given time. For example, it is known to enter poultry houses and kill many chickens; on the other hand, it may also reside close to such houses and never disturb a single bird. The long-tailed weasel also does not always consume its entire prey on the spot but may choose to move it to a burrow. In addition, it caches large prey. These activities lead to the belief that the weasel is ruthless and simply kills for the fun

of it; such is not the case. Food taken to the burrow may be fed to young, and large, cached carcasses provide meals for several days.

Despite its fierceness, the long-tailed weasel is beset with many enemies. It is preyed upon by raptorial birds such as great-horned and barred owls, goshawks, and rough-legged, broad-winged, and red-tailed hawks. Among carnivorous mammals, red and gray foxes, coyotes, bobcats, and domestic cats kill *M. frenata*, although they seldom eat it because of its strong, musky odor and presumably offensive taste. Snakes such as copperheads, rattlesnakes, and black rat snakes are reported to eat long-tailed weasels. Automobiles also take a toll on *M. frenata*, and some animals occasionally meet their demise as a result of an encounter with a porcupine.

External parasites including fleas, lice, mites, chiggers, and ticks infest the long-tailed weasel. Internal parasites are tapeworms, flukes, and an abundance of roundworms. The nasal nematode, also known to infect other mustelids, invades the nasal sinuses of *M. frenata*, exerting pressure on the brain, thus resulting in convulsions and possibly death. *Mustela frenata* harbors canine distemper and tularemia, both of which probably play an important role in the population biology of the long-tailed weasel.

Behavior

The long-tailed weasel is active year-round, foraging mainly during darkness, although it sometimes hunts during daylight. In winter, it commonly weaves, undetected, within the subnivean environment in search of mice, voles, and shrews. Its presence is evidenced by its tracks in the snow. Its gait is characterized by a bounding lope with an arched back; upon coming down, its hindfeet land nearly in the tracks left by the forefeet. Although *M. frenata* is an agile climber and swims well, it spends most of its time on the ground.

The home of *M. frenata* can be found in ground burrows, under stumps, or beneath rock piles. This weasel does not usually excavate its own burrows but commonly uses those abandoned by chipmunks. The nest chamber is located about 60 centimeters (2 ft.) from the burrow entrance and measures some 22 to 30 centimeters (9–12 in.) in diameter. It is lined with dried grasses and the fur of victims, and remnants of bones and skins of prey may litter the burrow. The long-tailed weasel defecates both in the nest and outside the burrow entrance.

With well-developed anal scent glands, *M. frenata* produces a musky, pungent odor. Unlike skunks, it does not spray its musk but drags and rubs its body over surfaces, presumably leaving its scent. This odor probably serves to identify individuals and delimits territories. Except during breeding and while young are being reared, the long-tailed weasel leads a solitary life.

The long-tailed weasel has acute senses of sight, smell, and hearing. Its vocalizations include purrs of contentment and squeals, hisses, and screeches proclaiming annoyance or pain. When irritated, it commonly stomps its feet.

Reproduction and Development

Mating takes place in July or August, with implantation of the fertilized egg on the uterine wall delayed until about March. The entire gestation period is about 10 months, with actual embryonic development occurring only during the last four weeks of this period. The adaptive significance of this behavior is to time the arrival of the young to that season when hunting is easiest, namely spring when small mammals are plentiful.

A single litter of five to eight young is born in April or May. Newborns are pink, sparsely haired, and blind. They weigh only 3 grams (0.1 oz.), about the weight of a hummingbird. Growth is rapid; by three weeks they are well furred, can crawl outside the nest, and even feed on meat supplied by both parents. Pups weigh between 21 and 27 grams (0.7–1 oz.) at this time. At five weeks of age, their eyes open, they are rather rambunctious and vocal, and weaning is under way. A week later, the young emerge from the nest and accompany the female on hunting trips. By autumn, young are full grown and the family disbands. Females breed when three to four months old, whereas males reach sexual maturity at about 15 to 18 months of age.

Mink

SCIENTIFIC NAME
Mustela vison (*Mustela* is Latin for "weasel." The derivation of *vison* is uncertain. It is either from the Icelandic or Swedish word *vison*, meaning "a kind of weasel," or from the Latin word *visor*, meaning "scout." The common name is derived from the Swedish word *maenk*.)

SUBSPECIES IN PENNSYLVANIA
Mustela vison mink; Mustela vison vison

ALSO CALLED
Vison, common mink, woods mink, water weasel, least otter

TOTAL LENGTH
460–684 mm (17.9–26.7 in.)

LENGTH OF TAIL
155–235 mm (6.0–9.2 in.)

WEIGHT
520–723 g (1.1–1.7 lbs.)

MAMMAE
Three pairs

POPULATION DENSITY
1–8/km² (3–21/mi.²)

HOME RANGE
8–125 ha (20–309 acres)

LONGEVITY
3–6 yrs. in the wild; 8–12 yrs. in captivity

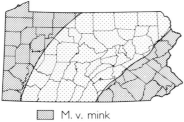

M. v. mink
M. v. vison

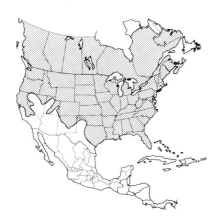

Description

Like other weasels (*Mustela*), the mink has a small, flattened head and short, sturdy legs. Even the dentition and skull of the mink are similar to those of other weasels, except for being larger. What best distinguishes *M. vison* from its cousins are its larger body size, uniform coloration, long bushy tail, and aquatic habits.

The mink is probably best known for its luxuriant, chocolate brown fur coat with white patches on the chin and throat. Thick, soft, and glossy—mink fur consists of a dense, wooly underfur overlaid by long, coarse, shiny guard hairs. Overlapping scales along the shaft of each guard hair cause light to be reflected, thereby enhancing the pelage. Juveniles, with few guard hairs, are a little

Mink (*Mustela vison*).
Photo by James F. Parnell.

paler than adults. By virtue of the water-repellent quality of its fur, *M. vison* is well adapted for an aquatic life. Its short, rounded ears and partially webbed toes further enhance its amphibious life-style.

The spring molt of *M. vison* commences in late March and produces summer pelage by mid- to late July. The autumn molt begins in late August or early September and produces the prime winter coat by late November or early December. In contrast with weasels, the mink does not turn white in winter; an occasional albino individual, however, may be found in the wild. Males are appreciably larger than females.

Ecology

Widespread throughout Pennsylvania, the mink ranges from tidal flats of the Delaware River in the east to mountain ridges of Somerset County in the west. It seldom wanders far from water and is most abundant along the banks of streams and rivers or the marshy shorelines of ponds and lakes. There, *M. vison* finds suitable brushy or rocky cover for shelter and adequate food resources, especially a healthy population of muskrats.

Mustela vison feeds on a varied carnivorous diet governed by seasonal availability. During summer, crayfish top the menu, followed by muskrats, frogs, fish, snakes, small mammals, and waterfowl, especially flightless young and molting adults. During winter, muskrats are a staple. Because *M. vison* spends more time foraging away from water at this time, it also commonly feasts on small mammals such as voles, mice, shrews, cottontails, and, occasionally, squirrels.

A skillful and dedicated hunter with poor senses of sight and hearing, the mink relies on its keen sense of smell to locate prey. Its killing tactics are similar to those of other weasels: It inflicts a series of deadly bites to the neck and base of the skull. If the mink kills more prey than it can consume on the spot, it carries the victim by the neck to a den and stores the carcass for winter. Such caches may be quite large; one biologist reported a cache containing over a dozen muskrats, two mallard ducks, and an American coot (Yeager, 1943).

Great horned owls, foxes, coyotes, and bobcats occasionally prey on the mink. With its pelt netting about $13 each in Pennsylvania, the principal predators of *M. vison* are humans. During 1982–1983, nearly 4,500 minks were harvested for their pelts in the state, even though mink ranching accounts for most fur sold commercially. Trapping undoubtedly takes a toll on minks each year, as do natural predators and disease. Even greater mortality results from habitat destruction by stream channelization, drainage of wetlands, and dam construction in the Commonwealth.

Mustela vison harbors many ec-toparasites such as fleas, lice, mites, chiggers, and ticks. Internally, the mink is infested with roundworms, flukes, tapeworms, spiny-headed worms, and several protozoans. As with other mustelids, the nasal nematode occurs in *M. vison*. Minks residing in "fur farms" are known to harbor a great many diseases, but only tularemia and canine distemper are reported for wild populations. Because residues of environmental pollutants such as DDT and polychlorinated biphenyls (PCBs) are concentrated in aquatic food chains, the mink as a secondary or tertiary consumer is highly vulnerable to poisoning by such toxic chemicals.

Behavior

The mink is active year-round, foraging principally during hours of darkness, with major bursts of activity near dawn and dusk. It may become inactive during winter but, like other weasels, does not hibernate or undergo torpidity. Its presence is evidenced by tracks easily identified in mud along stream banks or in fresh snow. Like river otters, the mink has been observed sliding down snow-covered slopes on its belly.

The mink is not as agile or speedy on land as its weasel cousins. Its gait is characterized by a series of bounds. But like its cousins, the mink has an extremely flexible backbone which permits it to arch its back greatly while in the air between bounds. A proficient swimmer, *M. vison* is able to swim underwater for distances of up to 30 meters (100 ft.) and dive to depths of nearly 6 meters (20 ft.).

Mustela vison is solitary and rather unsocial except during breeding and when rearing young. An individual establishes its territory along streams or ponds and delimits its territory by spraying rocks, logs, and other objects with an acrid-smelling musk, particularly strong during the breeding season, produced by prominent anal glands. It also scent marks its domain by "anal dragging," which spreads the highly odorous substance, or by depositing feces coated with the musky secretions. The cylindrical and sometimes segmented scats of *M. vison* measure about 12 to 15 centimeters (5–6 in.) long and may contain bits of crayfish, muskrat bones, and its victims' fur.

When irritated, excited, or injured, a mink commonly expels its pervasive odor, which may be as obnoxious as the well-known aroma of the skunk. When alarmed, the mink may hiss or snarl, whereas it purrs when content. Other vocalizations include grunts, growls, and barks.

The mink constructs dens along banks of streams or ponds, under stumps or logs, or in rock piles, or commonly appropriates abandoned muskrat houses. Dens typically are located some 30 to 90 centimeters (1–3 ft.) below ground and are marked by one to several burrow entrances of 10 to 15 centimeters (4–6 in.) in diameter located near a shoreline. The burrow itself may be quite long, up to 3.5 meters (12 ft.). An enlargement of the burrow forms the nesting chamber, which is about 30 centimeters (1 ft.) in diameter and lined with dry grasses, leaves, feathers, and fur of victims. A mink family may use many dens; one study reported 20 different dens for a single family in an area of 31 hectares (77 acres) (Schlandweiler and Storm, 1969).

Reproduction and Development

In Pennsylvania, *M. vison* breeds between February and March. At this time, males travel long distances in search of females in heat, and more than one male may mate with a single female. As in the ermine and long-tailed weasel, delayed implantation of the early embryo on the uterine wall occurs in the mink. Consequently, a gestation period of 40 to 75 days is common, but only about one month of that time is devoted to embryonic growth. Although females are polyestrous, only a single litter is born each year, usually in April or May. Litter size varies from four to nine, averaging about five young.

Kits are born naked, blind, and pink. They weigh about 8 grams (0.3 oz.) and measure about 87.5 millimeters (3.5 in.) long. They quickly develop a coat of fine, short, whitish hair. About three weeks after birth, their eyes open and they are covered with short, reddish gray fur. At the age of five to six weeks, weaning begins. Both parents assist in rearing the young by bringing fresh food to the natal nest. On land, parents commonly carry their young by the scruff of the neck; in water the youngsters often ride on their parents' backs. By eight weeks of age, the kits accompany adults on foraging trips and can practice stalking and pouncing on prey. In autumn, the family disbands, and the young are on their own. By 10 months of age, they are usually sexually mature.

Eastern Spotted Skunk

SCIENTIFIC NAME
Spilogale putorius (*Spilogale* is
derived from two Greek words
meaning "spotted weasel";
putorius is from the Latin word
putor, meaning "a stench.")

SUBSPECIES IN PENNSYLVANIA
Spilogale putorius putorius

ALSO CALLED
Spotted skunk, polecat, civet cat,
civet, hydrophobia skunk, weasel
skunk

TOTAL LENGTH
400–550 mm (15.6–21.5 in.)

LENGTH OF TAIL
180–220 mm (7–8.6 in.)

WEIGHT
475–1,250 g (1–2.7 lbs.)

MAMMAE
Four pairs

POPULATION DENSITY
2–9/km² (5–23/mi.²)

HOME RANGE
10–300 ha (25–741 acres)

LONGEVITY
4–5 yrs. in the wild; up to 10 yrs.
in captivity

STATUS IN PENNSYLVANIA
Vulnerable

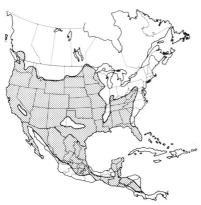

Description

The eastern spotted skunk has a
small head; short, stubby legs; a
long, bushy tail tipped with white;
and small, black, beady eyes that
shine a pale amber color at night.
Its jet black coat is marked by a
triangular white spot on the forehead and a unique pattern of
broken white stripes along the
back and sides. *Spilogale putorius*
was aptly described as a "little ani-
mated checkerboard" by Ernest
Thompson Seton, a renowned
turn-of-the-century naturalist, author, and artist (Jones et al., 1983).
This "checkerboard" coloration
readily distinguishes the spotted
skunk from the larger striped
skunk. Further, the pelage of the
spotted skunk is long and soft,
whereas the striped skunk has
coarse fur.

The sexes are colored alike, and
males are slightly larger than fe-

Eastern spotted skunk (*Spilogale putorius*).
Photo by John R. MacGregor.

males. The toes of *S. putorius* are slightly webbed, and this skunk employs a flat-footed (plantigrade) stance. As with most other Pennsylvania mustelids, the spotted skunk undergoes two annual molts, in spring and autumn.

Ecology

Pennsylvania represents the northeastern-most limit of the distribution of the spotted skunk in North America. In the Commonwealth, *S. putorius* is known to reside in only three southcentral counties: Bedford, Fulton, and Franklin. There, the species is most abundant in dry, rocky, montane forests characterized by the presence of oak, pitch pine, and Virginia pine. In nearby Maryland, the eastern spotted skunk resides in more diverse ecological communities such as forests of oak,

hickory, locust, and pine marked by dense tangles of wild grape.

The food habits of the eastern spotted skunk, an avid mouser, correspond closely to those of many of the weasels. During winter, small mammals may contribute up to 90 percent of its diet, with rabbits, voles, and mice predominating. Other winter foods include insects and carrion. During summer, the menu of the spotted skunk consists mainly of insects, especially ground beetles, crickets, and grasshoppers. Fruits, mice, frogs, crayfish, lizards, birds' eggs, and assorted invertebrates also are eaten at this time. The autumn menu reflects a shift to fleshy fruits and small mammals, as dictated by availability.

Spilogale putorius falls prey to great horned and barred owls, redtailed hawks, foxes, and domestic cats and dogs. Fur trappers periodically harvest spotted skunks even though their market value is rather low. Most trapping of *S. putorius* is accidental, with skunks being captured in traps set for more valuable furbearers. Spotted skunks are also killed on Pennsylvania highways.

The eastern spotted skunk harbors ectoparasites such as fleas, lice, mites, and ticks. Internal parasites include roundworms, tapeworms, flukes, and spiny-headed worms. Nasal roundworms infest the nasal sinuses of *S. putorius*, exerting pressure on the brain and, thus, resulting in convulsions and possibly death. Although no cases of rabies are known from Pennsylvania, the eastern spotted skunk is highly susceptible to this virus, hence, the vernacular name *hydrophobia skunk*. The spotted skunk is also known to host diseases such as canine distemper, tularemia, Q fever, and listeriosis.

Behavior

The eastern spotted skunk is nocturnal and active throughout the year. It does not hibernate or undergo torpidity but is known to exhibit short bouts of inactivity or "winter sleep" during severe cold spells. Although generally solitary, *S. putorius* may be found nesting communally in groups of up to three or more individuals during these cold spells or during the breeding season.

Spilogale putorius establishes its dens along fencerows, hollow logs, woodpiles, foundations of deserted outbuildings or in rock crevices. It commonly digs its own burrows but may use burrows abandoned by woodchucks. Dens, containing a nest chamber lined with dried grasses, do not appear to have a specific ownership; rather, they are shared property of a local population, although females with young have exclusive use during rearing.

The locomotion of the eastern spotted skunk is characterized by a flat-footed, bounding gait. Not very fast on foot, *S. putorius* reaches speeds of only about 7.5 kilometers per hour (4.5 mi./hr.). But this skunk is adept at climbing trees and commonly does so when escaping predators such as dogs and humans.

When threatened, the spotted skunk exhibits a unique and highly effective defense behavior. Initially, the skunk gives its intruder a warning: It displays an upright tail, erect hairs, and arched back, and even stomps its feet. These actions may be accompanied by growls, snarls, or hisses. Next, it employs some fancy acrobatics; it does a "handstand" on its forefeet. At this point, most predators retreat. Those that do not are quickly "educated." *Spilogale putorius* quickly drops to all fours, turns its body in a U-shaped position, with head and tail facing the intruder, takes aim, and sprays musk in the victim's face. Discharged from scent glands in the anus, the musk fluid resembles skim milk mixed with small white curds. With the active ingredient of mercaptan, a compound containing sulfur, the strongly acidic spray is quite nauseating and may cause momentary blindness.

Reproduction and Development

The eastern spotted skunk breeds during March and April in Pennsylvania. As with many mustelids, implantation of the fertilized egg is delayed, thus producing a gestation period of about 50 to 65 days. A litter of from four to nine young, usually five, is born in June. In Pennsylvania, only one litter is produced each year.

Newborn spotted skunks are naked and blind, measure about 100 millimeters (4 in.) long, and weigh some 9.5 grams (0.3 oz.). At birth, their distinctive black-and-white color pattern is evident. At three weeks of age, they are well furred; in less than two more weeks, their eyes open and tiny teeth protrude through the gums. The kits can now walk, although rather clumsily. When about six weeks old, they can lift their tail in the typical warning gesture and spray musk. Weaning occurs when the young are eight weeks old, at which time they are about half grown. They attain adult size between three and four months of age, and soon disperse from the natal nest for an independent life. Adult males do not assist in the care of the young. Male and female young are capable of breeding in the first year of their life.

Status in Pennsylvania

As aforementioned, the eastern spotted skunk is reported from only the southcentral portion of Pennsylvania where it exhibits low population densities. There, this skunk is potentially vulnerable to overexploitation because many specimens are captured in traps set for other more commercially valuable furbearers. Because of its low numbers and the accidental but unavoidable mortality induced by fur trappers, the Pennsylvania Biological Survey assigned the status of "vulnerable" to *S. putorius* in its report *Species of Special Concern in Pennsylvania* (Genoways and Brenner, 1985). Short of localized prohibition of trapping, little can be done to alleviate the dilemma of accidentally trapping a spotted skunk. The Survey, therefore, recommends that spotted skunks killed in traps be delivered to appropriate scientific institutions or state agencies. Information gained from these specimens will at least aid scientists in understanding the distribution and population biology of *S. putorius* in Pennsylvania.

Striped Skunk

SCIENTIFIC NAME
Mephitis mephitis (*Mephitis* is
from the Latin word *mephit,*
meaning "bad odor.")

SUBSPECIES IN PENNSYLVANIA
Mephitis mephitis nigra

ALSO CALLED
Skunk, polecat, lined skunk, wood
pussy

TOTAL LENGTH
539–665 mm (21–26 in.)

LENGTH OF TAIL
184–287 mm (7.2–11.2 in.)

WEIGHT
1.1–3.4 kg (2.4–7.5 lbs.)

MAMMAE
Six pairs

POPULATION DENSITY
1–9/km² (2–50/mi.²)

HOME RANGE
100–500 ha (247–1,235 acres)

LONGEVITY
2–4 yrs. in the wild; up to 10 yrs.
in captivity

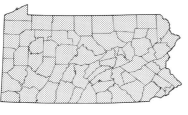

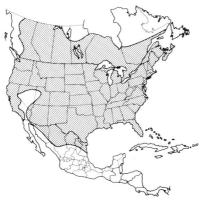

Description

The striped skunk's distinctive
smell and unique color pattern
make for easy identification of
this mammal of house cat size. Its
unique coloration consists of long
black fur marked by two prominent dorsal stripes meeting in a
cap on the head and shoulders.
Coarser than that of the spotted
skunk, the pelage is composed of
wooly underfur overlaid by shiny
guard hairs. Color variations include brown, white, cream, black,
and, occasionally, albino. During
April through late September or
early October, *M. mephitis* undergoes an annual molt, with the
prime pelt being produced during
midwinter. Sexes are colored
alike.

The head of the striped skunk,
which is small and triangular, is
equipped with short ears and
black, beady eyes which exhibit a
deep amber eyeshine at night. Its
tail is long and bushy, usually
with a white tip. The legs of *M.*

Striped skunk (*Mephitis mephitis*).

mephitis are short and stout, with each foot having five slightly webbed toes; the forefeet have long, curved claws evolved for digging, whereas the hindfeet have shorter, straighter claws. *Mephitis mephitis* employs a flat-footed (plantigrade) stance, and its foot pads are naked. Males are somewhat larger than females.

Ecology

Highly adaptable, the striped skunk occupies a wide variety of habitats in Pennsylvania—from montane forests to grassy meadows, cultivated land, and even suburban backyards. It is most abundant in farming areas where it prefers brushy, disturbed habitats such as fencerows, forest edges, and old fields supporting abundant food and suitable shelter.

Mephitis mephitis is omnivorous but exhibits dietary shifts reflecting seasonal availability of prey. During warm months, the striped skunk feeds mainly on insects such as grasshoppers, crickets, and beetles and their grubs. This mustelid is also fond of wasps and bees and commonly raids beehives or excavates yellow jacket nests with its strong front claws. Apparently, the skunk is not harmed by bee stings; individuals captured near hives have had many stings on the body, tongue, and even in the mouth. During autumn, the striped skunk is known to consume fruits and berries including blackberry, black cherry, blueberry, raspberry, and persimmon, in addition to grasses, roots, nuts, grains, and other assorted vegetation. Its winter menu consists mostly of small mammals—namely mice, voles, shrews, chipmunks, and young rabbits—which it captures and subdues house cat style. Birds and their eggs are eaten only occasionally. The skunk eats eggs by carefully biting off one end and licking out the contents; remaining shells are left more or less intact. Other foods eaten, as available, include salamanders, lizards, crayfish, earthworms, clams, and carrion. Skunks are not opposed to eating garbage and regularly visit camp sites and cabins at night in search of food.

The striped skunk has few natural enemies. Great horned and barred owls, mercifully lacking a good sense of smell, pose a threat to the skunk. If close to starvation, a coyote, fox, or bobcat may indulge. Although domestic dogs occasionally kill striped skunks, especially near farms, they are most frequently the victims of poor timing and receive a strong dose of musk head on!

Humans—the principal predators of *M. mephitis*—commonly poison, trap, shoot, gas, or give antifertility drugs to the skunk because of its depredation on beehives or because it sets up housekeeping under a barn foundation near human habitation. *Mephitis mephitis* is also commonly caught by accident in traps set for more commercially valuable furbearers. Although its pelts bring a price of only about $1.50, its musk may be used as a perfume base once the odor is removed. Many skunks are also killed by farm machinery and by automobiles in Pennsylvania, especially during autumn when the young are dispersing from the natal nest. The high mortality is due principally to the skunk's slow, ambling gait, coupled with its affinity for brushy roadside habitats.

The striped skunk hosts an abundance of parasites, perhaps because it lives in burrows and eats carrion. Ectoparasites include fleas, lice, mites, chiggers, and ticks. *Mephitis mephitis* also is known to host botfly larvae. Internal parasites include tapeworms, flukes, roundworms, and spiny-headed worms. Like other mustelids, the striped skunk harbors nematodes in the nasal sinuses, which exert pressure on the brain causing seizures and sometimes death. Several protozoans are known to infest *M. mephitis*. In addition, the species harbors canine distemper, tularemia, typhus, and a variety of other diseases. The striped skunk is the leading carrier of rabies in Pennsylvania and in the United States.

Behavior

The striped skunk is principally nocturnal. During autumn, it accumulates large quantities of body fat and becomes less active as cold weather approaches. Although the skunk does not hibernate, it dens up, sleeps, and lives off its accumulated fat during severe winter weather. On warm winter days, it arouses periodically and forages, as evidenced by tracks in the snow. Although the periods of "winter sleep" are generally brief and sporadic, one group of skunks is known to have remained in an underground burrow for almost four months. Up to 15 striped skunks are reported to nest communally in a single den.

Mephitis mephitis is terrestrial, rarely climbs, and is not especially fond of water. It typically progresses with a slow, ambling walk but can gallop at speeds of up to 16.5 kilometers per hour (10 mi./ hr.), if necessary. Nonaggressive and generally passive, the striped skunk appears oblivious of other skunks and animals. Its senses of sight, hearing, and smell are poorly developed, but its touch receptors are acute. The striped skunk is generally silent but occasionally grunts, growls, snarls, squeals, screeches, hisses, or twitters like a bird.

Although rather small in stature and quite timid, the striped skunk in Pennsylvania probably ranks second only to the black bear in its ability to command respect from humankind. Its talent for discharging musk effectively is the key to its successful intimidation. The yellowish, oily, nauseating, sulfur-alcohol compound is secreted from two anal scent glands. Each gland—containing about one tablespoon of musk, sufficient for up to six blasts—has a nipple-like outlet. When the tail is down, the nipples are hidden; once the tail is raised, the anus relaxes, the nipples protrude, and musk is released. The spray can cause nausea and momentary blindness if directed into the face or eyes. Most mammalogists agree that a skunk cannot easily expel musk if held in the air by its tail or if the tail is compressed tightly over the anus. There are no guarantees, however, and experimenta-

tion with techniques is not recommended for the novice.

If provoked, *M. mephitis* first turns and runs. If pursued, it elevates the tail, arches its back, and stomps its feet. As a last resort, the skunk quickly turns its body in a U-shaped position with head and tail facing the intruder, takes aim, and sprays. The musk is discharged as atomized spray or hits the target as a stream of rain-sized droplets. A top-notch marksman, the striped skunk is able to direct accurately the stream of musk up to 3 meters (10 ft.), and the smell may carry up to 2.5 kilometers (1.5 mi.) down wind.

Many antidotes are prescribed for ridding clothes and bodies of skunk scent. Although burning clothes sprayed with skunk musk is the most expeditious way of coping with the smell, washing them with ammonia may also eliminate the problem. Dogs or humans may require a thorough bath with tomato juice or vinegar to neutralize the scent. It may also be wise to keep a victimized pet in solitary confinement for several days.

The striped skunk usually resides in subsurface dens it digs itself or remodels from abandoned burrows of woodchucks, foxes, or other animals. During spring and summer, the striped skunk may also live beneath rock piles or in brush piles, hollow logs, or abandoned buildings. *Mephitis mephitis* seems to prefer to build its den on sunny, sloping terrain. Entrances are usually well hidden and number one to five, measuring some 20 centimeters (8 in.) in diameter. Burrows are typically 1.8

to 6 meters (6–20 ft.) long and reach some 1 to 1.2 meters (3–4 ft.) below ground where they meet, forming one to three chambers. These nest chambers are spherical, 30 to 38 centimeters (12–15 in.) in diameter, and lined with up to a bushel of dried leaves and grasses. During cold weather, the nest material may be used to plug entrances.

Reproduction and Development

The striped skunk is polygamous and typically breeds once per year. From mid-February to early March, females undergo a four- to five-day period of heat, during which time they may mate with several males. The male wanders from den to den in search of a receptive female. To mate, the male grasps the female by the neck with his teeth and assumes a rear mount position. Following a gestation period of about 63 days, a litter of four to six young is born in April or May.

At birth, kits are blind and wrinkled and have a sparse covering of hair. They weigh about 32 to 35 grams (1–1.2 oz.), measure some 138 millimeters (5.5 in.) long, and have the characteristic black-and-white color markings and well-developed front claws. The young are fully furred at two weeks of age; in another week, their eyes open and they can assume a defensive posture and even discharge a small amount of musk. Highly solicitous of her young, the mother carries them about the nest in her mouth and cleans them regularly. Weaning occurs between the ages of six and eight weeks, at which time tiny teeth penetrate the gums. Kits now follow the mother on evening hunting excursions. These family outings are rather comical, with the mother and kits marching single file through the woods in a formation similar to that of a brood of baby ducks. During late summer, family ties become loose. Some kits remain with the mother until spring, whereas others opt for independence and disperse from the natal nest. Young are capable of breeding in the spring following their birth.

River Otter

SCIENTIFIC NAME
Lutra canadensis (*Lutra* is Latin for "otter"; *canadensis* is Latin for "of Canada," the country where the first specimen was collected.)

SUBSPECIES IN PENNSYLVANIA
Lutra canadensis lataxina

ALSO CALLED
Northern river otter, Canadian otter, land otter; fish otter

TOTAL LENGTH
900−1,200 mm (35.1−46.8 in.)

LENGTH OF TAIL
300−450 mm (11.7−17.6 in.)

WEIGHT
5−11 kg (11−24.3 lbs.)

MAMMAE
Three pairs

POPULATION DENSITY
Up to 2/km² (up to 5/mi.²)

HOME RANGE
Linear; along watercourses: 3−42 km (1.3−26 mi.)

LONGEVITY
8−10 yrs in the wild; 15−20 yrs. in captivity

STATUS IN PENNSYLVANIA
Vulnerable

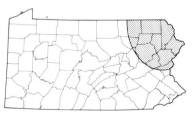

Description

With its torpedo-shaped, muscular body; short, stocky legs; long, tapered tail; and rich brown fur, *L. canadensis* can be confused with no other Pennsylvania mammal. Its dark brown upperparts appear nearly black when wet, and its underparts range from pale brown to gray. Long whiskers, extremely sensitive to touch, frame the otter's whitish muzzle. Juveniles are similar in color to adults, and the annual molts take place in spring and autumn. Although rare in the wild, color variations such as black, white, slate, and albino are known to occur. Males are slightly larger than females.

The river otter is superbly adapted for aquatic life. Its coat— composed of thick, oily underfur overlaid by long, glistening guard hairs—is nearly impervious to

River otter (*Lutra canadensis*).
Photo by A. Woolf.

water. Its muscular tail provides propulsion, while large, webbed paws act as swim fins. When submerged, *L. canadensis* can close its small, valvular ears and nose. Even the placement of its eyes is an adaptation to its amphibious life: Because the eyes are near the top of its broad, flattened head, this mustelid can see above water while it skims kayak-like along the surface.

Lutra canadensis is the only Pennsylvania carnivore with five cheekteeth on each side of both the upper and lower jaws. Its total number of teeth equals 36—more than any other mustelid in the state.

Ecology

In Pennsylvania, the river otter resides only in the Pocono Plateau region of the northeastern corner of the state. Here, this water-loving mustelid lives along rivers and streams in rather isolated, forested habitats.

Lutra canadensis is mainly carnivorous; its menu varies with habitat and seasonal availability of prey. As its mainstay, the otter relies on fish and crayfish. It also feasts on frogs, salamanders, snails, snakes, muskrats, earthworms, and larvae of aquatic invertebrates. Fish consumed are mainly nongame species such as minnows, carp, and suckers. Panfish and game fish such as sunfish and trout represent only a small portion of its diet.

In water, *L. canadensis* captures prey with its mouth. Small prey is consumed as the otter floats on its back, whereas large prey is carried to land. When devouring a victim, *L. canadensis* eats the head first, then the body; it normally discards the tail fins of fish. Occasionally, the otter hunts on land, guided by its well-developed sense of smell. Here, quarry in the form of birds, rodents, and rabbits round out the menu. Carrion is also included in the diet of the river otter.

Coyotes, domestic dogs, foxes, and great horned owls occasionally kill an unwary kit or possibly even an adult river otter, but natural predators exert a minimal impact on otter populations. Humans, on the other hand, greatly diminish the numbers of otters. In the past, trapping aimed at procuring the otter's beautiful, durable fur decimated large populations. In 1954, trapping of *L. canadensis* was prohibited in Pennsylvania. Today, mortality results from habitat destruction in the form of channelization of rivers, dam construction, increased groundwater acidity because of mining operations, and drainage of wetlands. Further, like the mink, *L. canadensis* is a primary consumer in the aquatic food web and, thus, is highly susceptible to poisoning by toxic chemicals. Tragically, residues of pesticides and toxic substances such as DDT, polychlorinated biphenyls (PCBs), and mercury are known to be concentrated in its tissue.

The river otter hosts a wide variety of parasites including ticks, flukes, tapeworms, spiny-headed worms, and numerous roundworms. Several of the roundworms may cause serious pathological damage, leading to a reduction in the numbers of otters in certain localities. As with other mustelids, the nasal roundworm infests the frontal sinuses of *L.*

canadensis, causing pressure to the brain and resulting in seizures and possibly death. The river otter is also susceptible to rabies, canine distemper, hepatitis, pneumonia, tuberculosis, and perhaps feline panleucopenia.

Behavior

Lutra canadensis is active year-round. Although foraging usually is confined to hours of darkness, it may be seen hunting or playing during the day.

The river otter is a strong, graceful swimmer. It moves by alternating hindlimb paddling with gliding. Its forelimbs are used mainly in turning maneuvers, while the tail acts as a rudder. When pursuing aquatic prey, the otter accomplishes maximum speed by rapidly moving the lower body and tail in a vertical direction. It can attain a swimming speed of up to 11 kilometers per hour (7 mi./hr.) and is known to outswim a trout in open water. Its endurance is also impressive; *L. canadensis* can swim up to 420 meters (0.3 mi.) underwater, remaining submerged for some eight minutes. Further, it can dive to depths of 13.5 meters (44.5 ft.).

Although a topnotch swimmer, the otter is rather slow on land, its movements characterized by an ungainly, loping gait, hindered no doubt by its short legs. *Lutra canadensis* compensates for this lack of speed on foot by excelling in the sport of "tobogganing"! Snow banks ending in drifts and stream banks emptying into deep pools set the stage for this amusing activity. Following a leaping take off, the otter slides headfirst on its chest and belly while holding its feet against the body. Several otters may join in the game, which is marked by antics of tumbling, chasing, and wrestling. Slides may be more than 7.5 meters (25 ft.) long, and the furrow-like trails measure some 20 centimeters (8 in.) in diameter. During "tobogganing," the otter commonly reaches speeds of up to 30 kilometers per hour (18.5 mi./hr.).

In contrast to its cousins the weasel and mink, the river otter is quite sociable and lives in family groups year-round. It is not highly vocal but is known to emit sounds such as grunts, snarls, and chuckles. Loud screams are common and act as distress calls heard over long distances. When foraging together, an otter family communicates by way of bird-like chirpings. Contentment is expressed by purring. Although generally playful and amiable, *L. canadensis* can be a fierce fighter, especially during the breeding season when females are known to make loud, howling noises.

The river otter customarily builds its home in bank dens close to streams, lakes, or ponds. It also nests under roots of large trees, beneath piles of rocks, or in abandoned beaver or muskrat houses. Bank dens often have entrances opening underwater and then sloping upward into the bank. The nest chamber, high above water, is commonly lined with sticks, grass, and leaves.

Reproduction and Development

Little is known of the reproductive biology of *L. canadensis* in Pennsylvania. In New York, the river otter is reported to breed in March or April, at which time males follow females in heat and commonly fight vigorously among themselves for mating rights. Copulation normally occurs in the water and lasts for about 15 to 25 minutes. The male mounts the female from the rear and holds on by the scruff of her neck. Implantation of the egg on the uterine wall is delayed for up to 9½ to 12½ months. Actual embryonic development is estimated to be only about 50 days. Kits are born in late winter or early spring, and females breed again while nursing their litter.

A river otter litter consists of one to five (typically three) kits. Newborns are blind and fully furred and have well-formed claws. At birth, they weigh about 130 grams (4.5 oz.) and measure some 275 millimeters (11 in.) long, slightly larger than an eastern chipmunk. Development is slow, and they are helpless for the first six weeks of life. At the age of about five weeks, their eyes open. Although the adult male may be nearby, he is usually excluded from the natal nest by the female until the young are several months old.

Kits emerge from the nest when they are about 10 to 12 weeks old. Swimming trials, attended by both parents, occur when the kits reach about 14 weeks of age. The learning process is slow; parents carry the young on their backs in the water and gradually coax them to swim. When the kits are stubborn and reluctant to swim, their parents may drag them into the water.

Weaning begins at 16 weeks of age. The kits remain with the parents in the natal den during the first winter but disperse in spring. Females usually breed for the first time when they are two years old, whereas males may not breed successfully until the age of six years.

Status in Pennsylvania

Little is known of the life history and ecology of *L. canadensis* in Pennsylvania. This fact, coupled with its restricted geographic distribution, has prompted the Pennsylvania Biological Survey to assign it the status of "vulnerable" in its report *Species of Special Concern in Pennsylvania* (Genoways and Brenner, 1985). To delimit the status of the river otter in Pennsylvania with respect to its present distribution, population structure, and habitat requirements, the Survey recommends initiation of a state-wide research program. Moreover, an effort must be made to improve the quality of aquatic habitats in the Commonwealth suitable for occupancy by this unique mustelid.

Cats

Family Felidae

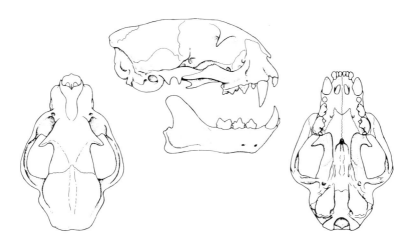

Skull of a felid (*Felis*, × ¼).

The Felidae are the most highly specialized group of carnivores. Members range in size from the tiny black-footed cat of the African steppe and savanna, weighing between 1 and 2 kilograms (2.2–4.4 lbs.), to the massive Siberian tiger, weighing up to 384 kilograms (845 lbs.) and measuring over 3.5 meters (11.5 ft.) long. The family is first known from the late Eocene Epoch of North America and Europe, some 38 million years ago. Four genera and 37 species occurring in all continents except Australia and Antarctica represent Felidae today.

Felids are typically separated into two basic groups. The big cats include lions, tigers, leopards, jaguars, and the cheetah, a total of seven species grouped within the genus *Panthera*. The genus *Felis*, consisting of the small cats—the lynx, bobcat, puma, ocelot, domestic cat, and many others—is quite diverse and comprises some 28 species. These two groups are distinguished by the presence in the big cats of a flexible cartilage at the base of the tongue which permits them to roar. Small cats—without the freedom of movement this cartilage allows—cannot roar; they purr instead.

Cats occur in many ecological settings, from deserts and tropical rain forests to the snow-covered coniferous forests of the Himalaya Mountains at elevations of up to 6,000 meters (19,700 ft.). Although they exhibit generalized habitat requirements, over 75 percent of all felid species are forest dwellers.

Like their habitat, the physical appearance of cats is quite variable. Soft and wooly, cats exhibit a basic color plan usually incorporating browns, grays, whites, blacks, golds, or yellows, patterned with dark circles, spots, rosettes, or stripes. They maintain their glossy appearance by frequent cleaning with their tongue and paws. They usually have long bodies and long, furred tails; exceptions are the lynx and the bobcat, which have short tails.

Highly carnivorous, most felids prey on any vertebrate they can overpower. Some species, such as the fishing cat, prefer fish and mollusks, and the flat-headed cat of southeastern Asia eats mainly fruit. But these are exceptions to the general rule of carnivorism.

Felids are highly adapted for capturing and consuming vertebrate prey. Their senses of smell and hearing are acute. Their eyes, larger than those of most carnivores, face forward, thus providing binocular vision and depth perception vital to locating prey. At night, their eyesight is six times more acute than that of humans. Also especially useful for foraging at night are their long, stiff, highly sensitive whiskers. Their long, sharp, usually retractile claws serve as effective meat hooks for capturing, slashing, and manipulating prey. For grasping prey, cats use their long, sharp canines, and they use their well-developed carnassials for shearing food. Finally, their tongue, covered with many sharply pointed papillae, is well suited for scraping meat from carcasses.

Since its stance is digitigrade, with five toes on the front foot and four on the back, the felid is highly adapted for cursorial locomotion, as exemplified by the cheetah—the fastest mammal, able to achieve speeds of up to 120 kilometers per hour (70 mi./hr.). All cats are adept climbers and readily climb trees when escaping predators. Hunting is done by stalking prey or lying in wait followed by a sudden rush and accurate pounce and bite. The combination of their well-furred feet and soft foot pads assists in their silent stalking of prey.

Most felids are nocturnal and solitary, usually intolerant of one another except during mating. Territories are marked with urine and feces as well as with tree scratches. The most gregarious species are the lions and cheetahs, commonly found in pairs or larger groups called prides.

Humans are the principal predators of cats. The lucrative trade of spotted skins, combined with trophy hunting, has resulted in bringing species such as the tiger, leopard, and ocelot near extinction. It is noteworthy that the pampered pussy cat—the most successful and widespread felid—is probably a descendant of the African wild cat domesticated in Egypt around 2,000 B.C.

Today, the only wild representative of the family Felidae residing in Pennsylvania is *Felis rufus*, the bobcat.

Bobcat

SCIENTIFIC NAME
Felis rufus (*Felis* is Latin for
"cat"; *rufus*, also Latin, means
"reddish.")

SUBSPECIES IN PENNSYLVANIA
Felis rufus rufus

ALSO CALLED
Wild cat, bay lynx, barred bobcat,
lynx cat

TOTAL LENGTH
710–1,200 mm (27.6–46.8 in.)

LENGTH OF TAIL
90–190 mm (3.5–7.4 in.)

WEIGHT
6–16 kg (13.2–35.2 lbs.)

MAMMAE
Two pairs

POPULATION DENSITY
Less than 2/km^2 (less than 5/mi.^{2})

HOME RANGE
500–15,600 ha (1,250–38,500
acres)

LONGEVITY
10–12 yrs. in the wild; 15–25 yrs.
in captivity

STATUS IN PENNSYLVANIA
Vulnerable

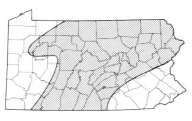

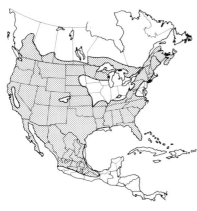

Description

The bobcat, the only wild felid in
Pennsylvania, might be mistaken
for a house cat at first glance. *Felis
rufus*, however, is about twice the
size of the average house cat and
has proportionally longer legs
equipped with well-furred paws.
Further, unlike the long-tailed
house cat, the bobcat has a short
tail with three to four brownish
black bars, the last of which is
broadest and darkest. The tip of
the tail and its underside are
white. Another distinguishing feature of the bobcat are its "sideburns"—characteristic ruffs of fur
from the ears down along the
sides of the cheeks.

The fur of *F. rufus* is short,
dense, and soft. Its underparts and
sides vary in color from yellowish
to reddish brown, often mixed
with a gray cast, streaked and

Bobcat (*Felis rufus*).

spotted with black. Two annual molts occur, in spring and autumn. The summer pelage is shorter and more reddish than the longer, grayer winter coat. Albino and melanistic (black) individuals occur occasionally in the wild. Although sexes are colored alike, males are slightly larger than females.

Felis rufus is digitigrade, that is, it walks on its toes, and has long, sharp, curved, retractile claws. Unlike its northern cousin the lynx, its foot pads lack fur. As in other cats, the tongue of the bobcat is generously equipped with small, rasping projections. Its eyes are prominent, and the pupils are elliptical when contracted in bright light, nearly round when dilated in dim light. Finally, the ears of *F. rufus* are pointed and marked by small tufts of black fur at the tips.

Ecology

The bobcat resides mainly in mountainous sections of Pennsylvania. Optimal habitats are woodlands interrupted by brushy thickets, old fields, and rocky outcrops. Strict isolation from human activity and the availability of prey and den sites are the key factors determining habitat selection.

Exclusively carnivorous, *F. rufus* feeds on a wide variety of prey. Rabbits top the menu and are joined by squirrels, chipmunks, mice, voles, woodchucks, birds such as grouse and turkey, frogs, fish, and assorted invertebrates. The bobcat occasionally preys on other carnivores such as foxes, raccoons, and skunks. They are also known to kill porcupines, but this animal understandably is given a low priority as a food source.

Felis rufus locates prey by its keen eyesight and hearing. It waits motionless near a game trail or stealthily stalks its prey. Then, from ambush, with several rapid bounds, it pounces on an unwary victim, quickly dispatching it with sword-like canines and sharp, retractile claws. The bobcat usually feeds on the spot, voraciously gorging itself on the victim. Surplus kill

may be buried under snow or leaves for future consumption.

The bobcat has few natural enemies. Humans and dogs top the list, and foxes, coyotes, and an occasional great horned owl may prey on unsuspecting young. Because of its solitary nature and infrequent consumption of carrion, *F. rufus* is not heavily infested with parasites. It does host external parasites such as fleas, ticks, lice, and mange mites and endoparasites such as tapeworms, flukes, roundworms, and spiny-headed worms. It is known to succumb to panleucopenia (feline distemper) and is susceptible to rabies, leptospirosis, and other wildlife diseases.

Behavior

The bobcat is active throughout the year, foraging mainly at night. It is solitary and rarely observed because of its shy, elusive nature. Ledges, rock piles, hollow trees, or a cavity beneath tree roots serve as den sites for the bobcat. Its nests—made of dried grass, leaves, and moss—are easily identified by a pervasive "cat odor."

An agile climber, the bobcat readily ascends trees if pursued by dogs or humans. Its characteristic gait is usually a walk or a gallop. Compared with the canids, *F. rufus* is a rather slow runner, reaching a maximum speed of about 24 kilometers per hour (15 mi./hr.). Although not particularly fond of water, the bobcat is a capable swimmer and readily crosses streams and even small rivers.

Felis rufus delimits its territories by scent marking with urine, feces, and highly aromatic secretions from anal scent glands. Tree trunks serving as scratching posts—sites for sharpening front claws—also aid in delimiting the bobcat's domain. *Felis rufus* further communicates by use of an impressive vocal repertoire which closely resembles that of the house cat but is magnified. The bobcat is most vocal during the breeding season when it emits piercing howls, wails, and screams. Like house cats, the bobcat indicates contentment by purring. If threatened, *F. rufus* hisses, growls, or spits.

Reproduction and Development

The female bobcat is polyestrous and may breed throughout the year, but most mating occurs in late winter. During this time, males are known to travel up to 67 kilometers (40 mi.) in search of a mate. Following a gestation period of about 60 days, one to four (usually two) kittens are born in spring.

At birth, kittens are blind and helpless but are well furred, spotted, and have sharp claws. Each weighs about 340 grams (12 oz.) and measure some 250 millimeters (10 in.) long. Development is rapid, and a well-fed kitten may gain up to 10 grams (0.4 oz.) per day. The young open their eyes at about 10 days of age, at which time they begin to play outside the den. The mother is highly solicitous and protective of her kittens, but, if continually harassed by humans or dogs, she may desert

them. The father usually does not participate in "child-care" chores. Weaning occurs at about two months of age. By autumn, the young weigh between 3 and 6 kilograms (7–13 lbs.) and are able to hunt alone. Shortly thereafter, they disperse from the natal den to pursue a solitary existence. Young may breed as yearlings, but most do not mate until two years of age.

Although rather rarely, *F. rufus* is known to breed with the house cat. In each case reported, a male bobcat bred with a female house cat. Their progeny included both spotted individuals with bobbed tails and individuals resembling typical house cats.

Status in Pennsylvania

The bobcat is restricted to isolated mountainous sections of Pennsylvania. Within this relatively broad geographic range, its populations are typified by low densities. As remote areas are developed for commercial and recreational activities, bobcat habitat is further limited and *F. rufus* may warrant consideration for a status of "threatened" in the future.

Because of its present low numbers and the dilemma of future decreases in the populations, the Pennsylvania Biological Survey has assigned the status of "vulnerable" to the bobcat in its report *Species of Special Concern in Pennsylvania* (Genoways and Brenner, 1985). The Survey recommends initiation of a thorough research program aimed at elucidating population levels and ecological requirements of *F. rufus* within the Commonwealth. Information derived from this research will aid in outlining measures necessary to preserve this unique native felid in the state. Further, complete protection of *F. rufus* must be continued under the auspices of the Pennsylvania Game Commission to "encourage" increased population growth of the bobcat within Pennsylvania.

EVEN-TOED HOOFED MAMMALS

Order Artiodactyla

Artiodactyls are important members of a large, diverse group of mammals collectively called ungulates—a name derived from the fact that these animals walk on their ungules ("nails"), or hooves, with the sole and heel of the foot raised off the ground. Living ungulates are divided into two orders: Perissodactyla and Artiodactyla. Perissodactyla are odd-toed ungulates such as horses, zebras, asses, tapirs, and rhinoceroses. Artiodactyla are even-toed ungulates, namely pigs, peccaries, camels, giraffes, hippopotami, deer, pronghorns, and bovids (bison, buffalo, cattle, sheep, goats, and antelopes).

The order Artiodactyla comprises nine living families of about 75 genera and 185 species first known from the early Eocene Epoch of Europe and North America, some 54 million years ago. Today, this order is represented throughout the world except in Australia, New Zealand, Antarctica, and many oceanic islands.

Members of the Artiodactyla occupy a diverse array of habitats ranging from deserts to tropical rain forests, from marshes to mountaintops. They range in size from the tiny mouse deer of Old World tropical forests, no bigger than a rabbit, to the massive hippopotamus of Africa, weighing up to 3,200 kilograms (7,055 lbs.). The tallest artiodactyl, the giraffe, also claims fame as the tallest mammal, reaching a height of some 5.3 meters (17 ft.).

Although there is great disparity in their size, the general architecture of artiodactyls is very similar. The head of an artiodactyl, held horizontally on the neck, has a long muzzle and may be adorned by horns or antlers. Most artiodactyls have barrel-shaped bodies with forelimbs and hindlimbs of equal length. Their skin is thick with coarse fur of blacks, browns, reds, and whites. Patterns of these colors commonly serve as protective camouflage.

In addition to having good senses of hearing and smell, artiodactyls have exceptional eyesight. Their vision is binocular with well-developed depth perception, vital to spotting potential predators.

The main distinguishing feature of the order is the foot. In artiodactyls, the main axis of the foot passes between the third and fourth digits, hence the weight of the animal is borne mainly on these digits. Although some artiodactyls—namely pigs, hippopotami, and chevrotains or mouse deer—have four functional digits, in most, the first digit is absent and the lateral second and fifth digits are reduced or rudimentary and not used. These modifications and many others associated with their limbs, girdles, and musculature serve to increase speed and enhance endurance. The adaptations presumably evolved to permit hoofed mammals to cover long distances with minimal effort and to optimize their survival when faced with highly cursorial feline predators such as those encountered on the African savanna.

Artiodactyls are primarily herbivorous, feeding on cellulose-rich herbs and grasses for which mammals lack digestive enzymes. Most artiodactyls, however, have a complex, four-chambered stomach with cellulose-digesting microorganisms that enable them to derive nutrients from these highly fibrous foods. Once food is procured by cropping or grazing, it immediately passes to the first and largest chamber of the network, the rumen. Both the rumen and the second chamber, the reticulum, knead the food and, with the aid of bacterial action, form the "cud." This softened mass is then regurgitated, and the animal "chews its cud," or "ruminates." At this time, the mass is further broken down by a potent enzyme, salivary amylase. The food is then swallowed a second time, entering the third chamber, the omasum, where muscular walls further knead it. The fourth and final chamber, the abomasum, is the true stomach, where the greatest digestive activity takes place. The adaptive advantage of this complex process is that it permits animals to feed quickly, reducing exposure to predators in open country. They can then retire to the safety of cover to chew their cud at a leisurely pace.

The teeth of artiodactyls are also highly adapted to their fibrous diet. The upper incisors and upper canines are usually absent. To crop grasses and foliage, their lower incisors bite against a callous pad on their upper gum. To grind tough plant material, they use their high-crowned cheekteeth with crescent-like surfaces. Pigs and peccaries are exceptions: They have upper incisors and low-crowned, squarish cheekteeth with rounded cusps well suited for a more generalized diet than other artiodactyls.

Artiodactyls and perissodactyls are the only mammals with head ornamentation in the forms of horns and antlers. True horns occur only in the family Bovidae. They are unbranched and permanent, composed of an inner bony core, an outgrowth of the skull, which is covered by a sheath of hardened epidermis (skin). A true horn grows throughout the adult life of the animal and may be present on both sexes or only on males.

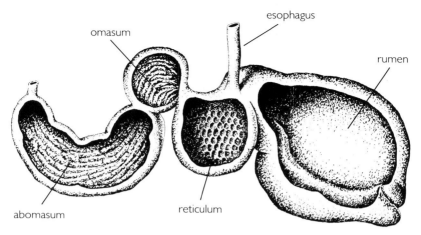

A generalized four-chambered stomach of a ruminant artiodactyl.

In contrast, antlers are found only in members of the family Cervidae (deer). They are branched, formed entirely of bone, and shed annually. Growing antlers are covered by a highly vascular layer of skin, the "velvet," which nourishes the growing bone. When the antler is fully grown, the velvet is sloughed off. Following the mating season in autumn, the antlers are shed; in spring, a new set begins to grow. Although normally found only in male deer, antlers are present on both sexes of caribou and reindeer.

Artiodactyls are an important source of food for humans as both game and domesticated animals. Some of mankind's most important domestic animals belong to this order, namely cows, sheep, goats, and pigs. The order is represented in Pennsylvania by one family occurring in the wild: the Cervidae.

Deer
Family Cervidae

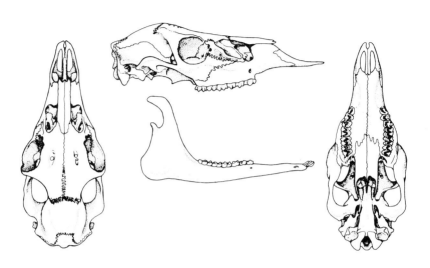

Skull of a cervid (*Odocoileus,* × ⅕).

The Cervidae is one of the most successful families of large mammals in the world. First known from the early Oligocene Epoch of Asia, some 35 million years ago, today the family comprises 17 genera and 38 species. Cervids are widely distributed and occur throughout the world except for Antarctica, southern South America, and some oceanic islands. They have been widely introduced in many areas, most notably in Australia, New Zealand, New Guinea, Hawaii, Cuba, and other islands. Today, they occupy a wide array of habitats including tropical rain forests, tundra, swamps, savannas, woodlands, thickets, and even paddy fields of southeast Asia.

This diverse group of mammals ranges in size from the beagle-sized South American pudu to the huge North American moose, standing up to 2.3 meters (7.5 ft.) tall at the shoulders and weighing some 800 kilograms (1,750 lbs.). Coat colors of cervids usually incorporate shades of gray, brown, red, and yellow; some adults and most young have spots. Underparts are usually lighter than the back, and many cervids have a light-colored "rump patch."

Despite differences in size and color, cervids have many things in common. They are exclusively herbivorous, feeding on grass, twigs, bark, or shoots of young trees, with some northern species even preferring a diet of lichens gleaned from the arctic tundra during winter. To deal with this highly fibrous diet, cervids, like other artiodactyls, have a modified digestive system and well-adapted teeth. Their four-chambered stomach with cellulose-digesting microorganisms permits the animals to feed quickly and then "chew their cud," or ruminate, at a leisurely pace. Without upper incisors, cervids bite off food between the lower incisors and a callous pad on their upper gum, and they grind fibrous plants with high-crowned cheekteeth that have crescent-shaped surfaces. Their canines are usually small, although in male water-deer, muntjacs, tufted deer, and musk deer of Asia, the canines develop into tusks used in fighting.

One feature clearly distinguishing cervids is their antlers (projections of their frontal bones). They use the antlers for defense or in combat with other members of the species during the breeding season. Only the water-deer and musk deer of Asia lack antlers. Except for caribou and reindeer, in which both sexes have antlers, usually only male cervids bear antlers.

These slim, long-legged artiodactyls have the characteristic even-toed, unguligrade stance, well-developed for running speed. They can reach speeds of up to 72 kilometers per hour (45 mi./hr.), clear fences 3 meters (10 ft.) high, and leap across streams 9 meters (30 ft.) wide. They are also excellent swimmers. Some, such as the caribou, undertake round-trip seasonal migrations covering a distance of 1,600 kilometers (1,000 mi.) each year.

Cervids are sociable, and most associate in groups of several to many individuals, especially during winter or during mass migrations as in the caribou. They are generally not domesticated. Exceptions are the reindeer, domesticated by the Lapps of Finland, Sweden, and Norway. More recently, red deer farming has become rather popular in New Zealand, Australia, and Great Britain.

Most species of deer are hunted for meat, and their antlers are prized as trophies. Throughout the world, nine species of the family Cervidae are presently regarded as "endangered." Within Pennsylvania, this family is represented by one species, *Odocoileus virginianus*, the white-tailed deer.

White-tailed Deer

SCIENTIFIC NAME
Odocoileus virginianus
(*Odocoileus*, from two Greek
roots meaning "hollow tooth,"
refers to the prominent depression
in the crown of the molar teeth;
virginianus is Latin for "of
Virginia," the locality cited in the
original description of this deer.)

SUBSPECIES IN PENNSYLVANIA
Odocoileus virginianus borealis

ALSO CALLED
Whitetail, Virginia deer, banner
tail, northern white-tailed deer

TOTAL LENGTH
1,340–2,060 mm (52.3–80.3 in.)

LENGTH OF TAIL
150–330 mm (5.9–12.9 in.)

WEIGHT
45–136 kg (100–300 lbs.)

MAMMAE
Two pairs

POPULATION DENSITY
5–25/km^2 (13–65/mi.^{2})

HOME RANGE
130–659 ha (321–1,628 acres)

LONGEVITY
3–8 yrs. in the wild; 15–20 yrs. in
captivity

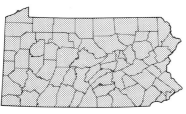

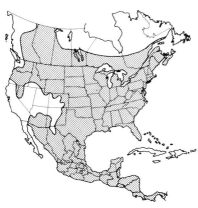

Description

The white-tailed deer is the "offi-
cial" Pennsylvania state mammal
and is so well known that it needs
little description. It is distinguished by its large size; fluffy
white tail; conspicuous ears; long,
spindly legs; and, in males, antlers. In summer, after a molt during May or June, this even-toed
ungulate dons a reddish brown
coat composed of short, thin,
straight hairs. The second annual
molt produces the winter coat by
mid-October. This grizzled grayish
brown pelage consists of long,
thick, hollow hairs that function
superbly as insulation against
cold.

The throat and underparts of
adults are white. Areas of white
also extend across the nose, encircle the eyes, and mark the in-
sides of the ears. *Odocoileus virginianus* has a white rump patch

White-tailed deer (*Odocoileus virginianus*).

partially obscured by its tail when relaxed. When bounding, this deer conspicuously displays its large white tail, or "flag." Fawns have reddish brown coats with white spots. Male white-tailed deer (bucks) are slightly larger than females (does).

When bucks reach about 10 months of age, they develop small swellings or protuberances on their frontal bones called "buttons." These structures usually do not penetrate the skin. During their second year of life, bucks produce antlers that are visible externally and normally consist of a single "spike." Older bucks develop branched antlers bearing many tines (points). Antlers normally occur only in male whitetailed deer and are grown and shed

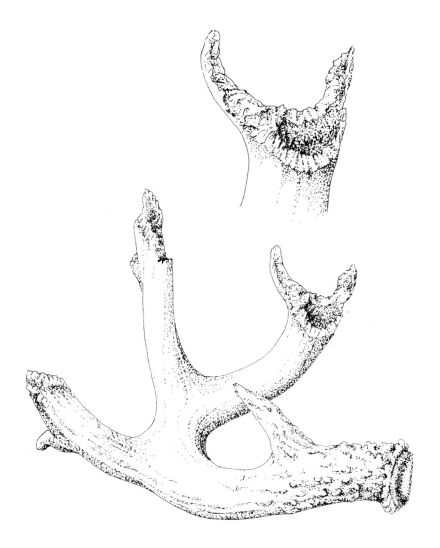

Antler of a white-tailed deer showing gnaw marks of rodents.

annually. Occasionally, female deer sport small, irregularly shaped antlers, but such cases are abnormalities due to hormonal imbalance.

In March or April, increasing day length triggers the pituitary gland to produce the hormone prolactin. This hormone, in turn, stimulates antler growth. As they grow, antlers are covered with soft, highly vascular skin called "velvet" which provides nutrients such as calcium, phosphorus, proteins, and other materials vital to growing antlers. In autumn, shortly before the breeding or rutting season, antlers reach their maximum size. At this time, the level of the male sex hormone, testosterone, is high because it is breeding season, and blood flow to the antlers is cut off. As a result, the "velvet" begins to dry and peel, and the buck rubs its antlers against limbs of trees and woody plants to scrape away the dead skin. The remaining hard, bony core is polished by additional rubbing. From late December to early February, antlers become loosened at their base and drop to the forest floor. Rabbits and rodents quickly consume the antlers for minerals and proteins.

The age of a buck cannot be determined by the size of its antlers or the number of tines. Nutritional, hormonal, and hereditary factors act in concert to regulate the size and structure of antlers.

Ecology

As a result of extensive lumbering and heavy deer hunting during the 19th century, the white-tailed deer was extremely rare in Pennsylvania at the turn of the century. Fortunately, the establishment of the Pennsylvania Game Commission in 1896 paved the way for regulations limiting the annual deer harvest. These restrictions—coupled with introductions of white-tailed deer from nearby states, lack of natural predators, and regrowth of previously logged or burned-over forests—are largely responsible for the resurgence of *O. virginianus* in the state during the past 80 years. Today, the white-tailed deer is abundant and widespread throughout Pennsyl-

vania. It is at home in a wide variety of habitats ranging from dense forests to agricultural land. The species is most prevalent along forest edges marked by brush, woody vegetation essential for concealment and food.

Odocoileus virginianus is exclusively herbivorous, with its diet strongly reflecting seasonal availability of forage. During spring and summer, the white-tailed deer browses extensively on twigs, leaves, and shoots of herbaceous and woody plants. In Pennsylvania, favored foods include maples, dogwoods, crabapple, hawthorn, sumac, black cherry, greenbriar, mountain ash, hickory, blueberry, and viburnums. Evergreens such as yew, hemlock, and pine are also eaten, but spruce and tamarack are given low priority. Grass and farm crops such as corn, alfalfa, and soybeans are also relished by *O. virginianus.*

During autumn, food preference shifts to fruits such as acorns, hickory nuts, beechnuts, persimmons, and other mast; also, many white-tailed deer congregate in apple orchards to feed on fallen fruit. In winter, as the fruit supply is exhausted, the white-tailed deer forages on buds, leaves of trees, twigs, and woody shrubs. It commonly frequents farmers' fields in search of waste corn. Certain plants show "immunity" from the white-tailed deer. These include rhododendron, mountain laurel, ironwood, witch hazel, and ninebark. This immunity, however, may be short-lived, when deer populations are high and preferred foods are depleted.

Since the white-tailed deer is the most important big game animal in the United States, harvesting by humans is the major cause of mortality of *O. virginianus* in Pennsylvania. In the state, both antlered and antlerless deer are hunted. In 1985, the total deer harvest equalled 161,425, with the greatest mortality occurring in the northcentral counties of the state. Current hunting pressure does not seem to affect adversely overall population numbers.

Collisions with automobiles, death by starvation or exhaustion in winter because of severe cold and lack of food, and predation by free-ranging domestic dogs also take a toll on deer populations. Natural predators such as foxes, bobcats, or coyotes kill an occasional adult but normally concentrate on fawns. Deer also die by entanglement in fences, by falling through ice and drowning, and as a result of forest fires.

The white-tailed deer hosts a plentiful array of parasites. Ectoparasites are fleas, ticks, mites, chiggers, and lice. Internally, they harbor tapeworms, flukes, and roundworms. Among protozoan diseases, coccidiosis is common, causing lesions in the liver and intestines and possibly proving fatal. The nose bot infests the nasal passages of the white-tailed deer; although two dozen or more larvae may be found in one deer, they are not known to cause deleterious effects. Bacterial diseases include actinomycosis (lumpy jaw), anthrax, brucellosis, leptospirosis, tularemia, and salmonellosis. Finally, *O. virginianus* is known to be susceptible to viral diseases such as bluetongue, epizootic hemorrhagic disease (EHD), canine distemper, and rabies. An ex-cellent review of the parasites infecting the white-tailed deer is provided by Hesselton and Hesselton (1982).

Behavior

The white-tailed deer is active year-round. Most daily activity occurs in early morning and shortly after dusk. At night, activity is not continuous, but *O. virginianus* exhibits brief foraging bouts alternating with periods of rest when it beds down. Also, the white-tailed deer occasionally feeds for brief times during the middle of the day.

The presence of a deer is evidenced by its characteristic "heart-shaped" hoof print. In good habitat, its travels are conspicuous through the forest by meandering trails, measuring some 25 to 30 centimeters (10–12 in.) wide, cut deeply into the soil. Along these paths, "buck rubs" may be evident. These consist of abraded bark on bushes or small trees caused by a buck rubbing off the velvet from its newly formed antlers. Also, vegetation adjacent to the trail may indicate deer browsing. Unlike rabbits, which neatly snip stems, deer, lacking upper incisors, tend to grasp and rip twigs and stems, leaving ragged edges. Further and conclusive proof of the presence of a deer are its scats; dark pellets, usually oblong shaped and about 2 centimeters (0.8 in.) long, are deposited in clumps or groups. Deer bedding sites are also conspicuous in forests and typified by an area of flattened vegetation forming a shallow depression about 1 meter (3 ft.) in diameter.

In fresh snow the bedding sites are easily recognized because the depression is formed by partially melted snow resulting from the deer's body warmth. Several animals may bed within a small area.

A white-tailed deer usually walks slowly and quietly. If startled, it shifts into a gallop interspersed with occasional high jumps as it vividly displays its "white flag." A graceful, speedy runner, the deer reaches speeds of up to 64 kilometers per hour (40 mi./hr.). Adept at jumping, it can easily clear a 2.5 meter (8 ft.) fence or jump a stream 9 meters (30 ft.) wide. *Odocoileus virginianus* is also a gifted swimmer and, in water, can maintain speeds of about 21 kilometers per hour (13 mi./hr.) for distances of up to 5.5 kilometers (3.5 mi.).

The white-tailed deer is rather social. During most of the year, it lives in family groups composed of an adult doe, her fawns, or yearlings. In spring, at the time of fawning, the female leaves her yearlings and lives alone to bear her young. Although yearling does rejoin their mother in autumn, yearling bucks usually do not return; instead, they join other bucks or remain alone.

Older bucks form groups of their own. In autumn, during the period of rut, bucks usually maintain bachelor groups except when pursuing a doe in heat. During winter in northern regions of the state, deer occasionally congregate in groups numbering from several to 50 individuals. These deer "yards" are usually located in protected valleys where food is abundant.

Although normally silent, *O.* *virginianus* loudly snorts or blows through its nose and stomps a hoof when nervous or alarmed. Does communicate with their fawn with a low, whining sound. When in pain, a deer commonly emits a sort of bleating cry. Most communication, however, is accomplished by means of scent marking, tail wagging, facial movements, and body postures.

The white-tailed deer has four pairs of prominent scent glands. Tarsal glands, identified by a tuft of long, coarse hair, are located on the inside of each hindleg. Metatarsal glands can be found on the outside of each hindleg between the ankle and hoof, and interdigital glands are located between the toes on all four feet. Lastly, preorbital glands are situated at the inner corners of the eyes. These scent glands exude an oily secretion with a pronounced, pungent musky odor. Spreading the glandular secretion on shrubs and foliage serves to delimit an individual's domain. Further, scent marks permit a deer to retrace its steps or to relocate a fawn or mate. In addition to serving as lubricant for the eyes, secretions from the preorbital glands are used to scent twigs and branches.

Reproduction and Development

The rutting season lasts for about two months in autumn, reaching its height in November. During this time, bucks become aggressive and vigorously joust with other bucks for mating rights with selected does. This competition is fierce and involves combat using both antlers and hooves. Occasionally, these contests result in the death of one of the combatants.

The white-tailed deer does not form extended pair bonds nor does the species form harems. Females undergo a period of heat that lasts about 24 hours. If the female does not successfully mate during her first heat, she undergoes a second period of heat about one month later. By late December, most adult females have bred, and gestation lasts about six and one-half to seven months. Young are born between late May and early June. A doe typically has twins, but litter size varies from one to three. Yearlings and old females commonly produce a single offspring.

Fawns are born in a precocial state. They have a well-furred, spotted coat; their eyes are open; and they weigh between 1.8 to 3.2 kilograms (4–7 lbs.) and measure about 42.5 to 47.5 centimeters (17–19 in.) in total length.

Shortly after birth, they stand, although they are weak and rather wobbly. Their spotted coat lends camouflage, they emit no scent, and, thus, they are relatively safe from predation.

Fawns remain close to their birthplace for several weeks. At one month of age, they start to accompany their mother on brief outings and begin eating their first green vegetation. Weaning commences at this time, although some fawns continue to nurse until six months of age. During summer months, fawns routinely travel with the doe on foraging trips. In September, when about three months old, they begin to lose their spots. At this time, a male typically weighs between 27 to 36 kilograms (60–80 lbs.). Fawns normally remain with their mother during the first winter. The majority of young are capable of breeding when they are six to eight months old.

Species of Uncertain Occurrence

MARTEN

SCIENTIFIC NAME: *Martes americana*

ORDER: Carnivora

FAMILY: Mustelidae

About the size of a small house cat, the marten weighs from 0.5 to 1.6 kilograms (1–3.5 lbs.) and has a long, slender body with short legs. Its bushy tail is about 165 to 240 millimeters (6.5–10 in.) long, about half the length of its body, which measures some 513 to 682 millimeters (20–27 in.). The soft, glossy coat of *M. americana* is golden brown, grading to black on the tail and legs. Its throat and breast are pale buff. Males are slightly larger than females. An arboreal weasel, the marten has sharp, curved claws well adapted to climbing.

Martes americana resides in cool, moist, northern coniferous and mixed forests typified by the presence of spruce, fir, and hemlock. It dens in hollow trees, rock piles, or under logs or stumps. Its principal prey includes red-backed voles, meadow voles, and deer mice. Since it is adept at climbing, the marten also pursues red squirrels and flying squirrels. Snowshoe hares, birds, fruit, insects, and carrion round out its menu.

In optimal habitat population density ranges from 0.5 to 1.7 individuals per square kilometer (1–4/mi.²). The home range is extensive, varying from 400 to 2,000 hectares (1,000–5,000 acres).

The marten is polygamous. Like many other mustelids, female martens exhibit delayed implantation. A single annual litter is produced in spring, averaging three to four young.

Status in Pennsylvania

In North America, *M. americana* is distributed from northwestern Alaska, east across Canada, and southward along mountain ranges to California and New Mexico. In the east, the marten extends into northern New England and south into the Catskill Mountains of New York. In Pennsylvania, one specimen was collected from Wayne County in 1963 and another from Mercer County in 1970. Prior to these finds, scientists believed that the marten had been extirpated from the state around the turn of the century as a result of excessive trapping for fur and elimination of forests by lumbering. Based on the records of these sightings, *M. americana* may eventually become reestablished in forest habitats in Pennsylvania.

Because of its uncertain occurrence in the Commonwealth, the Pennsylvania Biological Survey assigned the status of "undetermined" to the marten in its report *Species of Species Concern in Pennsylvania* (Genoways and Brenner, 1985). A systematic program designed to assess the presence of *M. americana* along the northern border of Pennsylvania should be initiated to delimit more accurately the range and, consequently, the status of this arboreal mustelid in the state.

FISHER

SCIENTIFIC NAME: *Martes pennanti*

ORDER: Carnivora

FAMILY: Mustelidae

This fox-sized weasel weighs from 2 to 5.5 kilograms (4–12 lbs.) and measures some 830 to 1,033 millimeters (32–40 in.) long. Its bushy, tapered tail measures between 340 and 422 millimeters (13–16.5 in.) long. It has short, stubby legs; a wedge-shaped head; and dark brown luxuriant fur grading to brownish underparts. Several white patches occur on the neck and throat, and white-tipped hairs on the shoulders and face give this animal a grizzled appearance. Males are much larger than females. Well-developed anal scent glands are present.

Throughout its range, the fisher resides in large tracts of mixed hardwood and coniferous forest, usually in isolated mountainous regions. Its dens are located in hollow trees or logs, abandoned porcupine dens, or under large boulders. Although mainly terrestrial, *M. pennanti* is also at home in trees.

The fisher is a highly opportunistic feeder but has a strong predilection for porcupines, which it overpowers by inflicting a series of rapid bites to the head and face. It then flips its victims over and feeds on the abdominal region where no quills exist. Other important foods include snowshoe hares, small mammals, birds, insects, nuts, and carrion.

Population density in suitable habitat for *M. pennanti* is less than one per square kilometer (up to 1/mi.²). A great traveler, its home range varies from 13,000 to 39,000 hectares (32,000 to 100,000 acres).

The fisher breeds once per year. In early spring, mating occurs; females exhibit delayed implantation of the embryo, resulting in an extremely long gestation period of about 51 weeks. From one to four kits are born in the following March.

Status in Pennsylvania

During the 19th and early 20th centuries, the fisher declined greatly in abundance throughout its range in North America, because of habitat destruction by logging and excessive trapping for fur. Prior to colonial times, *M. pennanti* probably resided throughout Pennsylvania, except for the southeastern section.

Today, the fisher is distributed in North America from northwestern Canada south in the Sierra Nevada Mountains to northern California and in the Rocky Mountains to Utah. In the east, *M. pennanti* extends into northern New England, New York, and West Virginia. Since the turn of the century, only two specimens document the occurrence of the fisher in Pennsylvania: One specimen was collected from Clinton County in 1901 and another, from Lancaster County in 1921. Indirect evidence in the form of sightings of "black panthers" and large mustelid tracks suggest, however, that *M. pennanti* may currently reside in the Commonwealth. This indirect evidence was the impetus for the Pennsylvania Biological Survey to assign the status of "uncertain" to the fisher in its report *Species of Special Concern in Pennsylvania* (Genoways and Brenner, 1985). The Survey suggests that additional observations coupled with successful livetrapping programs will draw a more accurate picture of the occurrence of this large, elusive mustelid in the state.

BADGER

SCIENTIFIC NAME: *Taxidea taxus*

ORDER: Carnivora

FAMILY: Mustelidae

This stocky member of the weasel family has a flat, muscular body; short, bowed legs; and a distinctive white stripe running from its nose to its shoulders. Its cheeks are white, and black spots occur in front of its small, rounded ears. The shaggy coat of the badger is grizzled gray on the back, whereas the underparts and short, bushy tail are buff colored. As befits this highly fossorial mustelid, its large forefeet are equipped with long, powerful claws; the middle claw reaches up to 39 millimeters (1.5 in.) long. Like other mustelids, the badger is well endowed with paired anal scent glands. The total length of adult badgers ranges from 521 to 870 millimeters (20–35 in.). Its short tail measures some 98 to 155 millimeters (4–6 in.) long. Adults weigh from 3.6 to 10 kilograms (8–22 lbs.); males are larger and heavier than females.

Taxidea taxus inhabits dry open plains country and rolling farmlands. It also occurs in forest-edge communities. Its principal prey includes ground squirrels, pocket gophers, mice, and voles captured by digging the victim out of its burrow. Other foods are rabbits, snakes, ground-nesting birds, insects, and carrion. A badger's presence is usually known by the large holes it digs when pursuing prey; these holes measure from 20 to 30 centimeters (8–12 in.) across and have elliptically shaped entrances, necessary to accommodate its flat body.

Not very speedy, *T. taxus* usually walks in a slow gait or shifts into a lope for a short distance. Its home range varies from 100 to 240 hectares (250–600 acres). The population density may reach up to five individuals per square kilometer (13/mi.^{2}) in optimal habitat but is usually lower over most of its range.

Except during its breeding season, which occurs in August or September, the badger leads a solitary life. After a delayed implantation of the embryo and a gestation period that total about seven months, the female badger produces a litter of one to five young in March or early April.

Status in Pennsylvania

The geographic range of *T. taxus* extends from southcentral Canada south through western and central United States and into central Mexico. In the east, it occurs from southeastern Ontario, Canada, to central Ohio. The badger was probably a resident of Pennsylvania during precolonial times, al-

though its occurrence in the state is documented by only one record prior to 1900. Since 1946, four records of the badger exist: from Beaver, Fayette, Indiana, and Washington counties (Williams et al., 1985). Two explanations account for these occurrences. First, these badgers may have escaped or were released from commercial operations. Second, their occurrence could reflect a natural eastward dispersal from resident populations in Ohio. In defense of the second explanation, suitable habitat is available along grassland "corridors" associated with an eastern dispersal route into Pennsylvania. Even if suitable habitat does not account for the past records of *T. taxus* in the state, it may provide an avenue for invasion of the badger in the future.

Because of the precarious status of the badger in the Commonwealth, the Pennsylvania Biological Survey labeled *T. taxus* as "uncertain" in its report *Species of Special Concern in Pennsylvania* (Genoways and Brenner, 1985). To substantiate the status of the badger in the state, the Survey recommends that badgers killed on highways, inadvertently trapped, or merely observed be reported to (or specimens deposited at) appropriate scientific institutions in Pennsylvania.

MOUNTAIN LION

SCIENTIFIC NAME: *Felis concolor*

ORDER: Carnivora

FAMILY: Felidae

The mountain lion (also called panther, cougar, and puma) is the largest North American cat. Adults have soft, short, yellowish brown fur on the back and slightly paler fur on the belly. Dark spots occur on the sides of the muzzle, on the backs of the small, rounded ears, and at the tip of the mountain lion's tail, which measures from 53 to 81 centimeters (20–30 in.) long. Kittens are yellowish brown in color, marked by brownish black, irregular spots which disappear when they reach six months of age. The head of *F. concolor* is small and rounded; its limbs are stout and thick. Adults measure from 150 to 274 centimeters (60–110 in.) in total length and weigh from 36 to 103 kilograms (80–230 lbs.). Males are considerably larger than females.

The mountain lion hunts mainly during hours of darkness, preferring to forage within dense cover and along rocky, rugged terrain. It is the supreme carnivore; the deer is its principal prey. This skillful predator slowly and silently stalks its prey, then, with a well-timed leap, pounces on the victim's back and quickly dispatches the prey by inflicting bites to the back of the neck and throat. It usually drags its prey to a sheltered location and partly devours it. Remains are covered with leaves, sticks, brush, and soil and visited for additional meals during the next several days. An adult mountain lion requires about one deer per week for sustenance. Other prey include raccoons, foxes, porcupines, skunks, rabbits, mice, voles, birds, and even insects.

The mountain lion travels widely for prey and may cover a hunting circuit of up to about 40 kilometers (25 mi.) per night. It does not establish a permanent den but rests under rock crevices, in hollow logs, or simply in tall grass or underbrush. Except during the breeding season, males and females without young lead solitary lives. Maximum density in the wild is about one mountain lion per 25 to 50 square kilometers (10–19 mi.^{2}).

Like domestic cats, *F. concolor* shows contentment by purring, but it is usually silent. The occurrence of its fabled, bloodcurdling "scream" is much debated; evidence suggests that the mountain lion does emit very loud screams on rare occasions, possibly during mating.

Felis concolor begins breeding at three years of age. Following a gestation period of about three months, a litter of from one to six kittens (usually three) is born, normally in late spring or summer. The kittens are weaned at two to three months of age but may remain with the mother until two years old. Maximum longevity of the mountain lion in the wild is about 15 years.

Status in Pennsylvania

Originally, the mountain lion had the broadest geographic distribution of any mammal in the Western Hemisphere except for humankind. It ranged from northern British Columbia, across southern Canada, throughout the entire United States and south to Patagonia in South America. It resided in a diverse array of habitats, from coastal swamps to montane coniferous forests and from hot deserts of the American southwest to tropical rain forests of South America. With European settlement of the United States, the range of the mountain lion steadily contracted. Today, *F. concolor* is restricted mainly to the mountains of western North America. Small, isolated populations, however, are reported from southcentral Canada, New Brunswick, Arkansas, Missouri, Oklahoma, Louisiana, Florida, Texas, and localities along the Appalachian Mountains. The subspecies of mountain lion native to Pennsylvania and most eastern states (*F. concolor cougar*) is declared "endangered" in North America (U.S. Dept. of Interior, 1974).

In Pennsylvania before colonial times, *F. concolor* occurred throughout the state and was most abundant in the northcentral and northeastern sections. As a result of trapping and hunting, decimation of forest habitats, and overharvesting of the mountain lion's principal prey, the white-tailed deer, *F. concolor* rapidly declined in the Commonwealth. By the late 1800s, the once-widespread felid was virtually eliminated from Pennsylvania.

The present status of the mountain lion in the state is difficult to evaluate. There have been many undocumented reports of sightings. Some of these sightings may be of captive mountain lions which escaped from game parks or private owners and ventured into the wild. Because of this tenuous position, *F. concolor* has been assigned the status of "undetermined" by the Pennsylvania Biological Survey in its report *Species of Special Concern in Pennsylvania* (Genoways and Brenner, 1985). Additional sightings, well-documented with unambiguous photographs, will aid in establishing an accurate appraisal of the mountain lion in the state.

LYNX

SCIENTIFIC NAME: *Felis lynx*

ORDER: Carnivora

FAMILY: Felidae

Although the lynx is similar in size and basic form to its southern cousin, the bobcat, it is distinguished by its long, black ear tufts and longer legs. Further, the tail of *F. lynx*—some 95 to 125 millimeters (4–5 in.) long—is shorter than that of the bobcat and has a solid black tip rather than an incomplete black ring. Like the bobcat, the lynx displays grayish white sideburns along its cheeks. Otherwise, the general color of the animal is yellowish brown, with its back appearing frosted gray and its underparts buff in color. Its winter pelage is thick and long, casting a fluffy appearance and making the lynx look much larger than it is. The feet of the lynx—oversized and heavily furred above and below—are ideally suited for walking on deep snow. Adults range from 825 to 954 millimeters (30–40 in.) in total length, weighing from 6.8 to 16 kilograms (15–35 lbs.). Males are somewhat larger than females.

Throughout its range, the lynx resides in dense coniferous forests, where it finds shelter under rock ledges or fallen timber or in hollow logs. This secretive, nocturnal cat relies on the snowshoe hare as its mainstay. In a given year, a lynx is reported to consume up to 170 hares (Saunders, 1963). The reliance of the lynx on the hare is so great that its densities undergo cyclic fluctuations as a response to the population cycles of the snowshoe hare. These cycles are marked by intervals of about 9 to 10 years between peaks of abundance. When snowshoe hare density drops, the number of lynx declines, as a result of mortality of kittens due to insufficient food. During times of food scarcity, *F. lynx* exhibits extensive migrations in search of food. In Alberta, Canada, its peak population density fluctuates from 3 to 13 lynx per 130 square kilometers (1–50/mi.^{2}) during the course of this cycle.

Although the snowshoe hare heads its menu, lynx are also fond of ruffed grouse and other ground-dwelling birds, squirrels, chipmunks, voles, mice, and carrion. *Felis lynx* requires some 600 grams (1.5 lbs.) of food per day on the average. A solitary animal, the lynx usually avoids other members of its species except during the breeding season. Its average nightly hunting circuit consists of from 5 to 19 kilometers (3–11 mi.). Its home range is extensive, varying from 1,100 to 5,000 hectares (2,700–12,350 acres).

Felis lynx mates in February or March. Following a gestation period of about two months, a litter of from one to five young (usually four) is born in April or May. Kittens usually remain with the mother until the winter breeding season commences.

Status in Pennsylvania

Felis lynx is a Holarctic species occurring in both North America and northern Eurasia. In North America, it occurs from Alaska across Canada, and, originally, its range spread across much of the northern United States. Today, because of hunting and trapping during the 18th and 19th centuries, it is now uncommon to rare in New England and the Adirondack Mountains of New York. In Pennsylvania, the lynx may have been extirpated by the turn of the century. The only 20th century specimen of *F. lynx* from Pennsylvania was collected in 1923 from Tioga County.

Because of the scarcity of verified records of this felid in the Commonwealth, it is difficult to ascertain whether it resides within the state or periodically invades Pennsylvania in response to prey scarcity farther north. Because of this ambiguous position, the Pennsylvania Biological Survey assigned the status of "undetermined" to *F. lynx* in its report *Species of Special Concern in Pennsylvania* (Genoways and Brenner, 1985). Further documentation is required to assess more accurately the status of the lynx in the Commonwealth.

Extirpated Species

GRAY WOLF

SCIENTIFIC NAME: *Canis lupus*

ORDER: Carnivora

FAMILY: Canidae

The gray wolf, the largest free-roaming canid, resembles a large German shepherd. It is distinguished from its close relative the coyote by its larger size, broader nose pad, shorter ears, and larger feet and claws. Further, *C. lupus* carries its tail high when running, unlike the coyote, which carries its tail low.

Although the coat of the gray wolf generally is grizzled gray, it shows great color variation ranging from black to nearly white, as in many arctic populations. Its long, bushy tail, which is marked with a black tip, is about one-third to one-fourth of its total body length: Adults range from 100 to 205 centimeters (40–80 in.) long, and their tails reach lengths of 35 to 50 centimeters (15–20 in.). They weigh from 18 to 80 kilograms (40–175 lbs.). The largest wolves reside in Alaska and western Canada; the smallest, in Mexico. Males are slightly larger than females.

Canis lupus once occupied nearly all habitats of the Northern Hemisphere, short of tropical forests and arid deserts. Today, this primarily nocturnal animal occurs mainly in arctic tundra and coniferous forests where it finds shelter in ground burrows, under rock

crevices, or in hollow logs. Although caribou, moose, and deer make up the bulk of its diet, the gray wolf also feeds on small mammals, birds, fish, insects, and berries.

The gray wolf locates its prey usually by chance encounter or with its keen sense of smell. Once it locates quarry, the wolf first attempts to surprise it by an ambush. Contrary to myth, it will not chase prey for extended periods; the wolf will cover only a maximum of about 5 kilometers (3 mi.) to subdue its quarry. Many times, the chase is unsuccessful, especially when prey is strong and healthy. Analyses of predation indicate that *C. lupus* kills mainly young, old, and infirm individuals, with the rate of kill varying from about one deer per wolf every 18 days to one moose per wolf every 45 days (Mech, 1974). Adults eat about 9 kilograms (20 lbs.) of meat in one feeding!

A social animal, *C. lupus* generally hunts in packs, or family units, consisting of an adult pair and their offspring of one or more years. The male, known commonly as the "alpha male," dominates the adult female and pups to maintain order and discipline within the pack.

Packs are highly territorial, usually hostile to one another. Maintenance of territories is accomplished by vocalizations such as growls, barks, and howls; scent marking via scratching, defecation, and urination; and visual displays including the use of various body postures and facial expressions. The size of the home range varies according to prey availability, season, and number of wolves. In southern Canada wolves exhibit a small range of only about 18 square kilometers (7 mi.^{2}), whereas in Alaska its home range reaches up to 13,000 square kilometers (5,000 mi.^{2}). Likewise, population density is quite variable, ranging from a low of one wolf per 520 square kilometers (200 mi.^{2}) to a high of one individual per 26 square kilometers (10 mi.^{2}).

Wolves mate from February to March, and, following a gestation period of about two months, one to eleven (usually six) young are born between April and early June. While the mother tends the growing young, the father and other pack members hunt, returning to the den with food for the mother and pups. Like many other canids, the gray wolf feeds its young by regurgitation. At one month of age, the young emerge and play near the natal den entrance. Weaning commences at about five weeks, and, by early autumn, pups travel with the pack on hunting trips. Wolves become sexually mature in their second year of life but normally do not breed until they reach three years old.

Status in Pennsylvania

Canis lupus originally was distributed widely throughout Eurasia and most of North America south to Mexico. Since the advent of European colonization, humans have deliberately killed the gray wolf for its fur, because of its depredation on livestock, and because of its ability to compete with humans for big game. Further—although there are no documented cases of wolves attacking humans except for occasional rabid wolves (Mech, 1970)—humans eliminated *C. lupus* out of fear that it preyed on mankind. Today, because of this deliberate extermination, the range of the gray wolf in North America is restricted to Alaska; Canada; the northern Great Lakes region; parts of Montana, Idaho, and Washington; and perhaps areas of the Southwest. *Canis lupus* is also represented in Mexico. All populations of *C. lupus* residing in the continental United States and Mexico are designated as "endangered," except for those occurring in Minnesota, which are classified as "threatened" (U.S. Dept. Interior, 1980).

Although it once ranged widely throughout Pennsylvania, the gray wolf was exterminated from the state before the close of the 19th century by relentless hunting, trapping, and poisoning. The last record of a naturally occurring gray wolf in Pennsylvania was in Clearfield County in 1892 (Williams et al., 1985). In its report *Species of Special Concern in Pennsylvania* (Genoways and Brenner, 1985), the Pennsylvania

Biological Survey classified *C. lupus* as "extirpated" in the Commonwealth. It is highly unlikely that this canid will ever reside in Pennsylvania again.

WOLVERINE

SCIENTIFIC NAME: *Gulo gulo*

ORDER: Carnivora

FAMILY: Mustelidae

The wolverine—the largest terrestrial member of the weasel family—has an elongated, bear-like form; coarse brown pelage; and broad, yellowish bands running from its shoulders along the hips and meeting in a "V" over the tail. Extremely long guard hairs on the sides, hips, and tail give *G. gulo* a rather shaggy appearance. Its head, broad with beady eyes, is marked by pale gray patches on the forehead and cheeks. Its muscular legs are short, whereas its bushy tail is long, measuring some 19 to 26 centimeters (7.5 to 10 in.) in adults. Adults range in total length from 90 to 113 centimeters (35 to 45 in.) and weigh from 11 to 18.2 kilograms (25–40 lbs.). Males are slightly larger than females. Like other mustelids, the wolverine has well-developed anal scent glands. It also has oversized feet that act like snowshoes, enabling the animal to pursue hoofed mammals in winter.

This large mustelid inhabits tundra and boreal forests, finding shelter in small caves or rocky crevices, under a fallen tree, or in ground burrows excavated by other animals. It is primarily terrestrial, is not very speedy, and progresses by a bounding gallop with its back arched high and its head and tail held low. An adept scavenger, the wolverine may travel great distances for carrion, its mainstay. If a carcass is not immediately consumed, the wolverine may dismember it and hide the parts in widely scattered caches. Females may visit these depositories up to six months later when searching for food for their young. *Gulo gulo* also eats birds, small mammals, berries, and, occasionally, moose, caribou, or deer. In addition, it is infamous for raiding trap lines and ransacking camps in search of food, a habit that has put the wolverine in strong disfavor with mankind and ultimately helped to contribute to its decline.

Although primarily nocturnal, the wolverine occasionally is active during daylight. It is solitary except during the breeding season. Its home range is extensive, sometimes exceeding 2,600 square kilometers (1,000 mi.²) during winter. *Gulo gulo* has a keen sense of smell but poor eyesight and hearing. Communication with other wolverines is accomplished by scent marking in the form of urination.

Gulo gulo mates between spring and midsummer. Like many other mustelids, delayed implantation of the fertilized egg occurs, resulting in an extended gestation period. A litter of from two to five young is born in late spring of the following year. Only the highly solicitous female cares for the young, which mature rapidly and disperse from the natal nest in autumn when five to six months of age. Young may breed when they are two years old.

Status in Pennsylvania

A Holarctic species, the wolverine originally occurred in both North America and Eurasia. In North America, its former range extended throughout Alaska and Canada and as far south as central California, southern Colorado, Indiana, and Pennsylvania. Today, *Gulo gulo* is found in northern Canada and, in the United States, only in Alaska; along the Cascade,

Sierra Nevada, and Rocky Mountain chains; in northeastern Minnesota; and possibly in Iowa and South Dakota. Its decline in numbers has resulted not only from its status of "nuisance" but from overharvesting by fur trappers. Its coarse fur is prized as lining for parka hoods because its oily, glossy hairs preclude the buildup of frost resulting from a person's breath.

In historical times, Pennsylvania probably represented the southern terminus of the geographic range of the wolverine in the east. Based on records principally from northcentral Pennsylvania, the wolverine was always rare in the state and disappeared from the Commonwealth during the mid- to late 19th century. The Pennsylvania Biological Survey has declared *Gulo gulo* as "extirpated" in the Commonwealth in its report *Species of Special Concern in Pennsylvania* (Genoways and Brenner, 1985). Like the gray wolf, it is highly unlikely that this large mustelid will reside in the Commonwealth again.

WAPITI

SCIENTIFIC NAME: *Cervus elaphus*

ORDER: Artiodactyla

FAMILY: Cervidae

The wapiti or elk is second in size only to the moose among members of the family Cervidae. Adults range from 203 to 254 centimeters (80–100 in.) in total length and weigh from 200 to 495 kilograms

(440–1,100 lbs.). The wapiti is heaviest during late summer. At this time, its dark, reddish brown coat begins to change to its brownish gray winter pelage. Throughout the year, a dark mane hangs to the lower chest, and a buffy white rump patch extends above the white tail. In adults, the tail measures only 10 to 13 centimeters (4–5 in.) long.

The muzzle of *C. elaphus* is naked, and its ears are conspicuous. A metatarsal scent gland is situated on the inside of each ankle and marked by coarse, ruffled hair. Unlike other North American cervids, *C. elaphus* has a functional pair of upper canine teeth known as "elk teeth," once treasured as charms. Males (bulls), about 25 percent larger than females (cows), have large, widely branching antlers that sweep upward and backward. The antlers of a big bull elk may weigh nearly 12 kilograms (25 lbs.) and exhibit a spread of some 1.5 meters (5 ft.). As in white-tailed deer, females lack antlers.

The wapiti, chiefly nocturnal, is an inhabitant of forest edges and open meadows. During summer, it grazes mainly on grasses and forbs, whereas in winter it browses on leaves, bark, and twigs. Its diet varies with seasonal availability of forage.

Cervus elaphus is a highly gregarious species. During winter in the Rocky Mountains, large herds, often of up to several hundred animals, congregate in sheltered valleys. As spring approaches, the large winter herds break up, sorting into smaller bands which follow the retreating snow line to higher elevations.

The rutting season for *C. elaphus* begins in autumn. Bulls, having shed their velvet and now sporting polished antlers, are prepared for competition for mating rights. One mating ritual charac-

teristic of the wapiti is "bugling." A bull elk begins this vocalization as a deep bellow and quickly changes it into a shrill whistle which echoes over long distances. Dominance over other males is declared by jousting rival bulls with antlers, scent marking, and wallowing in mud and stagnant ponds.

As a result of the elaborate mating ritual, the wapiti—the most polygamous cervid in North America—rounds up harems of up to 60 cows. By late October, most mating has occurred. In June, after a gestation period of about eight and one-half months, a cow leaves the herd and gives birth to a single calf weighing about 14 kilograms (30 lbs.). As with the white-tailed deer, young wapiti are born with a spotted coat and are highly precocial. By late summer, weaning is completed. Cows may become sexually mature at three years of age, whereas bulls usually do not acquire a harem and mate until they are four or five years old.

Because of its large size, the wapiti has few natural enemies, but it is an important game animal in North America. In the wild, *C. elaphus* lives 15 or more years.

Status in Pennsylvania

Cervus elaphus, a Holarctic species, originally ranged throughout North America and Eurasia. In the eastern United States, it was found from northern New York to central Georgia. Since the advent of European settlement, the wapiti has been extirpated over most of its former range in North America. Today, it resides chiefly in the Rocky Mountains and western states, except for small reintroduced populations across the continent.

In Pennsylvania specifically, the wapiti historically occurred throughout the state, with the greatest abundance existing in the Allegheny Mountains. With the arrival of European settlers in the Commonwealth, the numbers of wapiti dwindled because of hunting and the elimination of forest habitats for farmlands. By the mid-19th century, *C. elaphus* was restricted to the northcentral region of the state. By 1877, because of persecution by mankind, the wapiti had been exterminated from Pennsylvania. In its report *Species of Special Concern in Pennsylva-*

nia (Genoways and Brenner, 1985), the Pennsylvania Biological Survey classified the native population of *C. elaphus* as "extirpated" in the Commonwealth.

Today, as a result of reintroduction by the Pennsylvania Game Commission, a small population of wapiti resides within an area of Cameron, Elk, and McKean counties that measures about 200 square kilometers (80 mi.²). There, the population was estimated at some 135 individuals in 1982. It is noteworthy that this site of the present population of wapiti in the state is only about 120 kilometers (75 mi.) from the location of the last historical record of native wapiti in the Commonwealth.

MOOSE

SCIENTIFIC NAME: *Alces alces*

ORDER: Artiodactyla

FAMILY: Cervidae

The moose, about the size of a horse, is the largest member of the family Cervidae. In total length, adults range from 206 to 279 centimeters (80–110 in.); they weigh from 315 to 630 kilograms (700–1,400 lbs.), with males (bulls) about 25 percent heavier than females (cows). The huge stature of *Alces alces* is only one of its distinguishing features. It is also typified by the presence of a broad muzzle and a heavy mane equipped with a pendulous flap ("bell") of skin hanging from the throat. Males are further identified by

their massive, palm-like antlers which commonly exhibit a spread of 1.2 to 1.5 meters (4–5 ft.).

The coat of the moose consists of coarse, thick hairs. In summer, the pelage is blackish brown; in winter, it takes on a slightly grayish appearance. The ungainly moose has long legs; large, conspicuous ears; and a very short tail which measures only 7 to 12 centimeters (3–5 in.). Unlike the young of other cervids, the calves of moose are never spotted but, rather, sport a reddish brown coat.

Throughout its range, the moose

resides mainly in spruce forests, bogs, and aspen and willow thickets that border ponds, lakes, and watercourses. Primarily a browser, *A. alces* feeds on leaves, twigs, and bark of woody plants such as willow, aspen, birch, alder, maples, and dogwoods. It commonly wades into ponds and lakes in search of aquatic plants such as pond lilies, arrowheads, and pondweeds. During winter, when snowcover prohibits foraging on ground plants, the moose shifts to a diet of twigs and bark of conifer and hardwood trees. *Alces alces* requires about 19.5 kilograms (45 lbs.) of food per day (Morow, 1976).

A rather solitary animal, the moose is active chiefly at dawn and dusk. As a rule, it is not very sociable to others of its own species, but during summer several may congregate and feed in a pond. *Alces alces* is a good wader and swimmer and may lie in shallow water to escape torment from blackflies. Its vision is generally poor, but its hearing and smell are acute. Home ranges are rather small, varying from 2.2. to 16.9 square kilometers (0.85–6.5 mi.^{2}). Population density usually does not exceed two moose per square kilometer (5.2 moose/mi.^{2}) in optimum habitat.

In early autumn, the rutting season begins. Bulls, sporting polished antlers, travel widely in search of receptive cows. Like other male cervids, they compete vigorously for mating rights by jousting rival bulls with their huge antlers and by an elaborate repertoire of threat displays. Cows, not passive at this time, may actively pursue bulls. They frequently indicate their presence by emitting a long, moaning sound. Unlike the bull wapiti, the bull moose does not assemble a harem but remains with one cow for a week or two before moving on to mate with another. Mating is concluded usually by mid-October.

Following a gestation period of about eight months, a single young or twins are born in May or June. The young weigh between 11.3 and 15.9 kilograms (25–35 lbs.) at birth. Although fully furred, newborns are rather wobbly and helpless, but growth is rapid and they are weaned by six months of age. The young remain with their mother for about one year. In the wild, moose live from 18 to 23 years.

Status in Pennsylvania

Alces alces is a Holarctic species, originally occurring throughout much of northern North America and northern Eurasia. In North America, its range has retreated northward in recent times and, today, extends south from Alaska and Canada into northern New England, northern Minnesota, and south in the Rocky Mountains to northeastern Utah and western Wyoming.

The lack of historical records of the moose in Pennsylvania suggests that the species was always poorly represented in this state. With the encroachment of colonial settlements, the numbers of moose declined rapidly because of excessive hunting for meat and hides. *Alces alces* was extirpated in Pennsylvania probably by the late 18th century. The Pennsylvania Biological Survey has declared the native population of *A. alces* in Pennsylvania "extirpated" in its report *Species of Special* *Concern in Pennsylvania* (Genoways and Brenner, 1985).

BISON

SCIENTIFIC NAME: *Bison bison*

ORDER: Artiodactyla

FAMILY: Bovidae

The bison is the largest land mammal in North America. Adults range in length from 198 to 380 centimeters (6.5 – 12 ft.) and weigh from 410 to 900 kilograms (900 – 2,000 lbs.). In addition to its large size, *B. bison* is distinguished by its humped back, large head, and long beard. Short, upturned horns with a spread of up to 90 centimeters (3 ft.) adorn both sexes. Whereas adults wear a brown, shaggy coat, young calves are colored reddish brown. Males (bulls) are considerably larger than females (cows) and have larger humps and thicker necks and horns. Tails of adults range from 43 to 81.5 centimeters (1.5 – 3 ft.) long.

Within its range, the habitats of *B. bison* vary from primarily plains and grasslands to foothills and mountains. Mainly a grazer, it feeds on grasses, sedges, and forbs. During winter, it can be seen pushing snow aside with its hooves and head to uncover vegetation.

The bison is most active at dawn and dusk, but, during the heat of midday, it may be seen taking a "dust bath" to expel insects and to relieve itching. It devotes much time to resting and chewing its cud. The average daily movement of the bison is only about 3 kilometers (2 mi.). Formerly, bison residing in the Great Plains made extensive annual migrations of several hundred kilometers between summer and winter ranges. Today, some Canadian populations still travel up to 250 kilometers (160 mi.) each autumn and spring, roaming from wooded hills to the Peace River Valley of Alberta, Canada.

Bison bison is notably gregarious. It forms herds ranging in size from 11 to 20 individuals, composed of cows and calves. Bulls, however, for much of the year, are rather solitary or occasionally may form small groups. Rutting begins in midsummer and extends to early autumn. During this time, bulls compete fiercely for cows, mainly by head-to-head ramming. The successful combatant pairs with a cow for several days but then moves on to mate with other females.

In May, after a gestation period of about nine and one-half months, the female retreats to a secluded site and bears one calf. Occasionally, twins are born. Highly precocial, the newborn is fully furred and weighs about 30 kilograms (66 lbs.). It stands to nurse on wobbly legs about one-half hour after birth. In a few days, it joins the herd with its mother. Most calves are weaned by early autumn. In two to three years, the bison reaches sexual maturity. The life span of *B. bison* in the wild averages about 20 years.

Status in Pennsylvania

Originally, the bison ranged in North America from the Rocky Mountains and eastern Oregon in the west to the Appalachian Mountains and even to the Atlantic Coast in the east. It roamed from the Gulf of Mexico in the south to the Northwest Territories of Canada. Prior to the arrival of the first Europeans, the North American population of bison numbered about 70 million. By the year 1900, the numbers had dropped to fewer than 1,000 individuals. This demise was attributable to killing for hides, food, and sport. Today, the bison is represented in North America only by wild and semiwild herds maintained on private ranches, several national parks, and in public reserves.

During historic times, bison inhabited valleys, foothills, and forests of Pennsylvania. With the arrival of the first European settlers and increasing hunting pressure, the numbers of bison rapidly declined in the Commonwealth. The last bison reported to be killed in Pennsylvania was from Union County in 1801 (Williams et al., 1985). By 1825, *B. bison* was extirpated from the eastern United States. In its report *Species of Special Concern in Pennsylvania* (Genoways and Brenner, 1985), the Pennsylvania Biological Survey classified the native population of bison in the state as "extirpated."

APPENDIX

GLOSSARY

SELECTED REFERENCES

INDEX AND CHECKLIST

Appendix: Observing Mammals in the Wild

Most wild mammals are nocturnal or active at dawn or dusk, and most actively avoid contact with humans whenever possible. Unless seen along the roadside in the glare of headlights, they remain quite elusive. To detect their presence and identity, one must learn to interpret the clues they leave behind during their outings and activities.

You can begin tracking mammals by looking for their footprints. To supplement your "detective" work, refer to the section titled "Selected Tracks." Note, however, that even by using the individual prints coupled with the adjacent gait patterns in this section, you can only touch the surface of the complex art of tracking. Not only do you need to do further research, but you also need to search out and study lots of tracks.

To comprehend fully the activities and behaviors of wild mammals, you must think like a wild mammal. This can only be done by learning the habits and complex behaviors of mammals and gathering all possible clues left behind during their outings. These clues include fecal droppings (scats), scratches on trees, a chewed antler, trails or pathways, remains of feeding activities, smells, and even sounds. You can also locate their homes and tunnels. If an animal has died, perhaps only a skull is left to indicate its past presence. In that case, the section called "Dental Formulae" will assist you in identifying the species.

Among the more conspicuous signs of mammals are their homes. These range from the grapefruit-sized nests of meadow voles hidden within a tussock of grass to huge, hemispheric beaver lodges. The homes of Pennsylvania mammals are described and sometimes illustrated in each species account to aid in your identification of this important evidence. As you inspect these homes in the wild, look carefully around the entrances for scats which may confirm the identity of the occupant. The study of scats (scatology) reveals much about a mammal's activities and diet, in addition to acting as a vital clue to identity. Scatology is not treated in this guide, but excellent books that deal with this interesting subject include Murie (1954), Halfpenny (1986), and others cited in "Selected References."

A mammal's activity is also indicated by its excavations. Golf course groundkeepers are usually quite familiar with the surface tunnels and hills produced by moles, and the burrowing activities of muskrats are easily discovered by inspecting the banks of most Pennsylvania farm ponds. Short-tailed shrews are excellent burrowers, and their underground subways commonly emerge below backyard bird feeders. The entrances of woodchuck dens are a common feature along fencerows and in pasturelands of rural Pennsylvania.

Marks on trees and neatly severed twigs are signs that mammals have been in the area. The most obvious mammalian "chewers" are the porcupine and beaver, whereas bears, deer, rabbits, and voles commonly debark trees. Deer scrape bark from trees during the autumn as they rub the velvet off their newly grown antlers. The resulting antler trees or "buck rubs" are well known as a sign of deer activity. Further, bears commonly leave characteristic vertical claw and tooth marks on trees and use trees as rubbing posts for scent marking or to relieve itching. Many members of the dog and cat families also use trees for scent marking, rubbing, chewing, and clawing.

The activities of mammals also can be detected by their trails. The well-worn "game trail" characteristic of the white-tailed deer is familiar to most naturalists. Small mammals such as voles also make miniature versions of these game trails. Voles produce intricate, well-concealed runway systems which crisscross grassy fields, and shrews establish elaborate runways beneath the forest leaf litter. Evidence of the foraging activities of beavers and muskrats is revealed by pathways from the water's edge to fields and wetlands where they feed.

The feeding activities of mammals may act as a clue to their identity. Food caches in the form of piles of seeds and cone scales (middens) placed on stumps reveal the presence of red squirrels. Their close relative the gray squirrel chooses to bury nuts singly below the ground to be relocated and consumed during winter; a hole left in the ground after excavation of a nut is a sure sign of squirrel activity. Deer mice and white-footed mice establish elaborate food caches in hollow logs and even cache seeds and nuts in old boots and teapots in rural cabins.

Smells and sounds further suggest the presence of mammals. The nauseating, musky, pervasive odor of the striped skunk is well known to most Pennsylvanians and needs little description. The staccato "cherr" of an agitated red squirrel is a sure sign of its presence and familiar to most hikers. Likewise, the high-pitched "chip" of our eastern chipmunk alerts those nearby to its presence well before it is seen.

Signs of wild mammals are abundant and common in the environments of Pennsylvania. Careful observation of their habitats and continuing study of the natural history of mammals will aid the outdoor enthusiast in gathering and interpreting clues to the secretive lives of Pennsylvania's wild mammals.

Selected Tracks

Illustrated here are prints and gait patterns of 31 genera representing all 17 families in the 7 orders of Pennsylvania mammals. Tracks of the domestic dog (*Canis familiaris*) and the domestic cat (*Felis catus*) are included, because they are frequently encountered in the woodlands and thickets of the state. These tracks are arranged in conventional phylogenetic sequence, as are the accounts of the species.

Reading tracks is a difficult job, because their legibility varies greatly with the substrate frequented and the locomotor activity of the mammal. Footprints or tracks are best represented in soft mud along lakes, ponds, rivers, and streams. Dusty or sandy paths and, during winter, fresh snow also afford excellent tracking substrates. Once tracks are

VIRGINIA OPOSSUM

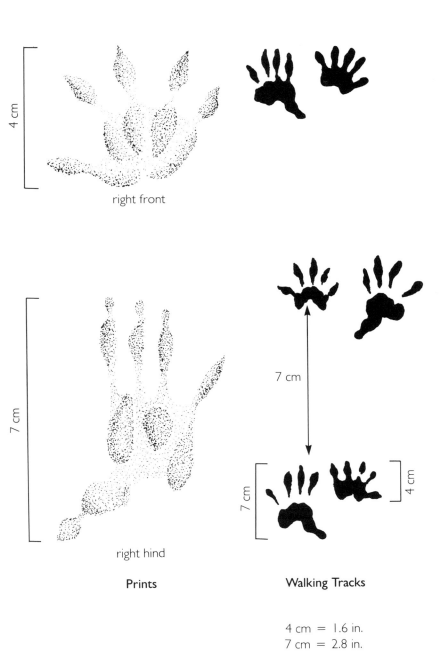

4 cm

right front

7 cm

7 cm

7 cm

4 cm

right hind

Prints

Walking Tracks

4 cm = 1.6 in.
7 cm = 2.8 in.

NORTHERN SHORT-TAILED SHREW

EASTERN COTTONTAIL

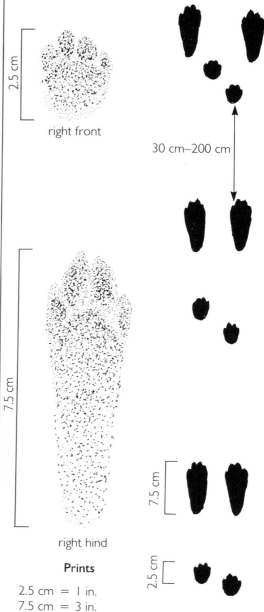

7 mm

right front

8 mm

right hind

Prints

7 mm = 0.3 in.
8 mm = 0.3 in.

2.5 cm

right front

30 cm–200 cm

7.5 cm

right hind

Prints

2.5 cm = 1 in.
7.5 cm = 3 in.
30 cm = 12 in.
200 cm = 80 in.

7.5 cm

2.5 cm

Hopping Tracks

SNOWSHOE HARE

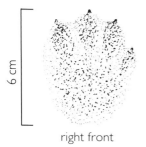

6 cm

right front

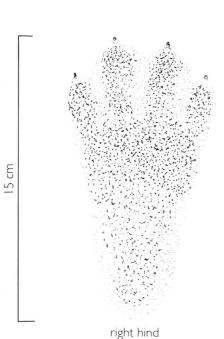

15 cm

right hind

Prints

6 cm = 2.4 in.
15 cm = 6 in.
30 cm = 12 in.
300 cm = 120 in.

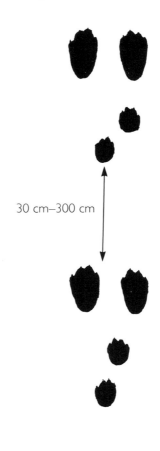

30 cm–300 cm

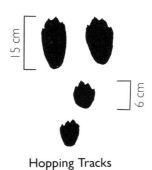

15 cm

6 cm

Hopping Tracks

EASTERN CHIPMUNK

1.5 cm

right front

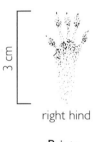

3 cm

right hind

Prints

22 cm

3 cm

1.5 cm

1.5 cm = 0.6 in.
3 cm = 1.2 in.
22 cm = 8.8 in.

Bounding Tracks

WOODCHUCK

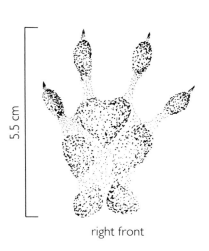

right front

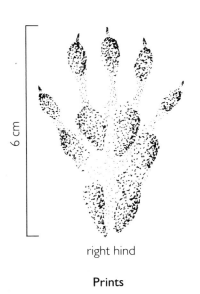

right hind

Prints

5.5 cm = 2.2 in.
6 cm = 2.4 in.

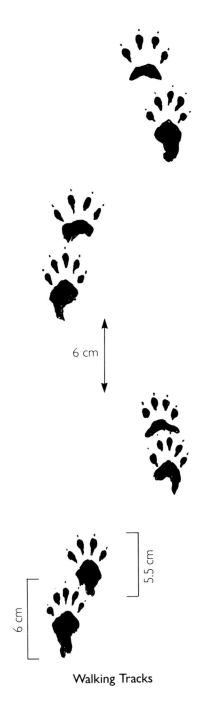

6 cm

Walking Tracks

GRAY SQUIRREL

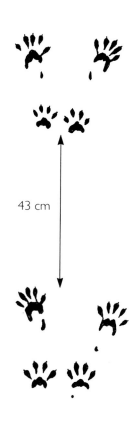

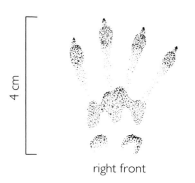

right front

43 cm

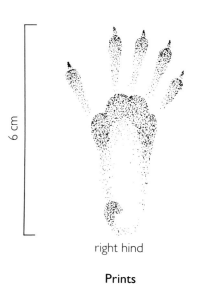

right hind

Prints

6 cm

4 cm

4 cm = 1.6 in.
6 cm = 2.4 in.
43 cm = 17.2 in.

Bounding Tracks

RED SQUIRREL

2.5 cm

right front

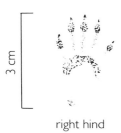

3 cm

right hind

Prints

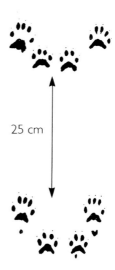

25 cm

2 cm = 0.8 in.
2.5 cm = 1 in.
3 cm = 1.2 in.
25 cm = 10 in.

2 cm

2 cm

Bounding Tracks

SOUTHERN FLYING SQUIRREL

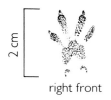

2 cm

right front

2 cm

right hind

Prints

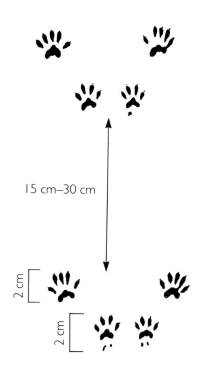

15 cm–30 cm

2 cm

2 cm

Bounding Tracks

2 cm = 0.8 in.
15 cm = 6 in.
30 cm = 12 in.

BEAVER

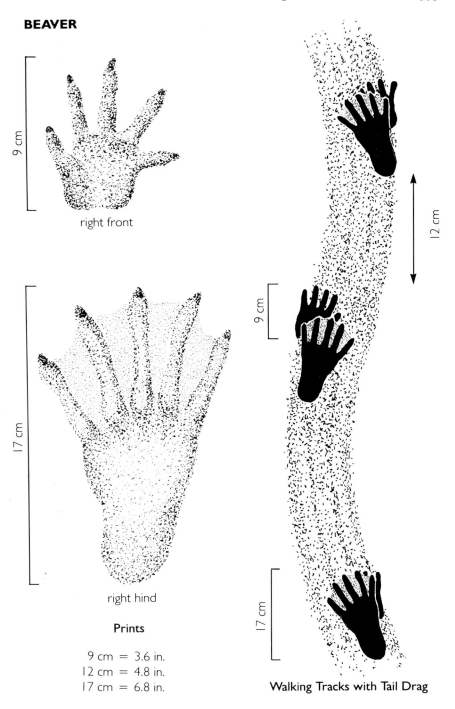

9 cm

right front

17 cm

right hind

Prints

9 cm = 3.6 in.
12 cm = 4.8 in.
17 cm = 6.8 in.

9 cm

12 cm

17 cm

Walking Tracks with Tail Drag

MARSH RICE RAT

right front

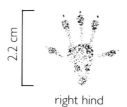

right hind

Prints

3 cm

1.5 cm = 0.6 in.
2.2 cm = 0.9 in.
3 cm = 1.2 in.

Walking Tracks

DEER MOUSE

0.5 cm

right front

1.3 cm

right hind

Prints

10 cm

1.3 cm

0.5 cm

0.5 cm = 0.2 in.
1.3 cm = 0.5 in.
10 cm = 4 in.

Bounding Tracks

Bounding Tracks
with Tail Held in Air

EASTERN WOODRAT

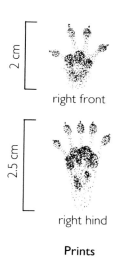

right front

right hind

Prints

20 cm

2.5 cm

2 cm

Bounding Tracks

2 cm = 0.8 in.
2.5 cm = 1 in.
20 cm = 8 in.

SOUTHERN RED-BACKED VOLE

right front

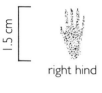

right hind

Prints

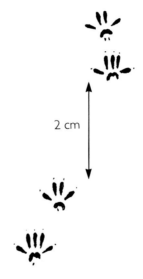

2 cm

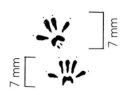

Walking Tracks

7 mm = 0.3 in.
1 cm = 0.4 in.
1.5 cm = 0.6 in.
2 cm = 0.8 in.

MEADOW VOLE

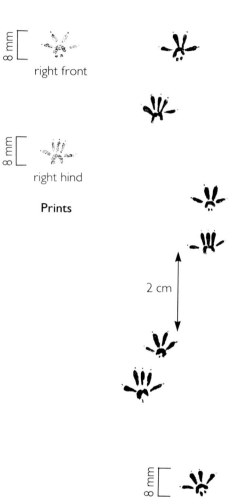

8 mm [right front

8 mm [right hind

Prints

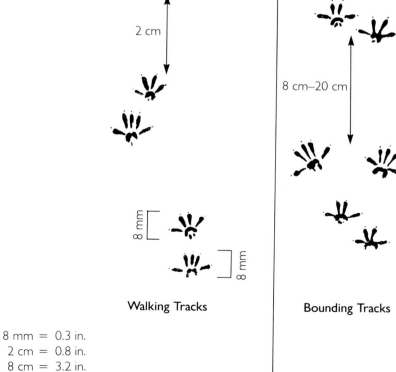

2 cm

8 cm–20 cm

8 mm [

] 8 mm

Walking Tracks

Bounding Tracks

8 mm = 0.3 in.
2 cm = 0.8 in.
8 cm = 3.2 in.
20 cm = 8 in.

MUSKRAT

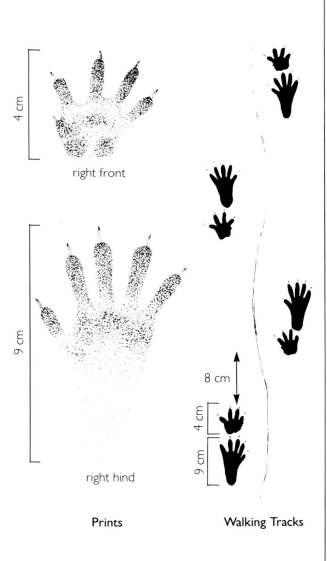

4 cm

right front

9 cm

right hind

8 cm

4 cm

9 cm

Prints

Walking Tracks

27 cm

Galloping Tracks

4 cm = 1.6 in.
8 cm = 3.2 in.
9 cm = 3.6 in.
27 cm = 10.8 in.

NORWAY RAT

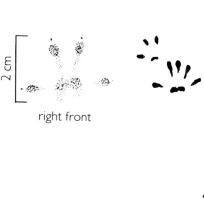

right front

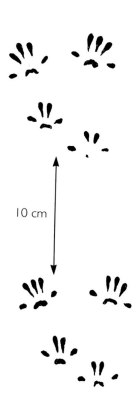

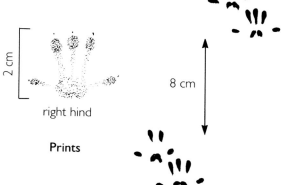

right hind

Prints

8 cm

10 cm

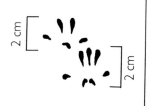

2 cm = 0.8 in.
8 cm = 3.2 in.
10 cm = 4 in.

Walking Tracks

Hopping Tracks

MEADOW JUMPING MOUSE

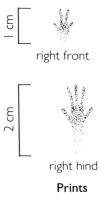

1 cm

right front

2 cm

right hind

Prints

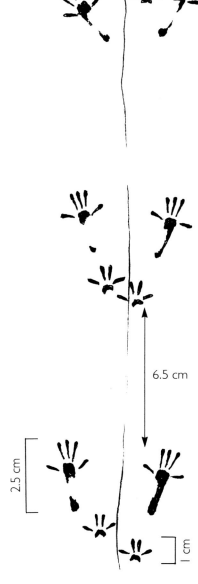

6.5 cm

2.5 cm

1 cm

1 cm = 0.4 in.
2 cm = 0.8 in.
2.5 cm = 1 in.
6.5 cm = 2.6 in.

Hopping Tracks

PORCUPINE

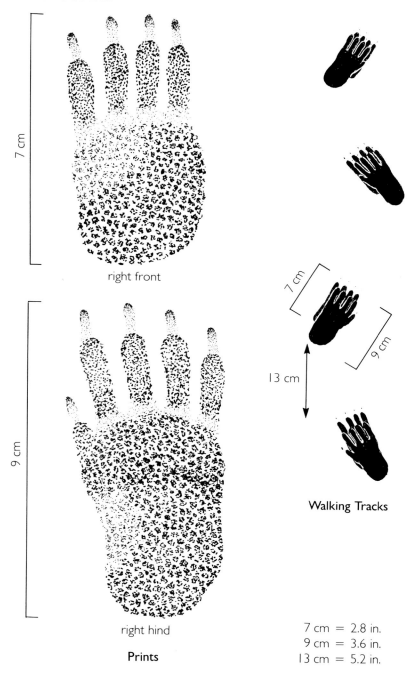

7 cm

right front

7 cm

9 cm

13 cm

Walking Tracks

9 cm

right hind

Prints

7 cm = 2.8 in.
9 cm = 3.6 in.
13 cm = 5.2 in.

RED FOX

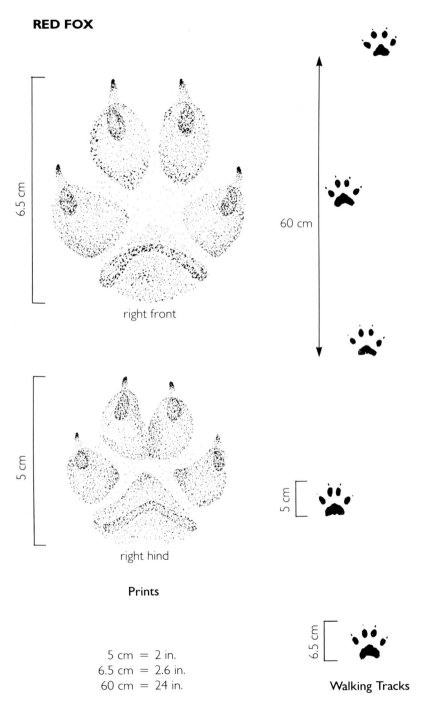

6.5 cm

right front

60 cm

5 cm

right hind

5 cm

Prints

5 cm = 2 in.
6.5 cm = 2.6 in.
60 cm = 24 in.

6.5 cm

Walking Tracks

GRAY FOX

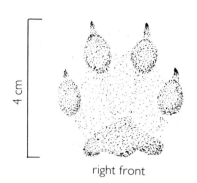

right front

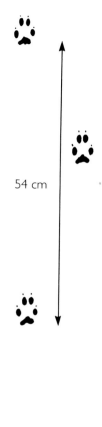

54 cm

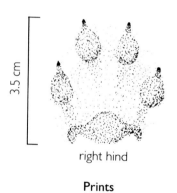

right hind

Prints

3.5 cm

3.5 cm = 1.4 in.
4 cm = 1.6 in.
54 cm = 21.6 in.

4 cm

Walking Tracks

BLACK BEAR

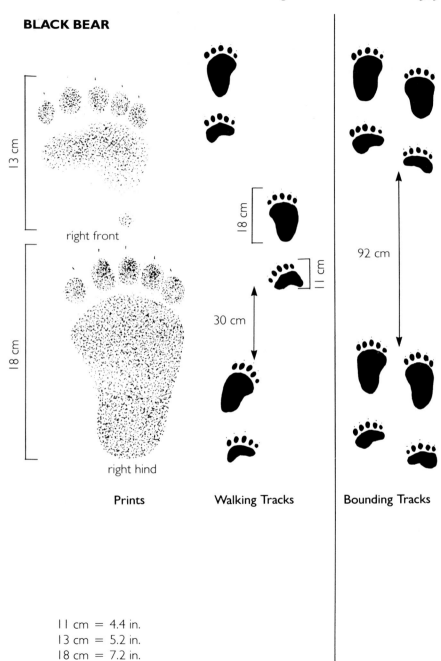

13 cm

right front

18 cm

right hind

18 cm

11 cm

30 cm

92 cm

Prints

Walking Tracks

Bounding Tracks

11 cm = 4.4 in.
13 cm = 5.2 in.
18 cm = 7.2 in.
30 cm = 12 in.
92 cm = 36.8 in.

RACCOON

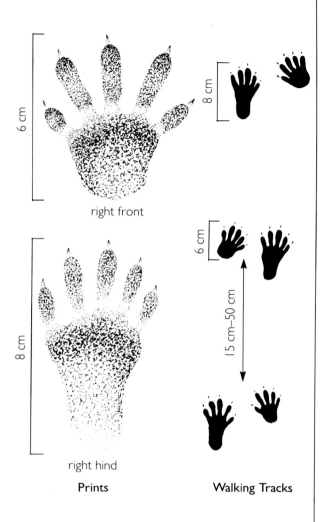

6 cm

right front

8 cm

right hind

Prints

8 cm

6 cm

15 cm–50 cm

Walking Tracks

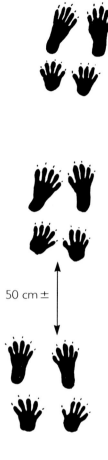

50 cm ±

Galloping Tracks

6 cm = 2.4 in.
8 cm = 3.2 in.
15 cm = 6 in.
50 cm = 20 in.

LONG-TAILED WEASEL

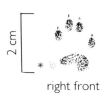

2 cm

right front

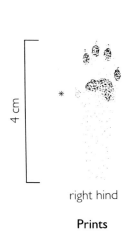

4 cm

right hind

Prints

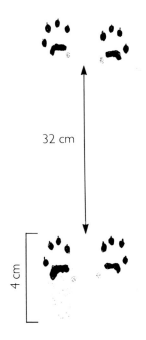

32 cm

4 cm

2 cm

Bounding Tracks

2 cm = 0.8 in.
4 cm = 1.6 in.
*Inner toe occasionally registers.   32 cm = 12.8 in.

MINK

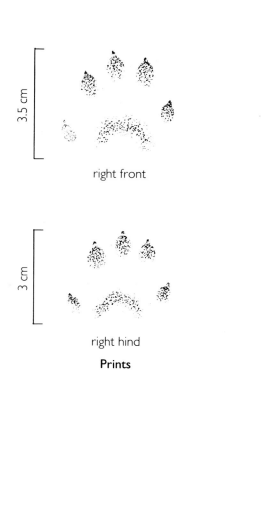

3.5 cm

right front

3 cm

right hind

Prints

28 cm

3 cm

3.5 cm

Galloping Tracks

3 cm = 1.2 in.
3.5 cm = 1.4 in.
28 cm = 11.2 in.

STRIPED SKUNK

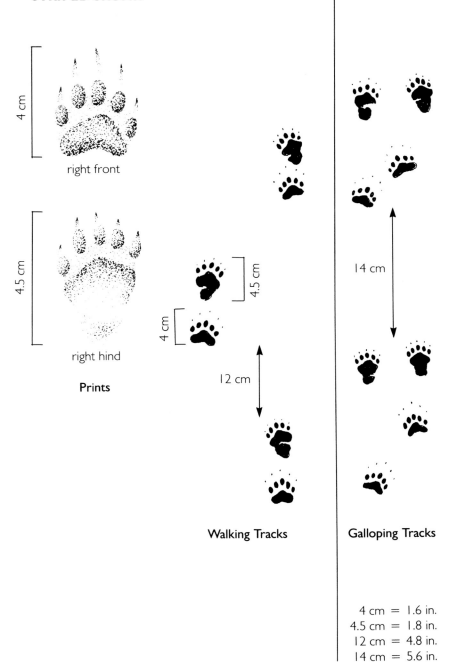

right front

right hind

Prints

Walking Tracks

Galloping Tracks

4 cm = 1.6 in.
4.5 cm = 1.8 in.
12 cm = 4.8 in.
14 cm = 5.6 in.

RIVER OTTER

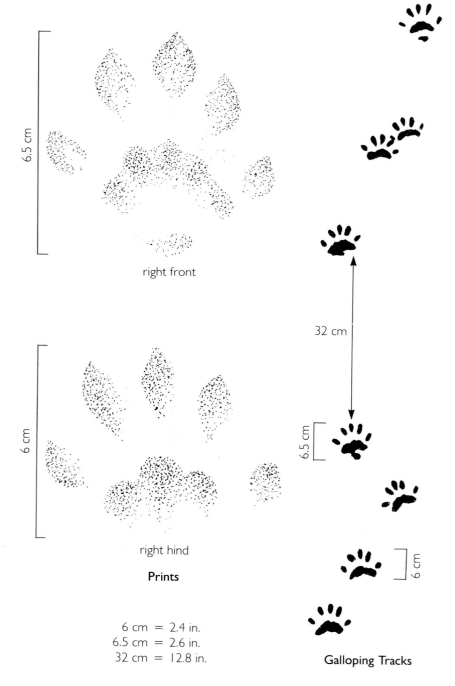

6.5 cm

right front

6 cm

right hind

Prints

32 cm

6.5 cm

6 cm

6 cm = 2.4 in.
6.5 cm = 2.6 in.
32 cm = 12.8 in.

Galloping Tracks

BOBCAT

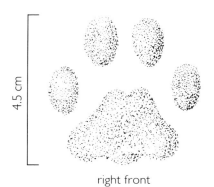

right front

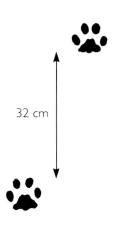

32 cm

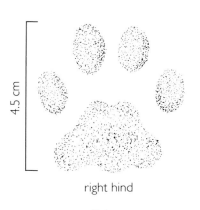

right hind

Prints

4.5 cm

4.5 cm

4.5 cm = 1.8 in.
32 cm = 12.8 in.

Walking Tracks

DOMESTIC CAT

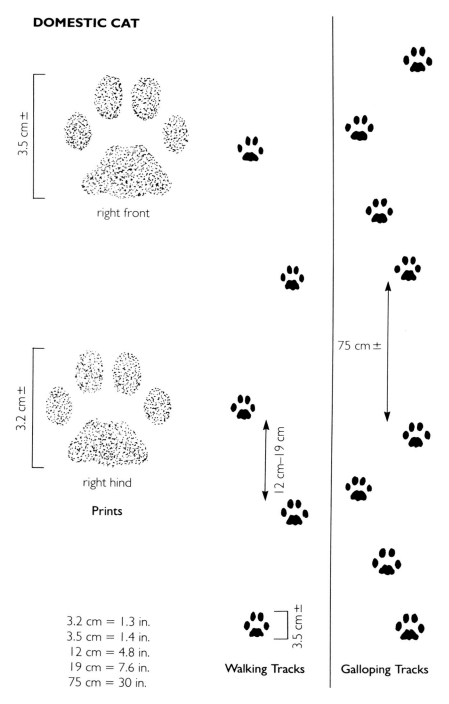

3.5 cm ±

right front

3.2 cm ±

right hind

Prints

75 cm ±

12 cm–19 cm

3.5 cm ±

3.2 cm = 1.3 in.
3.5 cm = 1.4 in.
12 cm = 4.8 in.
19 cm = 7.6 in.
75 cm = 30 in.

Walking Tracks

Galloping Tracks

DOMESTIC DOG

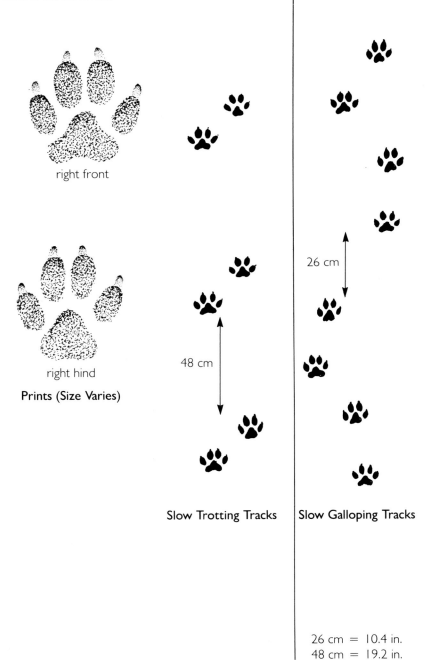

right front

right hind

Prints (Size Varies)

48 cm

26 cm

Slow Trotting Tracks

Slow Galloping Tracks

26 cm = 10.4 in.
48 cm = 19.2 in.

WHITE-TAILED DEER

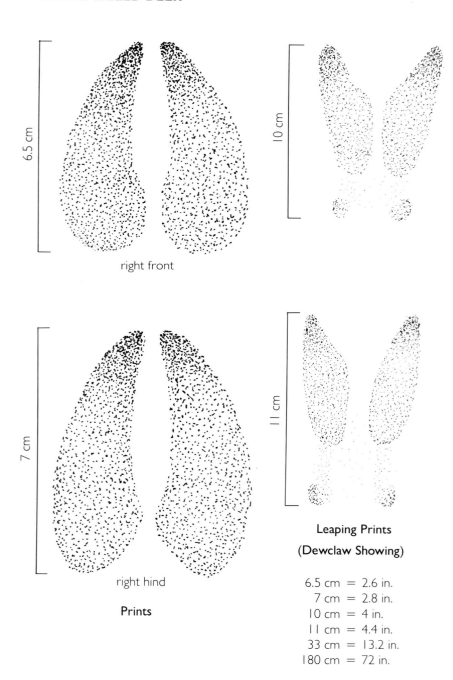

right front

right hind

Prints

Leaping Prints
(Dewclaw Showing)

6.5 cm = 2.6 in.
7 cm = 2.8 in.
10 cm = 4 in.
11 cm = 4.4 in.
33 cm = 13.2 in.
180 cm = 72 in.

WHITE-TAILED DEER

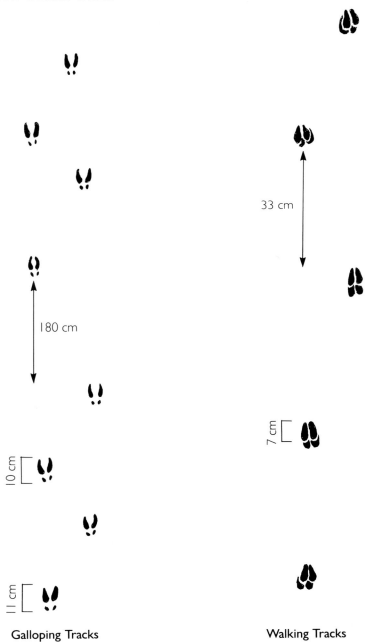

33 cm

180 cm

10 cm

7 cm

11 cm

Galloping Tracks   Walking Tracks

found, the difficult task begins. First, assess the size and shape of the prints. Are they hand-like in appearance? Are claw marks present or lacking? Take a look at the gait pattern. Does a tail drag show? Do the tracks end or begin at the base of a tree or enter an earthen hole? By the process of elimination, you may rule out one mammal after another and, with a bit of luck, arrive at the group of mammals or even the species that left the tracks.

You should not rely on reading tracks alone to substantiate the presence of a mammal. Other signs left behind during outings such as tunnels, scratches on trees, and fecal droppings will assist you in identifying Pennsylvania's mammalian fauna and enhance your understanding of these animals' habits and complex behaviors.

Dental Formulae

A dental formula specifies the types, arrangement, and numbers of teeth for a given species of mammal. Scientists commonly use this formula to aid in identifying a species of mammal when only the skull is available as evidence of its presence.

The teeth of mammals are set in sockets. They occur in two developmental sets called milk ("deciduous") and permanent teeth. Further, mammals have "heterodont" teeth—that is, teeth differentiated on the basis of their function. Heterodont teeth include incisors, canines, premolars, and molars.

It is easy to use a dental formula. The numbers of upper teeth are given above a horizontal line; the numbers of lower teeth are written below the line. Teeth are listed from the front to the rear of the skull and grouped in the appropriate heterdont category, that is, as incisors, canines, premolars, or molars. Because the two halves of each jaw of a mammal have the same number of teeth, the dental formula is written to describe only one side. The total number of teeth, thus, is determined by multiplying by two.

The table in this section contains the dental formulae for all genera of wild mammals and many domesticated mammals in Pennsylvania. For comparison, the dental formula for humans is also included. Before attempting to use this table, you might find it helpful to review the examples given.

Example 1
Assume you found a skull of the Virginia opossum (*Didelphis virginiana*) in the forest (see figure 1). Its dental formula is written:

$$\frac{5 - 1 - 3 - 4}{4 - 1 - 3 - 4} = \frac{26}{24} = 50$$

The skull of *Didelphis* is the only North American land mammal with 50 teeth; therefore, identification can be made solely by using the den-

Dental Formulae

Incisors	Canines	Premolars	Molars	Upper/ Lower	Total Teeth	Genera of Mammals in Pennsylvania
$\dfrac{5-1-3-4}{4-1-3-4}$				$= \dfrac{26}{24} =$	50	*Didelphis*
$\dfrac{3-1-4-3}{3-1-4-3}$				$= \dfrac{22}{22} =$	44	*Parascalops, Condylura, Sus**
$\dfrac{3-1-4-2}{3-1-4-3}$				$= \dfrac{20}{22} =$	42	*Vulpes, Urocyon, Canis latrans, Canis familiaris,** *Ursus*
$\dfrac{3-1-4-2}{3-1-4-2}$				$= \dfrac{20}{20} =$	40	*Procyon*
$\dfrac{3-1-4-1}{3-1-4-2}$				$= \dfrac{18}{20} =$	38	*Martes, Gulo*
$\dfrac{2-1-3-3}{3-1-3-3}$				$= \dfrac{18}{20} =$	38	*Myotis*
$\dfrac{3-(0-1)-(3-4)-3}{3-(0-1)-\ \ 3\ \ -3}$				$= \dfrac{18-22}{18-20} =$	36–42	*Equus**
$\dfrac{3-1-3-3}{2-0-3-3}$				$= \dfrac{20}{16} =$	36	*Scalopus*
$\dfrac{2-1-2-3}{3-1-3-3}$				$= \dfrac{16}{20} =$	36	*Lasionycteris*
$\dfrac{3-1-4-1}{3-1-3-2}$				$= \dfrac{18}{18} =$	36	*Lutra*
$\dfrac{2-1-2-3}{3-1-2-3}$				$= \dfrac{16}{18} =$	34	*Pipistrellus*
$\dfrac{3-1-3-1}{3-1-3-2}$				$= \dfrac{16}{18} =$	34	*Mustela, Mephitis, Spilogale, Taxidea*
$\dfrac{0-1-3-3}{3-1-3-3}$				$= \dfrac{14}{20} =$	34	*Cervus*
$\dfrac{2-1-2-3}{2-1-2-3}$				$= \dfrac{16}{16} =$	32	*Homo*
$\dfrac{3-1-3-3}{1-1-1-3}$				$= \dfrac{20}{12} =$	32	*Sorex, Blarina*
$\dfrac{2-1-1-3}{3-1-2-3}$				$= \dfrac{14}{18} =$	32	*Eptesicus*

Incisors	Canines	Premolars	Molars	Upper/ Lower	Total Teeth	Genera of Mammals in Pennsylvania
$\dfrac{1-1-2-3}{3-1-2-3}$				$=\dfrac{14}{18}=$	32	*Lasiurus*
$\dfrac{0-0-3-3}{3-1-3-3}$				$=\dfrac{12}{20}=$	32	*Odocoileus, Alces, Ovis,* * *Capra,* * *Bos,* * *Bison*
$\dfrac{3-1-2-3}{1-1-1-3}$				$=\dfrac{18}{12}=$	30	*Cryptotis*
$\dfrac{1-1-1-3}{3-1-2-3}$				$=\dfrac{12}{18}=$	30	*Nycticeius*
$\dfrac{3-1-3-1}{3-1-2-1}$				$=\dfrac{16}{14}=$	30	*Felis catus,* * *Felis concolor*
$\dfrac{3-1-2-1}{3-1-2-1}$				$=\dfrac{14}{14}=$	28	*Felis rufus, Felis lynx*
$\dfrac{2-0-3-3}{1-0-2-3}$				$=\dfrac{16}{12}=$	28	*Sylvilagus, Lepus*
$\dfrac{1-0-2-3}{1-0-1-3}$				$=\dfrac{12}{10}=$	22	*Marmota, Tamiasciurus,* * * *Sciurus carolinensis, Glaucomys*
$\dfrac{1-0-1-3}{1-0-1-3}$				$=\dfrac{10}{10}=$	20	*Tamias, Tamiasciurus, Sciurus niger, Castor, Erethizon*
$\dfrac{1-0-1-3}{1-0-0-3}$				$=\dfrac{10}{8}=$	18	*Zapus*
$\dfrac{1-0-0-3}{1-0-0-3}$				$=\dfrac{8}{8}=$	16	*Peromyscus, Neotoma, Clethrionomys, Synaptomys, Microtus, Ondatra, Rattus, Mus, Oryzomys, Napaeozapus*

*Domestic mammals: *Sus* (hog), *Canis familiaris* (dog), *Equus* (horse), *Ovis* (sheep), *Capra* (goat), *Bos* (cow), *Felis catus* (house cat).
* *In *Tamiasciurus*, a small pair of premolars is sometimes present, resulting in a tooth count of 22.

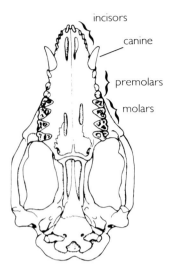

Figure 1. Skull of an opossum (*Didelphis*, × ½).

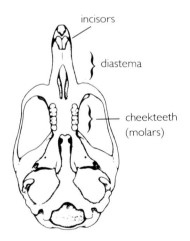

Figure 2. Skull of a rodent (*Peromyscus*, × 2¼).

tal formula. If one finds a skull with 42 teeth, it may be *Vulpes, Urocyon, Canis,* or *Ursus*. In this case, skull diagrams, photographs, or a key to skulls should be used to differentiate correctly between the genera.

Example 2
Some Pennsylvania mammals such as ungulates, lagomorphs, and rodents may lack incisors, canines, or premolars. In such cases, especially

in rodents, there will be a large space ("diastema") present, as shown in the skull illustration of the deer mouse (*Peromyscus*) (see figure 2). Its dental formula is written:

$$\frac{1 - 0 - 0 - 3}{1 - 0 - 0 - 3} = \frac{8}{8} = 16$$

In this formula, the zeros indicate the absence of canines and premolars on both upper and lower jaws, which results in a wide diastema. Once again, adding up the upper and lower totals and multiplying by two yields the total number of teeth found in *Peromyscus*.

Note
Because of the presence of milk teeth, fitting a dental formula to a skull of a young mammal may be confusing. Milk dentition does not include molar teeth.

For additional assistance in identifying skulls found in the wild, consult the skull illustrations at the beginning of each family section throughout this guidebook.

Glossary

Aestivation: A physiological state of dormancy or inactivity, characterized by a decrease in body temperature, that occurs in some species of mammals in response to heat or drought during summer.

Albino: An animal with white hair and pink skin and eyes, a condition resulting from the absence of all pigmentation.

Allantois: A sac-like outgrowth of the embryonic gut of reptiles, birds, and mammals. In embryos of mammals, it is situated between the chorion and amnion and functions in excretion, nutrition, and respiration.

Altricial: Pertaining to young which at birth are blind, naked, and entirely dependent on parental care. Most mammals are altricial at birth.

Amnion: The fluid-filled sac enclosing the embryos of reptiles, birds, and mammals.

Annulated: Composed of rings or having a serially ringed appearance.

Aquatic: Living in water.

Arboreal: Living in trees.

Arthropod: Any member of the invertebrate phylum Arthropoda, such as insects and spiders.

Avian: Of or pertaining to the class Aves (birds).

Buff: Dull, brownish yellow color.

Calcar: The cartilaginous, spur-like projection on the ankle of bats which helps to support the uropatagium (interfemoral membrane).

Cambium: Plant tissue, usually under the bark of trees, consisting of cells that, by repeated division, increase the girth of the stem, adding new wood and bark.

Canopy: In a forest, the uppermost layer of tree branches.

Carnivorous: Pertaining to those animals that feed mainly on meat.

Carrion: A dead body or dead and decaying flesh.

Cheekteeth: Collectively, the premolars and molars.

Chorioallantoic placenta: A type of placenta consisting of an outer chorion and inner allantoic membranes. Marsupial bandicoots and all eutherian mammals have a chorioallantoic placenta.

Chorion: The embryoic membrane that envelops the embryo. In mammals, the chorion makes up most of the placenta.

Choriovitelline placenta: The type of placenta—consisting of a chorion membrane and yolk sac—that occurs in all marsupials except the bandicoots. The choriovitelline placenta is the most primitive type of mammalian placenta.

Cloaca: A chamber at the terminal part of the gut into which the reproductive, digestive, and urinary systems empty and from which waste products leave the body.

Coniferous forest: A forest consisting chiefly of cone-bearing evergreen trees such as pines, spruces, and firs.

Conspecific: Of the same species.

Coprophagy: The habit of feeding upon feces. Rabbits, for example, practice coprophagy.

Crepuscular: Pertaining to twilight (dawn and dusk); active during periods of twilight.

Cursorial: Adapted for running locomotion.

Cusp: A small projection or bump on the biting surface of a mammalian molar tooth.

Deciduous forest: A forest consisting chiefly of trees which shed their leaves annually, usually in autumn.

Digitigrade: Walking on the toes with the heels not touching the ground. Cats and dogs exhibit this stance.

Distemper: Several infectious diseases of animals, especially members of the dog family, characterized by fever, lethargy, loss of appetite, and a discharge from the eyes and nose.

Diurnal: Pertaining to the day; active during daylight hours.

Dorsal: Pertaining to the back or dorsum of an animal; opposite of "ventral."

Echolocation: A process by which an animal orients itself by emitting high-frequency sounds and interpreting the reflected sound waves. Most bats navigate and locate prey by this method.

Estrus: See "Heat."

Eutherian: A mammal of the subclass Eutheria, the dominant group of mammals which includes the true placental mammals.

Extirpation: The extinction of a species in a particular geographic region.

Forb: An herb other than grass.

Fossorial: Pertaining to life under the surface of the ground. Some animals exhibit structural modification adapted for digging and burrowing. Moles of the class Mammalia best exemplify these adaptations.

Gestation period: The period of development of the embryo in the uterus.

Gregarious: Living in groups or herds; sociable.

Grizzled: Coloration which is gray or streaked with gray.

Guard hairs: Long, stiff outer hairs which lie over the underfur of most mammals.

Heat: The period during which a female mammal is sexually receptive to a male; also called "estrus."

Herbaceous: Resembling or having the characteristics of an herb; a nonwoody plant.

Hibernation: The period of winter inactivity during which normal physiological processes are reduced and a significant decrease in body temperature occurs. In Pennsylvania, true hibernation is displayed only by woodchucks, jumping mice, and bats.

Holarctic: Pertaining to the land mass of the entire northern region of the continents of the Old World and New World.

Homeothermic: Warm-blooded; having a body temperature that remains fairly constant regardless of external temperatures.

Home range: The area that an animal traverses during its normal activities of food gathering, mating, and caring for its young.

Implantation: The process by which the blastocyst (embryo) imbeds in the lining of the uterus.

Inguinal: Of or pertaining to the region of the groin.

Insectivorous: Pertaining to those animals that feed mainly on insects. Mammals such as shrews, moles, and most bats are insectivorous.

Keel: A ridge-like projection that provides expanded surface for the attachment of muscles.

Lactation: The production of milk by mammary glands.

Larva: A developmental form of some insects, frogs, and many marine invertebrates that is fundamentally unlike the adult in appearance. Grubs, maggots, and caterpillars are larvae.

Leptospirosis: A disease produced by a spirochaete bacterium (*Leptospira*) transmitted to humans and other mammals by contact with contaminated water, soil, and vegetables. Symptoms include fever, chills, headaches, malaise, abdominal pains, nausea, and vomiting.

Mammary glands: Milk-producing glands unique to mammals. Growth and activity are governed by hormones of the ovary, uterus, and pituitary gland. Mammae develop in both sexes but are rudimentary in males.

Mast: Fruit of various forest trees such as acorns, beechnuts, and hickory nuts.

Melanism: Unusual darkening of coloration because of large deposits of the melanin pigment in the skin or hair.

Mesic: Pertaining to an area or habitat characterized by moisture and dampness.

Metabolic rate: The speed at which the chemical processes of the body occur.

Migration: Movement, usually seasonal, from one region to another for the purpose of feeding or breeding.

Molt: The process of periodically shedding and replacing hair.

Monestrous: Having a single estrous cycle (period of heat) per year.

Montane: Pertaining to or inhabiting mountainous country.

Murine typhus: Infectious disease caused by the *Rickettsia* bacterium transmitted by arthropods. *Murine* pertains to the family Muridae (Old World Rats and Mice).

New World: All the land masses of the Western Hemisphere.

Niche: The role or "profession" of an organism in the environment.

Nictitating membrane: A thin, transparent membrane that can be drawn over the surface of the eyeball from the inner angle of the eye. Often called a "third eyelid," this membrane is common in reptiles and birds, occurs in some sharks and amphibians, and is present in a few mammals, such as the beaver.

Nocturnal: Pertaining to the night; active during the night.

Nymph: A young insect that looks somewhat like an adult but with juvenile features.

Occlusal: Pertaining to the grinding surface of the upper and lower teeth.

Old World: All the land masses of the Eastern Hemisphere.

Omnivorous: Pertaining to those animals that eat both animal and vegetable food.

Ovulation: The release of an egg or eggs from the ovary.

Parturition: The act of giving birth to offspring; the process by which the fetus of mammals separates from the mother's uterine wall and is born.

Patagium: The gliding membrane in flying squirrels and bats that typically stretches down the side of the body between the forelimb and hindlimb and occasionally includes the tail.

Pelage: The entire coat of a mammal, including fur, wool, hair, quills, and bristles.

Pinna: The external ear, which consists of a thin flap of skin protruding from the head. Pinnae are absent in many aquatic and fossorial mammals.

Placenta: The vascular structure formed by the union of uterine tissue of the mother and membranes of the developing embryo. The placenta provides for the transfer of gases, nutrients, and waste materials between mother and fetus. Only placental mammals have a well-developed placenta. Marsupials have either a rudimentary placenta or none, and monotremes lay eggs.

Plantigrade: Walking on the soles of the feet with the heel touching the ground. Bears and humans, for example, have a plantigrade foot stance.

Poikilothermic: Cold-blooded; having a body temperature that varies with that of the environment.

Polyestrous: Having more than one estrous cycle (period of heat) per year.

Population: A group of individuals of a single species; a reproductive unit.

Postpartum heat: The ability of a female to become receptive to a male soon after giving birth; also called "postpartum estrus."

Precocial: Pertaining to young which at birth are fully furred, have open eyes, and are able to move immediately. Snowshoe hares, deer, porcupines, and livestock have precocial young.

Prehensile: Pertaining to appendages adapted for grasping and seizing by curling or wrapping. Many New World monkeys and the opossum, for example, have prehensile tails.

Pupa: The dormant or inactive stage in the development of some insects (between the larval and adult stages). During this stage, the insect is usually enclosed within a protective covering such as an earthen cell, cocoon, or puparium.

Rickettsia: A bacterium-like organism of the genus *Rickettsia* which exhibits certain protozoan characteristics. This organism commonly is transmitted by arthropods and causes typhus fever, Rocky Mountain spotted fever, Q fever, trench fever, and Rickettsial pox.

Riparian: Pertaining to the bank or shore of a river, lake, or stream.

Rut: A breeding season, usually referring to the annual recurrent state of sexual excitement in the male deer.

Scansorial: Pertaining to arboreal animals that climb by means of sharp, curved claws. Tree squirrels, for example, are scansorial.

Species: A group of interbreeding natural populations that are reproductively isolated from other such groups.

Stenotopic: Pertaining to a species characterized by a restricted geographic range because of its limited tolerance of ecological conditions.

Submaxillary gland: A small gland under the lower jaw that supplies saliva to the mouth.

Subnivean: Beneath the snow.

Subspecies: A recognizable subpopulation of a single species, typically having a distinct geographic range.

Subterranean: Below the surface of the ground.

Succession: The gradual replacement of one kind of community by another kind. The plant changes that occur during replacement of a prairie by shrubland are an example of succession.

Talus: A slope formed by rocky debris at the base of a cliff or on a hillside.

Tawny: Brownish yellow color.

Territory: The portion of the home range that an individual defends against members of the same or sometimes different species.

Torpidity: The relatively short-term period of winter inactivity when the body temperature drops and the rate of metabolism is slightly reduced. In Pennsylvania, chipmunks, deer mice, and white-footed mice undergo torpidity.

Tubercle: A small, rounded projection, such as is found on the crown of a tooth or on the sole of a foot.

Tularemia: A bacterial disease contracted by humans principally through the bites of flies, fleas, ticks, and lice which infest rabbits, hares, and rodents. This bacterium (*Pasteurella tularensis*) may also be transmitted to humans by direct contact with an infected animal. The disease is characterized by ulceration at the point of inoculation, fever, and inflammation of the lymph glands.

Tundra: The treeless area in arctic and alpine regions where vegetation is dominated by low shrubs, grasses, forbs, lichens, and mosses.

Understory: A layer of herbs, shrubs, and small trees beneath the forest canopy.

Unguligrade: Positioning the foot so only the unguis (hoof) is in contact with the ground. Deer, for example, have an unguligrade foot stance.

Uropatagium: The web of skin extending between the hindlegs of bats which frequently encloses the tail; also called "interfemoral membrane."

Ventral: Pertaining to the underside or belly (venter) of an animal; opposite of "dorsal."

Vibrissae: Long, stiff facial whiskers or hairs around the nose or mouth of certain mammals.

Selected References

This bibliography is divided into the following sections:

I. Literature Cited
II. Environment of Pennsylvania
III. General Publications on Mammals
   A. Pennsylvania Faunas
   B. Faunas of Eastern United States and Canada
   C. Field Guides
IV. Publications on Specific Mammals

I. Literature Cited

Allen, E. G. 1938. The habits and life history of the eastern chipmunk (*Tamias striatus lysteri*). Bull. New York State Mus., 314:1–122.
Bailey, V. 1924. Breeding, feeding, and other life habits of meadow mice (*Microtus*). J. Agri. Res., 27:523–535.
Bekoff, M. 1982. Coyote. Pp. 447–459, *in* Wild mammals of North America: Biology, management, and economics (J. A. Chapman and G. A. Feldhamer, eds.). Johns Hopkins Univ. Press, Baltimore, Maryland, 1147 pp.
Chapman, J. A., and G. A. Feldhamer, eds. 1982. Wild mammals of North America: Biology, management, and economics. Johns Hopkins Univ. Press, Baltimore, Maryland. 1147 pp.
DeBlase, A. F., and R. E. Martin. 1981. A manual of mammalogy with keys to families of the world. Second ed. William C. Brown Co., Dubuque, Iowa, 436 pp.
Doutt, J. K., C. A. Heppenstall, and J. E. Guilday. 1977. Mammals of Pennsylvania. Fourth ed. Pennsylvania Game Commission, Harrisburg, Pennsylvania, 288 pp.
Erdman, K. S., and P. G. Wiegman. 1974. Preliminary list of natural areas in Pennsylvania. Western Pennsylvania Conservancy, Pittsburgh, Pennsylvania, 106 pp.
Ferguson, R. M. 1968. The timber resources of Pennsylvania. Resource Bull., U.S. Forest Service, Washington, D.C., no. NE-8.
Genoways, H. H., and F. J. Brenner, eds. 1985. Species of special concern in Pennsylvania. Carnegie Mus. Nat. Hist., Pittsburgh, Pennsylvania, 430 pp.
Gilbert, B. 1985. A groundhog's "day" means more to us than it does to him. Smithsonian, 15:60–68.
Godin, A. J. 1977. Wild mammals of New England. Johns Hopkins Univ. Press, Baltimore, Maryland, 304 pp.
Halfpenny, J. 1986. A field guide to mammal tracking in western America. Johnson Books, Boulder, Colorado, 111 pp.

Hall, E. R. 1927. An outbreak of house mice in Kern County, California. Publ. Zool., Univ. California, Berkeley, 30:189–203.

———. 1981. Mammals of North America. Second ed. John Wiley and Sons, New York, 2 vols., 1373 pp.

Hamilton, W. J., Jr. 1938. Life history notes on the northern pine mouse. J. Mamm., 19:163–170.

Hesselton, W. T., and R. M. Hesselton. 1982. White-tailed deer. Pp. 878–901, *in* Wild mammals of North America: Biology, management, and economics (J. A. Chapman and G. A. Feldhamer, eds.). Johns Hopkins Univ. Press, Baltimore, Maryland, 1147 pp.

Jackson, H. H. T. 1961. Mammals of Wisconsin, Univ. Wisconsin Press, Madison, Wisconsin, 517 pp.

Jones, J. K., Jr., D. C. Carter, H. H. Genoways, R. S. Hoffmann, and D. W. Rice. 1982. Revised checklist of North American mammals north of Mexico. Occas. Papers Mus., Texas Tech Univ., 80:1–22.

Jones, J. K., Jr., D. M. Armstrong, R. S. Hoffmann, and C. Jones. 1983. Mammals of the northern Great Plains. Univ. Nebraska Press, Lincoln, 379 pp.

Kuchler, A. W. 1964. Manual to accompany the map of potential natural vegetation of the conterminous United States. Spec. Publ., Amer. Geog. Soc., 36:1–116.

Lowery, G. H. 1974. The mammals of Louisiana and its adjacent waters. Louisiana State Univ. Press, Baton Rouge, 587 pp.

McCarley, W. H. 1959. An unusually large nest of *Cryptotis parva*. J. Mamm., 40:243.

Mech, L. D. 1970. The wolf: The ecology and behavior of an endangered species. Natural History Press, New York, 384 pp.

———. 1974. Canis lupus. Mamm. Species, 37:1–6.

Morow, K. 1976. Food habits of moose from Augustow Forest. Acta. Theriol., 21:101–116.

Murie, O. J. 1954. A field guide to animal tracks. Houghton Mifflin Co., Boston, Massachusetts, 374 pp.

Raynor, G. S. 1960. Three litters in a pine mouse nest. J. Mamm., 41:275.

Richmond, N. D., and R. D. McDowell. 1952. The least weasel (*Mustela rixosa*) in Pennsylvania. J. Mamm., 33:251–253.

Saunders, J., Jr. 1963. Food habits of the lynx in Newfoundland. J. Wildlife Mgmt., 27:384–390.

Schlandweiler, J. L., and G. L. Storm. 1969. Den-use by mink. J. Wildlife Mgmt., 33:1025–1026.

Schwartz, C. W., and E. R. Schwartz. 1981. The wild mammals of Missouri. Univ. Missouri Press, Columbia, 356 pp.

Seton, E. T. 1929. Lives of game animals. Doubleday, Doran and Co., Garden City, New York, 4 vols.

U.S. Dept. of Interior. 1974. Endangered fauna. U.S. Fish and Wildlife Service, Washington, D.C., 22 pp.

———. 1980. Re-publication of the lists of endangered and threatened species and correction of technical errors in final rules. Federal Register, 45:33768–33781.

Whitaker, J. O., Jr. 1980. The Audubon Society field guide to North American mammals. Alfred A. Knopf, New York, 745 pp.
Williams, S. L., S. B. McLaren, and M. A. Burgwin. 1985. Paleo-archaeological and historical records of selected Pennsylvania mammals. Ann. Carnegie Mus. Nat. Hist., 54:77–188.
Yeager, L. E. 1943. Storing of muskrats and other food by minks. J. Mamm., 24:100–101.

II. Environment of Pennsylvania

Brenner, F. J. 1985. Aquatic and terrestrial habitats in Pennsylvania. Pp. 7–17, in Species of special concern in Pennsylvania (H. H. Genoways and F. J. Brenner, eds.). Carnegie Mus. Nat. Hist., Pittsburgh, Pennsylvania, 430 pp.
Erdman, K. S., and P. G. Wiegman. 1974. Preliminary list of natural areas in Pennsylvania. Western Pennsylvania Conservancy, Pittsburgh, Pennsylvania, 106 pp.
Ferguson, R. M. 1968. The timber resources of Pennsylvania. Resource Bull., U.S. Forest Service, Washington, D.C., no. NE-8.
Grimm, W. C. 1950. The trees of Pennsylvania. Stackpole and Heck, Inc., New York, 363 pp.
Guilday, J. E. 1985. The physiographic provinces of Pennsylvania. Pp. 19–29, in Species of special concern in Pennsylvania (H. H. Genoways and F. J. Brenner, eds.). Carnegie Mus. Nat. Hist., Pittsburgh, Pennsylvania, 430 pp.
Hunt, C. B. 1967. Physiography of the United States. W. H. Freeman and Co., San Francisco, California, 480 pp.
———. 1974. Natural regions of the United States and Canada. W. H. Freeman and Co., San Francisco, California, 725 pp.
Jennings, O. E. 1953. Wildflowers of western Pennsylvania and the upper Ohio basin. Univ. Pittsburgh Press, Pittsburgh, Pennsylvania, 574 pp.
Kuchler, A. W. 1964. Manual to accompany the map of potential natural vegetation of the conterminous United States. Spec. Publ., Amer. Geog. Soc., 36:1–116.
Powell, D. S., and F. J. Considine, Jr. 1982. An analysis of Pennsylvania forest resources. Resource Bull., U.S. Forest Service, Washington, D.C., no. NE-69:1–96.
Shiffer, C. 1985. Drainage patterns in Pennsylvania. Pp. 31–34, in Species of special concern in Pennsylvania (H. H. Genoways and F. J. Brenner, eds.). Carnegie Mus. Nat. Hist., Pittsburgh, Pennsylvania, 430 pp.
Wiegman, P. G. 1985. Plants. Pp. 39–78, in Species of special concern in Pennsylvania (H. H. Genoways and F. J. Brenner, eds.). Carnegie Mus. Nat. Hist., Pittsburgh, Pennsylvania, 430 pp.
Willard, B. 1962. Pennsylvania geology summarized. Ed. Ser., Dept. Environmental Resources, Bur. Topographic and Geologic Survey, Harrisburg, Pennsylvania, 4:1–17.

III. General Publications on Mammals

Boitani, L., and S. Bartoli. 1983. Simon and Schuster's guide to mammals (S. Anderson, ed.). Simon and Schuster, New York, 511 pp.

Chapman, J. A., and G. A. Feldhamer, eds. 1982. Wild mammals of North America: Biology, management, and economics. Johns Hopkins Univ. Press, Baltimore, Maryland, 1147 pp.

DeBlase, A. F., and R. E. Martin. 1981. A manual of mammalogy with keys to families of the world. Second ed. William C. Brown Co., Dubuque, Iowa, 436 pp.

Hall, E. R. 1981. Mammals of North America. Second ed. John Wiley and Sons, New York, 2 vols., 1373 pp.

Jones, J. K., Jr., D. C. Carter, H. H. Genoways, R. S. Hoffmann, and D. W. Rice. 1982. Revised checklist of North American mammals north of Mexico. Occas. Papers Mus., Texas Tech Univ., 80:1–22.

Lawlor, T. E. 1979. Handbook to the orders and families of living mammals. Mad River Press, Eureka, California, 327 pp.

Macdonald, D., ed. 1984. The encyclopedia of mammals. Equinox, Ltd., Oxford, 895 pp.

Nowak, R. M., and J. L. Paradiso. 1983. Walker's mammals of the world. Fourth ed. Johns Hopkins Univ. Press, Baltimore, Maryland, 2 vols., 1362 pp.

U.S. Dept. of Interior. 1974. Endangered fauna. U.S. Fish and Wildlife Service, Washington, D.C., 22 pp.

―――. 1980. Re-publication of the lists of endangered and threatened species and correction of technical errors in final rules. Federal Register, 45:33768–33781.

Vaughan, T. A. 1986. Mammalogy. Third ed. Saunders Publ. Co., Philadelphia, Pennsylvania, 576 pp.

A. PENNSYLVANIA FAUNAS

Doutt, J. K., C. A. Heppenstall, and J. E. Guilday. 1977. Mammals of Pennsylvania. Fourth ed. Pennsylvania Game Commission, Harrisburg, Pennsylvania, 288 pp.

Genoways, H. H., and F. J. Brenner, eds. 1985. Species of special concern in Pennsylvania. Carnegie Mus. Nat. Hist., Pittsburgh, Pennsylvania, 430 pp.

Gifford, C. L., and R. Whitebread. 1951. Mammal survey of southcentral Pennsylvania. Final Rpt., Pittman-Robertson Proj. 38-R, Pennsylvania Game Commission, Harrisburg, Pennsylvania, 74 pp.

Grimm, W. C., and H. A. Roberts. 1950. Mammal survey of southwestern Pennsylvania. Final Rpt., Pittman-Robertson Proj. 24-R, Pennsylvania Game Commission, Harrisburg, Pennsylvania, 99 pp.

Grimm, W. C. and R. Whitebread. 1952. Mammal survey of northeastern Pennsylvania. Final Rpt., Pittman-Robertson Proj. 42-R, Pennsylvania Game Commission, Harrisburg, Pennsylvania, 82 pp.

Rhoads, S. N. 1903. The mammals of Pennsylvania and New Jersey. Privately published, Philadelphia, Pennsylvania, 266 pp.

Richmond, N. D., and H. R. Roslund. 1949. Mammal survey of northwestern Pennsylvania. Final Rpt., Pittman-Robertson Proj. 20-R, Pennsylvania Game Commission, Harrisburg, Pennsylvania, 67 pp.

Roberts, H. A., and R. C. Early. 1952. Mammal survey of southeastern Pennsylvania. Final Rpt., Pittman-Robertson Proj. 43-R, Pennsylvania Game Commission, Harrisburg, Pennsylvania, 70 pp.

Roslund, H. R. 1951. Mammal survey of northcentral Pennsylvania. Final Rpt., Pittman-Robertson Proj. 37-R, Pennsylvania Game Commission, Harrisburg, Pennsylvania, 55 pp.

Rupprecht, C. E., and T. J. Wiktor. 1987. Antigenic variants of rabies in Pennsylvania wildlife. From North American Symposium on Rabies in Wildlife held by Pan-American Health Organization. Pan-American Health Organization, Washington, D.C., forthcoming.

Williams, S. L., S. B. McLaren, and M. A. Burgwin. 1985. Paleo-archaeological and historical records of selected Pennsylvania mammals. Ann. Carnegie Mus. Nat. Hist., 54:77–188.

B. FAUNAS OF EASTERN UNITED STATES AND CANADA

Baker, R. H. 1983. Michigan mammals. Michigan State Univ. Press, East Lansing, 642 pp.

Barbour, R. W., and W. H. Davis. 1974. Mammals of Kentucky. Univ. Kentucky Press, Lexington, 322 pp.

Burt, W. H. 1946. The mammals of Michigan. Univ. Michigan Press, Ann Arbor, 288 pp.

———. 1972. Mammals of the Great Lakes Region. Univ. Michigan Press, Ann Arbor, 246 pp.

Godin, A. J. 1977. Wild mammals of New England. Johns Hopkins Univ. Press, Baltimore, Maryland, 304 pp.

Gottschang, J. L. 1981. A guide to the mammals of Ohio. Ohio State Univ. Press, Columbus, 176 pp.

Hamilton, W. J., Jr., and J. O. Whitaker, Jr. 1979. Mammals of the eastern United States. Second ed. Comstock Publ. Assoc., Div. of Cornell Univ. Press, New York, 346 pp.

Handley, C. O., Jr., and C. P. Patton. 1947. Wild mammals of Virginia. Virginia Comm. Game and Inland Fisheries, Richmond, 220 pp.

Linzey, A. V., and D. W. Linzey. 1971. Mammals of Great Smoky Mountains National Park. Univ. Tennessee Press, Knoxville, 114 pp.

Mumford, R. E., and J. O. Whitaker, Jr. 1982. Mammals of Indiana. Indiana Univ. Press, Bloomington, 537 pp.

Paradiso, J. L. 1969. Mammals of Maryland. N. Amer. Fauna Ser., U.S. Dept. Interior, Washington, D.C., 66:1–193.

Schwartz, C. W., and E. R. Schwartz. 1981. The wild mammals of Missouri. Univ. Missouri Press, Columbia, 356 pp.

Van Zyll de Jong, C. G. 1983. Handbook of Canadian mammals. Vol. 1: Marsupials and insectivores. National Mus. Canada, Ottawa, 210 pp.

————. 1985. Handbook of Canadian mammals. Vol. 2: Bats. National Mus. Canada, Ottawa, 212 pp.

Webster, W. D., J. F. Parnell, and W. C. Briggs, Jr. 1985. Mammals of the Carolinas, Virginia, and Maryland. Univ. North Carolina Press, Chapel Hill, 255 pp.

C. FIELD GUIDES

Brown, T., and B. Morgan. 1983. Tom Brown's field guide to nature observation and tracking. Berkley Books, New York, 282 pp.

Burt, W. H., and R. P. Grossenheider. 1976. A field guide to the mammals. Third ed. Houghton Mifflin Co., Boston, Massachusetts, 289 pp.

Cox, G. 1975. Winter signs in the snow. Michael Kensend Publishing Ltd., New York, 80 pp.

Halfpenny, J. 1986. A field guide to mammal tracking in western America. Johnson Books, Boulder, Colorado, 111 pp.

Headstrom, R. 1971. Identifying animal tracks of mammals, birds, and other animals of the eastern United States. Dover Publications, Inc., New York, 141 pp.

Miller, D. 1981. Track finder: A guide to mammal tracks of eastern North America. Nature Study Guild, Berkeley, California, 61 pp.

Murie, O. J. 1954. A field guide to animal tracks. Houghton Mifflin Co., Boston, Massachusetts, 374 pp.

Ormond, C. 1975. How to track and find game. Outdoor Life Books, Funk and Wagnalls, New York, 152 pp.

Rue, L. L., III. 1968. Sportsman's guide to game animals. Outdoor Life Books, Harper & Row, New York, 655 pp.

Seton, E. T. 1958. Animal tracks and hunter signs. Macmillan of Canada, Toronto, Ottawa, Canada, 160 pp.

Smith, R. P. 1982. Animal tracks and signs of North America. Stackpole Books, Harrisburg, Pennsylvania, 271 pp.

Whitaker, J. O., Jr. 1980. The Audubon Society field guide to North American mammals. Alfred A. Knopf, New York, 745 pp.

IV. Publications on Specific Mammals

A. NEW WORLD OPOSSUMS: FAMILY DIDELPHIDAE

Gardner, A. L. 1982. Virginia opossum. Pp. 3–36, *in* Wild mammals of North America (Chapman and Feldhamer, eds.). See section III.

Llewellyn, L. M., and F. H. Dale. 1964. Notes on the ecology of the opossum in Maryland. J. Mamm., 45:113–122.

McManus, J. J. 1974. Didelphis virginiana. Mamm. Species, 40:1–6.

B. SHREWS: FAMILY SORICIDAE

Diersing, V. E. 1980. Systematics and evolution of the pygmy shrews (subgenus *Microsorex*) of North America. J. Mamm., 61:76–101.

George, S. B., J. R. Choate, and H. H. Genoways. 1986. Blarina brevicauda. Mamm. Species, 261:1–9.

Hamilton, W. J., Jr. 1930. The food of the Soricidae. J. Mamm., 11: 26–39.

———. 1940 The biology of the smoky shrew (*Sorex fumeus fumeus* Miller). Zoologica, 25:473–492.

———. 1944. The biology of the little short-tailed shrew, *Cryptotis parva*. J. Mamm., 24:1–7.

Kirkland, G. L., Jr. 1977. A re-examination of the subspecific status of the Maryland shrew, Sorex cinereus fontinalis Hollister. Proc. Pennsylvania Acad. Sci., 51:43–46.

Kirkland, G. L., Jr., A. M. Wilkinson, J. V. Planz, and J. E. Maldonado. 1987. *Sorex (Microsorex) hoyi* in Pennsylvania. J. Mamm., 68, in press.

Long, C. A. 1972. Notes on habitat preference and reproduction in pigmy shrews, *Microsorex*. Canadian Field-Nat., 86:155–160.

———. 1974. Microsorex hoyi and Microsorex thompsoni. Mamm. Species, 146:1–4.

McCarley, W. H. 1959. An unusually large nest of *Cryptotis parva*. J. Mamm., 40:243.

Martin, I. G. 1981. Venom of the short-tailed shrew (*Blarina brevicauda*) as an insect immobilizing agent. J. Mamm., 62:189–192.

Merritt, J. F. 1986. Winter survival adaptations of the short-tailed shrew (*Blarina brevicauda*) in an Appalachian montane forest. J. Mamm., 67:450–464.

Prince, L. A. 1940. Notes on the habits of the pigmy shrew (*Microsorex hoyi*) in captivity. Canadian Field-Nat., 54:97–100.

Tomasi, T. E. 1978. Function of venom in the short-tailed shrew, *Blarina brevicauda*. J. Mamm., 59:852–854.

Whitaker, J. O., Jr. 1974. Cryptotis parva. Mamm. Species, 43:1–8.

C. MOLES: FAMILY TALPIDAE

Conaway, C. H. 1959. The reproductive cycle of the eastern mole. J. Mamm., 40:180–194.

Eadie, W. R. 1939. A contribution to the biology of *Parascalops breweri*. J. Mamm., 20:150–173.

Guilday, J. E. 1961. Prehistoric record of *Scalopus* from western Pennsylvania. J. Mamm., 42:117–118.

Hallett, J. G. 1978. Parascalops breweri. Mamm. Species, 98:1–4.

Hamilton, W. J., Jr. 1931. Habits of the star-nosed mole, *Condylura cristata*. J. Mamm., 12:345–355.

Peterson, K. E., and T. L. Yates. 1980. Condylura cristata. Mamm. Species, 129:1–4.

Yates, T. L., and R. J. Pedersen. 1982. Moles. Pp. 37–51, *in* Wild mammals of North America (Chapman and Feldhamer, eds.). See section III.
Yates, T. L., and D. J. Schmidly. 1978. Scalopus aquaticus. Mamm. Species, 105:1–4.

D. BATS: FAMILY VESPERTILIONIDAE

Allen, G. M. 1939. Bats. Harvard Univ. Press, Cambridge, Massachusetts, 368 pp.
Barbour, R. W., and W. H. Davis. 1969. Bats of America. Univ. Press Kentucky, Lexington, 286 pp.
Brenner, F. J. 1974. A five-year study of a hibernating colony of *Myotis lucifugus*. Ohio J. Sci., 74:239–244.
Fenton, M. B., and R. M. R. Barclay. 1980. Myotis lucifugus. Mamm. Species, 142:1–8.
Fitch, J. H., and K. A. Shump, Jr. 1979. Myotis keenii. Mamm. Species, 121:1–3.
Fujita, M. S., and T. H. Kunz. 1984. Pipistrellus subflavus. Mamm. Species, 228:1–6.
Hall, J. S. 1962. A life history and taxonomic study of the Indiana bat, *Myotis sodalis*. Sci. Publ., Reading Public Museum and Art Gallery, Reading, Pennsylvania, 12:68.
Humphrey, S. R. 1982. Bats. Pp. 52–70, *in* Wild mammals of North America (Chapman and Feldhamer, eds.). See section III.
Kunz, T. H. 1982. Lasionycteris noctivagans. Mamm. Species, 172:1–5.
Leen, N., and A. Novick. 1969. The world of bats. Holt, Rinehart, and Winston, New York, 171 pp.
Mohr, C. O. 1933. Pennsylvania bats of the genus *Myotis*. Proc. Pennsylvania Acad. Sci., 7:39–43.
Poole, E. L. 1932. Breeding of the hoary bat in Pennsylvania. J. Mamm., 13:365–367.
———. 1938. Notes on the breeding of *Lasiurus* and *Pipistrellus* in Pennsylvania. J. Mamm., 19:249.
Shump, K. A., Jr., and A. U. Shump. 1982. Lasiurus borealis. Mamm. Species, 183:1–6.
———. 1982. Lasiurus cinereus. Mamm. Species, 185:1–5.
Thomson, C. E. 1982. Myotis sodalis. Mamm. Species, 163:1–5.
Watkins, L. C. 1972. Nycticeius humeralis. Mamm. Species, 23:1–4.

E. RABBITS AND HARES: FAMILY LEPORIDAE

Aldous, C. M. 1937. Notes on the life history of the snowshoe hare. J. Mamm., 18:46–57.
Bittner, S. L., and O. J. Rongstad. 1982. Snowshoe hare and allies. Pp. 146–163, *in* Wild mammals of North America (Chapman and Feldhamer, eds.). See section III.
Chapman, J. A. 1975. Sylvilagus transitionalis. Mamm. Species, 55:1–4.

Chapman, J. A., J. G. Hockman, and M. M. Ojeda C. 1980. Sylvilagus floridanus. Mamm. Species, 136:1−8.
Chapman, J. A., J. G. Hockman, and W. R. Edwards. 1982. Cottontails. Pp. 83−123, *in* Wild mammals of North America (Chapman and Feldhamer, eds.). See section III.
Keith, L. B., and L. A. Windberg. 1978. A demographic analysis of the snowshoe hare cycle. Wildlife Monogr., 58:1−70.

F. SQUIRRELS: FAMILY SCIURIDAE

Allen, E. G. 1938. The habits and life history of the eastern chipmunk (*Tamias striatus lysteri*). Bull. New York State Mus., 314:1−122.
Arsenault, J. R., and R. F. Romig. 1985. Plants eaten by woodchucks in three northeastern Pennsylvania counties. Proc. Pennsylvania Acad. Sci., 59:131−134.
Dolan, P. G., and D. C. Carter. 1977. Glaucomys volans. Mamm. Species, 78:1−6.
Flyger, V., and J. E. Gates. 1982. Fox and gray squirrels. Pp. 209−229, *in* Wild mammals of North America (Chapman and Feldhamer, eds.). See section III.
———. 1982. Pine squirrels. Pp. 230−238, *in* Wild mammals of North America (Chapman and Feldhamer, eds.). See section III.
Gilbert, B. 1985. A groundhog's "day" means more to us than it does to him. Smithsonian, 15:60−68.
Layne, J. N. 1954. The biology of the red squirrel, *Tamiasciurus hudsonicus loquax* (Bangs) in central New York. Ecol. Monogr., 24:227−267.
Lee, D. S., and J. B. Funderburg. 1982. Marmots. Pp. 176−191, *in* Wild mammals of North America (Chapman and Feldhamer, eds.). See section III.
MacClintock, D. 1970. Squirrels of North America. Van Nostrand Reinhold Co., New York, 184 pp.
Snyder, D. P. 1982. Tamias striatus. Mamm. Species, 168:1−8.
Weigl, P. D. 1978. Resource overlap, interspecific interactions and the distribution of the flying squirrels, Glaucomys volans and G. sabrinus. Amer. Midl. Nat., 100:83−96.
Wells-Gosling, N., and L. R. Heaney. 1984. Glaucomys sabrinus. Mamm. Species, 229:1−8.

G. BEAVERS: FAMILY CASTORIDAE

Hill, E. P. 1982. Beaver. Pp. 256−281, *in* Wild mammals of North America (Chapman and Feldhamer, eds.). See section III.
Jenkins, S. H., and P. E. Busher. 1979. Castor canadensis. Mamm. Species, 120:1−8.
Rue, L. L., III. 1964. The world of the beaver. J. B. Lippincott Co., Philadelphia, Pennsylvania, 155 pp.

H. NATIVE RATS, MICE, AND VOLES: FAMILY CRICETIDAE

Bailey, V. 1924. Breeding, feeding, and other life habits of meadow mice (*Microtus*). J. Agri. Res., 27:523–535.

Boonstra, R., and F. H. Rodd. 1983. Regulation of breeding density in *Microtus pennsylvanicus*. J. Anim. Ecol., 52:757–780.

Connor, P. F. 1959. The bog lemming *Synaptomys cooperi* in southern New Jersey. Publ. Mus. (Biol. Ser.), Michigan State Univ., 1:165–248.

Erickson, H. R. 1966. Muskrat burrowing damage and control procedures in New York, Pennsylvania, and Maryland. New York Fish and Game J., 13:176–187.

Errington, P. L. 1963. Muskrat populations. Iowa State Univ. Press, Ames, 665 pp.

———. 1978. Muskrats and marsh management. Univ. Nebraska Press, Lincoln, 183 pp.

Hamilton, W. J., Jr. 1937. The biology of microtine cycles. J. Agri. Res., 54:779–790.

———. 1938. Life history notes on the northern pine mouse. J. Mamm., 19:163–170.

Johnson, M. L., and S. Johnson. 1982. Voles. Pp. 326–354, *in* Wild mammals of North America (Chapman and Feldhamer, eds.). See section III.

King, J. A., ed. 1968. Biology of *Peromyscus* (Rodentia). Spec. Publ., Amer. Soc. Mamm., 2:593.

Kirkland, G. L., Jr. 1975. Taxonomy and geographic distribution of *Peromyscus maniculatus nubiterrae* Rhoads (Mammalia: Rodentia). Ann. Carnegie Mus. Nat. Hist., 45:213–229.

Kirkland, G. L., Jr., and F. J. Jannett, Jr. 1982. Microtus chrotorrhinus. Mamm. Species, 180:1–5.

Krebs, C. J., and J. H. Myers. 1974. Population cycles in small mammals. Pp. 267–399, *in* Advances in ecological research, (A. MacFadyen, ed.). Academic Press, New York, 418 pp.

Lackey, J. A., D. G. Huckaby, and B. G. Ormiston. 1985. Peromyscus leucopus. Mamm. Species, 247:1–10.

Linzey, A. V. 1983. Synaptomys cooperi. Mamm. Species, 210:1–5.

Merritt, J. F. 1981. Clethrionomys gapperi. Mamm. Species, 146:1–9.

Newcombe, C. L. 1930. An ecological study of the Allegheny cliff rat (*Neotoma pennsylvanica* Stone). J. Mamm., 11:204–211.

Perry, H. R., Jr. 1982. Muskrats. Pp. 282–325, *in* Wild mammals of North America (Chapman and Feldhamer, eds.). See section III.

Poole, E. L. 1940. A life history sketch of the Allegheny woodrat. J. Mamm., 21:249–270.

Raynor, G. S. 1960. Three litters in a pine mouse nest. J. Mamm., 41:275.

Reich, L. M. 1981. Microtus pennsylvanicus. Mamm. Species, 159:1–8.

Smolen, M. J. 1981. Microtus pinetorum. Mamm. Species, 147:1–7.

Tamarin, R. H., ed. 1985. Biology of New World *Microtus*. Spec. Publ., Amer. Soc. Mamm., 8:893.

Wiley, R. W. 1980. Neotoma floridana. Mamm. Species, 139:1–7.

Willner, G. R., G. A. Feldhamer, E. E. Zucker, and J. A. Chapman. 1980. Ondatra zibethicus. Mamm. Species, 141 : 1–8.
Wolfe, J. L. 1982. Oryzomys palustris. Mamm. Species, 176 : 1–5.
Wolff, J. O. 1985. Comparative population ecology of *Peromyscus leucopus* and *Peromyscus maniculatus.* Canadian J. Zool., 63 : 1548–1555.
Wolff, J. O., and D. S. Durr. 1986. Winter nesting behavior of *Peromyscus leucopus* and *Peromyscus maniculatus.* J. Mamm., 67 : 409–412.

I. OLD WORLD RATS AND MICE: FAMILY MURIDAE

Brown, R. Z. 1953. Social behavior, reproduction, and population changes in the house mouse (*Mus musculus*). Ecol. Monogr., 23 : 17–40.
Calhoun, J. B. 1962. The ecology and sociology of the Norway rat. Pub. Health Serv. Publ., U.S. Dept. Health, Educ., and Welfare, Washington, D.C., 1008 : 288.
Hall, E. R. 1927. An outbreak of house mice in Kern County, California. Publ. Zool., Univ. California, Berkeley, 30 : 189–203.
Jackson, W. B. 1982. Norway rat and allies. Pp. 1077–1088, *in* Wild mammals of North America (Chapman and Feldhamer, eds.). See section III.

J. JUMPING MICE: FAMILY ZAPODIDAE

Brower, J. E., and T. J. Cade. 1966. Ecology and physiology of *Napaeozapus insignis* (Miller) and other woodland mice. Ecology, 47 : 46–63.
Quimby, D. C. 1951. The life history and ecology of the jumping mouse, *Zapus hudsonius.* Ecol. Monogr., 21 : 61–95.
Whitaker, J. O., Jr. 1972. Zapus hudsonius. Mamm. Species, 11 : 1–7.
Whitaker, J. O., Jr., and R. E. Wrigley. 1972. Napaeozapus insignis. Mamm. Species, 14 : 1–6.
Wrigley, R. E. 1972. Systematics and biology of the woodland jumping mouse, *Napaeozapus insignis.* Illinois Biol. Monogr., Univ. Illinois Press, Urbana, 47 : 59–113.

K. NEW WORLD PORCUPINES: FAMILY ERETHIZONTIDAE

Costello, D. F. 1966. The world of the porcupine. J. B. Lippincott Co., Philadelphia, Pennsylvania, 157 pp.
Dodge, W. E. 1982. Porcupine. Pp. 355–366, *in* Wild mammals of North America (Chapman and Feldhamer, eds.). See section III.
Woods, C. A. 1973. Erethizon dorsatum. Mamm. Species, 29 : 1–6.

L. DOGS AND FOXES: FAMILY CANIDAE

Bekoff, M. 1977. Canis latrans. Mamm. Species, 79 : 1–9.
———, ed. 1978. Coyotes: Biology, behavior, and management. Academic Press, New York, 384 pp.

————. 1982. Coyote. Pp. 447–459, *in* Wild mammals of North America (Chapman and Feldhamer, eds.). See section III.

Fritzell, E. K., and K. J. Haroldson. 1982. Urocyon cinereoargenteus. Mamm. Species, 189 : 1–8.

McGinnis, H. J. 1979. Pennsylvania coyotes and their relationship to other wild *Canis* populations in the Great Lakes region and the northeastern United States. Unpubl. M.S. thesis, Pennsylvania State Univ., University Park, 227 pp.

Mech, L. D. 1970. The wolf: The ecology and behavior of an endangered species. Natural History Press, New York, 384 pp.

————. 1974. Canis lupus. Mamm. Species, 37 : 1–6.

Paradiso, J. L., and R. M. Nowak. 1982. Wolves. Pp. 460–474, *in* Wild mammals of North America (Chapman and Feldhamer, eds.). See section III.

Rue, L. L., III. 1969. The world of the red fox. J. B. Lippincott Co., Philadelphia, Pennsylvania, 204 pp.

Rutter, R. J., and D. H. Pimlott. 1968. The world of the wolf. J. B. Lippincott Co., Philadelphia, Pennsylvania, 202 pp.

Samuel, D. E., and B. B. Nelson. 1982. Foxes. Pp. 475–490, *in* Wild mammals of North America (Chapman and Feldhamer, eds.). See section III.

Van Wormer, J. 1964. The world of the coyote. J. B. Lippincott Co., Philadelphia, Pennsylvania, 150 pp.

M. BEARS: FAMILY URSIDAE

Alt, G. L. 1982. Reproductive biology of Pennsylvania's black bear. Pennsylvania Game News, 53 : 9–15.

————. 1983. Timing of parturition of black bears (*Ursus americanus*) in northeastern Pennsylvania. J. Mamm., 64 : 305–307.

————. 1984. Cub adoption in the black bear. J. Mamm., 65 : 511–512.

Alt, G. L., and J. M. Gruttadauria. 1984. Reuse of black bear dens in northeastern Pennsylvania. J. Wildlife Mgmt., 48 : 236–239.

Pelton, M. R. 1982. Black bear. Pp. 504–514, *in* Wild mammals of North America (Chapman and Feldhamer, eds.). See section III.

Van Wormer, J. 1966. The world of the black bear. J. B. Lippincott Co., Philadelphia, Pennsylvania, 163 pp.

N. RACCOONS: FAMILY PROCYONIDAE

Kaufmann, J. H. 1982. Raccoon and allies. Pp. 567–585, *in* Wild mammals of North America (Chapman and Feldhamer, eds.). See section III.

Kennedy, M. L., G. D. Baumgardner, M. E. Cope, F. R. Tabatabai, and O. S. Fuller. 1986. Raccoon (*Procyon lotor*) density as estimated by the census-assessment line technique. J. Mamm., 67 : 166–168.

Lotze, J. H., and S. Anderson. 1979. Procyon lotor. Mamm. Species, 119 : 1–8.

Rue, L. L., III. 1964. The world of the raccoon. J. B. Lippincott Co., Philadelphia, Pennsylvania, 145 pp.

O. WEASELS AND ALLIES: FAMILY MUSTELIDAE

Godin, A. J. 1982. Striped and hooded skunks. Pp. 674–687, *in* Wild mammals of North America (Chapman and Feldhamer, eds.). See section III.
Hall, E. R. 1951. American weasels. Univ. Kansas Publ., Mus. Nat. Hist., 4:1–466.
Hawley, V. D., and F. E. Newby. 1957. Marten home ranges and population fluctuations. J. Mamm., 38:174–184.
Howard, W. E., and R. E. Marsh. 1982. Spotted and hog-nosed skunks. Pp. 664–673, *in* Wild mammals of North America (Chapman and Feldhamer, eds.). See section III.
King, C. M. 1983. Mustela erminea. Mamm. Species, 195:1–8.
Kirkland, G. L., Jr. 1975. Parasitosis of the striped skunk (Mephitis mephitis) in Pennsylvania by the nasal nematode (Skrjabingylus chitwoodorum). Proc. Pennsylvania Acad. Sci., 49:51–53.
Latham, R. M., and C. R. Studholme. 1947. Spotted skunk in Pennsylvania. J. Mamm., 28:409.
Lindzey, F. G. 1982. Badger. Pp. 653–663, *in* Wild mammals of North America (Chapman and Feldhamer, eds.). See section III.
Linscombe, G., N. Kinler, and R. J. Aulerich. 1982. Mink. Pp. 629–643, *in* Wild mammals of North America (Chapman and Feldhamer, eds.). See section III.
Long, C. A. 1973. Taxidea taxus. Mamm. Species, 26:1–4.
Nugent, R. F., and J. R. Choate. 1970. Eastward dispersal of the badger, *Taxidea taxus*, into the northeastern United States. J. Mamm., 51: 626–627.
Powell, R. A. 1981. Martes pennanti. Mamm. Species, 156:1–6.
———. 1982. The fisher: Life history, ecology, and behavior. Univ. Minnesota Press, Minneapolis, 219 pp.
Richmond, N. D., and R. D. McDowell. 1952. The least weasel (*Mustela rixosa*) in Pennsylvania. J. Mamm., 33:251–253.
Strickland, M. A., C. W. Douglas, M. Novak, and N. P. Hunziger. 1982. Fisher. Pp. 586–598, *in* Wild mammals of North America (Chapman and Feldhamer, eds.). See section III.
———. 1982. Marten. Pp. 599–612, *in* Wild mammals of North America (Chapman and Feldhamer, eds.). See section III.
Svendsen, G. E. 1982. Weasels. Pp. 613–628, *in* Wild mammals of North America (Chapman and Feldhamer, eds.). See section III.
Toweill, D. E., and J. E. Tabor. 1982. River otter. Pp. 688–703, *in* Wild mammals of North America (Chapman and Feldhamer, eds.). See section III.
Verts, B. J. 1967. The biology of the striped skunk. Univ. Illinois Press, Urbana, 218 pp.

Wade-Smith, J., B. J. Verts. 1982. Mephitis mephitis. Mamm. Species, 173:1−7.
Wilson, D. E. 1982. Wolverine. Pp. 644−652, *in* Wild mammals of North America (Chapman and Feldhamer, eds.). See section III.
Yeager, L. E. 1943. Storing of muskrats and other food by minks. J. Mamm., 24:100−101.

P. CATS: FAMILY FELIDAE

Currier, M. J. P. 1983. Felis concolor. Mamm. Species, 200:1−7.
Dixon, K. R. 1982. Mountain lion. Pp. 711−727, *in* Wild mammals of North America (Chapman and Feldhamer, eds.). See section III.
Fuller, T. K., W. E. Berg, and D. W. Kuehn. 1985. Bobcat home range size and daytime cover-type use in northcentral Minnesota. J. Mamm., 66:568−571.
McCord, C. M., and J. E. Cardoza. 1982. Bobcat and lynx. Pp. 728−766, *in* Wild mammals of North America (Chapman and Feldhamer, eds.). See section III.
Nowak, R. M. 1976. The cougar in the United States and Canada. U.S. Fish and Wildlife Service and New York Zool. Soc., Washington, D.C., 190 pp.
Russell, K. P. 1978. Mountain lion. Pp. 207−226, *in* Big game of North America (J. L. Schmidt and D. L. Gilbert, eds.). Stackpole Books, Harrisburg, Pennsylvania, 494 pp.
Saunders, J., Jr. 1963. Food habits of the lynx in Newfoundland. J. Wildlife Mgmt., 27:384−390.
Van Wormer, J. 1963. The world of the bobcat. J. B. Lippincott Co., Philadelphia, Pennsylvania, 128 pp.
Young, S. P. 1978. The bobcat of North America. Univ. Nebraska Press, Lincoln, 193 pp.
Young, S. P., and E. A. Goldman. 1946. The puma, mysterious American cat. Amer. Wildlife Inst., Washington, D.C., 358 pp.

Q. DEER: FAMILY CERVIDAE

Coady, J. W. 1982. Moose. Pp. 902−922, *in* Wild mammals of North America (Chapman and Feldhamer, eds.). See section III.
Franzmann, A. W. 1981. Alces alces. Mamm. Species, 154:1−7.
Hesselton, W. T., and R. M. Hesselton. 1982. White-tailed deer. Pp. 878−901, *in* Wild mammals of North America (Chapman and Feldhamer, eds.). See section III.
Morow, K. 1976. Food habits of moose from Augustow Forest. Acta Theriol., 21:101−116.
Murie, O. J. 1951. The elk of North America. Stackpole Books, Harrisburg, Pennsylvania, 376 pp.
Peek, J. M. 1982. Elk. Pp. 851−861, *in* Wild mammals of North America (Chapman and Feldhamer, eds.). See section III.

Taylor, W. P., ed. 1956. The deer of North America. Stackpole Books, Harrisburg, Pennsylvania, 668 pp.

R. BISON: FAMILY BOVIDAE

McDonald, J. N. 1981. North American bison: Their classification and evolution. Univ. California Press, Berkeley, 316 pp.

Meagher, M. 1986. Bison bison. Mamm. Species, 266:1–8.

Reynolds, H. W., R. D. Glaholt, and A. W. L. Hawley. 1982. Bison. Pp. 972–1007, *in* Wild mammals of North America (Chapman and Feldhamer, eds.). See section III.

Roe, F. G. 1970. The North American buffalo. Second ed. Univ. Toronto Press, Toronto, Ottawa, Canada, 991 pp.

Index and Checklist

When you identify a species in the wild, put a check in the box next to its common name.